T0223213

Lecture Notes in Artificial Intelligence 1471

Subseries of Lecture Notes in Computer Science
Edited by J. G. Carbonell and J. Siekmann

Lecture Notes in Computer Science

Edited by G. Goos, J. Hartmanis and J. van Leeuwen

Springer
Berlin
Heidelberg
New York
Barcelona
Budapest
Hong Kong
London
Milan
Paris
Singapore
Tokyo

Jürgen Dix   Luís Moniz Pereira
Teodor C. Przymusinski (Eds.)

Logic Programming and Knowledge Representation

Third International Workshop, LPKR '97
Port Jefferson, New York, USA, October 17, 1997
Selected Papers

Springer

Series Editors

Jaime G. Carbonell, Carnegie Mellon University, Pittsburgh, PA, USA
Jörg Siekmann, University of Saarland, Saarbrücken, Germany

Volume Editors

Jürgen Dix
Universität Koblenz-Landau, Institut für Informatik
Rheinau 1, D-56075 Koblenz, Germany
E-mail: dix@uni-koblenz.de

Luís Moniz Pereira
Universidade Nova de Lisboa, Departamento de Informática
P-2825 Monte da Caparica, Portugal
E-mail: lmp@di.fct.unl.pt

Teodor C. Przymusinski
University of California at Riverside
College of Engineering, Department of Computer Science
E-mail: teodor@cs.ucr.edu

Cataloging-in-Publication Data applied for

Die Deutsche Bibliothek - CIP-Einheitsaufnahme

Logic programming and knowledge representation : third
international workshop ; selected papers / LPKR '97, Port Jefferson,
New York, USA, October 17, 1997. Jürgen Dix ... (ed.). - Berlin ;
Heidelberg ; New York ; Barcelona ; Budapest ; Hong Kong ;
London ; Milan ; Paris ; Singapore ; Tokyo : Springer, 1998
　　(Lecture notes in computer science ; Vol. 1471 : Lecture notes in
　　artificial intelligence)
　　ISBN 3-540-64958-1

CR Subject Classification (1991): I.2.3-4, F.4.1, D.1.6

ISBN 3-540-64958-1 Springer-Verlag Berlin Heidelberg New York

© Springer-Verlag Berlin Heidelberg 1998
Printed in Germany

Typesetting: Camera ready by author
SPIN 10638651　　　06/3142 – 5 4 3 2 1 0　　　Printed on acid-free paper

Preface

This book is the outcome of the compilation of extended and revised versions of selected papers presented at the workshop on *Logic Programming and Knowledge Representation* held in Port Jefferson (NY), USA, on October 17, 1997. A total of 15 papers were resubmitted, 8 of which were finally accepted by the PC and published in this volume. Background to this book is furnished through an invited introduction on knowledge representation with logic programs, by Brewka and Dix.

The development of machines that are able to reason and act intelligently is one of the most challenging and desirable tasks ever attempted by humanity. It is therefore not surprising that the investigation of techniques for representing and reasoning about knowledge has become an area of paramount importance to the whole field of Computer Science. Due to logic programming's declarative nature, and its amenability to implementation, it has quickly become a prime candidate language for knowledge representation and reasoning.

The impressive research progress of the last few years as well as the significant advances made in logic programming implementation techniques now provide us with a great opportunity to bring to fruition computationally efficient implementations of the recent extensions to logic programming and their applications.

This workshop is the third (after ICLP '94 and JICSLP '96) in a series of workshops which we have been organizing in conjunction with Logic Programming conferences. However, as shown by the following list of suggested topics in the call for papers, its scope is significantly broader than the previous ones:

LP Functionalities: abduction, communication, contradiction removal, declarative debugging, knowledge and belief revision, learning, reasoning about actions, updates,

LP Integrations: coupling knowledge sources, combining functionalities, logical agent architecture, multi-agents architecture,

LP Language Extensions: constructive default negation, disjunctive programs, default and epistemic extensions, metalevel programming, object-oriented programming, paraconsistency, reactive rules, strong and explicit negation,

LP Applications to Knowledge Representations: heterogeneous databases, model-based diagnosis, modeling production systems, planning, reactive databases, relations to non-monotonic formalisms, software engineering,

LP Implementations: computational procedures, implementations.

We would like to warmly thank the authors, the members of the program committee, and the additional reviewers listed below. They all have made this book possible and ensured its quality.

June 1998

Jürgen Dix, Koblenz
Luís Moniz Pereira, Lisboa
Teodor C. Przymusinski, Riverside

Papers in this Book

In order to facilitate reading of this volume, we now present a brief overview of the content of the presented papers. The aim of the first paper, invited by the organizers, is to serve as an introductory overview on the topic, and as a guide for the other articles.

Disjunctive Semantics

Three papers are concerned with *disjunctive semantics*. While Greco et al. introduce *nested rules* in the heads of rules to increase the expressivity, D. Seipel defines variants of the answer set semantics to remove the inconsistency problem. Yuan et al. use autoepistemic reasoning to classify disjunctive semantics with negation.

S. Greco et al.: The authors present an extension of disjunctive Datalog programs by allowing nested rules in the disjunctive head. They show that such programs allow one to naturally model several real-world situations. In fact they show that this enlarged class of programs has an *increased expressivity*: the *full second level* of the polynomial hierachy is captured.

D. Seipel: This paper considers the *inconsistency* problem of the stable and the partial stable semantics. It is well known that such models do not exist for all disjunctive deductive databases. The problem solved in the paper is to define an extension of these semantics such that (1) the new semantics coincides with the original if the original semantics is consistent, and (2) models always exist for the new semantics. The author also investigated abstract properties of the new semantics and compares them with the classical semantics.

L.-Y. Yuan et al.: The paper gives a classification of various semantics for disjunctive logic programs by using autoepistemic reasoning. *Consistency-based* as well as *minimal-model-based* semantics are shown to correspond to suitable *introspection* policies. The authors also observe three main *semantical* viewpoints (well-founded, stable, and partial stable) and thus propose a classification into six categories.

Abduction

The three papers involving abduction concern themselves with learning (E. Lamma et al.), describing action domains (R. Li et al.), and the semantics of disjunctive logic programs (K. Wang and H. Chen).

E. Lamma et al.: A system for learning abductive logic programs from an abductive background theory and examples is presented. It can make assumptions to cover positive examples and to avoid coverage of negative ones, and these assumptions can be further used as new training data. The system can be applied for learning in the context of incomplete knowledge, and for learning exceptions to classification rules.

R. Li et al.: The authors present an abductive methodology for describing action domains, starting from incomplete actions theories, i.e., those with more than one model. By performing tests to obtain additional information, a complete theory can be abduced. A high level language is used to describe incomplete domains and tests, and its sound and complete translation into abductive logic programs is provided. Via tests and abduction the original domain description can be refined to become closer to reality. The methodology, which has been implemented, allows for abductive planning, prediction, and explanation.

K. Wang and H. Chen: The authors treat argumentation in disjunctive logic programming as abduction, within a semantic framework in which disjuncts of negative literals are taken as possible assumptions. Three semantics are defined, by as many kinds of acceptable hypotheses, to represent credulous, moderate, and skeptical reasoning. The framework is defined for a broader class than disjunctive logic programs, thereby integrating and extending many key semantics such as minimal models, EGCWA, WFS, and SM, and serving as a unifying semantics for disjunctive logic programming.

Priorities

M. Gelfond and T.C. Son: A methodology for reasoning with prioritized defaults in logic programs under answer sets semantics is investigated. The paper presents, in a simple language, domain independent axioms for doing so in conjunction with particular domain descriptions. Sufficient conditions for consistency are given, and various examples from the literature are formalized. They show that in many cases the approach leads to simpler and more intuitive formalizations. A comparative discussion of other approaches is included.

Updates

J. Leite and L. M. Pereira: The paper defines what it is to update one logic program with another logic program defining the update. Furthermore, it shows how to obtain a third program as a result, whose semantics are as intended. The resulting program can in turn be updated. The classes of programs to be updated are those of extended programs under answer sets semantics, and of normal programs under stable model semantics. The concept of program update generalizes that of interpretation update, and solves important problems arising with the latter approach. Program updating opens up a whole new range of applications of logic programming, as well as the incremental approach to programming.

Organization

Previous Related Workshops

Sponsors

ESPRIT Compulog Network of Excellence, University of Koblenz

Organizing Committee

Jürgen Dix   University of Koblenz
Luís Moniz Pereira   Universidade Nova de Lisboa
Teodor Przymusinski   University of California at Riverside

Program Committee

Jürgen Dix   University of Koblenz, Germany
Phan Minh Dung   AIT, Bangkok, Thailand
Vladimir Lifschitz   University of Texas, U.S.A.
Jack Minker   University of Maryland, U.S.A.
Luís Moniz Pereira   Universidade Nova de Lisboa, Portugal
Teodor Przymusinski   University of California at Riverside, U.S.A.
Chiaki Sakama   University of Wakayama, Japan
Mirek Truszczynski   University of Kentucky at Lexington, U.S.A.
David S. Warren   SUNY at Stony Brook, U.S.A.

Additional Referees

C. Aravindan, P. Baumgartner, F. Toni, H. Turner

Table of Contents

Knowledge Representation with Logic Programs*

Gerhard Brewka[1] and Jürgen Dix[2]

[1] Universität Leipzig, Institut fuer Informatik
Augustusplatz 10/11, D-04109 Leipzig
brewka@informatik.uni-leipzig.de

[2] Universität Koblenz-Landau, Institut für Informatik,
Rheinau 1, D-56075 Koblenz
dix@mailhost.uni-koblenz.de

Abstract In this overview we show how Knowledge Representation (KR) can be done with the help of *generalized* logic programs. We start by introducing the core of PROLOG, which is based on *definite* logic programs. Although this class is very restricted (and will be enriched by various additional features in the rest of the paper), it has a very nice property for KR-tasks: there exist efficient *Query-answering procedures* — a *Top-Down* approach and a *Bottom-Up* evaluation. In addition we can not only handle ground queries but also queries with variables and compute *answer-substitutions*.

It turns out that more advanced KR-tasks can not be properly handled with definite programs. Therefore we extend this basic class of programs by additional features like *Negation-as-Finite-Failure*, *Default-Negation*, *Explicit Negation*, *Preferences*, and *Disjunction*. The need for these extensions is motivated by suitable examples and the corresponding semantics are discussed in detail.

Clearly, the more expressive the respective class of programs under a certain semantics is, the less efficient are potential Query-answering methods. This point will be illustrated and discussed for every extension. By well-known recursion-theoretic results, it is obvious that there do not exist complete Query-answering procedures for the general case where variables and function symbols are allowed. Nevertheless we consider it an important topic of further research to extract *feasible* classes of programs where answer-substitutions can be computed.

1 Knowledge Representation with Non-classical Logic

One of the major reasons for the success story (if one is really willing to call it a success story) of human beings on this planet is our ability to invent tools that help us improve our — otherwise often quite limited — capabilities. The invention of machines that are able to do interesting things, like transporting people from one place to the other (even through the air), sending moving pictures and

---

* This is a short version of Chapter 6 in D. Gabbay and F. Guenthner (editors), *Handbook of Philosophical Logic, 2nd Edition, Volume 6, Methodologies*, Reidel Publ., 1999

sounds around the globe, bringing our email to the right person, and the like, is one of the cornerstones of our culture and determines to a great degree our everyday life.

Among the most challenging tools one can think of are machines that are able to handle knowledge adequately. Wouldn't it be great if, instead of the stupid device which brings coffee from the kitchen to your office every day at 9.00, and which needs complete reengineering whenever your coffee preferences change, you could (for the same price, admitted) get a smart robot whom you can simply tell that you want your coffee black this morning, and that you need an extra Aspirin since it was your colleague's birthday yesterday? To react in the right way to your needs such a robot would have to know a lot, for instance that Aspirin should come with a glass of water, or that people in certain situations need their coffee extra strong.

Building smart machines of this kind is at the heart of Artificial Intelligence (AI). Since such machines will need tremendous amounts of knowledge to work properly, even in very limited environments, the investigation of techniques for representing knowledge and reasoning is highly important.

In the early days of AI it was still believed that modeling general purpose problem solving capabilites, as in Newell and Simon's famous GPS (General Problem Solver) program, would be sufficient to generate intelligent behaviour. This hypothesis, however, turned out to be overly optimistic. At the end of the sixties people realized that an approach using available knowledge about narrow domains was much more fruitful. This led to the expert systems boom which produced many useful application systems, expert system building tools, and expert system companies. Many of the systems are still in use and save companies millions of dollars per year[1].

Nevertheless, the simple knowledge representation and reasoning methods underlying the early expert systems soon turned out to be insufficient. Most of the systems were built based on simple rule languages, often enhanced with ad hoc approaches to model uncertainty. It became apparent that more advanced methods to handle incompleteness, defeasible reasoning, uncertainty, causality and the like were needed.

This insight led to a tremendous increase of research on the foundations of knowledge representation and reasoning. Theoretical research in this area has blossomed in recent years. Many advances have been made and important results were obtained. The technical quality of this work is often impressive.

On the other hand, most of these advanced techniques have had surprisingly little influence on practical applications so far. To a certain degree this is understandable since theoretical foundations had to be laid first and pioneering work was needed. However, if we do not want research in knowledge representation to remain a theoreticians' game more emphasis on computability and applicability seems to be needed. We strongly believe that the kind of research presented in this overview, that is research aiming at interesting combinations of ideas from

---

[1] We refer the interested reader to the recent book [104] which gives a very detailed and nice exposition of what has been done in AI since its very beginning until today.

logic programming and nonmonotonic reasoning, provides an important step into this direction.

1.1 Some History

Historically, logic programs have been considered in the logic programming community for more than 20 years. It began with [51, 82, 115] and led to the definition and implementation of *PROLOG*, a by now theoretically well-understood programming language (at least the declarative part consisting of Horn-clauses: *pure PROLOG*). Extensions of PROLOG allowing negative literals have been also considered in this area: they rely on the idea of *negation-as-finite-failure*, we call them *Logic-Programming-semantics* (or shortly *LP-semantics*).

In parallel, starting at about 1980, *Nonmonotonic Reasoning* entered into computer science and began to constitute a new field of active research. It was originally initiated because *Knowledge Representation* and *Common-Sense Reasoning* using classical logic came to its limits. Formalisms like classical logic are inherently monotonic and they seem to be too weak and therefore inadequate for such reasoning problems.

In recent years, independently of the research in logic programming, people interested in knowledge representation and nonmonotonic reasoning also tried to define declarative semantics for programs containing *default* or *explicit* negation and even *disjunctions*. They defined various semantics by appealing to (different) intuitions they had about programs.

This second line of research started in 1986 with the *Workshop on the Foundations of Deductive Databases and logic programming* organized by Jack Minker: the revised papers of the proceedings were published in [88]. The *stratified* (or the similar *perfect*) semantics presented there can be seen as a splitting-point: it is still of interest for the logic programming community (see [43]) but its underlying intuitions were inspired by nonmonotonic reasoning and therefore much more suitable for knowledge representation tasks. Semantics of this kind leave the philosophy underlying classical logic programming in that their primary aim is not to model *negation-as-finite-failure*, but to construct new, more powerful semantics suitable for applications in knowledge representation. Let us call such semantics *NMR-semantics*.

Nowadays, due to the work of Apt, Blair and Walker, Fitting, Lifschitz, Przymusinski and others, very close relationships between these two independent research lines became evident. Methods from logic programming, e.g. least fixpoints of certain operators, can be used successfully to define NMR-semantics.

The NMR-semantics also shed new light on the understanding of the classical nonmonotonic logics such as *Default Logic*, *Autoepistemic Logic* and the various versions of *Circumscription*. In addition, the investigation of possible semantics for logic programs seems to be useful because

1. parts of nonmonotonic systems (which are usually defined for full predicate logic, or even contain additional (modal)-operators) may be "implemented" with the help of such programs,

2. nonmonotonicity in these logics may be described with an appropriate treatment of negation in logic programs.

1.2 Non-monotonic Formalisms in KR

As already mentioned above, research in nonmonotonic reasoning has begun at the end of the seventies. One of the major motivations came from reasoning about actions and events. John McCarthy and Patrick Hayes had proposed their situation calculus as a means of representing changing environments in logic. The basic idea is to use an extra situation argument for each fact which describes the situation in which the fact holds. Situations, basically, are the results of performing sequences of actions. It soon turned out that the problem was not so much to represent what changes but *to represent what does not change* when an event occurs. This is the so-called *frame problem*. The idea was to handle the frame problem by using a default rule of the form

If a property P holds in situation S then P typically also holds in the situation obtained by performing action A in S.

Given such a rule it is only necessary to explicitly describe the changes induced by a particular action. All non-changes, for instance that the *real colour* of the kitchen wall does not change when the light is turned on, are handled implicitly. Although it turned out that a straightforward formulation of this rule in some of the most popular nonmonotonic formalisms may lead to unintended results the frame problem was certainly the challenge motivating many people to join the field.

In the meantime a large number of different nonmonotonic logics have been proposed. We can distinguish four major types of such logics:

1. Logics using nonstandard inference rules with an additional consistency check to represent default rules. Reiter's default logic and its variants are of this type.
2. Nonmonotonic modal logics using a modal operator to represent consistency or (dis-) belief. These logics are nonmonotonic since conclusions may depend on disbelief. The most prominent example is Moore's autoepistemic logic.
3. Circumscription and its variants. These approaches are based on a preference relation on models. A formula is a consequence iff it is true in all most preferred models of the premises. Syntactically, a second order formula is used to eliminate all non-preferred models.
4. Conditional approaches which use a non truth-functional connective $\succ$ to represent defaults. A particularly interesting way of using such conditionals was proposed by Kraus, Lehmann and Magidor. They consider p as a default consequence of q iff the conditional $q \succ p$ is in the closure of a given conditional knowledge base under a collection of rules. Each of the rules directly corresponds to a desirable property of a nonmonotonic inference relation.

The various logics are intended to handle different intuitions about nonmonotonic reasoning in a most general way. On the other hand, the generality leads to problems, at least from the point of view of implementations and applications. In the first order case the approaches are not even semi-decidable since an implicit consistency check is needed. In the propositional case we still have tremendous complexity problems. For instance, the complexity of determining whether a formula is contained in all extensions of a propositional default theory is on the second level of the polynomial hierarchy. As mentioned earlier we believe that logic programming techniques can help to overcome these difficulties.

Originally, nonmonotonic reasoning was intended to provide us with a *fast* but *unsound* approximation of classical reasoning in the presence of incomplete knowledge. Therefore one might ask whether the higher complexity of NMR-formalisms (compared to classical logic) is not a real drawback of this aim? The answer is that NMR-systems allow us to formulate a problem in a very *compact* way as a theory T. It turns out that any equivalent formulation in classical logic (if possible at all) as a theory T' is much larger: the size of T' is exponential in the size of T! We refer to [74] and [41, 42, 40] where such problems are investigated.

2 Knowledge Representation with Definite Logic Programs

In this section we consider the most restricted class of programs: *definite* logic programs, programs without any negation at all. All the extensions of this basic class we will introduce later contain at least some kind of negation (and perhaps additional features). But here we also allow the ocurrence of free variables as well as function symbols.

In Section 2.1 we introduce as a representative for the *Top-Down* approach the SLD-Resolution. Section 2.1 presents the main competing approach of SLD: *Bottom-Up Evaluation*. This approach is used in the Database community and it is efficient when additional assumptions are made (*finiteness-assumptions, no function symbols*). Finally in Section 2.2 we present and discuss two important examples in KR: *Reasoning in Inheritance Hierarchies* and *Reasoning about Actions*. Both examples clearly motivate the need of extending definite programs by a kind of *default-negation " not "*.

First some notation used throughout this paper. A language $\mathcal{L}$ consists of a set of relation symbols and a set of function symbols (each symbol has an associated arity). Nullary functions are called constants. Terms and atoms are built from $\mathcal{L}$ in the usual way starting with variables, applying function symbols and relation-symbols.

Instead of considering arbitrary $\mathcal{L}$-formulae, our main object of interest is a program:

Definition 1 (Definite Logic Program).
A definite logic program consists of a finite number of rules of the form

$$A \leftarrow B_1, \ldots, B_m,$$

where $A, B_1, \ldots, B_m$ are positive atoms (containing possibly free variables). We call A the head *of the rule and $B_1, \ldots, B_m$ its* body. *The comma represents conjunction $\wedge$.*

We can think of a program as formalizing our knowledge about the world and how the world behaves. Of course, we also want to derive new information, i.e. we want to ask queries:

Definition 2 (Query).
Given a definite program we usually have a definite query in mind that we want to be solved. A definite query Q is a conjunction of positive atoms $C_1 \wedge \ldots \wedge C_l$ which we denote by

$$?\text{-}\ C_1, \ldots, C_l.$$

These C_i may also contain variables. Asking a query Q to a program P means asking for all possible substitutions Θ of the variables in Q such that $Q\Theta$ follows from P. Often, Θ is also called an answer *to Q. Note that $Q\Theta$ may still contain free variables.*

Note that if a program P is given, we usually assume that it also determines the underlying language $\mathcal{L}$, denoted by $\mathcal{L}_P$, which is generated by exactly the symbols ocurring in P. The set of all these atoms is called the *Herbrand base* and denoted by $B_{\mathcal{L}_P}$ or simply B_P. The corresponding set of all ground terms is the *Herbrand universe*.

How are our programs related to classical predicate logic? Of course, we can map a program-rule into classical logic by interpreting "$\leftarrow$" as material implication "$\supset$" and universally quantifying. This means we view such a rule as the following universally quantified formula

$$B_1 \wedge \ldots \wedge B_m \ \supset\ A.$$

However, as we will see later, there is a great difference: a logic program-rule takes some orientation with it. This makes it possible to formulate the following principle as an underlying intuition of all semantics of logic programs:

Principle 01 (Orientation)
If a ground atom A does not unify with some head of a program rule of P, then this atom is considered to be false. In this case we say that "not A" is derivable from P to distinguish it from classical $\neg A$.

The orientation principle is nothing but a weak form of *negation-by-failure*. Given an intermediate goal *not A*, we first try to prove A. But if A does not unify with any head, A fails and this is the reason to derive *not A*.

2.1 Top-Down versus Bottom-Up

SLD-Resolution[2] is a special form of Robinson's general Resolution rule. While Robinson's rule is complete for full first order logic, SLD is complete for definite logic programs (see Theorem 1 on the facing page).

---

[2] **SL-resolution for Definite clauses. SL**-resolution stands for **L**inear resolution with **S**election function.

Definite programs have the nice feature that the intersection of all Herbrand-models exists and is again a Herbrand model of P. It is denoted by M_P and called the least Herbrand-model of P. Note that our original aim was to find substitutions Θ such that $Q\Theta$ is derivable from the program P. This task as well as M_P is closely related to SLD:

Theorem 1 (Soundness and Completeness of SLD).
The following properties are equivalent:

- *$P \models \forall\, Q\Theta$, i.e. $\forall\, Q\Theta$ is true in all models of P,*
- *$M_P \models \forall\, Q\Theta$,*
- *SLD computes an answer τ that subsumes[3] Θ wrt Q.*

Note that not any correct answer is computed, only the most general one is (which of course subsumes all the correct ones).

The main feature of SLD-Resolution is its *Goal-Orientedness*. SLD automatically ensures (because it starts with the Query) that we consider only those rules that are relevant for the query to be answered. Rules that are not at all related are simply not considered in the course of the proof.

Bottom-Up

We mentioned in the last section the least Herbrand model M_P. The bottom-up approach can be described as computing this least Herbrand model from below.

To be more precise we introduce the immediate consequence operator T_P which associates to any Herbrand model another Herbrand model.

Definition 3 (T_P).
Given a definite program P let $T_P : 2^{B_P} \longmapsto 2^{B_P}; \ \mathcal{I} \longmapsto T_P(\mathcal{I})$

$$T_P(\mathcal{I}) := \{A \in B_P : \ \textit{there is an instantiation of a rule in } P$$
$$\textit{s.t. } A \textit{ is the head of this rule and all}$$
$$\textit{body-atoms are contained in } \mathcal{I} \ \}$$

It turns out that T_P is monotone and continuous so that (by a general theorem of Knaster-Tarski) the least fixpoint is obtained after ω steps. Moreover we have

Theorem 2 (T_P and M_P).
$M_P = T_P{\uparrow}^\omega = lfp(T_P)$.

This approach is especially important in Database applications, where the underlying language does not contain function symbols (DATALOG) — this ensures the Herbrand universe to be finite. Under this condition the iteration stops after finitely many steps. In addition, rules of the form

$$p \leftarrow p$$

---

[3] i.e. $\exists \sigma : Q\tau\sigma = Q\Theta$.

do not make any problems. They simply can not be applied or do not produce anything new. Note that in the Top-Down approach, such rules give rise to infinite branches! Later, elimination of such rules will turn out to be an interesting property. We therefore formulate it as a principle:

Principle 02 (Elimination of Tautologies)
Suppose a program P has a rule which contains the same atom in its body as well as in its head (i.e. the head consists of exactly this atom). Then we can eliminate this rule without changing the semantics.

Unfortunately, such a bottom-up approach has two serious shortcomings. First, the goal-orientedness from SLD-resolution is lost: we are always computing the whole M_P, even those facts that have nothing to do with the query. The reason is that in computing T_P we do not take into account the query we are really interested in. Second, in any step facts that are already computed before are recomputed again. It would be more efficient if only new facts were computed. Both problems can be (partially) solved by appropriate refinements of the naive approach:

- *Semi-naive* bottom-up evaluation ([39, 114]),
- *Magic Sets* techniques ([16, 113]).

2.2 Why Going Beyond Definite Programs?

So far we have a nice query-answering procedure, SLD-Resolution, which is goal-oriented as well as sound and complete with respect to general derivability. But note that up to now we are not able to derive any *negative* information. Not even our queries allow this. From a very pragmatic viewpoint, we can consider " *not A*" to be derivable if A is not. Of course, this is not sound with respect to classical logic but it is with respect to M_P.

In KR we do not only want to formulate negative queries, we also want to express *default-statements* of the form

Normally, unless something abnormal holds, then ψ implies ϕ.

Such statements were the main motivation for nonmonotonic logics, like Default Logic or Circumscription). How can we formulate such a statement as a logic program? The most natural way is to use negation " *not* "

$$\phi \leftarrow \psi, \; not \; ab$$

where *ab* stands for *abnormality*. Obviously, this forces us to extend definite programs by negative atoms.

A typical example for such statements occurs in Inheritance Reasoning. We take the following example from [10]:

Example 1 (Inheritance Hierachies).
Suppose we know that birds typically fly and penguins are non-flying birds. We also know that Tweety is a bird. Now an agent is hired to build a cage for Tweety. Should the agent put a roof on the cage? After all it could be still the case that Tweety is a penguin and therefore can not fly, in which case we would not like to pay for the unneccessary roof. But under normal conditions, it should be obvious that one should conclude that Tweety is flying.

A natural axiomatization is given as follows:

$$P_{Inheritance} : \begin{aligned} flies(x) &\leftarrow bird(x), \quad not\ ab(r_1, x) \\ bird(x) &\leftarrow penguin(x) \\ ab(r_1, x) &\leftarrow penguin(x) \\ make\_top(x) &\leftarrow flies(x) \end{aligned}$$

together with some particular facts, like e.g. $bird(Tweety)$ and $penguin(Sam)$. The first rule formalizes our default-knowledge, while the third formalizes that the default-rule should not be applied in abnormal or exceptional cases. In our example, it expresses the famous *Specificity-Principle* which says that more specific knowledge should override more general one ([110, 112, 76]).

For the query "$make\_top(Tweety)$" we expect the answer "yes" while for the query "$make\_top(Sam)$" we expect the answer "no".

Another important KR task is to formalize knowledge for reasoning about action. We again consider a particular important instance of such a task, namely *temporal projection*. The overall framework consists in describing the initial state of the world as well as the effects of all actions that can be performed. What we want to derive is how the world looks like after a sequence of actions has been performed.

The common-sense argument from which this should follow is the

Law of Inertia: Things normally tend to stay the same.

Up to now we only have stated some very "natural" axiomatizations of given knowledge. We have motivated that something like default-negation " *not* " should be added to definite programs in order to do so and we have explicitly stated the answers to particular queries. What is still missing are solutions to the following very important problems

- *How should an appropriate query answering mechanism handling default-negation "not " look like?*
- *What is the formal semantics that such a procedural mechanism should be checked against?*

Such a semantics is certainly not classical predicate logic because of the default character of " *not* " — *not* is not classical ¬. Both problems will be considered in detail in Section 3.

2.3   What Is a Semantics?

In the last sections we have introduced two principles (*Orientation* and *Elimination of Tautologies*) and used the term *semantics of a program* in a loose, imprecise way. We end this section with a precise notion of what we understand by a semantics.

As a first attempt, we can view a semantics as a mapping that associates to any program a set of positive atoms and a set of default atoms. In the case of SLD-Resolution the positive atoms are the ground instances of all derivable atoms. But sometimes we also want to derive negative atoms (like in our two examples above). Our *Orientation*-Principle formalizes a minimal requirement for deriving such default-atoms.

Of course, we also want that a semantics SEM should *respect* the rules of P, i.e. whenever SEM makes the body of a rule true, then SEM should also make the head of the rule true. But it can (and will) happen that a semantics SEM does not always decide *all* atoms. Some atoms A are not derivable nor are their default-counterparts *not A*. This means that a semantics SEM can view the body of a rule as being *undefined*.

This already happens in classical logic. Take the theory

$$T := \{(A \wedge B) \supset C, \ \neg A \supset B\}.$$

What are the atoms and negated atoms derivable from T, i.e. true in all models of T? No positive atom nor any negated atom is derivable! The classical semantics therefore makes the truthvalue of $A \wedge B$ undefined in a sense.

Suppose a semantics SEM treats the body of a program rule as undefined. What should we conclude about the head of this rule? We will only require that this head is not treated as false by SEM — it could be true or undefined as well. This means that we require a semantics to be compatible with the program *viewed as a 3-valued theory* — the three values being "true", "false" and "undefined". For the understanding it is not neccessary to go deeper into 3-valued logic. We simply note that we interpret "←" as the Kleene-connective which is true for "*undefined ← undefined*" and false for "*false ← undefined*".

Definition 4 (SEM).
A semantics SEM is a mapping from the class of all programs into the powerset of the set of all 3-valued structures. SEM assigns to every program P a set of 3-valued models of P:

$$SEM(P) \subseteq MOD^{\mathcal{L}_P}_{3-val}(P).$$

This definition covers both the classical viewpoint (classical models are 2-valued and therefore special 3-valued models) as well as our first attempt in the beginning of this section.

Formally, we can associate to any semantics SEM in the sense of Definition 4 two entailment relations

sceptical: $SEM^{scept}(P)$ is the set of all atoms or default atoms that are true in *all models* of $SEM(P)$.

credulous: $SEM^{cred}(P)$ is the set of all atoms or default atoms that are true in *at least one model* of $SEM(P)$.

3 Adding Negation

In the last section we have illustrated that logic programs with negation are very suitable for KR — they allow a natural and straightforward formalization of default-statements. The problem still remained to define an appropriate semantics for this class and, if possible, to find efficient query-answering methods. Both points are adressed in this section.

We can distinguish between two quite different approaches:

LP-Approach: This is the approach taken mainly in the Logic Programming community. There one tried to stick as close as possible to SLD-Resolution and treat negation as "Finite-Failure". This resulted in an extension of SLD, called SLDNF-Resolution, a procedural mechanism for query answering. For a nice overview, we refer to [6].

NML-Approach: This is the approach suggested by non-monotonic reasoning people. Here the main question is *"What is the right semantics?"* I.e. we are looking first for a semantics that correctly fits to our intuitions and treats the various KR-Tasks in the right (or appropriate) way. It should allow us to jump to conclusions even when only little information is available. Here it is of secondary interest how such a semantics can be implemented with a procedural calculus. Interesting overviews are [89] and [61].

The LP-Approach is dealt with in Section 3.1. It is still very near to classical predicate logic — default negation is interpreted as *Finite-Failure*. To get a stronger semantics, we interpret " *not* " as *Failure* in Section 3.2. The main difference is that the principle *Elimination of Tautologies* holds. We then introduce a principle GPPE which is related to partial evaluation. In KR one can see this principle as allowing for definitional extensions — names or abbreviations can be introduced without changing the semantics.

All these principles do not yet determine a unique semantics — there is still room for different semantics and a lot of them have been defined in the last years. We do not want to present the whole zoo of semantics nor to discuss their merits or shortcomings. We refer the reader to the overview articles [6] and [61] and the references given therein. We focus on the two main competing approaches that still have survived. These are the Wellfounded semantics WFS (Section 3.3) and the Stable semantics STABLE (Section 3.4).

3.1 Negation-as-Finite-Failure

The idea of negation treated as *finite-failure* can be best illustrated by still considering definite programs, but queries containing default-atoms. How should we handle such default-atoms by modifying our SLD-resolution? Let us try this:

- If we reach a default-atom " *not A*" as a subgoal of our original query, we keep the current SLD-tree in mind and start a new SLD-tree by trying to solve "*A*".
- If this succeeds, then we falsified " *not A*", the current branch is failing and we have to backtrack and consider a different subquery.
- But it can also happen that the SLD-tree for "*A*" is *finite with only failing branches*. Then we say that *A finitely fails*, we turn back to our original SLD-tree, consider the subgoal " *not A*" as successfully solved and go on with the next subgoal in the current list.

It is important to note that an SLD-tree for a positive atom can fail without *being finite*. The SLD-tree for the program consisting of the single rule $p \leftarrow p$ with respect to the query p is infinite but failing (it consists of one single infinite branch).

Although this idea of *Finite-Failure* is very procedural in nature, there is a nice modeltheoretical counterpart — Clark's completion $comp(P)$ ([50]). The idea of Clark was that a program P consists not only of the implications, but also of the information that *these are the only ones*. Roughly speaking, he argues that one should interpret the "$\leftarrow$"-arrows in rules as equivalences "$\equiv$" in classical logic.

Definition 5 (Clark's Completion $comp(P)$).
Clark's semantics for a program P is given by the set of all classical models of the theory $comp(P)$.

We can now see the classical theory $comp(P)$ as the information contained in the program P. $comp(P)$ is like a sort of closed world assumption applied to P. We are now able to derive negative information from P by deriving it from $comp(P)$. In fact, the following soundness and completeness result for definite programs P and definite queries $Q = \bigwedge_i A_i$ (consisting of only *positive* atoms) holds:

Theorem 3 (COMP and Fair FF-Trees).
The following conditions are equivalent:

- $comp(P) \models \forall \neg Q$
- *Every fair SLD-tree for P with respect to Q is finitely failed.*

Note that in the last theorem we did not use default negation but classical negation $\neg$ because we just mapped all formulae into classical logic. We need the fairness assumption to ensure that the selection of atoms is reasonably well-behaving: we want that every atom or default-atom occurring in the list of preliminary goals will eventually be selected.

But even this result is still very weak — after all we want to handle not only negative queries but programs containing default-atoms. From now on we consider programs with default-atoms in the body. We usually denote them by

$$A \leftarrow B^+ \wedge not\ B^-,$$

where $\mathcal{B}^+$ contains all the positive body atoms and *not* $\mathcal{B}^-$ all default atoms "*not C*".

Our two motivating examples in Section 2.2 contain such default atoms. This gives rise to an extension of SLD, called SLDNF, which treats negation as *Finite-Failure*

$$\text{SLDNF} = \text{SLD} + not\ L \text{ succeeds, if } L \text{ finitely fails.}$$

The precise definitions of SLDNF-*resolution*, *tree*, etc. are very complex: we refer to [85, 5]. Recently, Apt and Bol gave interesting improved versions of these notions: see [6, Section 3.2]. In order to get an intuitive idea, it is sufficient to describe the following underlying principle:

Principle 03 (A "Naive" SLDNF-Resolution)
If in the construction of an SLDNF-tree a default-atom not L_{ij} *is selected in the list* $\mathcal{L}_i = \{L_{i1}, L_{i2}, \ldots\}$, *then we try to prove* L_{ij}.
If this fails finitely (it fails because the generated subtree is finite and failing), then we take not L_{ij} *as proved and we go on to prove* $L_{i(j+1)}$.
If L_{ij} *succeeds, then* not L_{ij} *fails and we have to backtrack to the list* $\mathcal{L}_{i-1}$ *of preliminary subgoals (the next rule is applied: "backtracking").*

Does SLDNF-Resolution properly handle Example 1? It does indeed:

Inheritance: The query $make\_top(Tweety)$ generates an SLD-tree with one main branch, the nodes of which are:

$$\begin{aligned} &flies(Tweety), \\ &bird(Tweety),\ not\ ab(r_1, Tweety), \\ &not\ ab(r_1, Tweety), \\ &Success. \end{aligned}$$

The third node has a sibling-node $penguin(Tweety)$, not $ab(r_1, Tweety)$ which immediately fails because $Tweety$ does not unify with Sam. The $Success$-node is obtained from not $ab(r_1, Tweety)$ because the corresponding SLD-tree for the atom $ab(r_1, Tweety)$ fails finitely (this tree consists only of $ab(r_1, Tweety)$ and $penguin(Tweety)$).

Up to now it seems that SLDNF-resolution solves all our problems. It handles our examples correctly, and is defined by a procedural calculus strongly related to SLD. There are two main problems with SLDNF:

– SLDNF can not handle free variables in negative subgoals,
– SLDNF is still too weak for Knowledge Representation.

The latter problem is the most important one. By looking at a particular example, we will motivate in Section 3.2 the need for a stronger semantics. This will lead us in the remaining sections to the wellfounded and the stable semantics.

For the rest of this section we consider the first problem, known as the *Floundering Problem*. This problem will also occur later in implementations of the

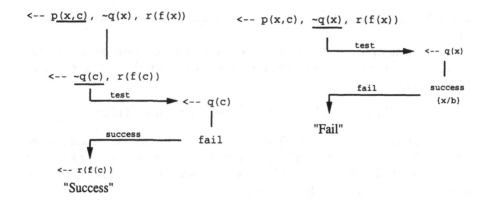

Figure1. The Floundering-Problem

wellfounded or the stable semantics. We consider the program $P_{flounder}$ consisting of the three facts

$$p(c, c), \ q(b), \ r(f(c)).$$

Our query is *?- $p(x, c)$, not $q(x), r(f(x))$* that is, we are interested in instantiations of x such that the query follows from the program. The situation is illustrated in Figure 1. Let us suppose that we always select the first atom or default-atom: it is underlined in the sequel. The SLDNF-tree of this trivial example is linear and has three nodes: the first node is the query itself

$$?\text{-} \ \underline{p(x, c)}, \ not \ q(x), r(f(x))$$

the second node is *?- not $q(c), r(f(c))$* Now, we enter the negation-as-failure mode and ask *?- $q(c)$* This query immediately fails (the generated tree exists, is finite and fails) so that we give back the answer "yes, the default atom *not $q(c)$* succeeds and can be skipped from the list". The last node is *?- $r(f(c))$* which immediately succeeds.

Note that in the last step, the test for *?-$q(c)$* has to be finished before the tree can be extended. If we get no answer, the SLDNF-tree simply does not exist: this can not happen with SLD-trees.

So far everything was fine. But what happens if we select the second atom in the first step

$$?\text{-}p(x, c), \ \underline{not \ q(x)}, r(f(x))$$

Example 2 (Floundering).
We again consider the program $P_{flounder}$ consisting of the three facts

$$p(c, c), \ q(b), \ r(f(c)).$$

Our query is *?-$p(x, c)$, not $q(x), r(f(x))$* and in the first step we will select the second default-atom, i.e. one with a free variable. Thus we enter the negation-as-failure mode with the query *?- not $q(x)$* In this case, x may be instantiated to b so that we have to give back the answer "no, the default-atom *not* $q(x)$ fails" and the whole query will fail. This is because SLDNF treats the subgoal as "$\forall x$ *not* $q(x)$" instead of "$\exists x$ *not* $q(x)$" which is intended. There exist approaches to overcome this shortcoming by treating negation as *constructive negation*: see [44, 45, 67].

3.2   Negation-as-Failure

Let us first illustrate that SLDNF answers quite easily our requirements of a semantics SEM (stated explicitly in Definition 4 on page 10). We can formulate these requirements as two program-transformations (they will be used later for computing a semantics). We call them *Reductions* for obvious reasons.

Principle 04 (Reduction)
Suppose we are given a program P with possibly default-atoms in its body. If a ground atom A does not unify with any head of the rules of P, then we can delete in every rule any occurrence of "not A" without changing the semantics.

Dually, if there is an instance of a rule of the form "$B \leftarrow$" then we can delete all rules that contain "not B" in their bodies.

It is obvious that SLDNF "implements" these two reductions automatically. The weakness of SLDNF for Knowledge Representation is in a sense inherited from SLD. When we consider rules of the form "$p \leftarrow p$", then SLD resolution gets into an infinite loop and no answer to the query $?\text{-}p$ can be obtained. This has often the effect that when we enter into negation-as-failure mode, the SLD-tree to be constructed is not finite, although it is not successful and therefore should be considered as failed.

Let us discuss this point with a more serious example.

Example 3 (The Transitive Closure).
Assume we are given a graph consisting of nodes and edges between some of them. We want to know which nodes are reachable from a given one. A natural formalization of the property "reachable" would be

$$reachable(x) \leftarrow edge(x, y), reachable(y).$$

What happens if we are given the following facts

$$edge(a, b), \ edge(b, a), \ edge(c, d)$$

and $reachable(c)$? Of course, we expect that neither a nor b are reachable because there is no path from c to either a or b.

But SLDNF-Resolution does not derive "*not reachable(a)*"!

How does this result relate to Theorem 3 on page 12? Note that our query has exactly the form as required there. Clark's completion of our program rule is

$$reachable(x) \ \equiv \ (x \doteq c \ \lor \ \exists y \, (reachable(y) \land edge(y, x)))$$

from which, together with our facts about the edge-relation, $\neg reachable(a)$ is indeed not derivable. This is due to the wellknown fact that transitive closure is not expressible in first order predicate logic.

Note also that our Principle 02 on page 8 does not help, because it simply does not apply. It turns out that we can augment our two principles by a third one, that constitutes together with them a very nice calculus handling the above example in the right way. This principle is related to *Partial Evaluation*, hence its name GPPE[4]. Let us motivate this principle with the last example. The query "*not reachable(a)*" leads to "*reachable(a) ← edge(a, b), reachable(b)*" and "*reachable(b)*" leads to "*reachable(b) ← edge(b, a), reachable(a)*". Both rules can be seen as definitions for $reachable(a)$ and $reachable(b)$ respectively. So it should be possible to replace in these rules the body atoms of $reachable$ by their definitions. Thus we obtain the two rules

$$reachable(a) \leftarrow edge(a, b), edge(b, a), reachable(a)$$
$$reachable(b) \leftarrow edge(b, a), edge(a, b), reachable(b)$$

that can both be eliminated by applying Principle 02 on page 8. So we end up with a program that does neither contain $reachable(a)$ nor $reachable(b)$ in one of the heads. Therefore, according to Principle 01 on page 6 both atoms should be considered false. The precise formulation of this principle is as follows:

Principle 05 (GPPE,[22, 106])

We say that a semantics SEM satisfies GPPE, if the following transformation does not change the semantics. Replace a rule $A \leftarrow B^+ \wedge not\ B^-$ where B^+ contains a distinguished atom B by the rules

$$A \cup \left(\mathcal{A}_i \setminus \{B\}\right) \leftarrow \left(B^+ \setminus \{B\}\right) \cup B_i^+ \wedge\ not\ \left(B^- \cup B_i^-\right)\ (i = 1, \ldots, n)$$

where $B \leftarrow B_i^+ \wedge not\ B_i^-\ (i = 1, \ldots, n)$ are all rules with head B.

Note that any semantics SEM satsfying GPPE and Elimination of Tautologies can be seen as extending SLD by doing some *Loop-checking*. We will call such semantics *NMR-semantics* in order to distinguish them from the classical *LP-semantics* which are based on SLDNF or variants of Clark's completion $comp(P)$:

– *NMR-Semantics = SLDNF + Loop-check.*

The following, somewhat artificial example illustrates this point.

Example 4 (COMP vs. NMR).

---
[4] Generalized Principle of Partial Evaluation

$$P_{NMR} : p \leftarrow p$$
$$q \leftarrow not\ p$$

$$P'_{NMR} : p \leftarrow p$$
$$q \leftarrow not\ p$$
$$r \leftarrow not\ r$$

$$comp(P_{NMR}) : p \equiv p$$
$$q \equiv \neg p$$

$$comp(P'_{NMR}) : p \equiv p$$
$$q \equiv \neg p$$
$$r \equiv \neg r$$

?-q: No (COMP).   ?-p: Yes (COMP).
Yes (NMR).   No (NMR).

For both programs, the answers of the completion-semantics do not match our NMR-intuition! In the case of P_{NMR} we expect q to be derivable, since we expect *not p* to be derivable: the only possibility to derive p is the rule $p \leftarrow p$ which, obviously, will never succeed. But $q \notin Th(\{q \equiv \neg p\}) = comp(P_{NMR})$! In the case of P'_{NMR} we expect p not to be derivable, for the same reason: the only possibility to derive p is the rule $p \leftarrow p$. But $p \in Fml = Th(\{r \equiv \neg r\}) = comp(P'_{NMR})$!

Note that the answers of the completion-semantics agree with the mechanism of SLDNF: $p \leftarrow p$ represents a loop. The completion of P' is inconsistent: this led Fitting to consider the three-valued version of $comp(P)$ mentioned at the end of Section 3.1. This approach avoids the inconsistency (the query *?-p* is not answered "yes") but it still does not answer "no" as we would like to have.

The last principle in this section is related to *Subsumption*: we can get rid of non-minimal rules by simply deleting them.

Principle 06 (Subsumption)
In a program P we can delete a rule $A \leftarrow B^+ \wedge$ not B^- whenever there is another rule $A \leftarrow B'^+ \wedge$ not B'^- with

$$B'^+ \subseteq B^+ \ and\ B'^- \subseteq B^-.$$

As a simple example, the rule $A \leftarrow B, C,\ not\ D,\ not\ E$ is subsumed by the 3 rules $A \leftarrow C,\ not\ D,\ not\ E$ or $A \leftarrow B, C,\ not\ E$ and by $A \leftarrow C,\ not\ E$.

3.3   The Wellfounded Semantics: WFS

The wellfounded semantics, originally introduced in [116], is the *weakest* semantics satisfying our 4 principles (see [30, 29, 60]). We call a semantics

$$\text{SEM}_1 \text{ weaker than } \text{SEM}_2, \text{ written } \text{SEM}_1 \leq_k \text{SEM}_2,$$

if for all programs P and all atoms or default-atoms l the following holds: $\text{SEM}_1(P) \models l$ implies $\text{SEM}_2(P) \models l$. I.e. all atoms derivable from SEM_1 with respect to P are also derivable from SEM_2. The notion $\leq_k$ refers to the knowledge ordering in three-valued logic. This is a nice theorem and gives rise to the following definition:

Theorem 4 (WFS, [30]).
There exists the weakest semantics satisfying our four principles Elimination of Tautologies, Reduction, Subsumption and GPPE. This semantics is called wellfounded semantics WFS.

It can also be shown, that for propositional programs, our transformations can be applied to compute this semantics.

Theorem 5 (Confluent Calculus for WFS,[29]).
The calculus consisting of these four transformations is confluent, i.e. whenever we arrive at an irreducible program, it is uniquely determined. The order of the transformations does not matter.

For finite propositional programs, it is also terminating: any program P is therefore associated a unique normalform $res(P)$. The wellfounded semantics of P can be read off from $res(P)$ as follows

$$WFS(P) = \{A: \ A \leftarrow \ \in res(P)\} \cup \{\text{not } A: \ A \text{ is in no head of } res(P)\}$$

We note that the size of the residual program is in general *exponential* in the size of the original program. Recently it was shown in [34, 31] how a small modification of the residual program, which still satisfies the nice characterization of computing WFS as given in Theorem 5, results in a *polynomial* computation.

Therefore the wellfounded semantics associates to every program P with negation a set consisting of atoms and default-atoms. This set is a 3-valued model of P. It can happen, of course, that this set is empty. But it is always consistent, i.e. it does not contain an atom A and its negation *not A*. Moreover, it extends SLDNF: whenever SLDNF derives an atom or default-atom and does not flounder, then WFS derives it as well. Therefore the two examples of Section 2.2 are handled in the right way. But also for Example 3 on page 15 we get the desired answers.

As we said above, loop-checking is in general undecidable. Therefore WFS is in the most general case where variables and function-symbols are allowed, undecidable. Only for finite propositional programs it is decidable. In fact, it is of quadratic complexity see [31].

Let us end this section with another example, which contains negation.

Example 5 (Van Gelder's Example).
Assume we are describing a two-players game like checkers. The two players alternately move a stone on a board. The moving player wins when his opponent has no more move to make. We can formalize that by

- wins(x) ← move_from_to(x,y), *not* wins(y)

meaning that

- the situation x is won (for the moving player A), if he can lead over[5] to a situation y that can never be won for B.

---

[5] With the help of a regular move, given by the relation *move_from_to/2*.

If we also have $move\_from\_to(a, b)$, $move\_from\_to(b, a)$ and $move\_from\_to(b, c)$. Our query to this program P_{game} is $?\text{-}wins(b)$ Here we have no problems with floundering, but using SLDNF we get an infinite sequence of oscillating SLD-trees (none of which finitely fails).

WFS, however, derives the right results

$$WFS(P_{game}) = \{\ not\ wins(c), wins(b),\ not\ wins(a)\}$$

which matches completely with our intuitions.

3.4   The Stable Semantics: STABLE

We defined WFS as the weakest semantics satisfying our four principles. This already indicates that there are even stronger semantics. One of the main competing approaches is the stable semantics STABLE. The stable semantics associates to any program P a set of 2-valued models, like classical predicate logic. STABLE satisfies the following property, in addition to those that have been already introduced:

Principle 07 (Elimination of Contradictions)
Suppose a program P has a rule which contains the same atom A and not A *in its body. Then we can eliminate this rule without changing the semantics.*

This principle can be used, in conjunction with the others to define the stable semantics

Theorem 6 (STABLE,[28]).
There exists the weakest semantics satisfying our five principles Elimination of Tautologies, Reduction, Subsumption, GPPE and Elimination of Contradictions.

If a semantics SEM satisfies *Elimination of Contradictions* it is based on 2-valued models ([28]). The underlying idea of STABLE is that any atom in an intended model should have a definite reason to be true or false. This idea was made explicit in [19, 20] and, independently, in [73]. We use the latter terminology and introduce the Gelfond-Lifschitz transformation: for a program P and a model $N \subseteq B_P$ we define

$$P^N := \{rule^N :\ rule \in P\}$$

where $rule := A \leftarrow B_1, \ldots, B_n$, not $C_1, \ldots$, not C_m is transformed as follows

$$(rule)^N := \begin{cases} A \leftarrow B_1, \ldots, B_n, & \text{if } \forall j : C_j \notin N, \\ \mathbf{t}, & \text{otherwise.} \end{cases}$$

Note that P^N is always a *definite* program. We can therefore compute its least Herbrand model M_{P^N} and check whether it coincides with the model N with which we started:

Definition 6 (STABLE).
N *is called a* stable *model[6] of P if and only if $M_{PN} = N$.*

What is the relationship between STABLE and WFS? We have seen that they are based on rather identical principles.

– Stable models N extend WFS: $l \in \mathrm{WFS}(P)$ implies $N \models l$.
– If $\mathrm{WFS}(P)$ is two-valued, then $\mathrm{WFS}(P)$ is the unique stable model.

But there are also differences. We refer to Example 5 on page 18 and consider the program P consisting of the clause

$$wins(x) \leftarrow move\_from\_to(x, y), \ not \ wins(y)$$

together with the following facts: $move\_from\_to(a, b)$, $move\_from\_to(b, a)$, as well as $move\_from\_to(b, c)$, and $move\_from\_to(c, d)$. In this particular case we have two stable models: $\{wins(a), \ wins(c)\}$ and $\{wins(b), \ wins(c)\}$ and therefore

$$\mathrm{WFS}(P) = \{wins(c), \ not \ wins(d)\} = \bigcap_{N \text{ a stable model of } P} N.$$

This means that the 3-valued wellfounded model is exactly the set of all atoms or default-atoms true in all stable models. But this is not always the case, as the program of $P_{splitting}$ shows:

Example 6 (Reasoning by cases).

$$P_{splitting} : a \leftarrow not \ b$$
$$b \leftarrow not \ a$$
$$p \leftarrow a$$
$$p \leftarrow b$$

Although neither a, nor b can be derived in any semantics based on two-valued models (as STABLE for example), the disjunction $a \vee b$, thus also p, is true. In this way the example is handled by the completion semantics, too. $\mathrm{WFS}(P)$, however, is empty; if the WFS cannot decide between a or $not \ a$, then a is undefined.

The main differences between STABLE and WFS are

– STABLE is not always consistent,
– STABLE does not allow for a goal-oriented implementation.

The inconsistency comes from odd, negative cycles

$$STABLE(p \leftarrow not \ p) = \emptyset.$$

---

[6] Note that we only consider Herbrand models.

The idea to consider 2-valued models for a semantics neccessarily implies its inconsistency ([24]). Note that $WFS(p \leftarrow not\ p) = \{\emptyset\}$ which is quite different! Sufficient criteria for the existence of stable models are contained in [68, 70].

That STABLE does not allow for a Top-Down evaluation is a more serious drawback and has nothing to do with inconsistency.

We end this section with another description of WFS and STABLE that will be useful in later sections. It was introduced in [11, 12]:

Definition 7 (Antimonotone Operator γ_P).
For a program P and a set $N \subset B_P$ we define an operator γ_P mapping Herbrand-structures to Herbrand structures:

$$\gamma_P(N) := M_{P^N}.$$

It is easy to see that γ_P is antimonotone. Therefore its twofold application γ^2 is monotone ([109]).

Obviously, the stable models of a program P are exactly the fixpoints of γ_P. This is just a reformulation of Definition 6 on the preceding page. WFS is related to γ as follows

Theorem 7 (WFS and γ^2).
A positive atom A is in WFS(P) if and only if $A \in lfp(\gamma_P^2)$. A default-atom not A is in WFS(P) if and only if $A \notin gfp(\gamma_P^2)$:

$$WFS(P) = lfp(\gamma_P^2) \cup \{\,not\ A : A \notin gfp(\gamma_P^2)\}.$$

Atom or default-atoms that do occur in neither of the two sets are undefined.

4   Adding Explicit Negation

So far we have considered programs with one special type of negation, namely default negation. Default negation is particularly useful in domains where complete positive information can be obtained. For instance, if one wants to represent flight connections from Budapest to the US it is very convenient to represent all existing flights and to let default negation handle the derivation of negative information. There are domains, however, where the lack of positive information cannot be assumed to support (or support with enough strength) that this information is false. In such domains it becomes important to distinguish between cases where a query does not succeed and cases where the negated query succeeds. The following example was used by McCarthy to illustrate the issue. Assume one wants to represent the rule: cross the railroad tracks if no train is approaching. The straightforward representation of this rule with default negation would be

$$crosstracks \leftarrow not\ train$$

It seems obvious that in many practical settings the use of such a rule would not lead to intended behaviour, in fact it might even have disasterous consequences.

What seems to be needed here is the possibility of using a different negation symbol representing a stronger form of negation. This new negation — we will call it explicit negation — should be true only if the corresponding negated literal can actually be derived. We will use the classical negation symbol ¬ to represent explicit negation. The track crossing rule will be represented as

$$crosstracks \leftarrow \neg train$$

The idea is that this latter rule will only be applicable if ¬*train* has been proved, contrary to the first rule which is applicable whenever *train* is not provable.

In the next section we will shortly discuss that explicit negation is (or should not be) *classical* negation and how it should interfere with default negation. In the two following subsections we will generalize the semantics STABLE and WFS, respectively, to programs with explicit negation.

4.1   Explicit vs. Classical and Strong Negation

First we define the language we are using more precisely.

Definition 8 (Extended Logic Program).
An extended logic program consists of rules of the form

$$c \leftarrow a_1, \ldots, a_n, \text{not } b_1, \ldots, \text{not } b_m$$

where the a_i, b_j and c are literals, i.e., either propositional atoms or such atoms preceded by the classical negation sign. The symbol "not " denotes negation by failure (default negation), "¬" denotes explicit negation.

We have already motivated the need of a second kind of negation "¬" different from " *not* ". What should the semantics of "¬" be? Should it be just like in classical logic? Note that classical negation satisfies the law of excluded middle

$$A \lor \neg A.$$

The following example taken from [4] shows that classical negation is sometimes inappropriate for KR-tasks.

Example 7 (Behaviour of Classical Negation).
Suppose an employer has several candidates that apply for a job. Some of them are clearly qualified while others are not. But there may also be some candidates whose qualifications are not clear and who should therefore be interviewed in order to find out about their qualifications. If we express the situation by

$$hire(X) \leftarrow qualified(X) \text{ and } reject(X) \leftarrow \neg qualified(X)$$

then, interpreting "¬" as classical negation, we are forced to derive that every candidate must either be hired or rejected! There is no room for those that should be interviewed. Also, applying the law of excluded middle has a highly non-constructive flavor.

Let us now consider again the example $crosstracks \leftarrow \neg train$ from the beginning of this section. Suppose that we replace $\neg train$ by $free\_track$. We obtain

$$crosstracks \leftarrow free\_track.$$

From this program, "$not\ crosstracks$" will be derivable for any semantics. Therefore we should make sure that "$not\ crosstracks$" is also derivable from

$$crosstracks \leftarrow \neg train$$

After all, the second program is obtained from the first one by a simple syntactic operation. This means we have to make sure that default negation "not" treats positive and negative atoms symmetrically.

Such a negation, we will call it *explicit* will be introduced in the next two sections. Sometimes explicit negation is also called *strong* negation and denotes still a variant of our explicit negation. In [4] the authors introduce both a strong and explicit negation and discuss their relation with classical and default negation at length.

4.2   STABLE for Extended Logic Programs

The extension of STABLE to extended logic programs is based on the notion of answer sets which generalize the original notion of stable models in a rather straightforward manner. Let us first introduce some useful notation. We say a rule $r = c \leftarrow a_1, \ldots, a_n,\ not\ b_1, \ldots,\ not\ b_m \in P$ is defeated by a literal l iff $l = b_i$ for some $i \in \{1, \ldots, m\}$. We say r is defeated by a set of literals X if X contains at least one literal that defeats r. Furthermore, we call the rule obtained by deleting weakly negated preconditions from r the monotonic counterpart of r and denote it with $Mon(r)$. We also apply Mon to sets of rules with the obvious meaning.

Definition 9 (X-reduct).
Let P be an extended logic program, X a set of literals. The X-reduct of P, denoted P^X, is the program obtained from P by

- *deleting each rule defeated by X, and*
- *replacing each remaining rule r with its monotonic counterpart $Mon(r)$.*

Definition 10 (Consequences of Rules).
Let R be a set of rules without negation as failure. $Cn(R)$ denotes the smallest set of literals that is

1. *closed under R, and*
2. *logically closed, i.e., either consistent or equal to the set of all literals.*

Definition 11 (Answer set).
Let P be an extended logic program, X a set of literals. Define the operator γ_P as follows:

$$\gamma_P(X) = Cn(P^X)$$

X is an answer set of P iff $X = \gamma_P(X)$.

The definition of answer sets is thus based on a natural generalization of the operator γ_P (see Definition 7 on page 21) to extended logic programs.

A literal l is a consequence of a program P under the new semantics, denoted $l \in STABLE(P)$, iff l is contained in all answer sets of P.

It is not difficult to see that for programs without explicit negation stable models and answer sets coincide. Here is an example involving both types of negation. The example describes the strategy of a certain college for awarding scholarships to its students. It is taken from [10]:

$$P_{el} : \begin{array}{ll} (1)\ eligible(x) & \leftarrow\ highGPA(x) \\ (2)\ eligible(x) & \leftarrow\ minority(x), fairGPA(x) \\ (3)\ \neg eligible(x) & \leftarrow\ \neg fairGPA(x), \neg highGPA(x) \\ (4)\ interview(x) & \leftarrow\ not\ eligible(x), not\ \neg eligible(x) \end{array}$$

Assume in addition to the rules above the following facts about Anne are given:

$$fairGPA(Anne), \neg highGPA(Anne)$$

We obtain exactly one answer set, namely

$$\{fairGPA(Anne), \neg highGPA(Anne), interview(Anne)\}$$

Anne will thus be interviewed before a decision about her eligibility is made. If we use the above rules together with the facts

$$minority(Mike), fairGPA(Mark)$$

then the program entails $eligible(Mike)$.

We obtain the following result [83]:

Lemma 1 (Program Types).
Let P be an extended logic program. P satisfies exactly one of the following conditions:

- *P has no answer sets,*
- *P has an answer set, and all its answer sets are consistent,*
- *the only answer set for P is Lit,*

A program is consistent if the set of its consequences is consistent, and inconsistent otherwise. The former corresponds to the first two cases listed in the proposition, the latter to the third case.

It should be noted that extended logic programs under answer set semantics can be reduced to general logic programs as follows: for any predicate p occurring in a program P we introduce a new predicate symbol p' of the same arity representing the explicit negation of p. We then replace each occurrence of $\neg p$ in the program with p', thus obtaining the general logic program P'. It can be proved that a consistent set of literals S is an answer set of P iff the set S' is a stable model of P', where S' is obtained from S by replacing $\neg p$ with p'.

4.3   WFS for Extended Logic Programs

We now show how the second major semantics for general logic programs, WFS, can be extended to logic programs with explicit negation. For our purposes the characterization of WFS given in Theorem 7 on page 21 will be useful. WFS is based on a particular three-valued model. To simplify our presentation in this section we will restrict ourselves to the literals which are true in this three-valued model. The literals which are false will be left implicit. They can be added in a canonical way as follows: let T, the set of true literals, be defined as the least fixed point of a monotone operator composed of two antimonotone operators $op_1 op_2$. Then the literals which are false in the three-valued model are exactly those which are not contained in $op_2(T)$. Given this canonical extension to the full three-valued model we can safely leave the false literals implicit from now on.

A natural idea is to use the characterization of WFS in terms of the least fixed point of γ_P^2, as in Theorem 7 on page 21, where γ_P now is the new generalized operator from Definition 4.2 on page 23 [10, 83]. This works in some cases, but often leads to very weak results.

Consider the following program P_0 which has also been discussed by Baral and Gelfond [10]:

$$P_0 : (1)\ b\ \leftarrow\ not\ \neg b$$
$$(2)\ a\ \leftarrow\ not\ \neg a$$
$$(3)\ \neg a \leftarrow\ not\ a$$

The least fixed point of γ^2 is empty since $\gamma_{P_0}(\emptyset)$ equals Lit, the set of all literals, and the Lit-reduct of P_0 contains no rule at all. This is surprising since, intuitively, the conflict between (2) and (3) has nothing to do with $\neg b$ and b.

This problem arises whenever the following conditions hold:

1. a complementary pair of literals is provable from the monotonic counterparts of the rules of a program P, and
2. there is at least one proof for each of the complementary literals whose rules are not defeated by $Cn(P')$, where P' consists of the "strict" rules in P, i.e., those without negation as failure.

In this case well-founded semantics concludes l iff $l \in Cn(P')$. It should be obvious that such a situation is not just a rare limiting case. To the contrary, it can be expected that many commonsense knowledge bases will give rise to such undesired behaviour.

A minor reformulation of the fixpoint operator can overcome this weakness and leads to better results. Consider the following operator

$$\gamma_P^*(X) = Cl(P^X)$$

where $Cl(R)$ denotes the minimal set of literals closed under the (classical) rules R. $Cl(R)$ is thus like $Cn(R)$ without the requirement of logical closedness. Now define a monotne operator as follows:

$$\Gamma_P^*(X) = \gamma_P(\gamma_P^*(X))$$

With this operator well founded semantics can be defined.

Definition 12 (WFS for extended programs).
Let P be an extended logic program. The set of well-founded conclusions of P, denoted $WFS(P)$, is the least fixpoint of Γ_P^*.

Consider the effects of this modification on our example P_0:

$$\gamma_{P_0}^*(\emptyset) = \{a, \neg a, b\}.$$

Rule (1) is contained in the $\{a, \neg a, b\}$-reduct of P_0 and thus $\Gamma_{P_0}^*(\emptyset) = \{b\}$. Since b is also the only literal contained in all answer sets of P_0 WFS actually coincides with answer set semantics in this case.

It can be shown that every well-founded conclusion is a conclusion under the answer set semantics. Well-founded semantics can thus be viewed as an approximation of answer set semantics.

An alternative, somewhat stronger approach, was developed by Pereira and Alferes [98, 2, 3], the semantics WFSX. This semantics implements the intuition that a literal with default negation should be derivable from the corresponding explicitly negated literal. The authors call this the coherence principle. To satisfy the principle they use the seminormal version of a program P, denoted $S(P)$, which is obtained from P by replacing each rule

$$c \leftarrow a_1, \ldots, a_n, \text{ not } b_1, \ldots, \text{ not } b_m$$

by the rule

$$c \leftarrow a_1, \ldots, a_n, \text{ not } b_1, \ldots, \text{ not } b_m, \text{ not } -c$$

where $-c$ is the complement of c, i.e. $\neg c$ if c is an atom and a if $c = \neg a$. Based on this notion Pereira and Alferes consider the following monotone operator:

$$\Omega_P(X) = \gamma_P^* \gamma_{S(P)}^*(X)$$

The use of the seminormal version of the program in the first application of γ^* guarantees that a literal l is not considered a potential conclusion whenever the complementary literal is already known to be true. In the general case $S(P)^X$ contains fewer rules than P^X. Therefore, fewer literals are considered as potential conclusions and thus more conclusions are obtained in each iteration of the monotone operator. Here is an example [10]:

$$
\begin{aligned}
P_{WFSX} : (1)\ a &\leftarrow \text{ not } b \\
(2)\ b &\leftarrow \text{ not } a \\
(3)\ \neg a &\leftarrow
\end{aligned}
$$

The original version of WFS does not conclude b. In WFSX the set $X = \{\neg a\}$ is obtained after the first iteration of the monotone operator. Since rule (1) is not contained in the X-reduct of the seminormal version of the program the monotonic counterpart of (2) produces b after the second iteration.

Although a number of researchers consider WFSX to be the more adequate extension of well-founded semantics to extended logic programs the original formulation is still very often found in the literature. For this reason we will base our treatment of preferences in the next section on the earlier formulation based on Γ^*.

For the next section a minor reformulation turns out to be convenient. Instead of using the monotonic counterparts of undefeated rules we will work with the original rules and extend the definitions of the two operators Cn and Cl accordingly, requiring that default negated preconditions be neglected, i.e., for an arbitrary set of rules P with default negation we define $Cn(P) = Cn(Mon(P))$ and $Cl(P) = Cl(Mon(P))$. We can now equivalently characterize γ_P and γ_P^* by the equations

$$\gamma_P(X) = Cn(P_X)$$

$$\gamma_P^*(X) = Cl(P_X)$$

where P_X denotes the set of rules not defeated by X.

An alternative characterization of Γ_P^* will also turn out to be useful in the next section. It is based on the following notion:

Definition 13 (X-SAFE).
Let P be a logic program, X a set of literals. A rule r is X-safe wrt. P ($r \in SAFE_X(P)$) if r is not defeated by $\gamma_P^*(X)$ or, equivalently, if $r \in P_{\gamma_P^*(X)}$.

With this new notion we can obviously characterize Γ_P^* as follows:

$$\Gamma_P^*(X) = Cn(P_{\gamma_P^*(X)}) = Cn(SAFE_X(P))$$

It is this last formulation that we will modify. More precisely, the notion of X-safeness will be weakened to handle preferences adequately.

5   Adding Preferences

In this section we describe an extension of well-founded semantics for logic programs with two types of negation where information about preferences between rules can be expressed in the logical language. Conflicts among rules are resolved whenever possible on the basis of derived preference information.

After giving some motivation in Section 5.1 we introduce our treatment of preferences in Section 5.2. We show that our conclusions are, in general, a superset of the well-founded conclusions. Section 5.3 illustrates the expressive power of our approach using a legal reasoning example.

5.1   Motivation

Preferences among defaults play a crucial role in nonmonotonic reasoning. One source of preferences that has been studied intensively is specificity [99, 110, 111] — we already discussed it in Example 1 on page 9. In case of a conflict between defaults we tend to prefer the more specific one since this default provides more reliable information. E.g., if we know that students are adults, adults are normally employed, students are normally not employed, we want to conclude "Peter is not employed" from the information that Peter is a student, thus preferring the student default over the conflicting adult default.

Specificity is an important source of preferences, but not the only one, and at least in some applications not necessarily the most important one. In the legal domain it may, for instance, be the case that a more general rule is preferred since it represents federal law as opposed to state law [100]. In these cases preferences may be based on some basic principles regulating how conflicts among rules are to be resolved. Also in other application domains, like model based diagnosis or configuration, preferences play a fundamental role.

The relevance of preferences is well-recognized in nonmonotonic reasoning, and prioritized versions for most of the nonmonotonic logics have been proposed, e.g., prioritized circumscription [84], hierarchic autoepistemic logic [81], prioritized default logic [35]. In these approaches preferences are handled in an "external" manner in the following sense: some ordering among defaults is used to control the generation of the nonmonotonic conclusions. For instance, in the case of prioritized default logic this information is used to control the generation of extensions. However, the preference information itself is not expressed in the logical language.

Here we want to go one step further and represent also this kind of information in the language. This makes it possible to reason not only *with*) but also *about* preferences. This is necessary in legal argumentation, for instance, where preferences are context-dependent, and the assessment of the preferences among involved conflicting laws is a crucial (if not the most crucial) part of the reasoning.

The presentation in this section is based on [37]. A treatment of prioritized logic programs under answer set semantics is described in [38].

5.2 Handling Preferences

In order to handle preferences we need to be able to express preference information explicitly. Since we want to do this *in* the logical language we have to extend the language. We do this in two respects:

1. we use a set of rule names N together with a naming function *name* to be able to refer to particular rules,
2. we use a special (infix) symbol $\prec$ that can take rule names as arguments to represent preferences among rules.

Intuitively, $n_1 \prec n_2$ where n_1 and n_2 are rule names means the rule with name n_1 is preferred over the rule with name n_2.[7]

---

[7] Note that for historical reasons we follow the convention that the minimal rules are the preferred ones.

Definition 14 (Prioritized Program).

A prioritized logic program is a pair $(R, name)$ where

- *R is a set of rules containing all ground instances of the schemata*

$$N_1 \prec N_3 \leftarrow N_1 \prec N_2, N_2 \prec N_3$$

   and

$$\neg(N_2 \prec N_1) \leftarrow N_1 \prec N_2$$

   where N_i are parameters for names, and
- *name a a partial injective naming function that assigns a name $n \in N$ to some of the rules in R.*

Note that not all rules do necessarily have a name. The reason is that names will only play a role in conflict resolution among defeasible rules, i.e., rules with weakly negated preconditions. For this reason names for strict rules, i.e., rules in which the symbol *not* does not appear, won't be needed.

In our examples we leave the instances of the schemata for $\prec$ implicit. We also assume that N and the function *name* are given implicitly. We write:

$$n_i : c \leftarrow a_1, \ldots, a_n, \; not \; b_1, \ldots, \; not \; b_m$$

to express that $name(c \leftarrow a_1, \ldots, a_n, \; not \; b_1, \ldots, \; not \; b_m) = n_i$.

Before introducing our new definitions we would like to point out how we want the new explicit preference information to be used. Our approach follows two principles:

1. *We want to extend well-founded semantics, i.e. we want that every $WFS^\star$-conclusion remains a conclusion in the prioritized approach.*
2. *We want to use preferences to solve conflicts whenever this is possible without violating principle 1.*

Let us first explain what we mean by conflict here. Rules may be conflicting in several ways. In the simplest case two rules may have complementary literals in their heads. We call this a type-I conflict.

Definition 15 (Type-I Conflict).

Let r_1 and r_2 be two rules. We say r_1 and r_2 are type-I conflicting iff the head of r_1 is the complement of the head of r_2.

Conflicts of this type may render the set of well-founded conclusions inconsistent, but do not necessarily do so. If, for instance, a precondition of one of the rules is not derivable or a rule is defeated the conflict is implicitly resolved. In that case the preference information will simply be neglected. Consider the following program P_1:

$$n_1 : b \leftarrow \; not \; c$$
$$n_2 : \neg b \leftarrow \; not \; b$$
$$n_3 : n_2 \prec n_1$$

There is a type-I conflict between n_1 and n_2. Although the explicit preference information gives precedence to n_2 we want to apply n_1 here to comply with the first of our two principles. Technically, this means that we can apply a preferred rule r only if we are sure that r's application actually leads to a situation where literals defeating r can no longer be derived.

The following two rules exhibit a different type of conflict:

$$a \leftarrow not\ b$$
$$b \leftarrow not\ a$$

The heads of these rules are not complementary. However, the application of one rule defeats the other and vice versa. We call this a direct type-II conflict. Of course, in the general case the defeat of the conflicting rule may be indirect, i.e. based on the existence of additional rules.

Definition 16 (Type-II Conflict).
Let r_1 and r_2 be rules, R a set of rules. We say r_1 and r_2 are type-II conflicting wrt. R iff

1. $Cl(R)$ *neither defeats r_1 nor r_2,*
2. $Cl(R + r_1)$ *defeats r_2, and*
3. $Cl(R + r_2)$ *defeats r_1*

Here $R + r$ abbreviates $R \cup \{r\}$. A direct type-II conflict is thus a type-II conflict wrt. the empty set of rules. Note that the two types of conflict are not disjoint, i.e. two rules may be in conflict of both type-I and type-II. Consider the following program P_2, a slight modification of P_1:

$$n_1 : b \leftarrow not\ c,\ not\ \neg b$$
$$n_2 : \neg b \leftarrow not\ b$$
$$n_3 : n_2 \prec n_1$$

Now we have a type-II conflict between n_1 and n_2 (more precisely, a direct type-II and a type-I conflict) that is not solvable by the implicit mechanisms of well-founded semantics alone. It is this kind of conflict that we try to solve by the explicit preference information. In our example n_2 will be used to derive $\neg b$. Note that now the application of n_2 defeats n_1 and there is no danger that a literal defeating n_2 might become derivable later. Generally, a type-II conflict between r_1 and r_2 (wrt. some undefeated rules of the program) will be solved in favour of the preferred rule, say r_1, only if applying r_1 excludes any further possibility of deriving an r_1-defeating literal.

After this motivating discussion let us present the new definitions. Our treatment of priorities is based on a weakening of the notion of X-safeness (Definition 13 on page 27). In Section 4 we considered a rule r as X-safe whenever there is no proof for a literal defeating r from the monotonic counterparts of X-undefeated rules. Now in the context of a prioritized logic program we will consider a rule r as X-safe if there is no such proof from monotonic counterparts *of a certain subset* of the X-undefeated rules. The subset to be used depends on the rule r and consists of those rules that are not "dominated" by r. Intuitively, r' is dominated by r iff r' is

1. known to be less preferred than r and
2. defeated when r is applied together with rules that already have been established to be X-safe.

It is obvious that whenever there is no proof for a defeating literal from all X-undefeated rules there can be no such proof from a subset of these rules. Rules that were X-safe according to our earlier definition thus remain to be X-safe. Here are the precise definitions:

Definition 17 (Dominated Rules).
Let $P = (R, name)$ be a prioritized logic program, X a set of literals, Y a set of rules, and $r \in R$. The set of rules dominated by r wrt. X and Y, denoted $Dom_{X,Y}(r)$, is the set

$$\{r' \in R \mid name(r) \prec name(r') \in X \text{ and } Cl(Y + r) \text{ defeats } r'\}$$

Note that $Dom_{X,Y}(r)$ is monotonic in both X and Y. We can now define the X-safe rules inductively:

Definition 18 $(SAFE_X^{pr}(P))$.
Let $P = (R, name)$ be a prioritized logic program, X a set of literals. The set of X-safe rules of P, denoted $SAFE_X^{pr}(P)$, is defined as follows: $SAFE_X^{pr}(P) = \bigcup_{i=0}^{\infty} R_i$, *where*

$R_0 = \emptyset$, *and for* $i > 0$,
$R_i = \{r \in R \mid r \text{ not defeated by } Cl(R_X \setminus Dom_{X,R_{i-1}}(r))\}$

Note that X-safeness is obviously monotonic in X. Based on this notion we introduce a new monotonic operator Γ_P^{pr}:

Definition 19 (WFS^{pr}).
Let $P = (R, name)$ be a prioritized logic program, X a set of literals. The operator Γ_P^{pr} is defined as follows:

$$\Gamma_P^{pr}(X) = Cn(SAFE_X^{pr}(P))$$

As before we define the (prioritized) well-founded conclusions of P, denoted $WFS^{pr}(P)$, as the least fixpoint of Γ_P^{pr}. If a program does not contain preference information at all, i.e., if the symbol $\prec$ does not appear in R, the new semantics coincides with WFS since in that case no rule can dominate another rule. In the general case, since the new definition of X-safeness is weaker than the one used earlier we may have more X-safe rules and for this reason obtain more conclusions than via Γ_P^*.

Consider the following prioritized program P:

$n_1 : b \leftarrow not\ c$
$n_2 : c \leftarrow not\ b$
$n_3 : n_2 \prec n_1$

We first apply Γ_P^{pr} to the empty set. Besides the instances of the transitivity and anti-symmetry schema that we implicitly assume only n_3 is in $SAFE_\emptyset^{pr}(P)$. We thus obtain

$$S_1 = \{n_2 \prec n_1, \neg(n_1 \prec n_2)\}$$

We next apply Γ_P^{pr} to S_1. Since $n_2 \prec n_1 \in S_1$ we have $n_1 \in Dom_{S_1,\emptyset}(n_2)$. $n_2 \in SAFE_{S_1}^{pr}(P)$ since $Cl(P_{S_1} \setminus \{n_1\})$ does not defeat n_2 and we obtain

$$S_2 = \{n_2 \prec n_1, \neg(n_1 \prec n_2), c\}$$

Further iteration of Γ_P^{pr} yields no new literals, i.e. S_2 is the least fixpoint. Note that c is not a conclusion under the original well-founded semantics.

The following nondeterministic algorithm computes the least fixed point of Γ_P^{pr} with time complexity of $O(n^3)$, where n is the number of rules:

Procedure WFS^{pr}
Input: A prioritized logic program $P = (R, name)$ with $|R| = n$
Output: the least fixed point of Γ_P^{pr}
$S_0 := \emptyset$;
$R_0 := \emptyset$;
for $i = 1$ to n do
    if there is a rule $r \in R_{S_{i-1}} \setminus R_{i-1}$ such that
    $Cl(R_{S_{i-1}} \setminus Dom_{S_{i-1}, R_{i-1}}(r))$ does not defeat r
    then $R_i := R_{i-1} + r; S_i := Cn(R_i)$
    else return S_{i-1}
endfor
end WFS^{pr}

5.3   A Legal Reasoning Example

In this section we show how our approach can be applied to legal reasoning problems. We will use an example first discussed by Gordon [75].

Example 8 (Legal Reasoning).
Assume a person wants to find out if her security interest in a certain ship is perfected. She currently has possession of the ship. According to the Uniform Commercial Code (UCC, §9-305) a security interest in goods may be perfected by taking possession of the collateral. However, there is a federal law called the Ship Mortgage Act (SMA) according to which a security interest in a ship may only be perfected by filing a financing statement. Such a statement has not been filed. Now the question is whether the UCC or the SMA takes precedence in this case. There are two known legal principles for resolving conflicts of this kind. The principle of *Lex Posterior* gives precedence to newer laws. In our case the UCC is newer than the SMA. On the other hand, the principle of *Lex Superior* gives precedence to laws supported by the higher authority. In our case the SMA has higher authority since it is federal law.

The available information can nicely be represented in our approach. To make the example somewhat shorter we use the notation

$$c \Leftarrow a_1, \ldots, a_n, \, not \; b_1, \ldots, \, not \; b_m$$

as an abbreviation for the rule

$$c \leftarrow a_1, \ldots, a_n, \, not \; b_1, \ldots, \, not \; b_m, \, not \; c'$$

where c' is the complement of c, i.e. $\neg c$ if c is an atom and a if $c = \neg a$. Such rules thus correspond to semi-normal or, if $m = 0$, normal defaults in Reiter's default logic [103].

We use the ground instances of the following named rules to represent the relevant article of the UCC, the SMA, Lex Posterior (LP), and Lex Superior (LS). The symbols d_1 and d_2 are parameters for rule names:

$UCC : perfected \Leftarrow possession$
$SMA : \neg perfected \Leftarrow ship, \neg fin\text{-}statement$
$LP(d_1, d_2) : d_1 \prec d_2 \Leftarrow more\text{-}recent(d_1, d_2)$
$LS(d_1, d_2) : d_1 \prec d_2 \Leftarrow fed\text{-}law(d_1), state\text{-}law(d_2)$

The following facts are known about the case and are represented as rules without body (and without name):

$possession$
$ship$
$\neg fin\text{-}statement$
$more\text{-}recent(UCC, SMA)$
$fed\text{-}law(SMA)$
$state\text{-}law(UCC)$

Let's call the above set of literals H. Iterated application of Γ_P^{pr} yields the following sequence of literal sets (in each case $S_i = (\Gamma_P^{pr})^i(\emptyset)$):

$$S_1 = H$$
$$S_2 = S_1$$

The iteration produces no new results besides the facts already contained in the program. The reason is that UCC and SMA block each other, and that no preference information is produced since also the relevant instances of Lex Posterior and Lex Superior block each other. The situation changes if we add information telling us how conflicts between the latter two are to be resolved. Assume we add the following information:[8]

$$LS(SMA, UCC) \prec LP(UCC, SMA)$$

---

[8] In realistic settings one would again use a schema here. In order to keep the example simple we use the relevant instance of the schema directly.

Now we obtain the following sequence:

$$S_1 = H \cup \{LS(SMA, UCC) \prec LP(UCC, SMA),$$
$$\neg LP(UCC, SMA) \prec LS(SMA, UCC)\}$$
$$S_2 = S_1 \cup \{SMA \prec UCC, \neg UCC \prec SMA\}$$
$$S_3 = S_2 \cup \{\neg perfected\}$$
$$S_4 = S_3$$

This example nicely illustrates how in our approach conflict resolution strategies can be specified declaratively, by simply asserting relevant preferences among the involved conflicting rules.

6   Adding Disjunction

In this section we will extend our programs to *disjunctive* statements. In Knowledge Representation it often occurs that we know $A \vee B \vee C$ without being sure which of these propositions hold. In fact, such a disjunction leaves it open: there might be states in the world where A holds or B or C or any combination thereof. Nevertheless, we can have information that A implies D and B implies D and C implies D from which we would like to derive that D holds for sure. It has been shown that even with disjunctive programs *without negation* we can already express relations which belong to the second level of the polynomial hierarchy.

Concerning the right semantics for such programs, we are in the same situation as in Section 3 — for positive programs there is general agreement while for disjunctive programs with default-negation there exist several competing approaches.

We present in Section 6.1 the generalized closed world assumption introduced by Minker. In Section 6.2 we show that our definition of WFS from Section 3.3 immediately carries over to the disjunctive case. The original definition of STABLE (Definition 6 on page 20) also carries over — we present it in Section 6.3.

6.1   GCWA

GCWA was defined by Minker ([87]) and can bee seen as a refined version of the CWA introduced by Reiter ([102]):

Definition 20 (CWA).

$$\text{CWA(DB)} = \text{DB} \cup \{\neg P(t) : \text{DB} \not\models P(t)\},$$

where $P(t)$ is a ground predicate instance.

That is, if a ground term cannot be inferred from the database, its negation is added to the closure. A weakness of CWA is that already for very simple theories, like $A \vee B$ it is inconsistent. Since neither A nor B is derivable, we have to add both their negations which makes the whole set inconsistent.

GCWA is defined for positive disjunctive programs consisting of rules of the form

$$A_1 \vee \ldots \vee A_n \leftarrow B_1, \ldots, B_m$$

by declaring all the minimal models to be the intended ones:

Definition 21 (GCWA).
The generalized closed world assumption GCWA of P is the semantics given by the set of all minimal Herbrand models of P:

$$GCWA(P) := Min\text{-}MOD(P)$$

GCWA is very important because it plays the same role for positive disjunctive programs as the least Herbrand model M_P does for definite programs.

Note also that as far as we consider deriving *positive* disjunctions, we stay entirely within classical logic — a positive disjunction is true in GCWA if and only if it follows from the program considered as a classical theory. Therefore this task can be accomplished be methods and techniques developed in theorem proving in the last 30 years. In fact this was one of the main starting points of the DisLoP-project in Koblenz (see Section 7.2).

In Sections 2 and 3 we have introduced the general notion of a semantics and various principles. Do they carry over to the disjunctive case? Fortunately, the answer is yes. In addition, GCWA not only satisfies all these properties, it is also uniquely characterized by them as the next theorem shows (we will introduce these properties in the next section).

Theorem 8 (Characterization of GCWA, [28]).
Let SEM be a semantics satisfying GPPE and Elimination of Tautologies.

a) *Then: $SEM(P) \subseteq Min\text{-}MOD_{2-val}(P)$ for positive disj. programs P.*
   I.e. any such semantics is already based on 2-valued minimal models. In particular, GCWA is the weakest semantics with these properties.
b) *If SEM is non-trivial and satisfies in addition[9] Isomorphy and* Relevance,
   then it coincides with GCWA on positive disjunctive programs.

We end this section with the discussion of a well-known example that can not be handled adequately by Circumscription:

Example 9 (Poole's Broken Arm).
Usually, a person's left arm is useable. But if the left arm is broken, it is an exception. The same statement holds for the right arm. Suppose that we saw Fred yesterday with a broken arm but we do not remember if it was the left or the right one. We also know that Fred can make out a cheque if he has at least

---

[9] See Section 7.1 for the precise definitions of Relevance and Isomorphy.

one useable arm (he is ambidextrous) but that he is completely disabled if both arms are broken. Here is the natural formalization:

$$
\begin{aligned}
left\_use(x) &\leftarrow not\ ab(left, x) \\
ab(left, x) &\leftarrow left\_brok(x) \\
right\_use(x) &\leftarrow not\ ab(right, x) \\
ab(right, x) &\leftarrow right\_brok(x) \\
left\_brok(Fred) \vee right\_brok(Fred) &\leftarrow \\
make\_cheque(x) &\leftarrow left\_use(x) \\
make\_cheque(x) &\leftarrow right\_use(x) \\
disabled(x) &\leftarrow left\_brok(x), right\_brok(x)
\end{aligned}
$$

Of course, we expect that Fred is able to make out a cheque even without knowing which arm he is actually using. Also we derive that he is not (completely) disabled.

For general Circumscription, the problem is to rule out the unintended model where both arms are broken and Fred is disabled. As we will see later, both D-WFS and DSTABLE derive that Fred is not disabled but only DSTABLE is strong enough to also conclude that Fred can make out a cheque.

6.2   D-WFS

Before we can state the definition of D-WFS we have to extend our principles to disjunctive programs with default-negation. We abbreviate general rules

$$A_1 \vee \ldots \vee A_k \leftarrow B_1, \ldots, B_m, not\ C_1, \ldots, not\ C_n,$$

by

$$\mathcal{A} \leftarrow \mathcal{B}^+, not\ \mathcal{B}^-$$

where $\mathcal{A} := \{A_1, \ldots, A_k\}$, $\mathcal{B}^+ := \{B_1, \ldots, B_m\}$, $\mathcal{B}^- := \{C_1, \ldots, C_n\}$. We also generalize our notion of a semantics slightly:

Definition 22 (Operator $\vdash\!\sim$, Semantics $\mathcal{S}_{\vdash\!\sim}$).
By a semantic operator $\vdash\!\sim$ we mean a binary relation between logic programs and pure disjunctions which satisfies the following three arguably obvious conditions:

1. *Right Weakening: If $P \vdash\!\sim \psi$ and $\psi \subseteq \psi'$[10], then $P \vdash\!\sim \psi'$.*
2. *Necessarily True: If $\mathcal{A} \leftarrow true \in P$ for a disjunction $\mathcal{A}$, then $P \vdash\!\sim \mathcal{A}$.*
3. *Necessarily False: If $A \notin Head\_atoms(P)$[11] for $\mathcal{L}$-ground atom A, then $P \vdash\!\sim not\ A$.*

Given such an operator $\vdash\!\sim$ and a logic program P, by the semantics $\mathcal{S}_{\vdash\!\sim}(P)$ of P determined by $\vdash\!\sim$ we mean the set of all pure disjunctions derivable by $\vdash\!\sim$ from P, i.e., $\mathcal{S}_{\vdash\!\sim}(P) := \{\psi \mid P \vdash\!\sim \psi\}$.

---

[10] I. e. ψ is a subdisjunction of ψ'.

[11] We denote by $Head\_atoms(P)$ the set of all (instantiations of) atoms ocurring in some rule-head of P.

In order to give a unified treatment in the sequel, we introduce the following notion:

Definition 23 (Invariance of $\mathrel{\mid\!\sim}$ under a Transformation).
Suppose that a program transformation Trans $: P \mapsto$ Trans(P) *mapping logic programs into logic programs is given. We say that the operator $\mathrel{\mid\!\sim}$ is invariant under* Trans *(or that* Trans *is a $\mathrel{\mid\!\sim}$-equivalence transformation) iff*

$$P \mathrel{\mid\!\sim} \psi \iff \text{Trans}(P) \mathrel{\mid\!\sim} \psi$$

for any pure disjunction ψ and any program P.

All our principles introduced below can now be naturally extended.

Definition 24 (Elimination of Tautologies, Non-Minimal Rules).
Semantics $S_{\mathrel{\mid\!\sim}}$ satisfies **a)** *the* Elimination of Tautologies, *resp.* **b)** *the* Elimination of Non-Minimal Rules *iff $\mathrel{\mid\!\sim}$ is invariant under the following transformations:*

a) *Delete a rule $\mathcal{A} \leftarrow \mathcal{B}^+ \wedge$ not $\mathcal{B}^-$ with $\mathcal{A} \cap \mathcal{B}^+ \neq \emptyset$.*
b) *Delete a rule $\mathcal{A} \leftarrow \mathcal{B}^+ \wedge$ not $\mathcal{B}^-$ if there is another rule*
   $\mathcal{A}' \leftarrow \mathcal{B}^{+'} \wedge$ not $\mathcal{B}^{-'}$ *with $\mathcal{A}' \subseteq \mathcal{A}$, $\mathcal{B}^{+'} \subseteq \mathcal{B}^+$, and $\mathcal{B}^{-'} \subseteq \mathcal{B}^-$.*

Our partial evaluation principle has now to take into account disjunctive heads. The following definition was introduced independently by Sakama/Seki and Brass/Dix ([22, 28, 106]):

Definition 25 (GPPE).
Semantics $S_{\mathrel{\mid\!\sim}}$ satisfies GPPE iff it is invariant under the following transformation: Replace a rule $\mathcal{A} \leftarrow \mathcal{B}^+ \wedge$ not $\mathcal{B}^-$ *where $\mathcal{B}^+$ contains a distinguished atom B by the rules*

$$\mathcal{A} \cup (\mathcal{A}_i \setminus \{B\}) \;\leftarrow\; (\mathcal{B}^+ \setminus \{B\}) \cup \mathcal{B}_i^+ \;\wedge\; not \left(\mathcal{B}^- \cup \mathcal{B}_i^-\right) \; (i = 1, \ldots, n)$$

where $\mathcal{A}_i \leftarrow \mathcal{B}_i^+ \wedge$ not $\mathcal{B}_i^-$ $(i = 1, \ldots, n)$ are all the rules with $B \in \mathcal{A}_i$.

Note that we are free to select a specific positive occurrence of an atom B and then perform the transformation. The new rules are obtained by replacing B by the bodies of all rules r with head literal B and adding the remaining head atoms of r to the head of the new rule.

Here is the analogue of Principle 04 on page 15:

Definition 26 (Positive and Negative Reduction).
Semantics $S_{\mathrel{\mid\!\sim}}$ satisfies **a)** Positive, *resp.* **b)** Negative *Reduction iff $\mathrel{\mid\!\sim}$ is invariant under the following transformations:*

a) *Replace $\mathcal{A} \leftarrow \mathcal{B}^+ \wedge$ not $\mathcal{B}^-$ by $\mathcal{A} \leftarrow \mathcal{B}^+ \wedge$ not $(\mathcal{B}^- \cap Head\_atoms(P))$.*
b) *Delete $\mathcal{A} \leftarrow \mathcal{B}^+ \wedge$ not $\mathcal{B}^-$ if there is a rule $\mathcal{A}' \leftarrow$ true with $\mathcal{A}' \subseteq \mathcal{B}^-$.*

Now the definition of a disjunctive counterpart of WFS is straightforward:

Definition 27 (D-WFS).
There exists the weakest semantics satisfying positive and negative Reduction, GPPE, Elimination of Tautologies and non-minimal Rules. We call this semantics D-WFS.

As it was the case for WFS, our calculus of transformations is also confluent ([25, 27]).

Theorem 9 (Confluent Calculus for D-WFS, [29]).
The calculus consisting of our four transformations is confluent and terminating for propositional programs. I.e. we always arrive at an irreducible program, which is uniquely determined. The order of the transformations does not matter.

Therefore any program P is associated a unique normalform $res(P)$. The disjunctive wellfounded semantics of P can be read off from $res(P)$ as follows

$$\psi \in D\text{-}WFS(P) \iff \text{there is } A \subseteq \psi \text{ with } A \leftarrow true \in res(P) \quad \text{or}$$
$$\text{there is not } A \in \psi \text{ and } A \notin Head\_atoms(res(P)).$$

Note that the original definition of WFS, or any of its equivalent characterizations, does not carry over to disjunctive programs in a natural way.

Let us see how Example 9 on page 35 is handled by D-WFS. Applying GPPE and Reduction gives us the following residual program (we consider just the $Fred$-instantiations):

$$
\begin{array}{ll}
left\_use(F) & \leftarrow not\ ab(left, F) \\
ab(left, F) \vee right\_brok(F) & \leftarrow \\
right\_use(F) & \leftarrow not\ ab(right, F) \\
ab(right, F) \vee left\_brok(F) & \leftarrow \\
left\_brok(F) \vee right\_brok(F) & \leftarrow \\
make\_cheque(F) & \leftarrow not\ ab(left, F) \\
make\_cheque(F) & \leftarrow not\ ab(right, F)
\end{array}
$$

Therefore we derive *not disabled*(F), because it does not appear in any head of the residual program. All the remaining atoms are undefined.

Two properties of D-WFS are worth noticing

- For positive disjunctive programs, D-WFS coincides with GCWA.
- For non-disjunctive programs with negation, D-WFS coincides with WFS.

6.3   DSTABLE

Unlike the wellfounded semantics, the original definition of stable models carries over to disjunctive programs quite easily:

Definition 28 (DSTABLE).
N is called a stable model[12] of P if and only if $N \in Min\text{-}Mod(P^N)$.

---

[12] Note that we only consider Herbrand models.

In the last definition P^N is the positive disjunctive program obtained from P by applying the Gelfond/Lifschitz transformation (as introduced before Definition 6 on page 20 — its generalization to disjunctive programs is obvious).

Analogously to D-WFS the following two properties of DSTABLE hold:

- For positive disjunctive programs, DSTABLE coincides with GCWA.
- For non-disjunctive programs with negation, DSTABLE coincides with STA-BLE.

What about our transformations introduced to define D-WFS? Do they hold for DSTABLE? Yes, they are indeed true. The most difficult proof is the one for GPPE. It was proved in [26, 106] independently that stable models are preserved under GPPE. Moreover, Brass/Dix proved in [24] that STABLE can be almost uniquely determined by GPPE:

Theorem 10 (Characterization of DSTABLE, [28]).
Let SEM be a semantics satisfying GPPE, Elimination of Tautologies, *and* Elimination of Contradictions. *Then:* $SEM(P) \subseteq STABLE(P)$.
Moreover, DSTABLE is the weakest semantics satisfying these properties.

DSTABLE is stronger than D-WFS as can be seen from Example 9 on page 35. There we have exactly two stable models

1. $left\_use(F)$, $not\ ab(left, F)$, $ab(right, F)$, $not\ right\_use(F)$,
   $right\_brok(F)$, $not\ left\_brok(F)$, $make\_cheque(F)$, $not\ disabled(F)$,
2. $right\_use(F)$, $not\ ab(right, F)$, $ab(left, F)$, $not\ left\_use(F)$,
   $left\_brok(F)$, $not\ right\_brok(F)$, $make\_cheque(F)$, $not\ disabled(F)$.

In all of them, Fred is not disabled and can make out a cheque.

Of course, DSTABLE inherits the shortcomings of STABLE such as inconsistency and no goal-orientedness.

7   What Do We Want and What Is Implemented?

In this part we first consider the question *Is there an optimal semantics?* (Section 7.1) and give in Section 7.2 an overview of all the existing implementations we are aware of. We also describe theoretical approaches that have not yet been implemented.

7.1   What Is the Best Semantics?

Most probably there is no definite answer to the question in the title. Different knowledge representation tasks may ask for different semantics. Some might be better suited in special domains than others. What are reasonable properties that semantics should be checked against?

While many people defined in the last years new semantics by considering only few examples and appealing to their own personal intuitions they had about how these few examples should be handled, Dix tried to adjust and investigate abstract properties known in general nonmonotonic reasoning to semantics of logic programs ([56, 58–60]). He showed for example that WFS is cumulative and rational and that a semantics defined independently by Schlipf and Dix is the weakest extension of WFS satisfying *Cut* and *Supraclassicality*.

Besides such properties (which he calls *strong*) he defined also *weak* properties — these are conditions that any reasonable semantics should satisfy ([57, 60]). The principles we have introduced in Sections 2, 3 belong to this sort. Let us take a closer look into some weak properties already mentioned (but not yet defined). We start with a property that is satisfied for any semantics we know:

Definition 29 (Isomorphy).
A semantics SEM satisfies Isomorphy, if and only if

$$SEM(\mathcal{I}(P)) = \mathcal{I}(SEM(P))$$

for all programs P and isomorphisms $\mathcal{I}$ on the Herbrand base B_P.

Isomorphy formalizes the intuition that a renaming of the program should have no influence on the semantics, as long as we also apply this same renaming to the semantics.

The next property gives a formal definition of the notion *Goal-Orientedness*. To state these conditions, we need the classical notion of the *Dependency-Graph* and the two definitions

- *dependencies_of*$(X) := \{A : X$ depends on $A\}$, and
- *rel_rul*(P, X) is the set of *relevant rules* of P with respect to X, i.e. the set of rules that contain an $A \in$ *dependencies_of*(X) in their head.

Given any semantics SEM and a program P, it is perfectly reasonable that the truthvalue of a literal L, with respect to SEM(P), only depends on the subprogram formed from the *relevant rules* of P with respect to L.[13] This idea is formalized by:

Definition 30 (Relevance).
The principle of Relevance states: $L \in SEM(P)$ *iff* $L \in SEM(rel\_rul(P, L))$.

Note that the set of relevant rules of a program P with respect to a literal L contains all rules, that could ever contribute to L's derivation (or to its nonderivability). In general, L depends on a large set of atoms: *dependencies_of*$(L) := \{A : L$ depends on $A\}$. But rules that do not contain these atoms in their heads, will never contribute to their derivation or non-derivation. Therefore, these rules should not affect the meaning of L in P. STABLE does not satisfy this principle. This is due to the nonexistence of stable models by adding a clause "$c \leftarrow not\ c$" to a program.

We have already introduced GPPE above. In fact, even a weaker property is not satisfied for the semantics defined by Minker and his group:

---

[13] Let *dependencies_of*$(not\ X) :=$ *dependencies_of*(X), and *rel_rul*$(P, not\ X) :=$ *rel_rul*(P, X).

Example 10 (Extension-by-Definition, [56]).
We consider the following two programs:

$$P_{GWFS} : p \leftarrow not\ b \qquad P_{GWFS_c} : p \leftarrow not\ b$$
$$a \leftarrow not\ b \qquad\qquad\quad a \leftarrow not\ b$$
$$b \leftarrow c \qquad\qquad\qquad\quad b \leftarrow p,\ not\ a$$
$$c \leftarrow p,\ not\ a \qquad\qquad c \leftarrow p,\ not\ a$$

$\text{GWFS}(P_{GWFS})$ entails $not\ c$, because $\text{Min-MOD}(P_{GWFS}) = \{\ \{p, a\},\ \{b\}\ \}$ and thus also (by simple negation-as-failure reasoning) $not\ b$, p and a. Also we have the identity $\text{Min-MOD}(P_{GWFS_c}) = \{\ \{p, a\},\ \{b\}\ \}$ but negation-as-failure can not be applied like before. Therefore $\text{GWFS}(P_{GWFS_c})$ does not entail $not\ b$, nor p nor a.

P_{GWFS_c} *partial evaluates* P_{GWFS}: the last but one clause was transformed into another one by expanding the definition of c. Obviously, a semantics should assign the same meaning to these programs: unfortunately GWFS does not!
Typical results of Dix are

- WFS is the weakest semantics satisfying some of these weak properties,
- WFS can be uniquely characterized if some strong properties are added.

Properties of Logic-Programming Semantics						
Semantics Reference	Domain	Taut.	GPPE	Red.	NMin.	Rel.
comp Cla78	Nondis.	—	•	•	•	—
GCWA Min82	Pos.	•	•	•	•	•
WGCWA RosTop88	Pos.	—	•	•	—	•
DSTABLEGelLif91	Dis.	•	•	•	•	—
WFS vGeld.etal88	Nondis.	•	•	•	•	•
$\mathcal{STN}$ Prz91	Dis.	•	•	•	•	•
STATIC Prz95	Dis.	•	•	•	•	•
D-WFS BraDix95	Dis.	•	•	•	•	•
DWFS Dix92	Dis.	•	•	•	•	•
Str. WFS Ros92	Dis.	—	—	•	—	•
WD-WFS BraDix95	Dis.	—	•	•	—	•
WDWFS Dix92	Dis.	—	•	•	—	•
PMS SakIno94	Dis.	—	—	•	—	—

Table1. Semantics and Their Equivalence-Transformations

We conclude with Table 1: an overview of the properties of some semantics mentioned above.

The bad properties of the PMS (failure of Relevance) stem from the fact that it was originally based on stable models. But the underlying idea of PMS is to transform disjunctive programs into non-disjunctive ones and then applying a semantics for non-disjunctive programs. By choosing semantics different from STABLE, PMS inherits other properties (see [105]).

7.2 Query-Answering Systems and Implementations

In this section we give a rough overview of what semantics have been implemented so far and where they are available. As already mentioned our NMR-semantics are undecidable in general. Nevertheless we think it is very important to have running systems that

1. can handle programs with free variables, and
2. are Goal-Oriented.

To ensure *completeness* (or *termination*) we need then additional requirements like *allowedness* (to prevent floundering, see Section 3.1) and no function symbols.

Although these restrictions ensure the Herbrand-universe to be finite (and thus we are really considering a propositional theory) we think that such a system has great advantages over a system that can just handle ground programs. For a language $\mathcal{L}$, the fully instantiated program can be quite large and difficult to handle effectively.

The goal-orientedness (or *Relevance* as introduced in Section 7.1) is also important — after all this was one reason of the success of SLD-Resolution. As noted above, such a goal-oriented approach is not possible for STABLE.

LP-Semantics Various commercial PROLOG-systems perform variants of SLDNF-Resolution. Chan's constructive negation has also been implemented as part of the master-theses [86, 117].

Currently, a library of implemented logic programming systems and interesting test-cases for such systems is collected as a project of the artificial intelligence group at Koblenz. We refer to http://www.uni-koblenz.de/ag-ki/LP/>.

Non-Disjunctive NMR-Semantics There are many theoretical papers that deal with the problem of implementation ([21, 80, 53, 71]) but only few running systems. The problem of handling and representing ground programs given a non-ground one has also been adressed [78, 79, 69].

In [17, 18] the authors showed how the problem of computing stable models can be transformed to an Integer-Linear Programming Problem. This has been extended in [64] to disjunctive programs.

Inoue et. al. show in [77] how to compute stable models by transforming programs into propositional theories and then using a model-generation theorem prover.

In Berne, Switzerland, a group around G. J"ager is building a non-monotonic reasoning system which incorporates various monotonic and non-monotonic logics. We refer to http://lwbwww.unibe.ch:8080/LWBinfo.html.

Extended logic programs under the well-founded semantics are considered by Pereira and his colleagues: [97, 1, 3]. The REVISE system, which deals with contradiction removal pro paraconsistent programs in this semantics, can be found in <http://www.uni-koblenz.de/ag-ki/LP/> too.

In [96], an implementation of WFS and STABLE with a special eye on complexity is described.

The most advanced system has been implemented by David Warren and his group in Stony Brook based on OLDT-algorithm of [108]. They first developed a meta-interpreter (SLG, see [49]) in PROLOG and then directly modified the WAM for a direct implementation of WFS (XSB). They use tabling-methods and a mixture of Top-Down and bottom-up evaluation to detect loops. Their system is complete and terminating for non-floundering DATALOG. It also works for general programs but termination is not guaranteed. This system is described in [47, 46, 48], and is available by anonymous ftp from ftp.cs.sunysb.edu/pub/XSB/.

Disjunctive NMR-Semantics   There are theoretical descriptions of implementations that have not yet been implemented: [72, 90, 52]. Also Sakama and Seki describe an approach for first-order disjunctive programs ([107]).

Here are some implemented systems. Inoue et. al. show in [77] how to compute stable models for extended disjunctive programs in a bottom-up-fashion using a theorem prover.

The approach of Bell et. al. ([93]) was used by Dix/Müller to implement versions of the stationary semantics of Przymusinski ([101]): [92, 63, 91].

Brass/Dix have implemented both D-WFS and DSTABLE for allowed DATALOG programs ([23][14]). An implementation of static semantics is described in [33][15].

Seipel has implemented in his DisLog-system various (modified versions of) semantics of Minker and his group. His system is publicly available at the URL http://sunwww.informatik.uni-tuebingen.de:8080/dislog/dislog.tar.Z. However we again point to the very irregular behaviour of these semantics illustrated by Example 10 on page 41.

Finally, there is the DisLoP project undertaken by the Artificial Intelligence Research Group at the University of Koblenz and headed by J. Dix and U. Furbach ([54, 8, 9]). This project aims at extending certain theorem proving concepts, such as restart model elimination [13] and hyper tableaux [14] calculi, for disjunctive logic programming. The hyper tableaux calculus can handle positive queries with respect to positive disjunctive logic programs and seems to facilitate minimal model generation. Restart model elimination calculus does not use any contrapositives of the given clauses and thus allows for their procedural reading. Moreover, it is answer complete for positive queries [15]. Thus, they are suitable for implementing an interpreter for positive progams and the DisLoP system extends this further for non-monotonic negations too.

---

[14] ftp://ftp.informatik.uni-hannover.de/software/index.html
[15] ftp://ftp.informatik.uni-hannover.de/software/static/static.html

Currently, DisLoP system can perform minimal model reasoning based on GCWA, WGCWA. Minimal model reasoning is an important problem to tackle, since any well-known semantics for negation is a conservative extension of that. DisLoP can perform minimal model reasoning in both top-down and bottom-up manners. The bottom-up approach employs the hyper tableaux calculus to generate potential minimal models and then uses a novel technique to check the minimality of the generated model without any reference to other models. This approach is described in [94, 95]. The top-down approach is based on an abductive framework studied in [7]. This introduces an inference rule, negation as failure to explain, which allows us to assume the negation of a sentence if there are no abductive explanations for that. The DisLoP system uses a modified restart model elimination calculus to generate abductive explanations of the given sentence and employs *negation-as-failure-to-explain* inference rule for minimal model reasoning.

This system can be extended to handle non-monotonic semantics such as D-WFS, STATIC etc. In particular, an implementation of D-WFS for general disjunctive programs which works *in polynomial space* is available ([32]). Currently, an extension to first-order programs is on its way ([65, 66]). Information on the DisLoP project and related publications can be obtained from the WWW page <http://www.uni-koblenz.de/ag-ki/DLP/>.

An important outcome of the Dagstuhl Seminar 9627 ([62]) was to construct a web page to collect and disseminate information on various logic programming systems that concentrate on non-monotonic aspects (different kinds of negation, disjunction, abduction etc.). This web page is actively maintained at the URL <http://www.uni-koblenz.de/ag-ki/LP/>. In addition the *Logic Programming and Nonmonotonic Reasoning*-conference 1997 ([55]) contains a special track on implementations and working systems.

References

1. J. J. Alferes, Carlos Viegas Damasio, and L. M. Pereira. A logic programming system for non-monotonic reasoning. *Journal of Automated Reasoning*, 14(1):93–147, 1995.
2. Jose Julio Alferes and Luiz Moniz Pereira. An argumentation theoretic semantics based on non-refutable falsity. In J. Dix, L. Pereira, and T. Przymusinski, editors, *Nonmonotonic Extensions of Logic Programming*, LNAI 927, pages 3–22. Springer, Berlin, 1995.
3. Jose Julio Alferes and Luiz Moniz Pereira, editors. *Reasoning with Logic Programming*, LNAI 1111, Berlin, 1996. Springer.
4. Jose Julio Alferes, Luiz Moniz Pereira, and Teodor Przymusinski. Strong and Explicit Negation in Non-Monotonic Reasoning and Logic Programming. In J.J Alferes, L.M. Pereira, and E. Orlowska, editors, *Logics in Artificial Intelligence (JELIA '96)*, LNCS 1126, pages 143–163. Springer, 1996.
5. Krzysztof R. Apt. Logic programming. In J. van Leeuwen, editor, *Handbook of Theoretical Computer Science, Vol. B*, chapter 10, pages 493–574. Elsevier Science Publishers, 1990.

6. Krzysztof R. Apt and Roland N. Bol. Logic Programming and Negation: A Survey. *Journal of Logic Programming*, 19-20:9–71, 1994.
7. Chandrabose Aravindan. An abductive framework for negation in disjunctive logic programming. In J. J. Alferes, L. M. Pereira, and E. Orlowska, editors, *Proceedings of Joint European workshop on Logics in AI*, number 1126 in Lecture Notes in Artificial Intelligence, pages 252–267. Springer-Verlag, 1996. A related report is available on the web from <http://www.uni-koblenz.de/~arvind/papers/>.
8. Chandrabose Aravindan, Jürgen Dix, and Ilkka Niemelä. Dislop: A research project on disjunctive logic programming. *AI Communications*, 10(3/4):151–165, 1997.
9. Chandrabose Aravindan, Jürgen Dix, and Ilkka Niemelä. DisLoP: Towards a Disjunctive Logic Programming System. In J. Dix, U. Furbach, and A. Nerode, editors, *Logic Programming and Non-Monotonic Reasoning, Proceedings of the Fourth International Conference*, LNAI 1265, pages 342–353, Berlin, June 1997. Springer.
10. Chitta Baral and Michael Gelfond. Logic Programming and Knowlege Representation. *Journal of Logic Programming*, 19-20:73–148, 1994.
11. Chitta Baral and V.S. Subrahmanian. Dualities between Alternative Semantics for Logic Programming and Non-monotonic Reasoning. In Anil Nerode, Wiktor Marek, and V. S. Subrahmanian, editors, *Logic Programming and Non-Monotonic Reasoning, Proceedings of the first International Workshop*, pages 69–86, Cambridge, Mass., July 1991. Washington D.C, MIT Press.
12. Chitta Baral and V.S. Subrahmanian. Stable and Extension Class Theory for Logic Programs and Default Logics. *Journal of Automated Reasoning*, 8, No. 3:345–366, 1992.
13. P. Baumgartner and U. Furbach. Model Elimination without Contrapositives and its Application to PTTP. *Journal of Automated Reasoning*, 13:339–359, 1994. Short version in: Proceedings of CADE-12, Springer LNAI 814, 1994, pp 87–101.
14. P. Baumgartner, U. Furbach, and I. Niemelä. Hyper Tableaux. In *Proc. JELIA 96*, number 1126 in LNAI. European Workshop on Logic in AI, Springer, 1996. (Long version in: *Fachberichte Informatik*, 8–96, Universität Koblenz-Landau).
15. P. Baumgartner, U. Furbach, and F. Stolzenburg. Model Elimination, Logic Programming and Computing Answers. In *Proceedings of IJCAI '95*, 1995. (to appear, Long version in: Research Report 1/95, University of Koblenz, Germany).
16. Catril Beeri and Raghu Ramakrishnan. On the power of magic. *The Journal of Logic Programming*, 10:255–299, 1991.
17. Colin Bell, Anil Nerode, Raymond T. Ng, and V. S. Subrahmanian. Implementing Stable Semantics by Linear Programming. In Luis Moniz Pereira and Anil Nerode, editors, *Logic Programming and Non-Monotonic Reasoning, Proceedings of the Second International Workshop*, pages 23–42, Cambridge, Mass., July 1993. Lisbon, MIT Press.
18. Colin Bell, Anil Nerode, Raymond T. Ng, and V. S. Subrahmanian. Mixed Integer Programming Methods for Computing Non-Monotonic Deductive Databases. *Journal of the ACM*, 41(6):1178–1215, November 1994.
19. Nicole Bidoit and Christine Froidevaux. General logical Databases and Programs: Default Logic Semantics and Stratification. *Information and Computation*, 91:15–54, 1991.
20. Nicole Bidoit and Christine Froidevaux. Negation by Default and unstratifiable logic Programs. *Theoretical Computer Science*, 78:85–112, 1991.

21. Roland N. Bol and L. Degerstedt. Tabulated resolution for well–founded semantics. In *Proc. Int. Logic Programming Symposium'93*, Cambridge, Mass., 1993. MIT Press.

22. Stefan Brass and Jürgen Dix. A disjunctive semantics based on unfolding and bottom-up evaluation. In Bernd Wolfinger, editor, *Innovationen bei Rechen- und Kommunikationssystemen*, (IFIP '94-Congress, Workshop FG2: Disjunctive Logic Programming and Disjunctive Databases), pages 83–91, Berlin, 1994. Springer.

23. Stefan Brass and Jürgen Dix. A General Approach to Bottom-Up Computation of Disjunctive Semantics. In J. Dix, L. Pereira, and T. Przymusinski, editors, *Nonmonotonic Extensions of Logic Programming*, LNAI 927, pages 127–155. Springer, Berlin, 1995.

24. Stefan Brass and Jürgen Dix. Characterizations of the Stable Semantics by Partial Evaluation. In A. Nerode, W. Marek, and M. Truszczyński, editors, *Logic Programming and Non-Monotonic Reasoning, Proceedings of the Third International Conference*, LNCS 928, pages 85–98, Berlin, June 1995. Springer.

25. Stefan Brass and Jürgen Dix. D-WFS: A Confluent calculus and an Equivalent Characterization. Technical Report TR 12/95, University of Koblenz, Department of Computer Science, Rheinau 1, September 1995.

26. Stefan Brass and Jürgen Dix. Disjunctive Semantics based upon Partial and Bottom-Up Evaluation. In Leon Sterling, editor, *Proceedings of the 12th Int. Conf. on Logic Programming, Tokyo*, pages 199–213. MIT Press, June 1995.

27. Stefan Brass and Jürgen Dix. Characterizing D-WFS: Confluence and Iterated GCWA. In L.M. Pereira J.J. Alferes and E. Orlowska, editors, *Logics in Artificial Intelligence (JELIA '96)*, LNCS 1126, pages 268–283. Springer, 1996. (Extended version will appear in the *Journal of Automated Reasoning* in 1998.).

28. Stefan Brass and Jürgen Dix. Characterizations of the Disjunctive Stable Semantics by Partial Evaluation. *Journal of Logic Programming*, 32(3):207–228, 1997. (Extended abstract appeared in: Characterizations of the Stable Semantics by Partial Evaluation *LPNMR, Proceedings of the Third International Conference, Kentucky*, pages 85–98, 1995. LNCS 928, Springer.).

29. Stefan Brass and Jürgen Dix. Characterizations of the Disjunctive Well-founded Semantics: Confluent Calculi and Iterated GCWA. *Journal of Automated Reasoning*, 20(1):143–165, 1998. (Extended abstract appeared in: Characterizing D-WFS: Confluence and Iterated GCWA. *Logics in Artificial Intelligence, JELIA '96*, pages 268–283, 1996. Springer, LNCS 1126.).

30. Stefan Brass and Jürgen Dix. Semantics of (Disjunctive) Logic Programs Based on Partial Evaluation. *Journal of Logic Programming*, accepted for publication, 1998. (Extended abstract appeared in: Disjunctive Semantics Based upon Partial and Bottom-Up Evaluation, *Proceedings of the 12-th International Logic Programming Conference, Tokyo*, pages 199–213, 1995. MIT Press.).

31. Stefan Brass, Jürgen Dix, Burkhard Freitag, and Zukowski. Transformation-based bottom-up computation of the well-founded model. *Journal of Logic Programming*, to appear, 1999.

32. Stefan Brass, Jürgen Dix, Ilkka Niemelä, and Teodor. C. Przymusinski. A Comparison of the Static and the Disjunctive Well-founded Semantics and its Implementation. In A. G. Cohn, L. K. Schubert, and S. C. Shapiro, editors, *Principles of Knowledge Representation and Reasoning: Proceedings of the Sixth International Conference (KR '98)*, pages 74–85. San Francisco, CA, Morgan Kaufmann, May 1998. appeared also as TR 17/97, University of Koblenz.

33. Stefan Brass, Jürgen Dix, and Teodor. C. Przymusinski. Super Logic Programs. In L. C. Aiello, J. Doyle, and S. C. Shapiro, editors, *Principles of Knowledge Representation and Reasoning: Proceedings of the Fifth International Conference (KR '96)*, pages 529–541. San Francisco, CA, Morgan Kaufmann, 1996.

34. Stefan Brass, Ulrich Zukowski, and Burkhardt Freitag. Transformation Based Bottom-Up Computation of the Well-Founded Model. In J. Dix, L. Pereira, and T. Przymusinski, editors, *Nonmonotonic Extensions of Logic Programming*, LNAI 1216, pages 171–201. Springer, Berlin, 1997.

35. G. Brewka. Adding priorities and specificity to default logic. In *Logics in Artificial Intelligence, Proc. JELIA-94, York*. Springer, 1994.

36. Gerd Brewka, Jürgen Dix, and Kurt Konolige. *Nonmonotonic Reasoning: An Overview*. CSLI Lecture Notes 73. CSLI Publications, Stanford, CA, 1997.

37. Gerhard Brewka. Well-founded semantics for extended logic programs with dynamic preferences. *Journal of Artificial Intelligence Research*, 4:19–36, 1996.

38. Gerhard Brewka and Thomas Eiter. Preferred answer sets. In Anthony Cohn, Lenhart Schubert, and Stuart Shapiro, editors, *Proceedings of the 6th Conference on Principles of Knowledge Representation and Reasoning, Trent, Italy*, pages 86–97. Morgan Kaufmann, 1998.

39. François Bry. Query evaluation in recursive databases: bottom-up and top-down reconciled. *Data & Knowledge Engineering*, 5:289–312, 1990.

40. M. Cadoli, F. M. Donini, P. Liberatore, and M. Schaerf. The size of a revised knowledge base. In *PODS '95*, pages 151–162, 1995.

41. Marco Cadoli, Francesco M. Donini, and Marco Schaerf. Is intractability of nonmonotonic reasoning a real drawback? *Artificial Intelligence Journal*, 88:215–251, 1996.

42. Marco Cadoli, Francesco M. Donini, Marco Schaerf, and Riccardo Silvestri. On compact representations of propositional circumscription. *Theoretical Computer Science*, 182:183–202, 1997. (Extended abstract appeared in: On Compact Representations of Propositional Circumscription. *STACS '95*, pages 205–216, 1995.).

43. L. Cavedon and J.W. Lloyd. A Completeness Theorem for SLDNF-Resolution. *Journal of Logic Programming*, 7:177–191, 1989.

44. David Chan. Constructive negation based on the completed database. In *Proc. 1988 Conf. and Symp. on Logic Programming*, pages 111–125, September 1988.

45. David Chan and Mark Wallace. An Experiment with programming using pure Negation. Technical Report TR, ECRC, July 1989.

46. Weidong Chen, Terrance Swift, and David S. Warren. Efficient Top-Down Computation of Queries under the Well-Founded Semantics. *Journal of Logic Programming*, 24(3):219–245, 1995.

47. Weidong Chen and David S. Warren. A Goal Oriented Approach to Computing The Well-founded Semantics. *Journal of Logic Programming*, 17:279–300, 1993.

48. Weidong Chen and David S. Warren. Computing of Stable Models and its Integration with Logical Query Processing. *IEEE Transactions on Knowledge and Data Engineering*, 17:279–300, 1995.

49. Weidong Chen and David S. Warren. Tabled Evaluation with Delaying for General Logic Programs. *Journal of the ACM*, 43(1):20–74, January 1996.

50. Keith L. Clark. Negation as Failure. In H. Gallaire and J. Minker, editors, *Logic and Data-Bases*, pages 293–322. Plenum, New York, 1978.

51. A. Colmerauer, H. Kanoui, R. Pasero, and P. Roussel. Un système de communication homme-machine en français. Technical report, Groupe de Intelligence Artificielle Universite de Aix-Marseille II, 1973.

52. Stefania Costantini and Gaetano A. Lanzarone. Static Semantics as Program Transformation and Well-founded Computation. In J. Dix, L. Pereira, and T. Przymusinski, editors, *Nonmonotonic Extensions of Logic Programming*, LNAI 927, pages 156–180. Springer, Berlin, 1995.

53. Lars Degerstedt and Ulf Nilsson. Magic Computation of Well-founded Semantics. In J. Dix, L. Pereira, and T. Przymusinski, editors, *Nonmonotonic Extensions of Logic Programming*, LNAI 927, pages 181–204. Springer, Berlin, 1995.

54. J. Dix and U. Furbach. The DFG-Project DisLoP on Disjunctive Logic Programming. *Computational Logic*, 2(2):89–90, 1996.

55. J. Dix, U. Furbach, and A. Nerode, editors. *Logic Programming and Nonmonotonic Reasoning*, LNAI 1265, Berlin, 1997. Springer.

56. Jürgen Dix. Classifying Semantics of Logic Programs. In Anil Nerode, Wiktor Marek, and V. S. Subrahmanian, editors, *Logic Programming and Non-Monotonic Reasoning, Proceedings of the first International Workshop*, pages 166–180, Cambridge, Mass., July 1991. Washington D.C, MIT Press.

57. Jürgen Dix. A Framework for Representing and Characterizing Semantics of Logic Programs. In B. Nebel, C. Rich, and W. Swartout, editors, *Principles of Knowledge Representation and Reasoning: Proceedings of the Third International Conference (KR '92)*, pages 591–602. San Mateo, CA, Morgan Kaufmann, 1992.

58. Jürgen Dix. Classifying Semantics of Disjunctive Logic Programs. In K. R. Apt, editor, *LOGIC PROGRAMMING: Proceedings of the 1992 Joint International Conference and Symposium*, pages 798–812, Cambridge, Mass., November 1992. MIT Press.

59. Jürgen Dix. A Classification-Theory of Semantics of Normal Logic Programs: I. Strong Properties. *Fundamenta Informaticae*, XXII(3):227–255, 1995.

60. Jürgen Dix. A Classification-Theory of Semantics of Normal Logic Programs: II. Weak Properties. *Fundamenta Informaticae*, XXII(3):257–288, 1995.

61. Jürgen Dix. Semantics of Logic Programs: Their Intuitions and Formal Properties. An Overview. In Andre Fuhrmann and Hans Rott, editors, *Logic, Action and Information – Essays on Logic in Philosophy and Artificial Intelligence*, pages 241–327. DeGruyter, 1995.

62. Jürgen Dix, Donald Loveland, Jack Minker, and David. S. Warren. Disjunctive Logic Programming and databases: Nonmonotonic Aspects. Technical Report Dagstuhl Seminar Report 150, IBFI GmbH, Schloß Dagstuhl, 1996.

63. Jürgen Dix and Martin Müller. Abstract Properties and Computational Complexity of Semantics for Disjunctive Logic Programs. In *Proc. of the Workshop W1, Structural Complexity and Recursion-theoretic Methods in Logic Programming, following the JICSLP '92*, pages 15–28. H. Blair and W. Marek and A. Nerode and J. Remmel, November 1992. also available as Technical Report 13/93, University of Koblenz, Department of Computer Science.

64. Jürgen Dix and Martin Müller. Implementing Semantics for Disjunctive Logic Programs Using Fringes and Abstract Properties. In Luis Moniz Pereira and Anil Nerode, editors, *Logic Programming and Non-Monotonic Reasoning, Proceedings of the Second International Workshop*, pages 43–59, Cambridge, Mass., July 1993. Lisbon, MIT Press.

65. Jürgen Dix and Frieder Stolzenburg. Computation of Non-Ground Disjunctive Well-Founded Semantics with Constraint Logic Programming (preliminary report). In J. Dix, L. Pereira, and T. Przymusinski, editors, *Nonmonotonic Extensions of Logic Programming*, LNAI 1216, pages 202–226. Springer, Berlin, 1997.

66. Jürgen Dix and Frieder Stolzenburg. A Framework to incorporate Nonmonotonic Reasoning into Constraint Logic Programming. *Journal of Logic Programming*, 35(1,2,3):5—37, 1998. Special Issue on *Constraint Logic Programming*, Guest Editors: Kim Marriott and Peter Stuckey.

67. Wlodzimierz Drabent. What is failure? A constructive approach to negation. *Acta Informatica*, 32(1):27–29, 1994.

68. P. M. Dung. On the relations between stable and wellfounded semantics of logic programs. *Theoretical Computer Science*, 105:7–25, 1992.

69. T. Eiter, J. Lu, and V. S. Subrahmanian. Computing Non-Ground Representations of Stable Models. In J. Dix, U. Furbach, and A. Nerode, editors, *Logic Programming and Non-Monotonic Reasoning, Proceedings of the Fourth International Conference*, LNAI 1265, pages 198–217, Berlin, July 1997. Springer.

70. F. Fages. Consistency of Clark's completion and existence of stable models. *Methods of Logic in Computer Science*, 2, 1993.

71. J. A. Fernández, J. Lobo, J. Minker, and V.S. Subrahmanian. Disjunctive LP + Integrity Constraints = Stable Model Semantics. *Annals of Mathematics and Artificial Intelligence*, 8(3-4), 1993.

72. J. A. Fernández and J. Minker. Bottom-Up Computation of Perfect Models for Disjunctive Theories. *Journal of Logic Programming*, 25(1):33–51, 1995.

73. Michael Gelfond and Vladimir Lifschitz. The Stable Model Semantics for Logic Programming. In R. Kowalski and K. Bowen, editors, *5th Conference on Logic Programming*, pages 1070–1080. MIT Press, 1988.

74. Goran Gogic, Christos Papadimitriou, Bart Selman, and Henry Kautz. The Comparative Linguistics of Knowledge Representation. In *Proceedings of the 14th International Joint Conference on Artificial Intelligence*, pages 862–869, Montreal, Canada, August 1995. Morgan Kaufmann Publishers.

75. T. F. Gordon. *The Pleadings Game: An Artificial Intelligence Model of Procedural Justice*. PhD thesis, TU Darmstadt, 1993.

76. Jeff Horty, Richmond Thomason, and D. S. Touretzky. A skeptical Theory of Inheritance in Nonmonotonic Semantic Networks. *Artificial Intelligence*, 42:311–348, 1990.

77. Katsumi Inoue, M. Koshimura, and R. Hasegawa. Embedding negation-as-failure into a model generation theorem prover. In Deepak Kapur, editor, *Automated Deduction — CADE-11*, number 607 in LNAI, Berlin, 1992. Springer.

78. Vadim Kagan, Anil Nerode, and V. S. Subrahmanian. Computing Definite Logic Programs by Partial Instantiation. *Annals of Pure and Applied Logic*, 67:161–182, 1994.

79. Vadim Kagan, Anil Nerode, and V. S. Subrahmanian. Computing Minimal Models by Partial Instantiation. *Theoretical Computer Science*, 155:157–177, 1995.

80. David B. Kemp, Peter J. Stuckey, and Divesh Srivastava. Magic Sets and Bottom-Up Evaluation of Well-Founded Models. In Vijay Saraswat and Kazunori Ueda, editors, *Proceedings of the 1991 Int. Symposium on Logic Programming*, pages 337–351. MIT, June 1991.

81. Kurt Konolige. Partial Models and Non-Monotonic Reasoning. In J. Richards, editor, *The Logic and Aquisition of Knowledge*. Oxford Press, 1988.

82. R.A. Kowalski. Predicate logic as a programming language. In *Proceeedings IFIP' 74*, pages 569–574. North Holland Publishing Company, 1974.

83. V. Lifschitz. Foundations of declarative logic programming. In G. Brewka, editor, *Principles of Knowledge Representation*, chapter 3, pages 69–128. CSLI, 1996.

84. Vladimir Lifschitz. Computing Circumscription. In *Proceedings of the International Joint Conference on Artificial Intelligence, Los Angeles, California*, pages 121–127, 1985.

85. John W. Lloyd. *Foundations of Logic Programming*. Springer, Berlin, 1987. 2nd edition.

86. Bertram Ludäscher. CNF-Prolog: A Meta-Interpreter for Chan's Constructive Negation, Implementation. Technical report, Master Thesis, Karlsruhe University (in german), 1991.

87. Jack Minker. On indefinite databases and the closed world assumption. In *Proceedings of the 6th Conference on Automated Deduction, New York*, pages 292–308, Berlin, 1982. Springer.

88. Jack Minker. *Foundations of Deductive Databases*. Morgan Kaufmann, 95 First Street, Los Altos, CA 94022, 1st edition, 1988.

89. Jack Minker. An Overview of Nonmonotonic Reasoning and Logic Programming. *Journal of Logic Programming, Special Issue*, 17(2/3/4):95–126, 1993.

90. Jack Minker and Carolina Ruiz. Computing stable and partial stable models of extended disjunctive logic programs. In J. Dix, L. Pereira, and T. Przymusinski, editors, *Nonmonotonic Extensions of Logic Programming*, LNAI 927, pages 205–229. Springer, Berlin, 1995.

91. Martin Müller. Examples and Run-Time Data from KORF, 1992.

92. Martin Müller and Jürgen Dix. Implementing Semantics for Disjunctive Logic Programs Using Fringes and Abstract Properties. In Luis Moniz Pereira and Anil Nerode, editors, *Logic Programming and Non-Monotonic Reasoning, Proceedings of the Second International Workshop*, pages 43–59, Cambridge, Mass., July 1993. Lisbon, MIT Press.

93. Anil Nerode, Raymond T. Ng, and V.S. Subrahmanian. Computing Circumscriptive Deductive Databases. CS-TR 91-66, Computer Science Dept., Univ. Maryland, University of Maryland, College Park, Maryland, 20742, USA, December 1991.

94. Ilkka Niemelä. Implementing circumscription using a tableau method. In W. Wahlster, editor, *Proceedings of the European Conference on Artificial Intelligence*, pages 80–84, Budapest, Hungary, August 1996. John Wiley.

95. Ilkka Niemelä. A tableau calculus for minimal model reasoning. In P. Miglioli, U. Moscato, D. Mundici, and M. Ornaghi, editors, *Proceedings of the Fifth Workshop on Theorem Proving with Analytic Tableaux and Related Methods*, pages 278–294, Terrasini, Italy, May 1996. LNAI 1071, Springer-Verlag.

96. Ilkka Niemelä and Patrik Simons. Efficient Implementation of the Well-founded and Stable Model Semantics. In M. Maher, editor, *Proceedings of the Joint International Conference and Symposium on Logic Programming*, pages 289–303, Bonn, Germany, September 1996. The MIT Press.

97. L. M. Pereira, J. N. Aparício, and J. J. Alferes. Non-Monotonic Reasoning with Logic Programming. *Journal of Logic Programming*, 17:227–264, 1993.

98. L.M. Pereira and J.J. Alferes. Well founded semantics for logic programs with explicit negation. In Bernd Neumann, editor, *Proc. of 10th European Conf. on Artificial Intelligence ECAI 92*, pages 102–106. John Wiley & Sons, 1992.

99. D. Poole. On the comparison of theories: Preferring the most specific explanation. In *Proc. IJCAI-85, Los Angeles*, 1985.

100. H. Prakken. *Logical Tools for Modelling Legal Argument*. PhD thesis, VU Amsterdam, 1993.

101. Teodor Przymusinski. Stationary Semantics for Normal and Disjunctive Logic Programs. In C. Delobel, M. Kifer, and Y. Masunaga, editors, *DOOD '91, Proceedings of the 2nd International Conference*, Berlin, December 1991. Muenchen, Springer. LNCS 566.

102. Raymond Reiter. On closed world data bases. In Hervé Gallaire and Jack Minker, editors, *Logic and Data Bases*, pages 55–76, New York, 1978. Plenum.

103. Raymond Reiter. A Logic for Default-Reasoning. *Artificial Intelligence*, 13:81–132, 1980.

104. Stuart Russel and Peter Norvig. *Artificial Intelligence — A Modern Approach*. Prentice Hall, New Jersey 07458, 1995.

105. Ch. Sakama and K. Inoue. An Alternative Approach to the Semantics of Disjunctive Logic Programs and Deductive Databases. *Journal of Automated Reasoning*, 13:145–172, 1994.

106. Chiaki Sakama and Hirohisa Seki. Partial Deduction of Disjunctive Logic Programs: A Declarative Approach. In *Logic Program Synthesis and Transformation – Meta Programming in Logic*, LNCS 883, pages 170–182, Berlin, 1994. Springer.

107. Chiaki Sakama and Hirohisa Seki. Partial Deduction in Disjunctive Logic Programming. *Journal of Logic Programming*, 32(3):229–245, 1997.

108. H. Tamaki and T. Sato. OLD Resolution with Tabulation. In *Proceedings of the Third International Conference on Logic Programming, London*, LNAI, pages 84–98, Berlin, June 1986. Springer.

109. A. Tarski. A lattice-theoretical fixpoint theorem and its applications. *Pacific Journal of Mathematics*, 5:285–309, 1955.

110. D. S. Touretzky. *The Mathematics of Inheritance*. Research Notes in Artificial Intelligence. Pitman, London, 1986.

111. D. S. Touretzky, R. H. Thomason, and J. F. Horty. A skeptic's menagerie: Conflictors, preemptors, reinstaters, and zombies in nonmonotonic inheritance. In *Proc. 12th IJCAI, Sydney*, 1991.

112. David S. Touretzky, Jeff Horty, and Richmond Thomason. A Clash of Intuitions: The current State of Nonmonotonic Multiple IHS. In *Proceedings IJCAJ*, 1988.

113. Jeffrey D. Ullman. Bottom-up Beats Top-down for Datalog. In *Proc. of the Eight ACM SIGACT-SIGMOD-SIGART Symposium on Principles of Database Systems, Philadelphia, Pennsylvania*, pages 140–149. ACM Press, March 1989.

114. Jeffrey D. Ullman. *Principles of Database and Knowledge-Base Systems, Vol. 2*. Computer Science Press, Rockville, 1989.

115. M.H. van Emden and R.A. Kowalski. The semantics of predicate logic as a programming language. *JACM*, 23:733–742, 1976.

116. Allen Van Gelder, Kenneth A. Ross, and J. S. Schlipf. Unfounded Sets and well-founded Semantics for general logic Programs. In *Proceedings 7th Symposion on Principles of Database Systems*, pages 221–230, 1988.

117. Martin Vorbeck. CNF-Prolog: A Meta-Interpreter for Chan's Constructive Negation, Theory. Technical report, Master Thesis, Karlsruhe University (in german), 1991.

DATALOG with Nested Rules*

Sergio Greco[1], Nicola Leone[2], and Francesco Scarcello[3]

[1] DEIS
Università della Calabria
I-87030 Rende, Italy
email: greco@si.deis.unical.it

[2] Institut für Informationssysteme
Technische Universität Wien
Paniglgasse 16, A-1040 Wien, Austria
email: leone@dbai.tuwien.ac.at

[3] ISI-CNR
c/o DEIS, Università della Calabria
I-87030 Rende, Italy
email: scarcello@unical.it

Abstract. This paper presents an extension of disjunctive datalog (Datalog$^\vee$) by nested rules. Nested rules are (disjunctive) rules where elements of the head may be also rules. Nested rules increase the knowledge representation power of Datalog$^\vee$ both from a theoretical and from a practical viewpoint. A number of examples show that nested rules allow to naturally model several real world situations that cannot be represented in Datalog$^\vee$. An in depth analysis of complexity and expressive power of the language shows that nested rules do increase the expressiveness of Datalog$^\vee$ without implying any increase in its computational complexity.

1 Introduction

In this paper, we propose an extension of Datalog$^\vee$ by nested rules that we call Datalog$^{\vee,\hookleftarrow}$. Informally, a Datalog$^{\vee,\hookleftarrow}$ rule is a (disjunctive) rule where rules may occur in the head. For instance, $r : A \vee (B \hookleftarrow C) \leftarrow D$, where A and B are atoms and C and D are conjunctions of atoms is a Datalog$^{\vee,\hookleftarrow}$ rule. The intuitive meaning of r is the following: if D is true, then A or B could be derived from r; however, B can be derived from r *only if* C is also true, i.e., B cannot be derived *from rule* r if C is false.

Example 1. The organizer of a party wants to invite either *susan* or *john* and, in addition, either *mary* or *paul*. This situation can be expressed by means of

---

* This work has been supported in part by FWF (Austrian Science Funds) under the project *P11580-MAT "A Query System for Disjunctive Deductive Databases"*; by the *Istituto per la Sistemistica e l'Informatica, ISI-CNR*; and by a MURST grant (40% share) under the project "Interdata."

the following disjunctive Datalog program

$$susan \lor john \leftarrow$$
$$mary \lor paul \leftarrow$$

This program has four stable models giving all possible solutions: $M_1 = \{$ susan, mary $\}$, $M_2 = \{susan, paul\}$, $M_3 = \{john, mary\}$ and $M_4 = \{john, paul\}$.

Suppose now that you know that *john* will attend the party only if *mary* will attend the party too; this means that if *mary* will not attend the meeting, *john* will not attend the meeting too (therefore, inviting *john* makes sense only if also *mary* has been invited). This situation cannot be naturally expressed in disjunctive Datalog whereas can be naturally expressed by means of nested rules.

$$susan \lor (john \leftrightarrow mary) \leftarrow$$
$$mary \lor paul \leftarrow$$

The new program has only three stable models, namely M_1, M_2 and M_3 (see Section 2), that represent the three reasonable alternative sets of persons to be invited.   □

Thus, the addition of nested rules allows us to represent real world situations that cannot be represented in plain Datalog$^{\lor}$ programs.

Remarks.

- We point out that a nested rule $a \leftrightarrow b$, appearing in the head of a rule r, does not constraint the truth of a (to b) *globally* (it is not logically equivalent to $\neg b \rightarrow \neg a$); rather, $a \leftrightarrow b$ constraints the derivation of a *from the rule r*. For instance, the program consisting of rule $(a \leftrightarrow b) \leftarrow$ and of fact $a \leftarrow$ has only the stable model $\{a\}$, where a is true even if b is false.
- It is worth noting that nested rules could be simulated by using (possibly unstratified) negation; however, in cases like the example above, a nested rule allows us a more direct representation of the reality and it is therefore preferable.
- In this paper we will contrast disjunctive Datalog with nested rules (Datalog$^{\lor,\leftrightarrow}$) mainly against plain (i.e., negation free) disjunctive Datalog (Datalog$^{\lor}$), in order to put in evidence the types of disjunctive information that become expressible thanks to the introduction of nested rules.

The main contributions of the paper are the following:

- We add nested rules to disjunctive Datalog and define an elegant declarative semantics for the resulting language. We show that our semantics generalizes the stable model semantics [22, 11] of disjunctive Datalog programs. Moreover, we show how nested rules can be used for knowledge representation and commonsense reasoning.
- We analyze the complexity and the expressive power of Datalog$^{\lor,\leftrightarrow}$. It appears that, while nested rules do not affect the complexity of the language,

they do increase its expressive power. Indeed, as for Datalog$^\vee$, brave reasoning is Σ_2^P-complete for Datalog$^{\vee,\hookleftarrow}$ (that is, the complexity is the same). However, Datalog$^\vee$ allows to express only a strict subset of Σ_2^P (e.g., even the simple *even* query,[1] asking whether a relation has an even number of elements, is not expressible) [7], while Datalog$^{\vee,\hookleftarrow}$ expresses exactly Σ_2^P (that is, it allows to represent all and only the properties that are computable in polynomial time by a nondeterministic Turing machine endowed with an NP oracle).

To our knowledge this is the first paper proposing an extension of disjunctive Datalog with nested rules. Related to our work can be considered papers presenting other extensions of logic programming like, for instance, [2, 15, 20, 4, 12]. Related results on complexity and expressive power of Knowledge Representation languages are reported in [8, 13, 5, 18, 24, 23].

The sequel of the paper is organized as follows. Section 2 describes the Datalog$^{\vee,\neg,\hookleftarrow}$ language formally. The syntax is first given, then an elegant definition of the stable model semantics, based on the notion of unfounded set is provided; results proving that our notions generalize the classical definitions of unfounded set and stable model are also given in this section. Section 3 presents the results on complexity and expressive power of our language. Some examples on the use of nested rules for representing knowledge are reported in Section 4. Finally, Section 5 draws our conclusions and addresses ongoing work.

2   The Datalog$^{\vee,\neg,\hookleftarrow}$ Language

In this section, we extend disjunctive Datalog by nested rules. For the sake of generality, we will consider also negation in the rules' bodies (defining the language Datalog$^{\vee,\neg,\hookleftarrow}$).

2.1   Syntax

A *term* is either a constant or a variable[2]. An *atom* is $a(t_1, ..., t_n)$, where a is a *predicate* of arity n and $t_1, ..., t_n$ are terms. A *literal* is either a *positive literal* p or a *negative literal* $\neg p$, where p is an atom.

A *nested rule* is of the form:

$$A \hookleftarrow b_1, \cdots, b_k, \neg b_{k+1}, \cdots, \neg b_m, \qquad m \geq 0$$

where $A, b_1, \cdots, b_m$ are atoms. If $m = 0$, then the implication symbol "$\hookleftarrow$" can be omitted.

A *rule* r is of the form

$$A_1 \vee \cdots \vee A_n \leftarrow b_1, \cdots, b_k, \neg b_{k+1}, \cdots, \neg b_m, \qquad n > 0, m \geq 0$$

---

[1] See example 9.

[2] Note that function symbols are not considered in this paper.

where $b_1, \cdots, b_m$ are atoms, and $A_1, \cdots, A_n$ are nested rules. The disjunction $A_1 \vee \cdots \vee A_n$ is the *head* of r, while the conjunction $b_1, ..., b_k, \neg b_{k+1}, ..., \neg b_m$ is the *body* of r; we denote the sets $\{A_1, \cdots, A_n\}$ and $\{b_1, ..., b_k, \neg b_{k+1}, ..., \neg b_m\}$ by $Head(r)$ and $Body(r)$, respectively; moreover, we denote $\{b_1, ..., b_k\}$ and $\{\neg b_{k+1}, ..., \neg b_m\}$ by $Body^+(r)$ and $Body^-(r)$, respectively. Notice that atoms occurring in $Head(r)$ stand for nested rules with an empty body. If $n = 1$ (i.e., the head is $\vee$-free), then r is *normal*; if no negative literal appear in r (r is $\neg$-free), then r is *positive*; if $A_1, \cdots, A_n$ are atoms, then r is *flat*. We will use the notation $Body(r)$ and $Head(r)$ also if r is a nested rule. A Datalog$^{\vee,\neg,\leftarrow}$ program $\mathcal{P}$ is a set of rules; $\mathcal{P}$ is *normal* (resp., *positive*, *flat*) if all rules in $\mathcal{P}$ are normal (resp. positive, flat). We denote by: (i) Datalog$^{\vee,\leftarrow}$, (ii) Datalog$^{\vee,\neg}$, and (iii) Datalog$^\vee$, the fragments of Datalog$^{\vee,\neg,\leftarrow}$ where we disallow: (i) negation in the body, (ii) nested implication in the head, and (iii) both negation in the body and nested implication in the head, respectively. Moreover, if negation is constrained to be stratified [21], then we will use the symbol $\neg_s$ instead of $\neg$ (e.g., Datalog$^{\vee,\neg_s}$ will denote disjunctive Datalog with stratified negation).

Example 2. A rule may appear in the head of another rule. For instance,

$$r_1: \qquad a \vee (b \leftarrow \neg c) \leftarrow d$$

is an allowed Datalog$^{\vee,\neg,\leftarrow}$ rule. Moreover,

$$r_2: \qquad a \vee (b \leftarrow c) \leftarrow d$$

is a Datalog$^{\vee,\leftarrow}$ rule as well. Neither, r_1 nor r_2 belong to Datalog$^\vee$; while

$$r_3: \qquad a \vee b \leftarrow d$$

is in Datalog$^\vee$. $\qquad\qquad\qquad\qquad\qquad\qquad\qquad\qquad\qquad\qquad\qquad\quad\square$

2.2 Semantics

Let $\mathcal{P}$ be a Datalog$^{\vee,\neg,\leftarrow}$ program. The *Herbrand universe* $U_\mathcal{P}$ of $\mathcal{P}$ is the set of all constants appearing in $\mathcal{P}$. The *Herbrand base* $B_\mathcal{P}$ of $\mathcal{P}$ is the set of all possible ground atoms constructible from the predicates appearing in $\mathcal{P}$ and the constants occurring in $U_\mathcal{P}$ (clearly, both $U_\mathcal{P}$ and $B_\mathcal{P}$ are finite). The instantiation of the rules in $\mathcal{P}$ is defined in the obvious way over the constants in $U_\mathcal{P}$, and is denoted by $ground(\mathcal{P})$.

A *(total) interpretation* for $\mathcal{P}$ is a subset I of $B_\mathcal{P}$. A ground positive literal a is *true* (resp., *false*) w.r.t. I if $a \in I$ (resp., $a \notin I$). A ground negative literal $\neg a$ is *true* (resp., *false*) w.r.t. I if $a \notin I$ (resp., $a \in I$).

Let r be a ground nested rule. We say that r is *applied* in the interpretation I if (i) every literal in $Body(r)$ is true w.r.t. I, and (ii) the atom in the head of r is true w.r.t. I. A rule $r \in ground(\mathcal{P})$ is *satisfied* (or *true*) w.r.t. I if its body is false (i.e., some body literal is false) w.r.t. I or an element of its head is applied. (Note that for flat rules this notion coincides with the classical notion of truth).

Example 3. The nested rule $b \hookleftarrow \neg c \leftarrow$ is applied in the interpretation $I = \{b, d\}$, as its body is true w.r.t. I and the head atom b is in I. Therefore, rule $r_1 : a \vee (b \hookleftarrow \neg c) \leftarrow d$ is satisfied w.r.t. I. r_1 is true also in the interpretation $I = \{a, d\}$; while it is not satisfied w.r.t. the interpretation $I = \{c, d\}$.   □

A *model* for $\mathcal{P}$ is an interpretation M for $\mathcal{P}$ which satisfies every rule $r \in ground(\mathcal{P})$.

Example 4. For the flat program $\mathcal{P} = \{a \vee b \leftarrow\}$ the interpretations $\{a\}$, $\{b\}$ and $\{a, b\}$ are its models.
   For the program $\mathcal{P} = \{a \vee b \leftarrow; \quad c \vee (d \hookleftarrow a) \leftarrow\}$ the interpretations $\{a, d\}$, $\{a, c\}$, $\{b, c\}$, $\{a, b, d\}$, $\{a, b, c\}$, $\{a, c, d\}$, $\{a, b, c, d\}$ are models. $\{b, d\}$ is not a model, as rule $c \vee (d \hookleftarrow a) \leftarrow$ has a true body but neither c nor $d \hookleftarrow a$ are applied w.r.t. $\{b, d\}$ (the latter is not applied because a is not true).   □

As shown in [19], the intuitive meaning of positive (disjunctive) programs (i.e., Datalog$^\vee$ programs) is captured by the set of its minimal models (a model M is minimal if no proper subset of M is a model). However, in presence of negation and nested rules, not all minimal models represent an intuitive meaning for the programs at hand. For instance, the program consisting of the rule $a \vee (b \leftarrow c) \leftarrow$ has two minimal models: $M_1 = \{a\}$ and $M_2 = \{b, c\}$. However, the model M_2 is not intuitive since the atom c cannon be derived from the program.
   To define a proper semantics of Datalog$^{\vee, \neg, \hookleftarrow}$ programs, we define next a suitable notion of *unfounded sets* for disjunctive logic programs with nested rules which extends in a very natural way the analogous notion of unfounded sets given for normal and disjunctive logic programs in [26] and [16, 17], respectively.
   Unfounded sets with respect to an interpretation I are essentially set of atoms that are definitely not derivable from the program (assuming I), and, as a consequence, they can be declared false according to the given interpretation.

Definition 1. *Let $\mathcal{P}$ be a Datalog$^{\vee, \neg, \hookleftarrow}$ program and $I \subseteq B_\mathcal{P}$ an interpretation for $\mathcal{P}$. $X \subseteq B_\mathcal{P}$ is an* unfounded set *for $\mathcal{P}$ w.r.t. I if, for each $a \in X$, every rule r with a nested rule $r' : a \hookleftarrow Body(r')$ in $Head(r)$,[3] satisfies at least one of the following conditions (we also say r has a witness of unfoundness):*

1. *$Body(r) \cup Body(r')$ is false w.r.t. I, i.e., at least one literal in $Body(r) \cup Body(r')$ is false w.r.t. I;*
2. *$(Body^+(r) \cup Body^+(r')) \cap X \neq \emptyset$;*
3. *some nested rule in $Head(r)$ is applied w.r.t. $I - X$.*   □

Informally, if a model M includes any unfounded set, say X, then, in a sense, we can get a better model, according to the closed world principle, by declaring false all the atoms in the set X. Therefore, a "supported" model must contain no unfounded set. This intuition is formalized by the following definition of stable models.

---

[3] An atom A in $Head(r)$ is seen as a nested rule with empty body $a \hookleftarrow$.

Definition 2. *Let $\mathcal{P}$ be a Datalog$^{\vee,\neg,\hookleftarrow}$ program and $M \subseteq B_{\mathcal{P}}$ be a model for $\mathcal{P}$. M is a* stable model *for $\mathcal{P}$ if it does not contain any non empty unfounded set w.r.t. M (i.e., if both $X \subseteq M$ and $X \neq \emptyset$ hold, then X is not an unfounded set for $\mathcal{P}$ w.r.t. M).*   □

Example 5. Let $\mathcal{P} = \{a \vee b \leftarrow c, \quad b \leftarrow \neg a, \neg c, \quad a \vee c \leftarrow \neg b\}$. Consider $I = \{b\}$. It is easy to verify that $\{b\}$ is not an unfounded set for $\mathcal{P}$ w.r.t. I. Indeed, rule $b \leftarrow \neg a, \neg c$ has no witness of unfoundedness w.r.t. I. Thus, as I is a model for $\mathcal{P}$, then I is a stable model for $\mathcal{P}$ according to Definition 1.

Let $\mathcal{P} = \{a \vee (b \hookleftarrow \neg c) \leftarrow d, \quad d \vee c \leftarrow\}$. Consider the model $I = \{b, d\}$. It is easy to verify that $\{b, d\}$ is not an unfounded set w.r.t. I and neither $\{a\}$ nor $\{b\}$ is an unfounded set for $\mathcal{P}$ w.r.t. I. Therefore, I is a stable model of $\mathcal{P}$.

It is easy to see that the stable models of the program $\mathcal{P} = \{susan \vee (john \hookleftarrow mary) \leftarrow, \quad mary \vee paul \leftarrow\}$ of example 1 are: $M_1 = \{susan, mary\}$, $M_2 = \{susan, paul\}$, and $M_3 = \{john, mary\}$.   □

We conclude this section by showing that the above definitions of unfounded sets and stable models extend the analogous notions given for normal and disjunctive logic programs.

Proposition 1. *Let I be an interpretation for a flat program $\mathcal{P}$. $X \subseteq B_{\mathcal{P}}$ is an unfounded set for $\mathcal{P}$ w.r.t. I according to [16, 17] if and only if X is an unfounded set for $\mathcal{P}$ w.r.t. I according to Definition 1.*

Proof.   For a flat program $\mathcal{P}$, every nested rule r' is of the form $a \hookleftarrow$. Consequently, Condition 1 and Condition 2 of Definition 1 correspond exactly to the analogous conditions of the definition of unfounded set given in [16, 17] (as $Body(r') = \emptyset$). Moreover, in absence of nested rules with nonempty bodies, Condition 3 of Definition 1 just says that some head atom is true w.r.t. $I - X$ (which corresponds to Condition 3 of the definition of unfounded set given in [16, 17]).□

As a consequence, if $\mathcal{P}$ is a non disjunctive flat program, then the notion of unfounded set does coincide with the original one given in [26].

Corollary 1. *Let I be an interpretation for a normal flat program $\mathcal{P}$. $X \subseteq B_{\mathcal{P}}$ is an unfounded set for $\mathcal{P}$ w.r.t. I according to [26] if and only if X is an unfounded set for $\mathcal{P}$ w.r.t. I according to Definition 1.*

Proof.   In [16, 17], it is shown that the Definition of unfounded sets given there, coincides on normal programs with the classical definition of unfounded sets of [26]. The result therefore follows from Proposition 1.   □

Theorem 1. *Let $\mathcal{P}$ be a flat program and M a model for $\mathcal{P}$. Then, M is a stable model for $\mathcal{P}$ according to [22, 11] if and only if M is a stable model for $\mathcal{P}$ according to Definition 2.*

Proof.   It follows from Proposition 1 and the results in [16, 17].   □

Moreover, if $\mathcal{P}$ is a positive flat program, then the set of its stable models coincides with the set of its minimal models. Hence, for positive flat programs our stable models semantics coincide with minimal model semantics proposed for such programs in [19].

In fact the stable model semantics defined above, is a very natural extension of the widely accepted semantics for the various (less general) classes of logic programs, since it is based on the same concepts of minimality and supportedness, which follow from the closed world assumption.

3   Complexity and Expressiveness

3.1   Preliminaries

In the context of deductive databases, some of the predicate symbols correspond to database relations (the *extensional (EDB) predicates*), and are not allowed to occur in rule heads; the other predicate symbols are called *intensional (IDB) predicates*. Actual database relations are formed on a fixed countable domain U, from which also possible constants in a Datalog$^{\vee,\neg,\hookleftarrow}$ program are taken.

More formally, a Datalog$^{\vee,\neg,\hookleftarrow}$ program $\mathcal{P}$ has associated a relational database scheme $\mathcal{DB}_{\mathcal{P}} = \{r|\ r$ is an EDB predicate symbol of $\mathcal{P}\}$; thus EDB predicate symbols are seen as relation symbols. A database D on $\mathcal{DB}_{\mathcal{P}}$ is a set of finite relations on U, one for each r in $\mathcal{DB}_{\mathcal{P}}$, denoted by $D(r)$; note that D can be seen as a first-order structure whose universe consists of the constants occurring in D (the *active domain* of D).[4] The set of all databases on $\mathcal{DB}_{\mathcal{P}}$ is denoted by $\mathbf{D}_{\mathcal{P}}$.

Given a database $D \in \mathbf{D}_{\mathcal{P}}$, $\mathcal{P}_D$ denotes the following program:

$$\mathcal{P}_D = \mathcal{P} \cup \{r(t) \leftarrow\ |\ r \in \mathcal{DB}_{\mathcal{P}} \wedge t \in D(r)\}.$$

Definition 3. *A (bound Datalog$^{\vee,\neg,\hookleftarrow}$) query $\mathcal{Q}$ is a pair $\langle \mathcal{P}, G \rangle$, where $\mathcal{P}$ is a Datalog$^{\vee,\neg,\hookleftarrow}$ program and G is a ground literal (the query goal). Given a database D in $\mathbf{D}_{\mathcal{P}}$, the answer of $\mathcal{Q}$ on D is true if there exists a stable model M of $\mathcal{P}_D$ such that G is true w.r.t. M, and false otherwise.* [5]   □

Constraining $\mathcal{P}$ on fragments of Datalog$^{\vee,\neg,\hookleftarrow}$, we obtain smaller sets of queries. More precisely, we say that $\mathcal{Q} = \langle \mathcal{P}, G \rangle$ is a Datalog^{X} query, where $X \subseteq \{\vee, \hookleftarrow, \neg\}$, if $\mathcal{P}$ is a Datalog^{X} program (and G is a ground literal). Clearly, $\neg$ could also be replaced by $\neg_s$ to obtain queries of stratified fragments of Datalog$^{\vee,\neg,\hookleftarrow}$.

The constants occurring in $\mathcal{P}_D$ and G define the active domain of query $\mathcal{Q} = \langle \mathcal{P}, G \rangle$ on the database D. Observe that, in general, two queries $\langle \mathcal{P}, G \rangle$ and $\langle \mathcal{P}, \neg G \rangle$ on the same database need not give symmetric answers. That is, if

---

[4] We use here active domain semantics (cf. [1]), rather then a setting in which a (finite) universe of D is explicitly provided [9, 6, 27]. Note that Fagin's Theorem and all other results to which we refer remain valid in this (narrower) context; conversely, the results of this paper can be extended to that setting.

[5] We consider brave (also called possibility) semantics in this paper; however, complexity and expressiveness of cautious (also called skeptical) semantics can be easily derived from it.

e.g. $\langle P, G \rangle$ answers yes for D, it may be possible that also $\langle P, \neg G \rangle$ answers yes for D.

A bound query defines a Boolean C-generic query of [1], i.e., a mapping from $\mathbf{D}_P$ to $\{true, false\}$. As common, we focus in our analysis of the expressive power of a query language on generic queries, which are those mappings whose result is invariant under renaming the constants in D with constants from U. Genericity of a bound query $\langle P, G \rangle$ is assured by excluding constants in P and G. As discussed in [1, p. 421], this issue is not central, since constants can be provided by designated input relations; moreover, any query goal $G = (\neg)p(\cdots)$ can be easily replaced by a new goal $G' = (\neg)q$ and the rule $q \leftarrow p(\cdots)$, where q is a propositional letter. In the rest of this paper, we thus implicitly assume that constants do not occur in queries.

Definition 4. *Let $Q = \langle P, G \rangle$ be a (constant-free) query. Then the database collection of Q, denoted by $\mathcal{EXP}(Q)$, is the set of all databases D in $\mathbf{D}_P$ for which the answer of Q is true.*

The expressive power of $Datalog^X$ ($X \subseteq \{\vee, \leftarrow, \neg\}$), denoted $\mathcal{EXP}(Datalog^X)$, is the family of the database collections of all $Datalog^X$ queries, i.e.,

$$\mathcal{EXP}[Datalog^X] = \{\mathcal{EXP}(Q) \mid Q \text{ is a constant-free } Datalog^X \text{ query}\}. \qquad \square$$

The expressive power will be related to database complexity classes, which are as follows. Let C be a Turing machine complexity class (e.g., P or NP), $\mathbf{R}$ be a relational database scheme, and $\mathbf{D}$ be a set of databases on $\mathbf{R}$.[6] Then, $\mathbf{D}$ is C-*recognizable* if the problem of deciding whether $D \in \mathbf{D}$ for a given database D on $\mathbf{R}$ is in C. The *database complexity class* $DB\text{-}C$ is the family of all C-recognizable database collections. (For instance, $DB\text{-}P$ is the family of all database collections that are recognizable in polynomial time). If the expressive power of a given language (fragment of $Datalog^{\vee, \neg, \leftarrow}$) $\mathcal{L}$ coincides with some class $DB\text{-}C$, we say that the given language *captures* C, and denote this fact by $\mathcal{EXP}[\mathcal{L}] = C$.

Recall that the classes Σ_k^P, Π_k^P of the polynomial hierarchy [25] are defined by $\Sigma_0^P = P$, $\Sigma_{i+1}^P = NP^{\Sigma_i^P}$, and $\Pi_i^P = \text{co-}\Sigma_i^P$, for all $i \geq 0$. In particular, $\Pi_0^P = P$, $\Sigma_1^P = NP$, and $\Pi_1^P = \text{co-}NP$.

3.2 Results

Theorem 2. $\mathcal{EXP}[Datalog^{\vee, \neg_s}] \subseteq \mathcal{EXP}[Datalog^{\vee, \leftarrow}]$

Proof. We will show that every $Datalog^{\vee, \neg_s}$ query can be rewritten into an equivalent $Datalog^{\vee, \leftarrow}$ query.

It can be easily verified that every $Datalog^{\vee, \neg_s}$ program (i.e., disjunctive Datalog program with stratified negation) can be polynomially rewritten in a program where negative literals appear only in the body of rules of the form

$$r : \quad p(\overline{X}) \leftarrow q(\overline{Y}), \ \neg s(\overline{Z})$$

---

[6] As usual, adopting the data independence principle, it is assumed that $\mathbf{D}$ is generic, i.e., it is closed under renamings of the constants in U.

where p and s are not mutually recursive and r is the only rule having p as head predicate symbol. Let $\langle \mathcal{P}, G \rangle$ be a Datalog$^{\vee, \neg_s}$ query. Following the observation above, we assume that every rule $r \in \mathcal{P}$ such that r contains negative literals has the syntactic form just described. This means that, given any database $D \in \mathbf{D}_{\mathcal{P}}$, a stable model M for $\mathcal{P}_D$, and a ground instance $\bar{r}:\ p(\bar{a}) \leftarrow q(\bar{b}), \neg s(\bar{c})$ of r, we have $p(\bar{a})$ is derivable from $\bar{r}$ if and only if $q(\bar{b})$ is true and $s(\bar{c})$ is not true. Moreover, the rule $\bar{r}$ cannot be used to prove that the atom $s(\bar{c})$ is *true*.

Now, given the Datalog$^{\vee, \neg_s}$ program $\mathcal{P}$, we define a Datalog$^{\vee, \hookleftarrow}$ program $\mathcal{P}'$ such that, for any given database $D \in \mathbf{D}_{\mathcal{P}}$, $\mathcal{P}'_D$ has the same set of stable models as $\mathcal{P}_D$. We obtain such a program $\mathcal{P}'$ from the program $\mathcal{P}$ by simply replacing any rule of $\mathcal{P}$ having the form of the rule r above by the following Datalog$^{\vee, \hookleftarrow}$ rule r':

$$r':\ p(\overline{X}) \vee (s(\overline{Z}) \hookleftarrow s(\overline{Z})) \leftarrow q(\overline{Y})$$

Now, apply to r' the substitution that yields $\bar{r}$ from r. The resulting instance is $\bar{r}':\ p(\bar{a}) \vee (s(\bar{c}) \hookleftarrow s(\bar{c})) \leftarrow q(\bar{b})$. From the semantics of nested rules, we have that $p(\bar{a})$ is derivable from $\bar{r}'$ if and only if $q(\bar{b})$ is true and $s(\bar{c})$ is false (exactly like for $\bar{r}$) – note that a crucial role is played by the fact that s belongs to a stratum lower than p so that s is already evaluated when p is considered (e.g., if $s(\bar{c})$ is true, then the nested rule $s(\bar{c}) \hookleftarrow s(\bar{c})$ is already applied and $\bar{r}'$ cannot be used to derive $p(\bar{a})$). Thus, r and r' have exactly the same behaviour. Consequently, given a database D in $\mathbf{D}_{\mathcal{P}}$, we have that an interpretation M is a stable model for $\mathcal{P}_D$ if and only if M is a stable model for $\mathcal{P}'_D$. $\qquad\square$

Corollary 2. $\Sigma_2^P \subseteq \mathcal{EXP}[\text{Datalog}^{\vee, \hookleftarrow}]$

Proof. From [7], $\Sigma_2^P \subseteq \mathcal{EXP}[\text{Datalog}^{\vee, \neg_s}]$. Therefore, the result follows from Theorem 2. $\qquad\square$

Corollary 3. $\mathcal{EXP}[\text{Datalog}^{\vee}] \subset \mathcal{EXP}[\text{Datalog}^{\vee, \hookleftarrow}]$

Proof. From [7], Datalog$^{\vee}$ can express only a strict subset of Σ_2^P (e.g., the simple *even* query, deciding whether the number of tuples of a relation is even or odd, is not expressible in Datalog$^{\vee}$ [7]). Therefore, the result follows from Corollary 2. $\qquad\square$

We next prove that the inclusion of Corollary 2 is not proper.

Theorem 3. $\mathcal{EXP}[\text{Datalog}^{\vee, \neg, \hookleftarrow}] \subseteq \Sigma_2^P$.

Proof. To prove the theorem, we have to show that for any Datalog$^{\vee, \neg, \hookleftarrow}$ query $\mathcal{Q} = \langle \mathcal{P}, G \rangle$, recognizing whether a database D is in $\mathcal{EXP}(\mathcal{Q})$ is in Σ_2^P.

Observe first that recognizing whether a given model M of a Datalog$^{\vee, \neg, \hookleftarrow}$ program is stable can be done in co-NP. Indeed, to prove that M is not stable, it is sufficient to guess a subset X of M and check that it is an unfounded set. (Note that, since $\mathcal{Q}$ is fixed, $ground(\mathcal{P}_D)$ has size polynomial in D, and can be constructed in polynomial time.)

Now, D is in $\mathcal{EXP}(\mathcal{Q})$ iff there exists a stable model M of $\mathcal{P}_D$ such that $G \in M$. To check this, we may guess an interpretation M of $\mathcal{P}_D$ and verify that: (i) M is a stable model of $\mathcal{P}_D$, and (ii) $G \in M$. From the observation above,

(i) is done by a single call to an NP oracle; moreover, (ii) is clearly polynomial. Hence, this problem is in Σ_2^P. Consequently, recognizing whether a database D is in $\mathcal{EXP}(Q)$ is in Σ_2^P.   □

Corollary 4. $\mathcal{EXP}[Datalog^{\vee,\neg,\leftarrow}] = \mathcal{EXP}[Datalog^{\vee,\leftarrow}] = \mathcal{EXP}[Datalog^{\vee,\neg}] = \Sigma_2^P$

Proof.   It follows from Corollary 2, from Theorem 3, and from the results in [7].   □

The above results show that full negation, stratified negation and nested rules in disjunctive rules have the same expressivity. Moreover, the choice of the constructs which should be used depends on the context of the applications.

4   Some Examples

In this section we present some examples to show that classical graph problems can be expressed in Datalog$^{\vee,\leftarrow}$. For the sake of presentation we shall use the predicate $\neq$ which can be emulated by Datalog$^{\vee,\leftarrow}$. Assuming that the the database domain is denoted by the unary predicate d, the following two rules define the binary predicate neq (not equal):

$$neq(X,Y) \vee (eq(X,Y) \leftarrow X = Y) \leftarrow d(X), \ d(Y).$$
$$eq(X,X)$$

Thus, a tuple $neq(x,y)$ is true if let x and y two elements in the database is $x \neq y$. Observe that also stratified negation could be emulated by Datalog$^{\vee,\leftarrow}$. In the following examples we assume to have the graph $G = (V,E)$ stored by means of the unary relation v and the binary relation e.

Example 6. Spanning tree. The following program computes a spanning tree rooted in the node a for a graph $G = (V,E)$. The set of arcs in the spanning tree are collected by means of the predicate st.

$$st(root,a).$$
$$st(X,Y) \vee (no\_st(X,Y) \leftarrow no\_st(X,Y)) \leftarrow st(\_,X), \ e(X,Y).$$
$$no\_st(X,Y) \qquad\qquad\qquad\qquad \leftarrow st(X',Y), X \neq X'.$$

Observe that the nested rule forces to select for each value of Y a unique tuple for $st(X,Y)$. Indeed, if some stable model M contains two tuples of the form $t_1 = st(x_1,y)$ and $t_2 = st(x_2,y)$, from the last rule, M must contain also the tuples $no\_st(x_1,y)$ and $no\_st(x_2,y)$. But this implies that also the interpretation $N \subseteq M - \{t_i\}$ for $t_i \in \{t_1,t_2\}$ is a stable model and, therefore, M is not minimal. On the other side, assume now that there is some stable model M containing a tuple $no\_st(x',y)$ but not containing tuples of the form $st(x,y)$ for $x \neq x'$. This means that the tuple $no\_st(x',y)$ cannot be derived from the last rule and, therefore, it must belong to some unfounded set w.r.t. M.

Thus, there is a one-to-one correspondence between the stable models of the program and the spanning trees rooted in a of the graph.   □

Example 7. Simple path. In this example we compute a simple path in a graph G, i.e., a path passing through every node just once (if any). The set of tuples in the simple path are collected by means of the predicate sp below defined:

$$sp(root, X) \vee (no\_sp(root, X) \leftrightarrow no\_sp(root, X)) \leftarrow e(X, \_).$$
$$sp(X, Y) \vee (no\_sp(X, Y) \leftrightarrow no\_sp(X, Y)) \qquad \leftarrow sp(W, X), \; e(X, Y).$$

$$no\_sp(X, Y) \leftarrow sp(X', Y), \; X' \neq X.$$
$$no\_sp(X, Y) \leftarrow sp(X, Y'), \; Y' \neq Y.$$

As for the program computing a spanning tree, the nested rule forces to select for each value of X a unique tuple for $sp(X, Y)$ and for each value of Y a unique tuple for $sp(X, Y)$. The nested rules impose the constraint that the set of tuples for sp defines a chain. Thus, the first nested rule is used to select the starting node of the simple path, whereas the second nested rule is used to select the set of arcs belonging to the simple path.

The above program can be used to define the hamiltonian path problem checking if a graph G has simple path passing through all nodes (hamiltonian path). Therefore, the hamiltonian graph problem can be defined by adding the check that all nodes in G are in the simple path. □

Example 8. Shortest path. In this example we assume to have a weighted directed graph $G = (V, E)$. We assume that the database domain contains a finite subset of the integer numbers and that the weight argument of the arcs takes values from this domain. We assume also that the minimum weight of all paths between two nodes takes values from this domain. The arcs of the graph are stored by means of tuples of the form $e(x, y, c)$ where c is the weight of the arc from x to y. The minimum weights of the paths from a source node a to every node in the graph can be defined as follows:

$$mp(a, 0).$$
$$mp(Y, C) \vee (no\_mp(Y, C) \leftrightarrow no\_mp(Y, C)) \leftarrow mp(X, C_1), e(X, Y, C_2),$$
$$C = C_1 + C_2.$$
$$no\_mp(Y, C) \qquad\qquad\qquad\qquad \leftarrow mp(Y, C'), \; C' < C.$$

The predicate mp computes, for each node x, the minimum distance from the source node a to the node x. A stable model M contains for each tuple $mp(y, c')$ in M all tuples of the form $no\_mp(y, c)$ with $c > c'$. Thus, a tuple $mp(y, c)$ is in M iff there is no tuple $no\_mp(y, c)$ in M, i.e., if all tuples in no_mp with first argument y have cost greater than c. □

Example 9. Even query. We are given a relation d and we want to check whether its cardinality is even or not. This can be done by first defining a linear order on the elements of the relation and, then, checking whether the number of elements in the ordering is even.

$$succ(root, root).$$
$$succ(X, Y) \vee (no\_succ(X, Y) \leftrightarrow no\_succ(X, Y)) \leftarrow succ(\_, X), \; d(Y).$$

$no\_succ(X,Y) \leftarrow succ(X,Y'), \; Y' \neq Y, \; Y' \neq root, \; d(Y).$
$no\_succ(X,Y) \leftarrow succ(X',Y), \; X' \neq X, \; d(X).$

$odd(X) \qquad\quad \leftarrow succ(root, X), X \neq root.$
$even(X) \qquad\; \leftarrow odd(Z), succ(Z, X).$
$odd(X) \qquad\quad \leftarrow even(Z), succ(Z, Y).$
$even\_rel \qquad\; \leftarrow even(X), \neg has\_a\_succ(X).$
$has\_a\_succ(X) \leftarrow d(X), \; succ(X, \_).$

The first four rules define a linear order on the elements of the relation d (by using a nested implication). Once a linear order has been defined on the domain it is easy to check, by a simple stratified program, whether the cardinality is even. Thus, the predicate $even\_rel$ is true iff the relation d has an even number of elements.

Therefore, Datalog$^{\vee,\leftarrow}$ expresses the even query,[7] while it cannot be expressed in Datalog$^{\vee}$ [7].   □

We conclude by observing that the problems of the above examples could be expressed by means of disjunctive datalog with (unstratified) negation. However, programs with unstratified negation are neither intuitive nor efficiently computable (while Datalog$^{\vee,\leftarrow}$ has nice computational properties – see Section 5).

5 Conclusion

We have presented an extension of Disjunctive Datalog by nested rules. We have shown the suitability of the language to naturally express complex knowledge-based problems, which are not expressible by Datalog$^{\vee}$. A formal definition of the semantics of Datalog$^{\vee,\neg,\leftarrow}$ programs has been provided, and we have shown that it is a generalization of the classical stable model semantics. Finally, we have carefully analyzed both data-complexity and expressiveness of Datalog$^{\vee,\neg,\leftarrow}$ under the possibility (brave) semantics.

The results on the data-complexity and the expressiveness of Datalog$^{\vee,\neg,\leftarrow}$ are compactly represented in Table 1. [8]

	Datalog$^{\vee,\leftarrow}$	Datalog$^{\vee}$	Datalog$^{\vee,\neg}$	Datalog$^{\vee,\neg,\leftarrow}$
Expressive Power	$= \Sigma_2^P$	$\subset \Sigma_2^P$	$= \Sigma_2^P$	$= \Sigma_2^P$
Data Complexity	Σ_2^P-complete	Σ_2^P-complete	Σ_2^P-complete	Σ_2^P-complete

Table 1. *Expressibility and complexity results on Datalog$^{\vee,\neg,\leftarrow}$*

---

[7] Recall that both $\neq$ and stratified negation are used for simplicity, bu they can be easily emulated in Datalog$^{\vee,\leftarrow}$.

[8] Note that the results on data-complexity are immediately derived from the expressibility results of Section 3.2.

Each column in Table 1 refers to a specific fragment of Datalog$^{\vee,\neg,\hookleftarrow}$. The table clearly shows that the addition of nested rules does not increase the complexity of disjunctive Datalog; indeed, brave reasoning for Datalog$^{\vee,\hookleftarrow}$ is Σ_2^P-complete as for Datalog$^{\vee}$. Nevertheless, nested rules do increase the expressive power, as Datalog$^{\vee,\hookleftarrow}$ allows to express all Σ_2^P database properties; while, Datalog$^{\vee}$ expresses only a strict subset of them (e.g., the simple *even* query, that decides whether a relation has an even number of tuples, cannot be expressed in Datalog$^{\vee}$).

Clearly, the power of Datalog$^{\vee,\hookleftarrow}$ does not exceed that of Datalog$^{\vee,\neg}$, as nested rules could be simulated by means of unstratified negation. However, the increase of expressiveness w.r.t. Datalog$^{\vee}$ confirms that nested rule allow to express some useful forms of disjunctive information which are not expressible in plain disjunctive Datalog.

Ongoing work concerns the definition of a fragment of Datalog$^{\vee,\hookleftarrow}$ for which one stable model can be computed in polynomial time; this fragment, under nondeterministic semantics, allows to express *all* polynomial time properties. Moreover, the investigation of abstract properties of Datalog$^{\vee,\hookleftarrow}$ would also be interesting to see whether this language can be characterized as for the stable model semantics [3]. We conclude by mentioning that nested rules have been recently used as a vehicle for binding propagation into disjunctive rules to optimize the computation of standard disjunctive queries. [14]

References

1. Abiteboul, S., Hull, R., Vianu, V. (1995), *Foundations of Databases*. Addison-Wesley.
2. Baral, C. and Gelfond, M. (1994), Logic Programming and Knowledge Representation *Journal of Logic Programming*, **19/20**, 73–148.
3. S. Brass and J. Dix (1997), Characterizations of the Stable Semantics by Partial Evaluation. *Journal of Logic Programming*, 32(3):207–228.
4. S. Brass, J. Dix, and T.C. Przymusinski (1996), Super Logic Programs. *In* "Proc. of the Fifth International Conference on Principles of Knowledge Representation and Reasoning (KR'96)", Cambridge, MA, USA, Morgan Kaufmann, pp. 529–540.
5. M. Cadoli and M. Schaerf (1993), A Survey of Complexity Results for Non-monotonic Logics, *Journal of Logic Programming*, Vol. 17, pp. 127-160.
6. Chandra, A., Harel, D. (1982), Structure and Complexity of Relational Queries. *Journal of Computer and System Sciences*, 25:99–128.
7. Eiter, T., Gottlob, G. and Mannila, H. (1994), Adding Disjunction to Datalog, *Proc. ACM PODS-94*, pp. 267–278.
8. T. Eiter and G. Gottlob and H. Mannila (1997), Disjunctive Datalog, *ACM Transactions on Database Systems*, 22(3):364–418.
9. Fagin R. (1974), Generalized First-Order Spectra and Polynomial-Time Recognizable Sets, *Complexity of Computation*, SIAM-AMS Proc., Vol. 7, pp. 43-73.
10. Gelfond, M., Lifschitz, V. (1988), The Stable Model Semantics for Logic Programming, *in Proc. of Fifth Conf. on Logic Programming*, pp. 1070–1080, MIT Press.
11. Gelfond, M. and Lifschitz, V. (1991), Classical Negation in Logic Programs and Disjunctive Databases, *New Generation Computing*, **9**, 365–385.

12. Gelfond, M. and Son, T.C., Reasoning with Prioritized Defaults, *Proc. of the Workshop Logic Programming and Knowledge Representation - LPKR'97*, Port Jefferson, New York, October 1997.

13. Gottlob, G., Complexity Results for Nonmonotonic Logics, *Journal of Logic and Computation*, Vol. 2, N. 3, pp. 397-425, 1992.

14. Greco, S.(1990), Binding Propagation in Disjunctive Databases, Proc. Int. Conf. on Very Large Data Bases, New York City.

15. Herre H., and Wagner G. (1997), Stable Models Are Generated by a Stabel Chain, *Journal of Logic Programming*, 30(2): 165–177.

16. Leone, N., Rullo, P., Scarcello, F. (1995) Declarative and Fixpoint Characterizations of Disjunctive Stable Models, *in* " Proceedings of International Logic Programming Symposium (ILPS'95)", Portland, Oregon, pp. 399–413, MIT Press.

17. Leone, N., Rullo, P., Scarcello, F. (1997) Disjunctive Stable Models: Unfounded Sets, Fixpoint Semantics and Computation, *Information and Computation*, Academic Press, Vol. 135, No. 2, June 15, 1997, pp. 69-112.

18. Marek, W., Truszczyński, M., Autoepistemic Logic, *Journal of the ACM*, 38, 3, 1991, pp. 518-619.

19. Minker, J. (1982), On Indefinite Data Bases and the Closed World Assumption, *in* "Proc. of the 6th Conference on Automated Deduction (CADE-82)," pp. 292–308.

20. L. Pereira, J. Alferes, and J. Aparicio (1992), Well founded semantics for logic programs with explicit negation. *In* "Proc. of European Conference on AI".

21. Przymusinski, T. (1988), On the Declarative Semantics of Deductive Databases and Logic Programming, *in* "Foundations of deductive databases and logic programming," Minker, J. ed., ch. 5, pp.193–216, Morgan Kaufman, Washington, D.C.

22. Przymusinski, T. (1991), Stable Semantics for Disjunctive Programs, *New Generation Computing*, **9**, 401–424.

23. D. Saccà. The Expressive Powers of Stable Models for Bound and Unbound DATALOG Queries. *Journal of Computer and System Sciences*, Vol. 54, No. 3, June 1997, pp. 441–464.

24. Schlipf, J.S., The Expressive Powers of Logic Programming Semantics, *Proc. ACM Symposium on Principles of Database Systems* 1990, pp. 196-204.

25. Stockmeyer, L.J. (1977), The Polynomial-Time Hierarchy. *Theoretical Computer Science*, 3:1–22.

26. Van Gelder, A., Ross, K. A. and Schlipf, J. S. (1991), The Well-Founded Semantics for General Logic Programs, *Journal of ACM*, **38**(3), 620–650.

27. Vardi, M. (1982), Complexity of relational query languages, *in* "Proceedings 14th ACM STOC," pp. 137–146.

Partial Evidential Stable Models for Disjunctive Deductive Databases

Dietmar Seipel

University of Würzburg
Am Hubland,
D – 97074 Würzburg, Germany
seipel@informatik.uni-wuerzburg.de

Abstract. In this paper we consider the basic semantics of *stable* and *partial stable models* for disjunctive deductive databases (with default negation), cf. [9, 16]. It is well–known that there are disjunctive deductive databases where no stable or partial stable models exist, and these databases are called inconsistent w.r.t. the basic semantics.

We define a consistent variant of each class of models, which we call *evidential stable* and *partial evidential stable models*. It is shown that if a database is already consistent w.r.t. the basic semantics, then the class of evidential models coincides with the basic class of models. Otherwise, the set of evidential models is a subset of the set of minimal models of the database. This subset is non–empty, if the database is logically consistent. It is determined according to a suitable *preference relation*, whose underlying idea is to *minimize* the amount of *reasoning by contradiction*.

The technical ingredients for the construction of the new classes of models are two transformations of disjunctive deductive databases. First, the *evidential transformation* is used to realize the preference relation, and to define evidential stable models. Secondly, based on the tu–*transformation* the result is lifted to the three–valued case, that is, partial evidential stable models are defined.

Keywords

disjunctive logic programming, non–monotonic reasoning, stable and partial stable models, handling inconsistency, program transformations

1   Introduction

The semantics of *stable* and *partial stable models*, cf. Gelfond, Lifschitz [9, 10] and Przymusinski [16], are among the most prominent semantics for disjunctive databases. Unfortunately, there are databases which are logically consistent, but are inconsistent w.r.t. these semantics. For normal databases, i.e. databases that may contain negation but do not contain disjunctions, however, the partial stable models semantics is always consistent, and it is equivalent to the *well–founded semantics* of van Gelder, Ross and Schlipf [21].

For large databases, small inconsistent parts can prohibit the existence of stable models, and even of partial stable models. Thus, we will introduce two new variants of the stable model semantics, which are always consistent if the database is logically consistent: First, the two–valued semantics of *evidential stable models*, which is stronger than minimal model but weaker than stable model semantics. Secondly, a three–valued version, called *partial evidential stable models*, which for normal databases coincides with the well–founded semantics. For stratified–disjunctive databases both evidential semantics coincide with the perfect model semantics.

Consider the disjunctive database $\mathcal{P} = \{r\}$ consisting of one rule $r = q \leftarrow not\ a$. Among its two minimal models $M_1 = \{q\}$ and $M_2 = \{a\}$, the first model is *preferred* to the second. Intuitively, the reason is that in M_2 the truth of "a" has been derived by *contradiction*, i.e. r has been fulfilled by making its body *false*. In contrast, in M_1 the truth of "q" is derived constructively from the head of r. Thus, M_1 is the so–called *perfect model* of $\mathcal{P}$, and it is considered to be the intended model.

The *evidential transformation* $\mathcal{EP}$ is a positive–disjunctive database that is derived from $\mathcal{P}$ by moving default negated body literals to the rule heads and prefixing them with "$\mathcal{E}$". Thus, the rule r is translated to $q \vee \mathcal{E}a$. Additionally, rules relating atoms and evidential atoms are introduced: $\mathcal{E}q \leftarrow q$, $\mathcal{E}a \leftarrow a$. A similar construction has been used by Fernández et al., cf. [7], to characterize the stable models of $\mathcal{P}$. But our use of evidences has a different interpretation, and moreover we use additional *normality rules*, which are not needed in [7]. *Evidential stable models* are defined as minimal models M of $\mathcal{EP}$ which also minimize the set of atoms that are derived by contradiction solely: such atoms A are *false* in M, but $\mathcal{E}A$ is *true* in M. Then we call $\mathcal{E}A$ an $\mathcal{E}$–violation. In our example, the minimal models of $\mathcal{EP}$ are $M_1' = \{q, \mathcal{E}q\}$ and $M_2' = \{\mathcal{E}a\}$. In M_1' there is no $\mathcal{E}$–violation, whereas in M_2' there is the $\mathcal{E}$–violation "$\mathcal{E}a$". Thus, M_1' is the unique evidential stable model of $\mathcal{P}$. We will show, that for databases which have stable models the evidential stable models coincide with the stable models, when evidential atoms $\mathcal{E}A$ are interpreted as atoms A. Furthermore, evidential stable models always exist for logically consistent databases. E.g. the database $\mathcal{P}' = \{a \leftarrow not\ a\}$, which does not have any stable models, has the unique evidential stable model $M' = \{\mathcal{E}a\}$, which is interpreted as the model $M = \{a\}$ of $\mathcal{P}$.

The second type of transformation we use is the tu–*transformation* $\mathcal{P}^{tu}$ of a disjunctive database $\mathcal{P}$, which suitably *annotates* the atoms in $\mathcal{P}$ by the two truth values *true* ("t") and *undefined* ("u"), cf. [19]. We state a *characterization* of the partial stable models of $\mathcal{P}$ in terms of the stable models of $\mathcal{P}^{tu}$. Then, *partial evidential stable models* are defined based on the evidential stable models of $\mathcal{P}^{tu}$, where the characterization for partial stable models motivates the new definition. As in the two–valued case, partial evidential stable models always exist for a logically consistent database. If there exist partial stable models of the database, then the partial evidential stable models coincide with the partial stable models, when evidential atoms are interpreted as atoms.

The paper is organized as follows: In Sections 2 and 3 we review the basic definitions and notation for disjunctive databases, partial Herbrand interpretations and partial stable models. In Section 4 we introduce the evidential transformation and the evidential stable models of a disjunctive database $\mathcal{P}$. In Section 5 we define the tu–transformation $\mathcal{P}^{\text{tu}}$ of $\mathcal{P}$ and we state a characterization of the partial stable models of $\mathcal{P}$ in terms of the total stable models of $\mathcal{P}^{\text{tu}}$. This motivates the definition of partial evidential stable models in Section 6. In Sections 7 and 8 we compare the new semantics with other approaches known from the literature, and we briefly comment on some of their abstract properties.

2   Basic Definitions and Notations

Given a first order language $\mathcal{L}$, a *disjunctive database* $\mathcal{P}$ consists of logical inference rules of the form

$$r = A_1 \vee \ldots \vee A_k \leftarrow B_1 \wedge \ldots \wedge B_m \wedge not\, C_1 \wedge \ldots \wedge not\, C_n, \qquad (1)$$

where A_i, $1 \leq i \leq k$, B_i, $1 \leq i \leq m$, and C_i, $1 \leq i \leq n$, are atoms in the language $\mathcal{L}$; $k, m, n \in I\!N_0$, and *not* is the negation–by–default operator.[1] A rule is called a fact if $m = n = 0$. The set of all *ground instances* of the rules and facts in $\mathcal{P}$ is denoted by $gnd\,(\mathcal{P})$. A rule (or database) is called *positive-disjunctive* if it does not contain default negation (i.e. $n = 0$). A rule r of the form (1) above is denoted for short as:

$$r = \alpha \leftarrow \beta \wedge not \cdot \gamma, \qquad (2)$$

where $\alpha = A_1 \vee \ldots \vee A_k$, $\beta = B_1 \wedge \ldots \wedge B_m$, and $\gamma = C_1 \vee \ldots \vee C_n$.[2]

Herbrand Interpretations and Partial Herbrand Interpretations

The Herbrand base $H\!B_{\mathcal{P}}$ of a disjunctive database $\mathcal{P}$ contains all ground atoms over the language of $\mathcal{P}$. A *partial Herbrand interpretation* of $\mathcal{P}$ is given by a mapping $I \colon H\!B_{\mathcal{P}} \to \{\text{t},\text{f},\text{u}\}$ that assigns a truth value "t" (*true*), "f" (*false*) or "u" (*undefined*) to each ground atom in $H\!B_{\mathcal{P}}$. Thus, partial Herbrand interpretations are also called three–valued Herbrand interpretations. I is called a *total* or *total Herbrand interpretation*, if all atoms $A \in H\!B_{\mathcal{P}}$ are mapped to classical truth values t or f.

Equivalently, a partial Herbrand interpretation I can be represented by using the concept of *annotated atoms*. Given an atom $A = p(t_1, \ldots, t_n)$ and a truth value $\text{v} \in \{\,\text{t},\text{f},\text{u}\,\}$, we define $A^{\text{v}} = p^{\text{v}}(t_1, \ldots, t_n)$, where p^{v} is taken to be a new predicate symbol. We will use two ways of representing I as a set of annotated atoms, either by specifying the *true* and *false* atoms or by specifying the *true* and *undefined* atoms:

---

[1] By $I\!N_+$ we denote the set $\{\,1, 2, 3, \ldots\,\}$ of positive natural numbers, whereas $I\!N_0$ denotes the set $\{\,0, 1, 2, \ldots\,\}$ of all natural numbers.

[2] Note that γ is a disjunction, and, according to De Morgan's law, $not \cdot \gamma$ is taken to be a conjunction.

tf–*Representation:* $I^{tf} = I^t \cup I^f$,
tu–*Representation:* $I^{tu} = I^t \cup I^u$,

where I^t, I^u and I^f are given by:

$I^t = \{\, A^t \mid A \in HB_\mathcal{P} \wedge I(A) = t \,\}$,
$I^f = \{\, A^f \mid A \in HB_\mathcal{P} \wedge I(A) = f \,\}$,
$I^u = \{\, A^u \mid A \in HB_\mathcal{P} \wedge (\, I(A) = t \vee I(A) = u \,) \,\}$.

Note that in the tu–representation every *true* atom A is recorded as A^t and as A^u, which will become important later. Note also that the tf–representation is essentially the same as the conventional representation of I as a *set of literals*, where A^t becomes the atom A itself and A^f becomes the negative literal $\neg A$. For a set $\mathcal{I}$ of partial Herbrand interpretations we will use the same notations for $v \in \{\, \mathrm{tf}, \mathrm{tu} \,\}$: $\mathcal{I}^v = \{\, I^v \mid I \in \mathcal{I} \,\}$. By $\mathcal{I} =_v \mathcal{J}$, we denote that $\mathcal{J} = \mathcal{I}^v$ is the v–representation of $\mathcal{I}$.

Consider for instance the Herbrand base $HB_\mathcal{P} = \{a, b, c, d\}$. Then the partial Herbrand interpretation I with $I(a) = t$, $I(b) = t$, $I(c) = f$, and $I(d) = u$, is represented as follows:

$$I^{tf} = \{\, a^t, b^t, c^f \,\}, \quad I^{tu} = \{\, a^t, a^u, b^t, b^u, d^u \,\}.$$

Obviously, a total Herbrand interpretation I can simply be represented by the set $J = \{\, A \in HB_\mathcal{P} \mid I(A) = t \,\}$ of *true* atoms. Conversely, any set $J \subseteq HB_\mathcal{P}$ of ground atoms *induces* a total Herbrand interpretation $J^\Diamond$, where $J^\Diamond(A) = t$ iff $A \in J$. For a set $\mathcal{J}$ of sets of atoms, $\mathcal{J}^\Diamond = \{\, J^\Diamond \mid J \in \mathcal{J} \,\}$.

Truth Ordering and Knowledge Ordering

There are two common *partial orderings on truth values*, the truth ordering and the knowledge ordering, cf. Fitting [8], which are shown by Figure 1:

Truth Ordering $\leq_t$: $f \leq_t u$, $u \leq_t t$,
Knowledge Ordering $\leq_k$: $u \leq_k f$, $u \leq_k t$.

Given two truth values $v_1, v_2 \in \{\, t, f, u \,\}$, by $v_1 \geq_x v_2$ we denote the fact that $v_2 \leq_x v_1$, for $x \in \{\, t, k \,\}$.

These partial orderings have been generalized (pointwise) to partial orderings on partial Herbrand interpretations as follows. For $x \in \{\, t, k \,\}$:

$$I_1 \leq_x I_2, \text{ iff } (\, \forall A \in HB_\mathcal{P} : I_1(A) \leq_x I_2(A) \,).$$

The truth ordering on partial Herbrand interpretations corresponds to the subset ordering on their tu–representations: $I_1 \leq_t I_2$ iff $I_1^{tu} \subseteq I_2^{tu}$. The knowledge ordering corresponds to the subset ordering on the tf–representations: $I_1 \leq_k I_2$ iff $I_1^{tf} \subseteq I_2^{tf}$.

The *Boolean operations* "$\vee$", "$\wedge$" and "$\neg$" on truth values are defined based on the truth ordering, cf. Figure 2. The truth value of a disjunction $v_1 \vee v_2$ and

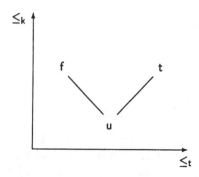

Fig. 1. Truth Ordering and Knowledge Ordering

∧	t	f	u
t	t	f	u
f	f	f	f
u	u	f	u

∨	t	f	u
t	t	t	t
f	t	f	u
u	t	u	u

¬	
t	f
f	t
u	u

Fig. 2. Boolean operations in three–valued logic

a conjunction $v_1 \wedge v_2$ of truth values are constructed by taking the *maximum* and the *minimum* of v_1 and v_2, respectively. "∨" and "∧" both are commutative and associative, and thus can be generalized to disjunctions and conjunctions, respectively, of more than one truth value.

Models and Partial Models, Minimality

Let M be a partial Herbrand interpretation of a disjunctive database $\mathcal{P}$. For $A_i \in HB_\mathcal{P}$, $1 \leq i \leq k$, and a connective $\otimes \in \{\vee, \wedge\}$ we define $M(A_1 \otimes \ldots \otimes A_k) = M(A_1) \otimes \ldots \otimes M(A_k)$. For $k = 0$, the empty disjunction (i.e. $\otimes = \vee$) evaluates to f, whereas the empty conjunction (i.e. $\otimes = \wedge$) evaluates to t. M is called a *partial model* of a ground rule $r = \alpha \leftarrow \beta \wedge not \cdot \gamma$ if

$$M(\alpha) \geq_t M(\beta) \wedge \neg M(\gamma). \tag{3}$$

M is called a *partial model* of $\mathcal{P}$ if M is a partial model of all ground instances $r \in gnd(\mathcal{P})$ of all rules of $\mathcal{P}$. This is denoted by $M \models_3 \mathcal{P}$.

Minimality of partial models is defined w.r.t. the truth ordering. M is called a *partial minimal model* of $\mathcal{P}$ if M is a partial model of $\mathcal{P}$ and there is no other partial model I of $\mathcal{P}$ such that $I \leq_t M$. The set of all partial minimal models of $\mathcal{P}$ is denoted by $\mathcal{MM}_3(\mathcal{P})$. A partial model M of a disjunctive database $\mathcal{P}$ that is total is called a *model* of $\mathcal{P}$. This is denoted by $M \models_2 \mathcal{P}$. A partial minimal model M of $\mathcal{P}$ that is total is called a *minimal model* of $\mathcal{P}$. The set of all minimal models of $\mathcal{P}$ is denoted by $\mathcal{MM}_2(\mathcal{P})$.

3 Stable and Partial Stable Models

The *Gelfond–Lifschitz transformation* (GL–transformation) of a disjunctive database P w.r.t. a partial Herbrand interpretation M is obtained from the ground instance $gnd\,(P)$ of P by replacing in every rule the negative body by its truth value $M(not\cdot\gamma) = \neg M(\gamma)$ w.r.t. M.[3]

Definition 1 (Gelfond–Lifschitz Transformation, [9, 16]).
Let M be a partial Herbrand interpretation of a disjunctive database P.

1. For $r = \alpha \leftarrow \beta \wedge not\cdot\gamma \in gnd\,(P)$ we define $r^M = \alpha \leftarrow \beta \wedge \neg M(\gamma)$.
2. The *Gelfond–Lifschitz transformation* of P is $P^M = \{\, r^M \mid r \in gnd\,(P)\,\}$.

The GL–transformation P^M is a ground positive–disjunctive database that has as additional atoms the truth values t, f and u. Note that these truth values must evaluate to themselves under all partial Herbrand interpretations I of P^M.

Definition 2 (Partial Stable Models, Stable Models, [9, 16]).
Let M be a partial Herbrand interpretation of a disjunctive database P.

1. M is called a *partial stable model* of P if $M \in \mathcal{MM}_3(P^M)$. The set of all partial stable models of P is denoted by $STABLE_3(P)$.
2. A partial stable model M of P that is total is called a *stable model* of P. The set of all stable models of P is denoted by $STABLE_2(P)$.

It can be shown that $STABLE_2(P) \subseteq STABLE_3(P)$ for all disjunctive databases. That is, the semantics of stable models is always stronger than the semantics of partial stable models. The following databases will be used as running examples throughout the paper.

Example 1 (Partial Stable Models).

1. For the disjunctive database

$$P_1 = \{\, a \vee b,\ q \leftarrow b \wedge not\,a,\ q \leftarrow a \wedge not\,b\,\},$$

we get the following set of partial stable models:

$$STABLE_3(P_1) =_{tf} \{\{\, a^t, q^t, b^f\,\}, \{\, b^t, q^t, a^f\,\}\}.$$

E.g. for $M^{tf} = \{\, a^t, q^t, b^f\,\}$ we get the GL–transformation $P_1^M = \{\, a \vee b,\ q \leftarrow b \wedge f,\ q \leftarrow a \wedge t\,\}$, and $\mathcal{MM}_3(P_1^M) =_{tf} \{\, M^{tf}, N^{tf}\,\}$, for $N^{tf} = \{\, b^t, a^f, q^f\,\}$. Here all partial stable models are also stable models, i.e. $STABLE_3(P_1) = STABLE_2(P_1)$. Since P_1 is stratified, the stable models coincide with the *perfect models*.

---

[3] If this truth value is "t", then "t" can be deleted from the body. If it is "f", then the whole rule can be deleted from P^M.

2. For the disjunctive database

$$\mathcal{P}_2 \;=\; \{\, a \leftarrow not\, b, \; b \leftarrow not\, c, \; c \leftarrow not\, a \,\},$$

there is a unique partial stable model, which is not stable:

$$\mathcal{STABLE}_3(\mathcal{P}_2) =_{\mathrm{tf}} \{\,\emptyset\,\}, \quad \mathcal{STABLE}_2(\mathcal{P}_2) =_{\mathrm{tf}} \emptyset.$$

3. The disjunctive database $\mathcal{P}_3 = \mathcal{P}_2 \cup \{\, a \vee b \vee c \,\}$, cf. also [16], is inconsistent w.r.t. the semantics of stable and partial stable models, i.e. $\mathcal{STABLE}_3(\mathcal{P}_3) = \mathcal{STABLE}_2(\mathcal{P}_3) = \emptyset$.

4 Evidential Stable Models

Given an atom $A = p(t_1, \ldots, t_n)$, we define the corresponding *evidential atom* $\mathcal{E}A = \mathcal{E}p(t_1, \ldots, t_n)$, where $\mathcal{E}p$ is taken to be a new predicate symbol. For a disjunction $\alpha = A_1 \vee \ldots \vee A_k$ and a conjunction $\beta = B_1 \wedge \ldots \wedge B_m$ of atoms we define $\mathcal{E}\alpha = \mathcal{E}A_1 \vee \ldots \vee \mathcal{E}A_k$ and $\mathcal{E}\beta = \mathcal{E}B_1 \wedge \ldots \wedge \mathcal{E}B_m$.

Definition 3 (Evidential Transformation).
Let $\mathcal{P}$ be a disjunctive database.

1. For a rule $r = \alpha \leftarrow \beta \wedge not \cdot \gamma \in \mathcal{P}$ we define

$$\mathcal{E}r = \alpha \vee \mathcal{E}\gamma \leftarrow \beta, \quad \mathcal{E}^2 r = \mathcal{E}\alpha \vee \mathcal{E}\gamma \leftarrow \mathcal{E}\beta.$$

2. The *evidential transformation* of $\mathcal{P}$ is

$$\mathcal{E}\mathcal{P} = \{\, \mathcal{E}r \mid r \in \mathcal{P} \,\} \cup \{\, \mathcal{E}^2 r \mid r \in \mathcal{P} \,\} \cup \{\, \mathcal{E}A \leftarrow A \mid A \in H_{B\mathcal{P}} \,\}.$$

A rule $\mathcal{E}r$ describes that, if the positive body β of r is *true*, then this gives rise to deriving either the head α "constructively" or an *evidence* for γ "by contradiction". The rules $\mathcal{E}^2 r$ could be compared with the *normality rules* from the *autoepistemic logic of beliefs*, cf. [17], and the rules $\mathcal{E}A \leftarrow A$ with the *necessitation rules*. For an implementation, $\mathcal{E}\mathcal{P}$ can be optimized: facts $\mathcal{E}^2 r = \mathcal{E}\alpha \vee \mathcal{E}\gamma$ obtained from rules $r = \alpha \leftarrow not \cdot \gamma \in \mathcal{P}$ with an empty positive body are *redundant*, since they are implied by $\mathcal{E}r = \alpha \vee \mathcal{E}\gamma$ and the necessitation rules.

Example 2 (Evidential Transformation).
For the disjunctive database $\mathcal{P}_1$ of Example 1 we get the following $\mathcal{E}\mathcal{P}_1$, where the fact $\mathcal{E}a \vee \mathcal{E}b$ is redundant:

$$\begin{aligned}
\mathcal{E}\mathcal{P}_1 = \;& \{\, a \vee b, \; q \vee \mathcal{E}a \leftarrow b, \; q \vee \mathcal{E}b \leftarrow a \,\} \;\cup \\
& \{\, \mathcal{E}a \vee \mathcal{E}b, \; \mathcal{E}q \vee \mathcal{E}a \leftarrow \mathcal{E}b, \; \mathcal{E}q \vee \mathcal{E}b \leftarrow \mathcal{E}a \,\} \;\cup \\
& \{\, \mathcal{E}a \leftarrow a, \; \mathcal{E}b \leftarrow b, \; \mathcal{E}q \leftarrow q \,\}.
\end{aligned}$$

Every pair of total Herbrand interpretations J and K of P induces a total Herbrand interpretation I of $\mathcal{E}P$, denoted by $J \cup \mathcal{E}K$, where for $A \in HB_P$:

$$(J \cup \mathcal{E}K)(A) = J(A), \quad (J \cup \mathcal{E}K)(\mathcal{E}A) = K(A).$$

Conversely, every total Herbrand interpretation I of $\mathcal{E}P$ can be represented as $J \cup \mathcal{E}K$. The total Herbrand interpretation K of P, that determines I on evidential atoms, will be denoted by $\mathcal{K}(I)$, i.e. $\mathcal{K}(J \cup \mathcal{E}K) = K$. $\mathcal{K}(I)$ will be considered to be the total Herbrand interpretation of P that corresponds to I. It ignores the part J, and interprets evidential atoms as (regular) atoms. For a set $\mathcal{I}$ of total Herbrand interpretations of $\mathcal{E}P$ we define $\mathcal{K}(\mathcal{I}) = \{ \mathcal{K}(I) \mid I \in \mathcal{I} \}$.

Based on a similar transformation $\mathcal{F}P = \{ \mathcal{E}r \mid r \in P \} \cup \{ \mathcal{E}A \leftarrow A \mid A \in HB_P \}$, which is a subset of $\mathcal{E}P$, and the set $\mathcal{C}P = \{ \leftarrow \mathcal{E}A \wedge not\ A \mid A \in HB_P \}$ of *test constraints*, a characterization of stable models has been given by Fernández et al.:

Theorem 1 (Characterization of Stable Models, [7]).
Given a disjunctive database P, then

$$\mathcal{S}TABLE_2(P) = \mathcal{K}(\{ I \in \mathcal{MM}_2(\mathcal{F}P) \mid I \models_2 \mathcal{C}P \}).$$

This characterization of stable models can also be proven for $\mathcal{E}P$ instead of $\mathcal{F}P$. It does not refer to the "normality rules" $\mathcal{E}^2 r$, since they are fulfilled automatically, if I strictly fulfills all of the test constraints in $\mathcal{C}P$. In our approach, however, they will be needed to guarantee that $\mathcal{K}(I)$ is a model of P if I is a model of $\mathcal{E}P$.

We propose the new concept of *evidential stable models*, which are minimal Herbrand models I of $\mathcal{E}P$, such that $\mathcal{K}(I) \in \mathcal{MM}_2(P)$. The strict requirement given by $\mathcal{C}P$ is relaxed to a *preference relation*: I' is preferred to I, if $\mathcal{V}(I') \subsetneq \mathcal{V}(I)$, where $\mathcal{V}(I)$ denotes the set of *violations* of test constraints.

Definition 4 (Evidential Stable Models).
Given a disjunctive database P and a set $\mathcal{I}$ of total Herbrand interpretations of $\mathcal{E}P$.

1. The set of $\mathcal{E}$-*violations* of $I \in \mathcal{I}$ is given by

$$\mathcal{V}(I) = \{ \mathcal{E}A \mid I \models_2 \mathcal{E}A \text{ and } I \not\models_2 A \},$$

   and $min_\mathcal{V}(\mathcal{I}) = \{ I \in \mathcal{I} \mid \not\exists I' \in \mathcal{I} : I \neq I' \wedge \mathcal{V}(I') \subsetneq \mathcal{V}(I) \}$ denotes the set of $\mathcal{V}$-*minimal* interpretations in $\mathcal{I}$.
2. The set of *evidential stable models* of P is

$$\mathcal{E}\mathcal{S}TABLE_2(P) = min_\mathcal{V}(\{ I \in \mathcal{MM}_2(\mathcal{E}P) \mid \mathcal{K}(I) \in \mathcal{MM}_2(P) \}),$$

and we further define $\mathcal{S}TABLE_2^{\bullet}(P) = \mathcal{K}(\mathcal{E}\mathcal{S}TABLE_2(P))$.

The name evidential stable models has been chosen, since an evidential stable model $I \in \mathcal{ESTABLE}_2(\mathcal{P})$ contains evidential atoms, and it can be shown that $\mathcal{K}(I)$ is a stable model of a suitably, minimally transformed database, where all atoms A, such that $\mathcal{E}A$ is an $\mathcal{E}$–violation in I, are moved from negative rule bodies to rule heads (see $\mathcal{P}'_2$ below).

An evidential stable model I provides more information than just about the truth of atoms A, namely the information of whether A was derived constructively, or solely by contradiction (i.e., $\mathcal{E}A$ is an $\mathcal{E}$–violation in I). In the models $\mathcal{K}(I) \in \mathcal{STABLE}_2^{\bigstar}(\mathcal{P})$, however, this information is ignored.

Example 3 (Evidential Stable Models).

1. For the disjunctive database $\mathcal{P}_1$ we get

$$\mathcal{STABLE}_2(\mathcal{P}_1) = \mathcal{STABLE}_2^{\bigstar}(\mathcal{P}_1) \subsetneq \mathcal{MM}_2(\mathcal{P}_1).$$

2. For the disjunctive database $\mathcal{P}_2$ we get the following $\mathcal{EP}_2$, where redundant facts have been left out:

$$\mathcal{EP}_2 = \{\, a \vee \mathcal{E}b, \, b \vee \mathcal{E}c, \, c \vee \mathcal{E}a \,\} \cup \{\, \mathcal{E}a \leftarrow a, \, \mathcal{E}b \leftarrow b, \, \mathcal{E}c \leftarrow c \,\}.$$

From $\mathcal{MM}_2(\mathcal{EP}_2)$, the first three models are $\mathcal{V}$–minimal:

$$\mathcal{MM}_2(\mathcal{EP}_2) = \{\, \{\, a, \mathcal{E}a, \mathcal{E}c \,\}, \, \{\, b, \mathcal{E}b, \mathcal{E}a \,\}, \, \{\, c, \mathcal{E}c, \mathcal{E}b \,\}, \, \{\, \mathcal{E}a, \mathcal{E}b, \mathcal{E}c \,\} \,\}^{\diamond}.$$

E.g. for $I = \{\, a, \mathcal{E}a, \mathcal{E}c \,\}^{\diamond}$ and $I' = \{\, \mathcal{E}a, \mathcal{E}b, \mathcal{E}c \,\}^{\diamond}$ we get

$$\mathcal{V}(I) = \{\, \mathcal{E}c \,\} \subsetneq \mathcal{V}(I') = \{\, \mathcal{E}a, \mathcal{E}b, \mathcal{E}c \,\}.$$

The meaning of I is that "a" is *true*, but there is only an evidence that "c" is *true*, i.e. "c" has been derived by contradiction:

$$\mathcal{STABLE}_2^{\bigstar}(\mathcal{P}_2) = \{\, \{a, c\}, \{a, b\}, \{b, c\} \,\}^{\diamond} = \mathcal{MM}_2(\mathcal{P}_2).$$

Finally, $\mathcal{K}(I) = \{\, a, c \,\}^{\diamond}$ is a stable model of the suitably, minimally transformed database $\mathcal{P}'_2$ for I:

$$\mathcal{P}'_2 = \{\, a \leftarrow not\, b, \, b \vee c, \, c \leftarrow not\, a \,\}.$$

3. For the disjunctive database $\mathcal{P}_3$ we get $\mathcal{STABLE}_2^{\bigstar}(\mathcal{P}_3) = \mathcal{STABLE}_2^{\bigstar}(\mathcal{P}_2)$.

The following theorem relates the evidential stable models of a disjunctive database to the minimal and the stable models.

Theorem 2 (Characterization of Evidential Stable Models).
Given a disjunctive database $\mathcal{P}$, then

1. *If $\mathcal{MM}_2(\mathcal{P}) \neq \emptyset$, then $\mathcal{STABLE}_2^{\bigstar}(\mathcal{P}) \neq \emptyset$.*
2. *If $\mathcal{STABLE}_2(\mathcal{P}) \neq \emptyset$, then $\mathcal{STABLE}_2^{\bigstar}(\mathcal{P}) = \mathcal{STABLE}_2(\mathcal{P})$.*
3. *$\mathcal{STABLE}_2(\mathcal{P}) \subseteq \mathcal{STABLE}_2^{\bigstar}(\mathcal{P}) \subseteq \mathcal{MM}_2(\mathcal{P})$.*

Proof.

1. Assume $\mathcal{MM}_2(\mathcal{P}) \neq \emptyset$. Every minimal model $M \in \mathcal{MM}_2(\mathcal{P})$ of $\mathcal{P}$ induces a Herbrand interpretation $M \cup \mathcal{E}M$, which obviously is a model of $\mathcal{EP}$. Thus, there exists a minimal model $I \in \mathcal{MM}_2(\mathcal{EP})$, such that $I = J \cup \mathcal{E}K \subseteq M \cup \mathcal{E}M$.[4] Since $\mathcal{E}K$ must be a model of $\mathcal{P}' = \{ \mathcal{E}^2 r \mid r \in \mathcal{P} \}$, and $\mathcal{E}M$ is a minimal model of $\mathcal{P}'$, and $\mathcal{E}K \subseteq \mathcal{E}M$, we get that $K = M$. Thus, $I = J \cup \mathcal{E}M \in \mathcal{MM}_2(\mathcal{EP})$ and $\mathcal{K}(I) = M \in \mathcal{MM}_2(\mathcal{P})$. This means that the set of interpretations which we minimize is not empty, i.e. $\mathcal{STABLE}_2^{\star}(\mathcal{P}) \neq \emptyset$.

2. The test condition (A) $I \models_2 \mathcal{CP}$ is equivalent to (B) $\mathcal{V}(I) = \emptyset$. Thus, for a stable model K of $\mathcal{P}$, the Herbrand interpretation $I = K \cup \mathcal{E}K$ of $\mathcal{EP}$ always is minimal w.r.t. violation, and thus I is evidential stable. Moreover, if there exists any stable model of $\mathcal{P}$, then all evidential stable models I of $\mathcal{P}$ must fulfill (B), i.e. they are of the form $I = K \cup \mathcal{E}K$, such that $K \in \mathcal{STABLE}_2(\mathcal{P})$.

3. First, the inclusion $\mathcal{STABLE}_2^{\star}(\mathcal{P}) \subseteq \mathcal{MM}_2(\mathcal{P})$ holds by definition. Secondly, the inclusion $\mathcal{STABLE}_2(\mathcal{P}) \subseteq \mathcal{STABLE}_2^{\star}(\mathcal{P})$ is an immediate consequence of part 2.

□

Note that the concept of evidential stable models cannot be lifted to the three-valued case by simply taking partial minimal models of $\mathcal{EP}$. The reason is that for positive-disjunctive databases (without default negation), such as $\mathcal{EP}$, the partial minimal models coincide with the minimal models.

5   Annotation of Databases and Partial Stable Models

We will use a special concept of annotating disjunctive rules, which encodes the condition that partial Herbrand models have to fulfill in terms of their tu-representation. Given a truth value $v \in \{t, u\}$, for a disjunction $\alpha = A_1 \vee \ldots \vee A_k$ and a conjunction $\beta = B_1 \wedge \ldots \wedge B_m$ of atoms we define $\alpha^v = A_1^v \vee \ldots \vee A_k^v$ and $\beta^v = B_1^v \wedge \ldots \wedge B_m^v$.

Definition 5 (Annotation of Databases).

1. For a disjunctive rule $r = \alpha \leftarrow \beta \wedge not \cdot \gamma$ we define the *annotated rules*

$$r^t = \alpha^t \leftarrow \beta^t \wedge not \cdot \gamma^u, \quad r^u = \alpha^u \leftarrow \beta^u \wedge not \cdot \gamma^t.$$

2. For a disjunctive database $\mathcal{P}$ we define $\mathcal{P}^t = \{ r^t \mid r \in \mathcal{P} \}$, $\mathcal{P}^u = \{ r^u \mid r \in \mathcal{P} \}$, and the *annotated database* $\mathcal{P}^{tu} = \mathcal{P}^t \cup \mathcal{P}^u \cup \{ A^u \leftarrow A^t \mid A \in HB_\mathcal{P} \}$.

Example 4 (Annotation of Databases).
For the disjunctive database $\mathcal{P}_1$ of Example 1 we get

$$\mathcal{P}_1^t = \{ a^t \vee b^t, q^t \leftarrow b^t \wedge not\, a^u, q^t \leftarrow a^t \wedge not\, b^u \},$$
$$\mathcal{P}_1^u = \{ a^u \vee b^u, q^u \leftarrow b^u \wedge not\, a^t, a^u \leftarrow q^u \wedge not\, b^t \},$$
$$\mathcal{P}_1^{tu} = \mathcal{P}_1^t \cup \mathcal{P}_1^u \cup \{ a^u \leftarrow a^t, b^u \leftarrow b^t, q^u \leftarrow q^t \}.$$

---

[4] Note that in this proof, total Herbrand interpretations are treated as their sets of *true* atoms, and they are compared like sets.

The construction of $\mathcal{P}^{tu}$ is motivated by the condition given in Equation (3), which every partial Herbrand model M of a ground rule $r = \alpha \leftarrow \beta \wedge not \cdot \gamma$ must fulfill. This condition can be encoded in the annotated rules r^t and r^u, since it is equivalent to the following:

$$((M(\beta) \geq_t t \wedge \neg(M(\gamma) \geq_t u) \implies M(\alpha) \geq_t t) \wedge$$
$$((M(\beta) \geq_t u \wedge \neg(M(\gamma) \geq_t t) \implies M(\alpha) \geq_t u).$$

The rules $A^u \leftarrow A^t$ are due to the fact that we want to perceive the Herbrand models of $\mathcal{P}^{tu}$ as Herbrand models of $\mathcal{P}$ in tu–representation.

Properties of the Annotated Database

It can be shown that annotation preserves stratification: Given a disjunctive database $\mathcal{P}$, the annotated disjunctive database $\mathcal{P}^{tu}$ is *stratified* if and only if $\mathcal{P}$ is stratified. Based on this, one can give an alternative proof of the well–known fact (see [16]) that the partial stable models of a stratified–disjunctive database $\mathcal{P}$ coincide with the perfect models of $\mathcal{P}$. This fact implies in particular that the partial stable models of a stratified–disjunctive database $\mathcal{P}$ are total.

The annotated database $\mathcal{P}^{tu}$ can be represented as a database over two predicate symbols "t" and "u". Then, annotated atoms A^t and A^u in rules can be represented by atoms $t(A)$ and $u(A)$, respectively, where "A" is seen as a term now. In this representation the (possibly infinite) set $\{ A^u \leftarrow A^t \mid A \in HB_\mathcal{P} \}$ of rules can simply be represented by one rule $u(X) \leftarrow t(X)$, where "X" is a variable symbol for atoms. Then $\mathcal{P}^{tu}$ has the size of $2 \cdot n + 1$ rules if $\mathcal{P}$ consists of n rules. This compact representation has been used for an implementation dealing with $\mathcal{P}^{tu}$.

Characterization of Partial Minimal and Partial Stable Models

The following theorem shows that the partial stable models of a disjunctive database $\mathcal{P}$ correspond to the total stable models of the annotated database $\mathcal{P}^{tu}$. For any total Herbrand interpretation I of $\mathcal{P}^{tu}$ we introduce the notation I^∇ for the partial Herbrand interpretation of $\mathcal{P}$ that is induced by I, i.e. for $A \in HB_\mathcal{P}$

$$I^\nabla(A) = \begin{cases} t \text{ if } I(A^t) = t \\ u \text{ if } I(A^u) = t \text{ and } I(A^t) = f \\ f \text{ if } I(A^u) = f \end{cases}$$

For a set $\mathcal{I}$ of total Herbrand interpretations of $\mathcal{P}^{tu}$, let $\mathcal{I}^\nabla = \{ I^\nabla \mid I \in \mathcal{I} \}$.

Theorem 3 (Partial Minimal and Partial Stable Models, [19]).
Given a disjunctive database $\mathcal{P}$, then

1. $\mathcal{MM}_3(\mathcal{P}) = \mathcal{MM}_2(\mathcal{P}^{tu})^\nabla$.
2. $\mathcal{STABLE}_3(\mathcal{P}) = \mathcal{STABLE}_2(\mathcal{P}^{tu})^\nabla$.

Example 5 (Partial Stable Models).

1. For the disjunctive database $\mathcal{P}_1$ of Example 1, whose annotated database $\mathcal{P}_1^{tu}$ has been given in Example 4, we get

$$\mathcal{STABLE}_3(\mathcal{P}_1) =_{tu} \{ \{ a^t, a^u, q^t, q^u \}, \{ b^t, b^u, q^t, q^u \} \}.$$

2. For the disjunctive database $\mathcal{P}_2$ of Example 1, we get the annotated database

$$\mathcal{P}_2^{tu} = \{ a^t \leftarrow not\, b^u,\ b^t \leftarrow not\, c^u,\ c^t \leftarrow not\, a^u,$$
$$a^u \leftarrow not\, b^t,\ b^u \leftarrow not\, c^t,\ c^u \leftarrow not\, a^t,$$
$$a^u \leftarrow a^t,\ b^u \leftarrow b^t,\ c^u \leftarrow c^t \}.$$

Thus, we get
$$\mathcal{STABLE}_3(\mathcal{P}_2) =_{tu} \{ \{ a^u, b^u, c^u \} \}.$$

For the restricted case of normal databases, i.e. databases that may contain negation but do not contain disjunctions, other characterizations of partial stable models are given in [4, 22]. The characterization of [4] is also based on the concept of annotation, but it needs more than the two truth values that we are annotating with here.

6 Partial Evidential Stable Models

For defining partial evidential stable models we can use the techniques described in the previous two sections. Partial evidential stable models are defined based on the evidential stable models of the tu–transformation of the database, i.e. Theorem 3 for partial stable models motivates the following definition.

Definition 6 (Partial Evidential Stable Models).
The set of *partial evidential stable models* of a disjunctive database $\mathcal{P}$ is

$$\mathcal{ESTABLE}_3(\mathcal{P}) = \mathcal{ESTABLE}_2(\mathcal{P}^{tu})^{\nabla},$$

and we further define $\mathcal{STABLE}_3^{\star}(\mathcal{P}) = \mathcal{K}(\mathcal{ESTABLE}_3(\mathcal{P}))$.

Thus, for constructing partial evidential stable models we need the evidential transformation $\mathcal{E}(\mathcal{P}^{tu})$ of the tu–transformation of $\mathcal{P}$. [5] As a consequence of its definition, for each rule $r = \alpha \leftarrow \beta \wedge not\cdot \gamma \in \mathcal{P}$, it contains two evidence rules $\mathcal{E}r^u$, $\mathcal{E}r^t$, and two normality rules $\mathcal{E}^2 r^u$, $\mathcal{E}^2 r^t$:

$$\mathcal{E}r^u = \alpha^u \vee \mathcal{E}\gamma^t \leftarrow \beta^u, \qquad \mathcal{E}r^t = \alpha^t \vee \mathcal{E}\gamma^u \leftarrow \beta^t,$$
$$\mathcal{E}^2 r^u = \mathcal{E}\alpha^u \vee \mathcal{E}\gamma^t \leftarrow \mathcal{E}\beta^u, \quad \mathcal{E}^2 r^t = \mathcal{E}\alpha^t \vee \mathcal{E}\gamma^u \leftarrow \mathcal{E}\beta^t.$$

Note that in an implementation, $\mathcal{E}(\mathcal{P}^{tu})$ can be represented compactly as a disjunctive database over four predicate symbols "t, u, $\mathcal{E}$t, $\mathcal{E}$u".

---

[5] We can identify evidential atoms $\mathcal{E}(A^{\vee})$ of $\mathcal{E}(\mathcal{P}^{tu})$ with annotated atoms $(\mathcal{E}A)^{\vee}$ of $(\mathcal{E}\mathcal{P})^{tu}$. But note that – even with this identification – the databases $\mathcal{E}(\mathcal{P}^{tu})$ and $(\mathcal{E}\mathcal{P})^{tu}$ are different if there is negation in $\mathcal{P}$.

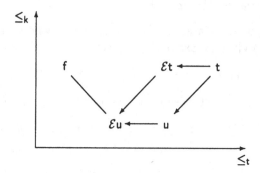

Fig. 3. Correlation between Annotated Atoms

The correlation between the four different types of atoms is specified by four generic rules in $\mathcal{E}(\mathcal{P}^{tu})$, cf. Figure 3: First, the rule $r = A^u \leftarrow A^t \in \mathcal{P}^{tu}$ gives rise to the two evidential rules $\mathcal{E}r = r$ and $\mathcal{E}^2 r = \mathcal{E}A^u \leftarrow \mathcal{E}A^t$. Secondly, we get the two necessitation rules $\mathcal{E}A^t \leftarrow A^t$ and $\mathcal{E}A^u \leftarrow A^u$, for A^t and A^u, respectively.

Analogously to evidential stable models, a partial evidential stable model I provides more information than just about the truth or undefinedness of atoms A, namely the information of whether an annotated atom A^v was derived constructively, or solely by contradiction (i.e. $\mathcal{E}A^v \in \mathcal{V}(I)$ is an $\mathcal{E}$–violation in I). Again, in the models $\mathcal{K}(I) \in \mathcal{STABLE}_3^+(\mathcal{P})$ this information is ignored, i.e., an evidential atom $\mathcal{E}A^v$ provides the same knowledge as a regular atom A^v (cf. the knowledge levels in Figure 3).

Example 6 (Partial Evidential Stable Models).

1. For the disjunctive database $\mathcal{P}_2$ of Example 1 we get

$$\mathcal{STABLE}_3^+(\mathcal{P}_2) = \mathcal{STABLE}_3(\mathcal{P}_2).$$

2. For the disjunctive database $\mathcal{P}_3$ of Example 1 we get $\mathcal{E}(\mathcal{P}_3^{tu})$, where the redundant facts $\mathcal{E}^2 r$ for rules $r \in \mathcal{P}_3^{tu}$ with empty positive bodies have been left out:

$$\mathcal{E}(\mathcal{P}_3^{tu}) = \{\, a^t \vee b^t \vee c^t,\ a^t \vee \mathcal{E}b^u,\ b^t \vee \mathcal{E}c^u,\ c^t \vee \mathcal{E}a^u \,\} \cup$$
$$\{\, a^u \vee b^u \vee c^u,\ a^u \vee \mathcal{E}b^t,\ b^u \vee \mathcal{E}c^t,\ c^u \vee \mathcal{E}a^t \,\} \cup$$
$$\{\, A^u \leftarrow A^t,\ \mathcal{E}A^u \leftarrow \mathcal{E}A^t,\ \mathcal{E}A^t \leftarrow A^t,\ \mathcal{E}A^u \leftarrow A^u \mid A \in HB_{\mathcal{P}_3} \,\}.$$

We get the set

$$\mathcal{MM}_2(\mathcal{E}(\mathcal{P}_3^{tu})) = \{\, I_1(a,b,c),\ I_2(a,b,c),\ I_1(c,a,b),\ I_2(c,a,b),$$
$$I_1(b,c,a),\ I_2(b,c,a) \,\}$$

of minimal models, where for $A, B, C \in HB_{\mathcal{P}_3}$:

$$I_1(A,B,C) = \{\, A^t,\ \mathcal{E}A^t,\ A^u,\ \mathcal{E}A^u,\ B^u,\ \mathcal{E}B^u,\ \mathcal{E}C^u \,\}^\diamond,$$
$$I_2(A,B,C) = \{\, A^t,\ \mathcal{E}A^t,\ A^u,\ \mathcal{E}A^u,\ \mathcal{E}C^t,\ \mathcal{E}C^u \,\}^\diamond.$$

Here, $\mathcal{V}(I_1(A,B,C)) = \{\,\mathcal{E}C^u\,\} \subsetneq \mathcal{V}(I_2(A,B,C)) = \{\,\mathcal{E}C^t, \mathcal{E}C^u\,\}$. Thus, we get

$$\mathcal{STABLE}_3^{\:\!\!\star}(\mathcal{P}_3) =_{tu} \{\,\{\,a^t, a^u, b^u, c^u\,\}, \{\,c^t, c^u, a^u, b^u\,\}, \{\,b^t, b^u, c^u, a^u\,\}\,\}.$$

3. For the (partial) evidential stable models of $\mathcal{P}_3$, it turns out that for each evidential stable model $I_2 \in \mathcal{STABLE}_2^{\:\!\!\star}(\mathcal{P}_3)$ there is a corresponding partial evidential stable model $I_3 \in \mathcal{STABLE}_3^{\:\!\!\star}(\mathcal{P}_3)$ that is weaker in the knowledge ordering: e.g. for $I_2^{tu} = \{\,a^t, a^u, c^t, c^u\,\}$ and $I_3^{tu} = \{\,a^t, a^u, b^u, c^u\,\}$ we get $I_3 \leq_k I_2$, since $I_3^{tf} = \{\,a^t\,\} \subsetneq \{\,a^t, b^f, c^t\,\} = I_2^{tf}$.

The following theorem relates the partial evidential stable models of a disjunctive database to the partial minimal and the partial stable models. It is a consequence of Definitions 4 and 6, and Theorems 2 and 3.

Theorem 4 (Characterization of Partial Evidential Stable Models).
Given a disjunctive database $\mathcal{P}$, then

1. *If $\mathcal{MM}_3(\mathcal{P}) \neq \emptyset$, then $\mathcal{STABLE}_3^{\:\!\!\star}(\mathcal{P}) \neq \emptyset$.*
2. *If $\mathcal{STABLE}_3(\mathcal{P}) \neq \emptyset$, then $\mathcal{STABLE}_3^{\:\!\!\star}(\mathcal{P}) = \mathcal{STABLE}_3(\mathcal{P})$.*
3. *$\mathcal{STABLE}_3(\mathcal{P}) \subseteq \mathcal{STABLE}_3^{\:\!\!\star}(\mathcal{P}) \subseteq \mathcal{MM}_3(\mathcal{P})$.*

Proof.
First, we will show that

$$\left(\mathcal{STABLE}_2^{\:\!\!\star}(\mathcal{P}^{tu})\right)^{\nabla} = \mathcal{STABLE}_3^{\:\!\!\star}(\mathcal{P}). \tag{4}$$

Due to Definition 4, $\left(\mathcal{STABLE}_2^{\:\!\!\star}(\mathcal{P}^{tu})\right)^{\nabla} = \left(\mathcal{K}(\mathcal{ESTABLE}_2(\mathcal{P}^{tu}))\right)^{\nabla}$. It is possible to switch: $\left(\mathcal{K}(\mathcal{ESTABLE}_2(\mathcal{P}^{tu}))\right)^{\nabla} = \mathcal{K}(\mathcal{ESTABLE}_2(\mathcal{P}^{tu})^{\nabla})$. According to Definition 6,

$$\mathcal{K}(\mathcal{ESTABLE}_2(\mathcal{P}^{tu})^{\nabla}) = \mathcal{K}(\mathcal{ESTABLE}_3(\mathcal{P})) = \mathcal{STABLE}_3^{\:\!\!\star}(\mathcal{P}).$$

1. Assume $\mathcal{MM}_3(\mathcal{P}) \neq \emptyset$. According to Theorem 3, part 1, this implies that $(\mathcal{MM}_2(\mathcal{P}^{tu}))^{\nabla} \neq \emptyset$. With Theorem 2, part 1, we get $(\mathcal{STABLE}_2^{\:\!\!\star}(\mathcal{P}^{tu}))^{\nabla} \neq \emptyset$. Using Equation (4), $\mathcal{STABLE}_3^{\:\!\!\star}(\mathcal{P}) \neq \emptyset$ can be concluded.
2. Assume $\mathcal{STABLE}_3(\mathcal{P}) \neq \emptyset$. According to Theorem 3, part 2, this implies that $(\mathcal{STABLE}_2(\mathcal{P}^{tu}))^{\nabla} \neq \emptyset$. With Theorem 2, part 2, we get

$$\left(\mathcal{STABLE}_2^{\:\!\!\star}(\mathcal{P}^{tu})\right)^{\nabla} = \left(\mathcal{STABLE}_2(\mathcal{P}^{tu})\right)^{\nabla}.$$

Using Equation (4) and Theorem 3, part 2, the desired result follows.
3. From Theorem 2, part 3, we get an inclusion chain, that is preserved by "∇": $\left(\mathcal{STABLE}_2(\mathcal{P}^{tu})\right)^{\nabla} \subseteq \left(\mathcal{STABLE}_2^{\:\!\!\star}(\mathcal{P}^{tu})\right)^{\nabla} \subseteq \left(\mathcal{MM}_2(\mathcal{P}^{tu})\right)^{\nabla}$. Applying Theorem 3, parts 1 and 2, to $(\mathcal{MM}_2(\mathcal{P}^{tu}))^{\nabla}$ and $(\mathcal{STABLE}_2(\mathcal{P}^{tu}))^{\nabla}$, respectively, and applying Equation (4) to $\left(\mathcal{STABLE}_2^{\:\!\!\star}(\mathcal{P}^{tu})\right)^{\nabla}$, we get the desired chain of inclusions.

$\square$

Partial evidential stable models provide a "consistent extension" of the well-founded semantics from normal databases to disjunctive databases $\mathcal{P}$, namely the set $\mathcal{STABLE}_3^{\star}(\mathcal{P})$ of partial Herbrand interpretations. For stratified–disjunctive databases, this extension coincides with the perfect models if there exist perfect models of $\mathcal{P}$ (which is for instance guaranteed for databases without denial rules).

7 Comparison with Other Approaches

Regular Models

The semantics of *regular models* has been introduced by You and Yuan, cf. [24, 25]: A regular model M is a justifiable model which has a minimal set M^u of undefined atoms. A *justifiable model* M is a minimal model of a variant $\mathcal{P}_\gamma^M$ of the three–valued Gelfond–Lifschitz transformation, where only those rules are selected whose negative bodies are *true* w.r.t. M (rather than *undefined* or *false*).

For a large class of disjunctive databases – including all examples considered so far in this paper – the partial evidential stable models coincide with the regular models. But, using an example database from [6], it can be shown that the regular models do not always coincide with the (partial) evidential stable models, neither with the (partial) stable models.

L–Stable and M–Stable Models

Eiter, Leone and Sacca [6] have investigated several interesting subsets of the set of partial stable models, like the *least undefined* and the *maximal partial stable models*, which they call *L–stable* and *M–stable models*, respectively.[6] For normal databases (without disjunctions), the M–stable models coincide with the regular models of You and Yuan.

Since L–stable and M–stable models always are partial stable models, they do not give a consistent interpretation for databases without partial stable models (like $\mathcal{P}_3$), while (partial) evidential stable models do so if the databases are logically consistent.

It tuns out that the concepts of minimizing undefinedness and maximizing knowledge can be combined with our concept of partial evidential stable models. That is, since $\mathcal{STABLE}_3^{\star}(\mathcal{P})$ is a set of partial Herbrand interpretations, it makes sense to look for the least undefined elements in that set, and also for the elements with maximal knowledge.

Abductive Variants of Stable Models

Given a disjunctive database $\mathcal{P}$, and a set $\mathcal{A} \subseteq HB_{\mathcal{P}}$ of ground atoms, called *abducibles*. A total Herbrand model I of $\mathcal{P}$ is called an $\mathcal{A}$–*belief model*, if there

---

[6] Within the set of all partial stable models, an L–stable model M must have a minimal set M^u of undefined atoms, whereas an M–stable model must have a maximal set M^{tf} of knowledge.

exists a set $A_I \subseteq A$ of abducibles, such that I is a stable model of $P \cup A_I$. I is called an A-*stable model* of P, if its set A_I is minimal among all A-belief models (i.e., if there exists no other A-belief model I' such that $A_{I'} \subsetneq A_I$).

This construction had been suggested by Gelfond[7], who allowed all ground atoms to be abducibles (i.e. $A = HB_P$). A slightly different variant had been proposed by Inoue and Sakama [11], who minimize the amount of abducibles in an A-stable model I by additionally requiring that $A_I = \{ A \in A \mid I(A) = t \}$ must hold for A-belief models.

In general, both definitions are different from evidential stable models. If there exist stable models, then Gelfond's approach also derives these stable models, but otherwise it does not necessarily derive only minimal models.[8] The approach of Inoue and Sakama is depending on particular useful sets of abducibles – for $A = \emptyset$ it derives the stable models, and for $A = HB_P$ it derives all minimal models.

There are, of course, similarities to evidential stable models, where the $\mathcal{E}$-violations (i.e. the atoms that are derived by contradiction solely) play the role of abducibles which must occur in negative bodies of ground rules.

Disjunctive Well–Founded Semantics

For achieving a consistent interpretation of disjunctive databases, several types of *well-founded semantics* have been proposed, cf. [1, 2, 14]. It seems that the semantics of evidential stable models are stronger than the semantics D-WFS of Brass and Dix [2], and still they are consistent.

8   Abstract Properties of the Evidential Semantics

In the following we will give a brief analysis of the two evidential semantics according to several *abstract properties* of semantics, cf. Brass and Dix [3]. A summary is given by Figure 4.

First, both evidential semantics have the property of *independence*. They even have the stronger property of *modularity*. This means that if a database can be decomposed into separate components that do not have any atoms in common, then the (partial) evidential stable models can be computed on the components separately. As a consequence, only on those parts of a disjunctive database that are inconsistent w.r.t. (partial) stable models we have to compute (partial) evidential stable models. On the consistent part of a database – which usually will be the main part – we can compute the basic (partial) stable model semantics.

---

[7] in discussions

[8] E.g., the disjunctive database $P = \{ q \leftarrow not\ a \wedge not\ q,\ a \leftarrow b \}$ has two evidential stable models $I_1^{tf} = \{ q^t, a^f, b^f \}$ and $I_2^{tf} = \{ a^t, b^f, q^f \}$. According to Gelfond's definition, besides I_1 and I_2 we get an extra A-stable model $I_3^{tf} = \{ a^t, b^t, q^f \}$, which is not minimal ($A = \{ a, b, q \}$, $A_{I_1} = \{ q \}$, $A_{I_2} = \{ a \}$, $A_{I_3} = \{ b \}$).

	Taut.	Contr.	GPPE	Indep.	Supra.
$STABLE_2$	+	+	+	—	+
$STABLE_3$	+	—	—	—	—
$STABLE_2^{\blacklozenge}$	+	+	—	+	+
$STABLE_3^{\blacklozenge}$	+	—	—	+	—
D-WFS	+	—	+	+	—
Regular	+	+	—	—	—

Fig. 4. Abstract properties of semantics

Secondly, evidential stable model semantics is *supraclassical*, i.e., it derives more consequences – by sceptical reasoning – than classical logic, since evidential stable models are also minimal models, cf. Theorems 2. On the other hand, partial evidential stable model semantics is not supraclassical, since for normal databases it is equivalent to the well–founded semantics, which is not supraclassical.

Thirdly, both evidential semantics allow for the *elimination of tautologies*. The semantics of evidential stable models also allows for the *elimination of contradictions*, whereas partial evidential stable models do not. This well matches with the conjecture of [3] that elimination of contradictions should be given up for (three–valued) semantics of general – i.e. non–stratified – disjunctive databases.

Fourth, both evidential semantics do not satisfy the *generalized property of partial evaluation* (GPPE). For partial evidential stable models this can be shown by an example that originally was used for showing that partial stable models do not satisfy GPPE [19]. Given the fact that evidential stable models satisfy elimination of tautologies and elimination of contradictions, using a theorem of [3] it can be concluded that evidential stable models cannot satisfy GPPE – the reason is that otherwise the set of evidential stable models always would have to be a subset of the set of stable models.

Finally, note that as a consequence of Theorem 3, the technique of partial evaluation can still be applied to the tu–transformation of a database – rather than the database itself – for computing its partial stable models, and consequently also the superset of partial evidential stable models.

9   Conclusions

The evidential semantics presented in this paper can be seen as a special case of the *general framework for revising non–monotonic theories* that was introduced by Witteveen and van der Hoek in [23]. In that case, the *intended models* would be the (partial) stable models, and the *backup models* – from among which the models are chosen if there exist no intended models – would be the (partial) minimal models, cf. Theorems 2 and 4.

The computation of (partial) evidential stable model semantics has been implemented within the system DISLOG for efficient reasoning in disjunctive databases, cf. [20]. It can be shown that the *time complexity* of computing (partial) evidential stable models is on the second level of the polynomial hierarchy, namely Σ_2^P, just as for computing (partial) stable models.

The detailed investigation of the properties and possible implementations of evidential stable models and partial evidential stable models will be the subject of future work.

Acknowledgements

The author would like to thank Adnan Yahya and Jia–Huai You for their comments on earlier drafts of this paper, and the anonymous referees for their useful remarks.

References

1. *C. Baral, J. Lobo, J. Minker:* WF^3: A Semantics for Negation in Normal Disjunctive Logic Programs, Proc. Intl. Symposium on Methodologies for Intelligent Systems (ISMIS'91), Springer LNAI 542, 1991, pp. 490–499.

2. *S. Brass, J. Dix:* A Disjunctive Semantics Based upon Partial and Bottom–Up Evaluation, Proc. Intl. Conference on Logic Programming (ICLP'95), MIT Press, 1995, pp. 199–213.

3. *S. Brass, J. Dix:* Characterizations of the Disjunctive Stable Semantics by Partial Evaluation, Proc. Third Intl. Conf. on Logic Programming an Non–Monotonic Reasoning (LPNMR'95), Springer LNAI 928, 1995, pp. 85–98, and: Journal of Logic Programming, vol. 32(3), 1997, pp. 207–228.

4. *C.V. Damásio, L.M. Pereira:* Abduction over 3–valued Extended Logic Programs, Proc. Third Intl. Conf. on Logic Programming an Non–Monotonic Reasoning (LPNMR'95), Springer LNAI 928, 1995, pp. 29–42.

5. *T. Eiter, N. Leone, D. Sacca:* The Expressive Power of Partial Models for Disjunctive Deductive Databases, Proc. Intl. Workshop of Logic in Databases (LID'96), Springer LNCS 1154, 1996, pp. 245–264.

6. *T. Eiter, N. Leone, D. Sacca:* On the Partial Semantics for Disjunctive Deductive Databases, Annals of Mathematics and Artificial Intelligence, to appear.

7. *J.A. Fernández, J. Lobo, J. Minker, V.S. Subrahmanian:* Disjunctive LP + Integrity Constrains = Stable Model Semantics, Annals of Mathematics and Artificial Intelligence, vol. 8 (3–4), 1993, pp. 449–474.

8. *M. Fitting:* Bilattices and the Semantics of Logic Programs, Journal of Logic Programming, vol. 11, 1991, pp. 91–116.

9. *M. Gelfond, V. Lifschitz:* The Stable Model Semantics for Logic Programming, Proc. Fifth Intl. Conference and Symposium on Logic Programming (ICSLP'88), MIT Press, 1988, pp. 1070–1080.

10. *M. Gelfond, V. Lifschitz:* Classical Negation in Logic Programs and Disjunctive Databases, New Generation Computing, vol. 9, 1991, pp. 365–385.

11. *K. Inoue, C. Sakama:* A Fixpoint Characterization of Abductive Logic Programs, Journal of Logic Programming, vol. 27(2), 1996, pp. 107–136.

12. *N. Leone, R. Rullo, F. Scarcello:* Stable Model Checking for Disjunctive Logic Programs, Proc. Intl. Workshop of Logic in Databases (LID'96), Springer LNCS 1154, 1996,pp. 265–278.

13. *J.W. Lloyd:* Foundations of Logic Programming, second edition, Springer, 1987.

14. *J. Lobo, J. Minker, A. Rajasekar:* Foundations of Disjunctive Logic Programming, MIT Press, 1992.

15. *I. Niemelä, P. Simons:* Efficient Implementation of the Well–founded and Stable Model Semantics, Proc. Joint Intl. Conference and Symposium on Logic Programming (JICSLP'96), MIT Press, 1996, pp. 289–303.

16. *T.C. Przymusinski:* Stable Semantics for Disjunctive Programs, New Generation Computing, vol. 9, 1991, pp. 401–424.

17. *T.C. Przymusinski:* Static Semantics for Normal and Disjunctive Logic Programs, Annals of Mathematics and Artificial Intelligence, vol. 14, 1995, pp. 323–357.

18. *D. Seipel, J. Minker, C. Ruiz:* Model Generation and State Generation for Disjunctive Logic Programs, Journal of Logic Programming, vol. 32(1), 1997, pp. 48–69.

19. *D. Seipel, J. Minker, C. Ruiz:* A Characterization of Partial Stable Models for Disjunctive Deductive Databases, Proc. Intl. Logic Programming Symposium (ILPS'97), MIT Press, 1997, pp. 245–259.

20. *D. Seipel:* DISLOG – A Disjunctive Deductive Database Prototype, Proc. Twelfth Workshop on Logic Programming (WLP'97), 1997, pp. 136–143.
    DISLOG is available on the WWW at
    "http://www-info1.informatik.uni-wuerzburg.de/databases/DisLog".

21. *A. Van Gelder, K.A. Ross, J.S. Schlipf:*, Unfounded Sets and Well–Founded Semantics for General Logic Programs, Proc. Seventh ACM Symposium on Principles of Database Systems (PODS'88), 1988, pp. 221–230.

22. *C. Witteveen, G. Brewka:* Skeptical Reason Maintenance and Belief Revision, Journal of Artificial Intelligence, vol. 61, 1993, pp. 1–36.

23. *C. Witteveen, W. van der Hoek:* A General Framework for Revising Nonmonotonic Theories, Proc. Fourth Intl. Conf. on Logic Programming an Non–Monotonic Reasoning (LPNMR'97), Springer LNAI 1265, 1997, pp. 258–272.

24. *J.H. You, L.Y. Yuan:* Three-Valued Formalisms of Logic Programming: Is It Needed ?, Proc. Ninth ACM Symposium on Principles of Database Systems (PODS'90), 1990, pp. 172–182.

25. *J.H. You, L.Y. Yuan:* On the Equivalence of Semantics for Normal Logic Programs, Journal of Logic Programming, vol. 22(3), 1995, pp. 211–222.

Disjunctive Logic Programming and Autoepistemic Logic

Li-Yan Yuan, Jia-Huai You, and Randy Goebel

Department of Computer Science
University of Alberta
Edmonton, Canada T6G 2H1
{yuan, you, goebel}@cs.ualberta.ca

Abstract. In this paper, we use autoepistemic reasoning semantics to classify various semantics for disjunctive logic programs with default negation. We have observed that two different types of negative introspection in autoepistemic reasoning present two different interpretations of default negation: consistency-based and minimal-model-based. We also observed that all logic program semantics fall into three semantical points of view: the skeptical, stable, and partial-stable. Based on these two observations, we classify disjunctive logic program semantics into six different categories, and discuss the relationships among various semantics.

1 Introduction

Recently the study of theoretical foundations of disjunctive logic programs with default negation has attracted considerable attention. This is mainly because the additional expressive power of disjunctive logic programs significantly simplifies the problem of modeling disjunctive statements of various nonmonotonic formalisms in the framework of logic programming, and consequently facilitates using logic programming as an inference engine for nonmonotonic reasoning.

One of the major challenges is how to define a suitable semantics for various applications. A semantics of logic programs is usually specified by how default negation is justified. Different ways of justification lead to different semantics. Though many promising semantics for disjunctive programs have been proposed, such as the answer set semantics [12], the static semantics [16], and the well-founded and stable circumscriptive semantics [22], searching for suitable semantics for disjunctive programs proved to be far more difficult than for normal programs (logic programs without disjunction) whose semantics is fairly well understood now.

Three major semantical points of view have been established for logic programs: the skeptical, stable, and partial-stable.

A skeptical semantics justifies a default negation **not**α with respect to a program Π if and only if α cannot possibly be derived from Π under any circumstance [1].

---

[1] We say α cannot be derived from Π under any circumstance if α cannot be derived from Π^N for any set N of default negations. Note that Π^N is a program obtained

A stable semantics is based on the idea of *perfect introspection*, in that the semantics entails **not**α if and only if it does not entails α. Obviously, a stable semantics disallows any *undefined atoms*. (Note that an atom α in a given semantics is considered undefined if neither α nor **not**α is true in the semantics.

A stable semantics characterizes an ideal (credulous) semantics for logic programs but a stable semantics of many less-than-ideal programs may not be consistent. For example, $\Pi = \{a \leftarrow \textbf{not}a\}$ has no stable models. This motivates the introduction of the third semantical point of view: the partial-stable semantics. A partial-stable semantics can be viewed as a relaxed stable semantics that allows a minimum number of undefined atoms.

The standard semantics in three semantical categories for normal programs are the well-founded semantics [9], the stable semantics [11], and the regular semantics [20], respectively.

Not surprisingly, many semantics for disjunctive programs have been proposed in each of these three semantical categories. For example, the static semantics, the well-founded circumscriptive semantics, and the disjunctive well-founded semantics [2–4] and the skeptical well-founded semantics [23] are representatives of the skeptical semantical category; and the answer set semantics and the stable extension semantics [14] (based on the autoepistemic translation of logic programs) are representatives of the stable semantical category. For the partial-stable semantical category, there are the partial-stable model semantics [15], the regular model semantics [20], and the maximal stable model semantics [8]. These three partial-stable semantics, as well as many others, defined weaker stable semantics for disjunctive programs but experienced various difficulties [8]. A notable new entry in the field is the the partial-stable assumption semantics [19]. The partial-stable assumption semantics extends the answer set semantics into the partial-stable semantical category in the same way as the regular semantics extends the stable semantics for normal programs.

In addition to three semantical points of view, it has also been realized that the interpretations for default negation can be divided into two camps: those in default logic and autoepistemic logic, which are *consistency-based*, and those in circumscription and the like, which are *minimal-model-based* [13]. In the former case, default assumptions are made on the basis of certain hypotheses being consistent with a current theory; in the latter case, default assumptions are made on the basis of their being true in all minimal models of a current theory.

In this paper, we use autoepistemic logic as a tool to classify disjunctive program semantics into six different semantical categories, according to three semantical points of view and two interpretations of default negation. We demonstrate that all the six semantics have been proposed earlier in various frameworks and that all promising semantics either coincide with, or are essentially the same as, one of these six semantics.

We also address computational aspects of various semantics, which is another important issue in the study of logic program semantics. In fact, we have

---

from Π by replacing all negations with their truth values in N. See Section 2 for details shown that among all six semantics, the consistency-based skeptical semantics has the lowest computational complexity: P^{NP}, which is not surprising because minimal-model entailment is inherently more difficult to compute than (consistency-based) classical entailment.

We use autoepistemic logic as a tool for classifying disjunctive logic program semantics for the following two reasons. First, default negation in logic programming and many other nonmonotonic reasoning frameworks can be precisely characterized by *negative introspection*, which is a process for a rational agent to derive disbeliefs according to the agent's perspective of the world, in autoepistemic reasoning [10]. Second, we have observed that the difference between consistency-based and minimal-model-based interpretations of default negation lies in the use of an axiom $\neg\alpha \subset \neg\mathbf{B}\alpha$, where $\neg\mathbf{B}\alpha$ standing for "not believing α" (or $\mathbf{not}\alpha$), in autoepistemic logic, which is quite interesting. In fact, we show that a minimal-model-based semantics can be precisely defined by the corresponding consistency-based semantics with one simple axiom in the context of autoepistemic logic semantics. The following example demonstrates the difference between the two interpretations of default negation and how they are related by the above axiom.

Example 1. Consider the following program Π_1:

$$driving \lor flying \leftarrow$$
$$fixing\_car \leftarrow \mathbf{not}\,flying$$
$$reserving\_seat \leftarrow \mathbf{not}\,driving$$

Π_1 can be represented by an autoepistemic theory A_1 below:

$$driving \lor flying$$
$$fixing\_car \subset \neg\mathbf{B}\,flying$$
$$reserving\_seat \subset \neg\mathbf{B}\,driving$$

The answer set semantics, which adopts the minimal-model-based default negation, of Π_1 has two answer sets, one conclude

$$\{driving; fixing\_car; \mathbf{not}\,flying; \mathbf{not}\,resering\_seat\}$$

and the other

$$\{flying; reserving\_seat; \mathbf{not}\,driving; \mathbf{not}\,fixing\_car\}.$$

The stable extension semantics [14], which is consistency-based, of A_1, on the other hand, contains a unique stable extension which concludes

$$\{driving \lor flying; fixing\_car; reserving\_seat; \neg\mathbf{B}\,driving; \neg\mathbf{B}\,flying\}$$

Let A_{1m} be obtained from A_1 by adding instantiated formulas of axiom $\neg\alpha \subset \neg\mathbf{B}\alpha$, i.e., $A_{1m} = A_1 \cup \{\neg driving \subset \neg\mathbf{B}\,driving; \neg flying \subset \neg\mathbf{B}\,flying\}$. Then the stable extension semantics of A_{1m} contains two stable extensions, one concludes

$$\{driving; fixing\_car; \neg\mathbf{B}\,flying; \neg\mathbf{B}\,resering\_seat\}$$

and the other

$$\{flying; reserving\_seat; \neg \mathbf{B}driving; \neg \mathbf{B}fixing\_car\},$$

which coincides with the answer set semantics of Π_1.

Our study provides much needed insights into the theoretical foundations of logic programming with default negation.

The rest of the paper is organized as follows: Section 2 and 3 briefly review logic program semantics and autoepistemic logic respectively. Section 4 defines three autoepistemic expansions according to three different semantical points of view. The six different semantics are redefined in Section 5. Semantical analysis and comparisons are given in Section 6.

2   Logic Programs with Default Negation

We consider instantiated programs in a finite language containing the binary connectives $\vee, \wedge, \leftarrow$, and a unary connective **not**. A logic program is a set of clauses of the form

$$A_1 \vee \cdots \vee A_q \leftarrow B_1, \ldots, B_m, \mathbf{not}C_1, \ldots, \mathbf{not}C_n,$$

where A_i, B_j, C_k are atoms, $\mathbf{not}C_k$ are *default negations*, also called *assumed negations*, and $q \geq 1$. Π is considered a *normal* program if $q = 1$; and a *positive* program if $n = 0$. We use $\Pi \vdash \alpha$ to denote the fact that α can be derived from Π in the sense of classical entailment.

Assume Π is a program. A *negation set N* is defined as a set of default negations that appear in Π, which represents a possible interpretation (values) of default negations contained in Π. The GL-translation Π^N is defined as a program obtained from Π by first deleting all $\mathbf{not}c_j s$ if $\mathbf{not}c_j \in N$ and then deleting all clauses with $\mathbf{not}c_k$ in the body if $\mathbf{not}c_k \notin N$.

The main challenge is how to define a suitable semantics for logic programs. Since a negation set specifies a set of default negations being assumed true and the intended meaning of Π under a given negation set N is determined by Π^N [2], a semantics of Π is usually given by one or more negation sets. Therefore, searching for a semantics of Π is a process of searching for a negation set that can be justified under a certain semantical point of view.

There are three major semantical points of view: the skeptical, stable, and partial-stable.

A skeptical semantics is the most conservative semantics in that it justifies a default negation $\mathbf{not}\alpha$ if and only if α cannot be derived from the current program in any circumstance, meaning α is not true with respect to Π^N for any negation set N. Both stable and partial-stable semantics justify a default

---

[2] Given Π and N, an atom α is considered true with respect to Π^N if either $\Pi^N \models \alpha$ as in a consistency-based semantics, or $(\Pi^N \cup \{\neg\beta \mid \mathbf{not}\beta \in N\}) \models \alpha$ as in the answer set semantics. See Section 5 for details.

negation $not\alpha$ only if α cannot be derived from the current program under the given negation set. The difference between the stable and partial-stable is that the former assigns a definite value, being true or assumed false, to each and every atom while the latter allows a minimum number of undefined atoms.

Consider normal (non-disjunctive) programs first. The following table lists all the major semantics proposed for normal programs.

Skeptical	Stable	partial-stable
Well-Founded Semantics [9]	Stable Semantics [11]	Regular Semantics [20]
		Preferential Semantics [7]
		Maximum Partial-Stable Semantics [17]
		Stable-Class Semantics [1]

Let Π be a normal program, and M and N negation sets of Π. We say M is compatible wrt N if $\Pi^N \not\models \alpha$ for any $not\alpha \in M$. Then N is justifiable wrt Π if $not\alpha \in N$ if and only if $\Pi^M \not\models \alpha$ for any M that is compatible wrt N. This leads to the following definition.

Definition 1. *Let Π be a normal program. A negation set N is said to be*

1. *a partial-stable set of Π if*
   (a) *N is compatible wrt itself, and*
   (b) *$N = \{not\alpha | \Pi^{\{not\beta \mid \Pi^N \not\models \beta\}} \not\models \alpha\}$.*
2. *a stable set of Π if $N = \{not\alpha \mid \Pi^N \not\models \alpha\}$.*

From this definition we can see that a partial-stable set N is a set of all default negations that can be justified under the rule of negation as failure. That is, $not\alpha \in N$ if and only if α cannot be derived from Π even all default negations $not\beta \in \{not\beta \mid \Pi^N \not\models \beta\}$ are assumed false. Obviously, a stable set is a partial-stable set, but not vice versa. A program has at least one partial-stable set, though it may not have any stable set. Further, it is easy to show that among all partial-stable sets of Π there exists the least stable set in the sense of set inclusion. The following proposition reveals that almost all semantics of normal programs can be characterized by partial-stable sets.

Proposition 1. ([21])

1. *The well-founded semantics is characterized by the least partial-stable set.*
2. *The stable semantics is characterized by the set of all stable sets.*
3. *The regular semantics, preferential semantics, maximum partial-stable semantics, and normal stable-class semantics coincide and are characterized by the set of maximal partial-stable sets, in the sense of set inclusion.*

This proposition demonstrates that the well-founded, stable, and the regular (including all other equivalent) semantics are the standard semantics for their respective categories.

While the normal program semantics is fairly understood, searching for suitable disjunctive programs proved to be much more difficult.

The following table lists all major semantics proposed for disjunctive programs.

Skeptical	Stable	Partial-Stable
Well-founded Circumscriptive Semantics [22]	Stable Circumscriptive Semantics [22]	Partial-stable Model Semantics [15]
Static Semantics [16]	Answer Set Semantics [12]	Regular Semantics [20]
Disjunctive Well-founded Semantics [2, 4]	Stable Extension Semantics [14]	Maximal Stable Model Semantics [8]
Skeptical Well-founded Semantics [23]		Partial-stable Assumption Semantics [19]
		Regularly-justified Set Semantics [23]

Both the static and the well-founded circumscriptive semantics were defined based on the same idea of minimal-model-based negative introspection. The specific form of this introspection was given in [22]. In fact, the first three skeptical semantics listed above are essentially the same [5]. The difference between the first three skeptical semantics and the skeptical well-founded semantics lies in the interpretation of default negation. The former adopts minimal-model-based default negation while the latter consistency-based default negation.

Example 2. Consider a simple program Π_2 below:

$$bird \leftarrow; \quad fly \lor abnormal \leftarrow bird; \quad fly \leftarrow bird, \mathbf{not} abnormal$$

Since *abnormal* is true in a minimal model of Π_2 with **not** *abnormal* being false while *abnormal* cannot be derived from Π_2 regardless of **not** *abnormal* being true or false, **not** *abnormal* can be justified under consistency-based default negation but not under minimal-model-based default negation.

The skeptical well-founded semantics adopts consistency-based default negation and thus concludes **not** *abnormal* and *fly*. On the other hand, the static as well as the well-founded circumscriptive and disjunctive well-founded semantics adopt minimal-model-based default negation and thus conclude neither **not** *abnormal* nor *fly*.

The answer set semantics is defined for extended logic programs that allow classical negation in both head and body while the stable circumscriptive semantics is defined for general autoepistemic theories, including the translated logic programs with default negation. Both semantics adopt minimal-model-based default negation and coincide in the context of disjunctive logic programs. On the other hand, the stable extension semantics and the stable set semantics [23] are a stable semantics that adopt consistency-based default negation.

Example 3. (Example 2 continued) The answer set semantics (as well as the stable circumscriptive semantics) of Π_2 is defined by two sets, the first one contains the set $\{bird, fly, \mathbf{not} abnormal\}$ and the second $\{bird, abnormal, \mathbf{not} fly\}$.

The stable set semantics, on the other hand, is defined by a unique negation set $\{\mathbf{not} abnormal\}$ and therefore implies $bird \land fly$.

All the partial-stable semantics, except the regularly-justified set semantics which is consistency-based, listed above are minimal-model-based but are different from each other. See [8] for detailed comparisons. The recently proposed partial-stable assumption semantics seems the only semantics that extends the answer set semantics in the same way as the regular semantics extends the stable semantics for normal programs [19].

Example 4. Consider the following program Π_4

$$work \lor sleep \lor tired \leftarrow$$
$$work \leftarrow \mathbf{not}tired$$
$$sleep \leftarrow \mathbf{not}work$$
$$tired \leftarrow \mathbf{not}sleep$$

Both partial-stable and maximal stable model semantics, listed in the table, of Π_4 are inconsistent while the partial-stable assumption semantics and the regularly-justified set semantics are characterized by an empty negation set $N = \emptyset$ which implies nothing but $work \lor sleep \lor tired$.

The difference between the partial-stable assumption and regularly-justified set semantics lies in the interpretation of default negation. For example, consider Π_2 in Example 2. The partial-stable assumption semantics of Π_2 coincides with the answer set semantics of Π_2 while the regularly-justified set semantics of Π_2 coincides with both the skeptical well-founded and the stable set semantics of Π_2.

Another important feature of a semantics is its computational complexity. Because of the inherent difficulty of computing minimal-model entailment, the computational complexity of consistency-based semantics is lower than that of minimal-model-based semantics.

3   Autoepistemic Logic

We consider here a propositional language augmented with a modal operator $\mathbf{B}$. An atomic formula (atom) is either a propositional symbol, or an epistemic atom, also called *belief atom*, $\mathbf{B}\alpha$, where α is a (well-formed) formula defined as usual. The intended meaning of $\mathbf{B}\alpha$ is "α is believed". For convenience, we also use $\mathbf{not}\alpha$, called *disbelief atom*, interchangeably for $\neg\mathbf{B}\alpha$, meaning α is disbelieved. ($\mathbf{not}\alpha$ is also viewed by many authors as a *default negation*.) An *belief theory* (or a theory for short) is a set of well-formed formulae, and a formula (or a theory) is *objective* if it contains no epistemic atoms, otherwise it is *subjective*. We denote by $P^+(A)$ and $P^-(A)$ the set of all propositions and the set of all negative literals that appear in A, and by $B^+(A)$ and $B^-(A)$ the set of all belief atoms and the set of all disbelief atoms that appear in A, respectively.

The logic has the following axioms and rules of inference.

Axioms.

PL. All propositional tautologies.

K. $\mathbf{B}(\alpha \supset \beta) \supset (\mathbf{B}\alpha \supset \mathbf{B}\beta)$.

D. $\neg\mathbf{B}$ (false)

Inference rules.

Modus Ponens (MP). $\dfrac{\alpha \supset \beta, \alpha}{\beta}$

A rational agent does not belief inconsistent conclusions which is expressed by
D. K means that if a conditional and its antecedent are both believed, then so
is the consequent. The importance of K is evidenced by the fact that K imposes
a constraint of normality on the language: $\mathbf{B}\alpha \equiv \mathbf{B}\beta$ whenever $\alpha \equiv \beta$. (Note
that by $\alpha \equiv \beta$ we mean $(\alpha \subset \beta) \wedge (\beta \subset \alpha)$.) MP is a usual inference rule for
propositional logic.

Let A be a theory and α a formula. By $A \vdash_{KD} \alpha$ we mean α can be derived
from A based on the aforementioned axioms and rules of inference. A is incon-
sistent if there exists a formula α such that $A \vdash_{KD} \alpha$ and $A \vdash_{KD} \neg\alpha$; otherwise,
it is consistent.

3.1   Belief Interpretation

A belief theory A is used to describe the knowledge base of a rational agent. Due
to incomplete information, an agent may have to hold a set of possible states
of epistemic belief, each of which represents a complete description about the
agent's belief. A (restricted) *belief interpretation* is thus introduced to characterize such a complete state of belief. Formally,

Definition 2.   *1. A restricted belief interpretation, or belief interpretation for
short, of A is a set I of belief atoms and disbelief atoms such that for any
belief atom $\mathbf{B}\alpha$ appearing in A, either $\mathbf{B}\alpha \in I$ or $\neg\mathbf{B}\alpha \in I$ (not both).*

   *2. A restricted belief model, or belief model for short, of A is a belief interpre-
tation I of A such that $A \cup I$ is consistent.*

Obviously, a theory is consistent if and only if it has at least one belief model.

Let A be a belief theory and I a belief model of A. An (objective) *perspective
theory* of A, denoted by A^I, is defined as an objective theory obtained from A
by replacing each belief atom in A with their corresponding truth value in I.
Obviously, a belief theory may have more than one perspective theory and each
of them represent the agent's perspective with respect to one restricted belief
model.

Example 5. The following autoepistemic theory is obtained from Π_2 in Example 2 above

$$A_5 = \{bird; \quad fly \vee abnormal \subset bird; \quad fly \subset bird \wedge \neg\mathbf{B}abnormal\}.$$

A_5 has two belief models and two corresponding perspective theories:

$I_1 = \{\mathbf{B}abnormal\}$ and $A_{51} = \{bird; fly \vee abnormal \subset bird\}$;
$I_2 = \{\neg\mathbf{B}abnormal\}$ and $A_{52} = \{bird; fly \vee abnormal \subset bird; fly \subset bird\}$.

3.2   Introspection

Introspection is a process of revising the agent' belief according to his perspective of the world. For example, Moore [14] uses the stable expansion T of A

$$T = \{\phi \mid A \cup \{\mathbf{B}\alpha \mid \alpha \in T\} \cup \{\neg \mathbf{B}\alpha \mid \alpha \notin T\} \vdash_{KD45} \phi\},$$

where $\vdash_{KD45}$ denotes derivation under logic KD45, to model introspective reasoning. The terms $\{\mathbf{B}\alpha \mid \alpha \in T\}$ and $\{\neg \mathbf{B}\alpha \mid \alpha \notin T\}$ express the positive and negative introspection of an agent respectively.

It is generally agreed that positive introspection is a process of concluding belief $\mathbf{B}\alpha$ if α can be derived while negative introspection is a process of concluding disbelief $\neg \mathbf{B}\alpha$ (or $\mathbf{B}\neg\alpha$) if α cannot be derived. Positive introspection is usually achieved by introducing the necessitation rule: derive $\mathbf{B}\alpha$ if α has been proved, as follows:

Necessitation (N). $$\frac{\alpha}{\mathbf{B}\alpha}$$

The interpretation of non-derivability for negative introspection, however, varies quite diversely. Two typical approaches are:

1. consistency-based introspection:
   deriving $\neg \mathbf{B}\alpha$ if $\neg\alpha$ is consistent with A, (or equivalently, $A \not\vdash_{KD} \alpha$); and
2. minimal-model-based p-introspection:
   deriving $\neg \mathbf{B}\alpha$ if $\neg\alpha$ is true in every minimal model of every perspective theory of A.

The closed world assumption, default logic, and Moore's autoepistemic logic use consistency-based negative introspection. This approach usually results in stronger negative introspection in that more disbeliefs may be concluded, and as such, many reasonable theories do not possess consistent introspective expansions. Minimal-model-based introspection, on the other hand, suffers from the inherent difficulties associated with minimal-model entailment [8].

In [24], we have argued that introspection should be consistency-based and be with respect to each and every possible belief world:

Deriving $\neg \mathbf{B}\alpha$ if $\neg\alpha$ is consistent with $A \cup I$ for every belief model I of A.

In the following we will formally define the inference rules of introspection. First we need to identify the classical entailment with respect to all possible belief worlds.

Definition 3. *Let A be a theory and α a formula.*

1. *$A \mathrel{|\!\sim} \alpha$ if $A \cup I \vdash_{KD} \alpha$ for every belief model I of A, and*
2. *$A \mathrel{\sim\!|} \alpha$ if $A \cup I \not\vdash_{KD} \alpha$ for every belief model I of A.*
   (Note that $A \cup \not\vdash_{KD} \alpha$ if and only if $\neg\alpha$ is consistent with $A \cup I$.)

If A has two belief models I_1 and I_2 such that $A \cup I_1 \vdash_{KD} \alpha$ and $A \cup I_2 \nvdash_{KD} \alpha$ then neither $A \mathrel{|\!\sim} \alpha$ nor $A \mathrel{\sim\!|} \alpha$. Further, if A is inconsistent then $A \mathrel{|\!\sim} \alpha$ and $A \mathrel{\sim\!|} \alpha$ for every formula α.

Now we are in a position to introduce the following two rules of inference for positive and negative introspection with respect to all possible belief worlds respectively.

Positive Introspection (PI). $\qquad \dfrac{\mathrel{|\!\sim} \alpha}{\mathbf{B}\alpha}$

Negative Introspection (NI). $\qquad \dfrac{\mathrel{\sim\!|} \alpha}{\neg\mathbf{B}\alpha}$

PI states that deriving $\mathbf{B}\alpha$ whenever $A \mathrel{|\!\sim} \alpha$ and NI that deriving $\neg\mathbf{B}\alpha$ whenever $A \mathrel{\sim\!|} \alpha$.

Remarks   *Because $A \mathrel{|\!\sim} \alpha$ if and only if $A \vdash_{KD} \alpha$, PI is the same as the necessitation rule N. We list PI as a rule of inference for positive introspection here to emphases its role in introspection. NI is not a usual inference rule in that its premise takes into account of the whole axioms. Rather, it is a content-based meta rule of inference.*

It is easy to see that PI is monotonic while NI is nonmonotonic. However, it has been shown that NI is cumulative in that $F \cup \{\neg\mathbf{B}\beta\}$ derives $\neg\mathbf{B}\alpha$, for any formula β, whenever F derives both $\neg\mathbf{B}\alpha$ and $\neg\mathbf{B}\beta$. Therefore, NI can be recursively applied in any ordering, which enable us to define a logic that is nonmonotonic in general but monotonic with respect to all belief and disbelief atoms, as follows.

Definition 4. *Assume A is a belief theory and α a formula. We say A introspectively implies α, denoted as $A \vdash_{IKD} \alpha$, if α can be derived from A by the following axioms and rules of inference:*
    Axioms: *PL, K, D*
Inference rule: *MP, PI, NI.*

Example 6. Consider A_5 in Example 5 again. Since $A_5 \mathrel{\sim\!|} abnormal$, $A_5 \vdash_{IKD}$ $\neg\mathbf{B}abnormal$. Consequently, $A_5 \vdash_{IKD} fly$ as well as $A_5 \vdash_{IKD} \mathbf{B}fly$.

The well-defined-ness of the epistemic entailment is evidenced by the fact that $\vdash_{IKD}$ is belief-monotonic, as described below.

Definition 5. *A relation $\vdash$ between a belief theory T and a formula α is said to be belief-monotonic if for any formula β, $T \cup \{\mathbf{B}\beta\} \vdash \alpha$ if $T \vdash \alpha$ and $T \cup \{\neg\mathbf{B}\beta\} \vdash \alpha$ if $T \vdash \alpha$.*

The introspective implication characterizes both positive and negative introspection, which is naturally nonmonotonic, but still remains belief monotonic. Therefore, the computation of the introspective logic can be carried out incrementally in any order, as long as the derived beliefs are preserved in the derivation.

The following example demonstrates that not every consistent theory is also consistent under introspective entailment.

Example 7. Let $A_7 = \{a \subset \neg \mathbf{B}b; \neg a \subset \neg \mathbf{B}b\}$. Since $A_7 \mathrel{\rlap{\sim}\dashv} b$, $A_7 \vdash_{IKD} \neg \mathbf{B}b$, but $A_7 \cup \{\neg \mathbf{B}b\}$ is not consistent. Note that A_7 is consistent for $\{\mathbf{B}b\}$ is a restricted belief model of A_7.

A theory A is said to be *introspectively consistent* if there exists no formula α such that $A \vdash_{IKD} \alpha$ and $A \vdash_{IKD} \neg \alpha$. Even though it is inherently difficult to check if a given theory is introspectively consistent, there exists a large class of theories that are introspectively consistent. For example, as discussed in Section 6, all belief theories representing disjunctive logic programs with negation are introspectively consistent.

The following observation, a direct consequence of axiom K, demonstrates the normal behavior of introspective logic. That is, for any formulae α and β,

$$\vdash_{IKD} \mathbf{B}\alpha \wedge \mathbf{B}\beta \equiv \mathbf{B}(\alpha \wedge \beta); \qquad \vdash_{IKD} \mathbf{B}\alpha \vee \mathbf{B}\beta \supset \mathbf{B}(\alpha \vee \beta).$$

4   Introspective Expansions

In this section, we define three classes of introspective expansions, in order to express the three semantical points of view in the context of autoepistemic logic.

Definition 6. *A belief theory T is said to be an* introspective expansion *of A if it satisfies the following fixpoint equation*

$$T = \{\phi \mid A \cup \{\neg \mathbf{B}\alpha \mid T \mathrel{\rlap{\sim}\dashv} \alpha\} \vdash_{IKD} \phi\}.$$

The introspective expansion characterizes the introspective reasoning process by expanding a given theory A using both rules of PI and NI.

It is worth noting that only the negative introspection $\{\neg \mathbf{B}\alpha \mid T \mathrel{\rlap{\sim}\dashv} \alpha\}$ is used in the above fixpoint equation. The use of inappropriate positive introspection in the equation, as indicated by Schwartz [18], may lead to ungrounded expansions.

Among all introspective expansions, the following three are of special interest.

Definition 7. *An introspective expansion T of A is said to be*

1. *the* ground expansion *of A if it is a subset of any introspective expansion;*
2. *a* stable expansion *of A if T is epistemically complete in that for any formula α, T contains either $\mathbf{B}\alpha$ or $\neg \mathbf{B}\alpha$; and*
3. *a* regular expansion *of A if there exists no introspective expansion T' of A such that $T' \supset T$.*

In fact, these three classes of expansions are defined to express the three semantical points of view, first developed in the context of normal programs.

Obviously, any stable expansion is a regular expansion, but not vice versa. For convenience we use $Cn_{IKD}(A)$ to denoted the set of all formulas introspectively implied by A, i.e., $Cn_{IKD}(A) = \{\alpha \mid A \vdash_{IKD} \alpha\}$.

Example 8. Consider

$$A_5 = \{bird; fly \lor abnormal \subset bird; fly \subset bird \land \neg \textbf{B}abnormal\}$$

in Example 5 again. A_5 has exactly one introspective expansion $T = Cn_{IKD}(A_5)$, which is also a stable expansion of A_5.

Example 9. Consider $A_9 = \{a \subset \textbf{B}a, b \subset \neg \textbf{B}a\}$. Then A_9 has two introspective expansions, that is, $T_1 = Cn_{IKD}(A_9) = \{\phi | A_9 \vdash_{IKD} \phi\}$ that contains neither $\textbf{B}a$ nor $\neg \textbf{B}a$, and $T_2 = Cn_{IKD}(A_9 \cup \{\neg \textbf{B}a\})$.

Note that $T_3 = Cn_{IKD}(A_9 \cup \{\textbf{B}a\})$ is not an introspective expansion of A_9 since a cannot be derived from A_9 with any set of disbelief atoms.

It turns out that any theory has the ground (least) expansion, though not necessarily a consistent one. Furthermore, the ground expansion is just the set of all introspective consequences of A.

Theorem 1.   *1. $T = \{\phi | A \vdash_{IKD} \phi\}$ is the ground expansion of A.*
  2. If A is introspectively consistent then any introspective expansion of A is consistent.

The proof of the theorem is straightforward and thus omitted.

5   Logic Program Semantics and Introspective Expansions

In this section, we will define various semantics of logic programs based on autoepistemic expansions.

5.1   Default Negation and Disbelief

Definition 8. *Let Π be a logic program. Then $AE(\Pi)$ is defined as an autoepistemic theory obtained from Π by translating each clause in Π into a formula of the form [10]*

$$A_1 \lor \cdots \lor A_q \subset B_1 \land \cdots \land B_m \land \neg \textbf{B}C_1 \land \cdots \land \textbf{not}\textbf{B}C_n$$

Example 10. Consider

$$\Pi_2 = \{bird \leftarrow; fly \lor abnormal \leftarrow bird; fly \leftarrow bird, \textbf{not}abnormal\}$$

again. Then $AE(\Pi) = \{bird; fly \lor abnormal \subset bird; fly \subset bird \land \neg \textbf{B}abnormal\}$.

Similar to negative introspection, default negations in disjunctive programs can also be interpreted in two different ways: consistency-based and minimal-model based. The former assumes $\textbf{not}\alpha$ if $\neg \alpha$ is consistent with the current program while the latter assumes $\textbf{not}\alpha$ if $\neg \alpha$ is true in every minimal model of the current program.

Example 11. (Example 10 continued) By consistency-based default negation, **not***abnormal* can be justified since *abnormal* cannot be derived from Π_2 no matter whether **not***abnormal* is true or false. On the other hand, by minimal-model based default negation, **not***abnormal* cannot be justified since *abnormal* is true in one of the minimal models of Π_2 when **not***abnormal* is not assumed.

Consistency-based default negation can be easily characterized by the translation given in Definition 8 since negative introspection of autoepistemic logic is consistency-based. The following translation is introduced to capture minimal-model based default negation.

Definition 9. *Let Π be a logic program, and $AE(\Pi)$ be the autoepistemic theory of Π. Then, the M-autoepistemic theory of Π, denoted as $MAE(\Pi)$ is defined as*

$$AE(\Pi) \cup \{\neg\alpha \subset \neg\mathbf{B}\alpha \mid \alpha \quad is\ an\ atom\ in \quad \Pi\}$$

$MAE(\Pi)$ *is also viewed as $AE(\Pi)$ augmented with an axiom $\neg\alpha \subset \neg\mathbf{B}\alpha$.*

Example 12. Consider Π_2 in Example 10 again. Then $MAE(\Pi_2)$ contains the following formulas:

$$
\begin{aligned}
&bird; \\
&fly \vee abnormal \subset bird; \\
&fly \subset bird \wedge \neg\mathbf{B}abnormal; \\
&\neg bird \subset \neg\mathbf{B}bird; \\
&\neg fly \subset \neg\mathbf{B}fly; \\
&\neg abnormal \subset \neg\mathbf{B}abnormal\}.
\end{aligned}
$$

Now, we are in a position to define declarative semantics of disjunctive programs in terms of translated autoepistemic theories of Π. Because each program has two different translated autoepistemic theories, corresponding to consistency-based and minimal-model based default negations, and each autoepistemic theory may have three different types of introspective expansions, corresponding to the skeptical, stable, and partial-stable semantical points of view, six different semantics are given below.

Definition 10. *Let Π be a disjunctive program, $AE(\Pi)$ and $MAE(\Pi)$ the corresponding autoepistemic theories of Π. Then we define*

1. *the C-ground (standing for consistency-based ground), C-stable (standing for consistency-based stable), and C-regular (standing for Consistency-based regular) semantics of Π by the ground expansion, the set of all stable expansions, and the set of all regular expansions, of $AE(\Pi)$ respectively; and*
2. *the ground, stable, and partial-stable semantics of Π by the ground expansion, the set of all stable expansions, and the set of all regular expansions, of $MAE(\Pi)$ respectively.*

By saying that a semantics is characterized by an introspective expansion we mean that (1) an objective formula α is true in the semantics if and only if α is contained in the expansion, and (2) a default negation **not**α *is true in the semantics if and only if ¬Bα is contained in the expansion.*

The following table summarizes all six different semantics.

	Skeptical	Stable	Partial-Stable
Consistency based	C-Ground Semantics: *the ground expansion of AE(Π)*	C-Stable Semantics: *all the stable expansions of AE(Π)*	C-Regular Semantics: *all the regular expansions of AE(Π)*
Minimal-model based	Ground Semantics: *the ground expansion of MAE(Π)*	Stable Semantics: *all the stable expansions of MAE(Π)*	Partial-stable Semantics: *all the regular expansions of MAE(Π)*

It is straightforward to show that for normal programs, consistency-based and minimal-model based semantics coincide, simply because an atom is true in the set of all minimal models of a Horn program if and only if it is a logical consequence of the program.

Example 13. Consider Π_2 in Example 10 again.

First, consider consistency-based default negation. Since *abnormal* cannot be derived from $AE(\Pi_2)$ in any circumstance, $AE(\Pi_2)$ has a unique expansion containing ¬**B***abnormal*. Thus, all three semantics, including the C-ground, C-stable, and C-regular, coincide and imply fly.

Now consider minimal-model based default negation. The skeptical semantics does not imply ¬**B***abnormal* since $I = \{\mathbf{B}bird, \neg\mathbf{B}fly, \mathbf{B}abnormal\}$ is a belief model of $MAE(\Pi_2)$ and $MAE(\Pi_2) \cup I \vdash_{KD} abnormal$. So the ground semantics does not imply fly either. In fact, it coincides with the static semantics.

The stable semantics, which coincide with the partial-stable semantics, of Π_2 is defined by two stable expansions, one contains $\{\mathbf{B}bird, \neg\mathbf{B}abnormal, \mathbf{B}fly\}$ and the other contains $\{\mathbf{B}bird, \mathbf{B}abnormal, \neg\mathbf{B}fly\}$.

6 Further Analysis

In this section, we will analyze relationships between various semantics.

First for normal programs, it is easy to show that both minimal-model-based and consistency-based semantics coincide.

Proposition 2. *Assume Π is a normal program. Then*

1. *The well-founded, C-ground, and ground semantics of Π coincide.*
2. *The stable and C-stable semantics coincide.*
3. *The regular, C-regular, and partial-stable semantics coincide.*

Both the answer set semantics and stable circumscriptive semantics are minimal-model-based and coincide with the stable semantics; and both the stable extension semantics and the stable set semantics are consistency-based and coincide with the C-stable semantics, as shown below. Again, the proof is straightforward and thus omitted.

Proposition 3. *1. Both the answer set and stable circumscriptive semantics coincide with the stable semantics.*

2. Both the stable extension semantics and the stable set semantics coincide with the C-stable semantics.

Among all the minimal-model-based semantics in the partial-stable category, the recently proposed partial-stable assumption semantics [19] coincides with the partial-stable semantics. Further, the C-partial-stable semantics coincides with the stable set semantics.

Proposition 4. *1. The partial-stable semantics coincides with the partial-stable assumption semantics.*

2. The C-partial-stable semantics coincides with the regularly-justified set semantics.

Proof. (1) It follows the following two facts.

First, the partial-stable assumption semantics utilizes an additional meta rule of inference $\frac{\alpha \vee \beta, \textbf{not} \beta}{\beta}$ while the partial-stable semantics utilizes a minimal-model axiom $\neg \alpha \subset \neg \textbf{B} \alpha$, which are essentially the same.

Second, the partial-stable assumption semantics is defined using the alternating fixpoint theory while the partial-stable semantics is defined using negative introspection with respect to all belief models. However, it is easy to show that, in the context of logic programming, the two are the same.

(2) It follows that the justification of default negation under the alternating fixpoint theory coincide with negative introspection with respect to all belief models. Note that the regularly-justified set semantics justifies a regular set using the alternating fixpoint theory.

Both the static and ground semantics are defined using minimal-model based introspection and thus are very much the same. The subtle difference between the two is due to the fact that the autoepistemic theory $MAE(\Pi)$ uses $\neg \textbf{B} \alpha$ to represent $\textbf{not} \alpha$ while the static semantics uses $\textbf{B} \neg \alpha$ to represent $\textbf{not} \alpha$.

6.1 Computational Complexity

It is a well-known fact that the computational complexity [3] of the well-founded semantics for normal program is polynomial while that of both the stable and regular semantics is NP-complete. Furthermore, it has been shown that the computational complexities for the answer set semantics and many other minimal-model-based partial-stable semantics are Σ_2^P [8]. This implies that the computational complexity of both the stable and partial-stable semantics for disjunctive programs are Σ_2^P.

The ground semantics and the static semantics have the same computational complexity which are also Σ_2^P-complete [6].

---

[3] By the computational complexity we mean the data complexity under possibility inference, i.e., the complexity of deciding if a given query is true in one partial-stable set under the given semantics [8]

The following proposition shows that the computational complexity of the consistency-based ground semantics is P^{NP} which is the lowest among all the semantics for disjunctive logic programs in the polynomial hierarchy.

Proposition 5. *The computational complexity of the consistency-based ground semantics is P^{NP}.*

Proof. Let $AE(\Pi)$ be a disjunctive theory and F a formula. We need only to show that deciding if $AE(\Pi) \vdash_{IKD} F$ is P^{NP}.

Let M_1 contain all disbeliefs and M_2 all beliefs. Then both M_1 and M_2 are belief models of $AE(\Pi)$. Furthermore, let B_1 and B_2 are objective perspective theories of B with respect to M_1 and M_2 respectively. Then for any formula α, $AE(\Pi) \mathrel{\mid\!\sim} \alpha$ if and only if $B_2 \vdash_{IKD} \alpha$ and $AE(\Pi) \mathrel{\mid\!\sim\!\!\!/} \alpha$ if and only if $B_1 \not\vdash_{IKD} \alpha$. This implies that a visit to an oracle for classical inference can determine the status of any $\neg \mathbf{B}C_i$ under the positive (or negative) introspection. Therefore, a linear calls to oracle are sufficient enough to determine if $AE(\Pi) \vdash_{IKD} F$.

This result is by no means surprising because (consistency-based) classical entailment is inherently more efficient to compute than minimal-model-based entailment.

References

1. C. R. Baral and V. S. Subrahmanian. Stable and extension class theory for logic programs and default logics. *Journal of Automated Reasoning*, 8:345–366, 1992.
2. S. Brass and J. Dix. Stefan Brass and Jürgen Dix. A disjunctive semantics based on unfolding and bottom-up evaluation. In Bernd Wolfinger, editor, *Innovationen bei Rechen- und Kommunikationssystemen*, (IFIP '94-Congress, Workshop FG2: Disjunctive Logic Programming and Disjunctive Databases), pages 83–91, Berlin, 1994. Springer.
3. Stefan Brass and Jürgen Dix. Characterizations of the Disjunctive Stable Semantics by Partial Evaluation. *Journal of Logic Programming*, 32(3):207–228, 1997. (Extended abstract appeared in: Characterizations of the Stable Semantics by Partial Evaluation *LPNMR, Proceedings of the Third International Conference, Kentucky*, pages 85–98, 1995. LNCS 928, Springer.).
4. Stefan Brass and Jürgen Dix. Characterizations of the Disjunctive Well-founded Semantics: Confluent Calculi and Iterated GCWA. *Journal of Automated Reasoning*, 20(1):143–165, 1998. (Extended abstract appeared in: Characterizing D-WFS: Confluence and Iterated GCWA. *Logics in Artificial Intelligence, JELIA '96*, pages 268–283, 1996. Springer, LNCS 1126.).
5. Stefan Brass, Jürgen Dix, Ilkka Niemelä, and Teodor. C. Przymusinski. A Comparison of the Static and the Disjunctive Well-founded Semantics and its Implementation. In A. G. Cohn, L. K. Schubert, and S. C. Shapiro, editors, *Principles of Knowledge Representation and Reasoning: Proceedings of the Sixth International Conference (KR '98)*, pages 74–85. San Francisco, CA, Morgan Kaufmann, May 1998. appeared also as TR 17/97, University of Koblenz.
6. J. Dix and T. Eiter. Personal communication.
7. P. M. Dung. Negations as hypotheses: An abductive foundation for logic programming. In *Proceedings of the 8th ICLP*, pages 3–17, 1991.

8. Thomas Eiter, Nicola Leone, and Domenico Sacc. The expressive power of partial models in disjunctive deductive databases. In *Logic in Databases*, pages 245–264, 1996.
9. A. Van Gelder, K. Ross, and J. Schlipf. The well-founded semantics for general logic programs. *JACM*, 38:620–650, 1991.
10. M. Gelfond. On stratified autoepistemic theories. In *Proceedings of AAAI-87*, pages 207–211. Morgan Kaufmann Publishers, 1987.
11. M. Gelfond and V. Lifschitz. The stable model semantics for logic programming. In *Proc. of the 5th ICLP*, pages 1070–1080, 1988.
12. M. Gelfond and V. Lifschitz. Classical negation in logic programs and disjunctive databases. *New Generation Computing*, 9:365–386, 1991.
13. H. J. Levesque. All i know: A study in autoepistemic logic. *AI*, 42:263–309, 1990.
14. R. C. Moore. Semantic considerations on non-monotonic logic. *AI*, 25:75–94, 1985.
15. T. C. Przymusinski. Stable semantics for disjunctive programs. *New Generation Computing*, 9:401–424, 1991.
16. T. C. Przymusinski. Static semantics for normal and disjunctive logic programs. *Annals of Mathematics and Artificial Intelligence*, 14:323–357, 1995.
17. D. Saccà and C. Zaniolo. Stable models and non-determinism in logic programs with negation. In *Proceedings of the 9th ACM PODS*, pages 205–217, 1990.
18. G. Schwarz. Bounding introspection in nonmonotonic reasoning. *KR'92*, pages 581–590, 1992.
19. J.-H. You, X. Wang, and L.-Y. Yuan. Disjunctive logic programming as constrainted inferences. In *Proc. of International Conference on Logic Programming*, 1997.
20. J.-H. You and L.-Y. Yuan. A three-valued semantics of deductive databases and logic programs. *Journal of Computer and System Sciences*, 49:334–361, 1994. A preliminary version appears in the Proc. of the 9th ACM PODS, page 171-182, 1990.
21. J.-H. You and L.-Y. Yuan. On the equivalence of semantics for normal logic programs. *Journal of Logic Programming*, 22(3):209–219, 1995.
22. L.-Y. Yuan and J.-H. You. Autoepistemic circumscription and logic programming. *Journal of Automated Reasoning*, 10:143–160, 1993.
23. L.-Y. Yuan and J.-H. You. On the extension of logic programming with negation though uniform proofs. In *Proc. of the 3rd International Conference on Logic Programming and Nonmonotonic Reasoning*, 1995.
24. L.-Y. Yuan and J.-H. You. An introspective logic of belief. In *Proc. of the Workshop on Logic Programming and Knowledge Representation, ILPS'97*, pages 157–170, 1997.

A System for Abductive Learning of Logic Programs

Evelina Lamma[1], Paola Mello[2], Michela Milano[1], and Fabrizio Riguzzi[1]

[1] DEIS, Università di Bologna,
Viale Risorgimento 2, I-40136 Bologna, Italy,
{elamma,mmilano,friguzzi}@deis.unibo.it

[2] Dip. di Ingegneria, Università di Ferrara,
Via Saragat 1, I-44100 Ferrara, Italy
pmello@ing.unife.it

Abstract. We present the system LAP (Learning Abductive Programs) that is able to learn abductive logic programs from examples and from a background abductive theory. A new type of induction problem has been defined as an extension of the Inductive Logic Programming framework. In the new problem definition, both the background and the target theories are abductive logic programs and abductive derivability is used as the coverage relation.

LAP is based on the basic top-down ILP algorithm that has been suitably extended. In particular, coverage of examples is tested by using the abductive proof procedure defined by Kakas and Mancarella [24]. Assumptions can be made in order to cover positive examples and to avoid the coverage of negative ones, and these assumptions can be used as new training data. LAP can be applied for learning in the presence of incomplete knowledge and for learning exceptions to classification rules.

Keywords: Abduction, Learning.

1 Introduction

Abductive Logic Programming (ALP) has been recognized as a powerful knowledge representation tool [23]. Abduction [22, 36] is generally understood as reasoning from effects to causes or explanations. Given a theory T and a formula G, the goal of abduction is to find a set of atoms Δ (explanation) that, together with T, entails G and that is consistent with a set of integrity constraints IC. The atoms in Δ are *abduced*: they are assumed true in order to prove the goal. Abduction is specially useful to reason in domains where we have to infer causes from effects, such as diagnostic problems [3]. But ALP has many other applications [23]: high level vision, natural language understanding, planning, knowledge assimilation and default reasoning. Therefore, it is desirable to be able to automatically produce a general representation of a domain starting from specific knowledge about single instances. This problem, in the case of standard Logic

Programming, has been deeply studied in Inductive Logic Programming (ILP) [7], the research area covering the intersection of Machine Learning [33] and Logic Programming. Its aim is to devise systems that are able to learn logic programs from examples and from a background knowledge. Recently, in this research area, a number of works have begun to appear on the problem of learning non-monotonic logic programs [4, 16, 8, 32].

Particular attention has been given to the problem of learning abductive logic programs [21, 26, 29, 30, 27] and, more generally, to the relation existing between abduction and induction and how they can integrate and complement each other [15, 17, 2]. Our work addresses this topic as well. The approach for learning abductive logic programs that we present in this paper is doubly useful. On one side, we can learn abductive theories for the application domains mentioned above. For example, we can learn default theories: in Section 5.1 we show an example in which we learn exceptions to classification rules. On the other side, we can learn theories in domains in which there is incomplete knowledge. This is a very frequent case in practice, because very often the data available is incomplete and/or noisy. In this case, abduction helps induction by allowing to make assumptions about unknown facts, as it is shown in the example in Section 5.2. In [29] we defined a new learning problem called Abductive Learning Problem. In this new framework we generate an abductive logic program from an abductive background knowledge and from a set of positive and negative examples of the concepts to be learned. Moreover, abductive derivability is used as the example coverage relation instead of Prolog derivability as in ILP.

We present the system LAP (Learning Abductive Programs) that solves this new learning problem. The system is based on the theoretical work developed in [21, 29] and it is an extension of a basic top-down algorithm adopted in ILP [7]. In the extended algorithm, the proof procedure defined in [24] for abductive logic programs is used for testing the coverage of examples in substitution of the deductive proof procedure of logic programming. Moreover, the abduced literals can be used as new training data for learning definitions for the abducible predicates.

The paper is organized as follows: in Section 2 we recall the main concepts of Abductive Logic Programming, Inductive Logic Programming, and the definition of the abductive learning framework. Section 3 presents the learning algorithm while its properties are reported in Section 4. In Section 5 we apply LAP to the problem of learning exceptions to rules and learning from incomplete knowledge. Related works are discussed in Section 6. Section 7 concludes and presents directions for future works.

2 Abductive and Inductive Logic Programming

2.1 Abductive Logic Programming

An *abductive logic program* is a triple $\langle P, A, IC \rangle$ where:

– P is a normal logic program;

- A is a set of *abducible predicates*;
- IC is a set of integrity constraints in the form of denials, i.e.:
  $\leftarrow A_1, \ldots, A_m, not\ A_{m+1}, \ldots, not\ A_{m+n}$.

Abducible predicates (or simply abducibles) are the predicates about which assumptions (or abductions) can be made. These predicates carry all the incompleteness of the domain, they can have a partial definition or no definition at all, while all other predicates have a complete definition.

Negation as Failure is replaced, in ALP, by Negation by Default and is obtained by transforming the program into its *positive version*: each negative literal *not p(t)*, where t is a tuple of terms, is replaced by a literal *not_p(t)*, where *not_p* is a new predicate symbol. Moreover, for each predicate symbol p in the program, a new predicate symbol *not_p* is added to the set A and the integrity constraint $\leftarrow p(X), not\_p(X)$ is added to IC, where X is a tuple of variables. Atoms of the form *not_p(t)* are called *default atoms*. In the following, we will always consider the positive version of programs. This allows us to abduce either the truth or the falsity of atoms.

Given an abductive theory $AT = \langle P, A, IC \rangle$ and a formula G, the goal of abduction is to find a (possibly minimal) set of ground atoms Δ (*abductive explanation*) of predicates in A which, together with P, entails G, i.e., $P \cup \Delta \models G$. It is also required that the program $P \cup \Delta$ be consistent with respect to IC, i.e. $P \cup \Delta \models IC$. When there exists an abductive explanation for G in AT, we say that AT *abductively entails* G and we write $AT \models_A G$.

As model-theoretic semantics for ALP, we adopt the *abductive model* semantics defined in [9]. We do not want to enter into the details of the definition, we will just give the following proposition which will be useful throughout the paper.

We indicate with $\mathcal{L}^A$ the set of all atoms built from the predicates of A (called *abducible atoms*), including also default atoms.

Proposition 1. *Given an abductive model M for the abductive program $AT = \langle P, A, IC \rangle$, there exists a set of atoms $H \subseteq \mathcal{L}^A$ such that M is the least Herbrand model of $P \cup H$.*

Proof. Straightforward from the definition of abductive model (definition 5.7 in [9]).

In [24] a proof procedure for abductive logic programs has been defined. This procedure starts from a goal and a set of initial assumptions Δ_i and results in a set of consistent hypotheses (abduced literals) Δ_o such that $\Delta_o \supseteq \Delta_i$ and Δ_o together with the program P allow deriving the goal. The proof procedure uses the notion of *abductive* and *consistency derivations*. Intuitively, an abductive derivation is the standard Logic Programming derivation suitably extended in order to consider abducibles. As soon as an abducible atom δ is encountered, it is added to the current set of hypotheses, and it must be proved that any integrity constraint containing δ is satisfied. For this purpose, a consistency derivation for δ is started. Since the constraints are denials only (i.e., goals), this corresponds to proving that every such goal fails. Therefore, δ is removed from all the constraints containing it, and we prove that all the resulting goals fail. In this consistency derivation, when an abducible is encountered, an abductive derivation for its complement is started in order to prove the abducible's failure, so that the initial constraint is satisfied. When the procedure succeeds for the goal G and the initial set of assumptions Δ_i, producing as output the set of assumptions Δ_o, we say that T *abductively derives* G or that G is *abductively derivable* from T and we write $T \vdash_{\Delta_i}^{\Delta_o} G$.

In [9] it has been proved that the proof procedure is *sound* and *weakly complete* with respect to the abductive model semantics defined in [9] under a number of restrictions. We will present these results in detail in Section 4.

2.2   Inductive Logic Programming

The ILP problem can be defined as [6]:
Given:

- a set $\mathcal{P}$ of possible programs
- a set E^+ of positive examples
- a set E^- of negative examples
- a logic program B (*background knowledge*)

Find:

- a logic program $P \in \mathcal{P}$ such that
  - $\forall e^+ \in E^+, B \cup P \vdash e^+$ (*completeness*)
  - $\forall e^- \in E^-, B \cup P \not\vdash e^-$ (*consistency*).

Let us introduce some terminology. The program P that we want to learn is the *target program* and the predicates which are defined in it are *target predicates*. The sets E^+ and E^- are called *training sets* and contain ground atoms for the target predicates. The program B is called *background knowledge* and contains the definitions of the predicates that are already known. We say that the program P *covers* an example e if $P \cup B \vdash e$[1], i.e. if the theory "explains" the example. Therefore the conditions that the program P must satisfy in order to be a solution to the ILP problem can be expressed as "P must cover all positive examples and must not cover any negative example". A theory that covers all positive examples is said to be *complete* while a theory that does not cover any negative example is said to be *consistent*. The set $\mathcal{P}$ is called the *hypothesis space*. The importance of this set lies in the fact that it defines the search space of the ILP system. In order to be able to effectively learn a program, this space must be restricted as much as possible. If the space is too big, the search could result infeasible.

---

[1] In the ILP literature, the derivability relation is often used instead of entailment because real systems adopt the Prolog interpreter for testing the coverage of examples, that is not sound nor complete.

The *language bias* (or simply *bias* in this paper) is a description of the hypothesis space. Many formalisms have been introduced in order to describe this space [7], we will consider only a very simple bias in the form of a set of literals which are allowed in the body of clauses for target predicates.

Initialize $H := \emptyset$
repeat (*Covering loop*)
    Generate one clause c
    Remove from E^+ the e^+ covered by c
    Add c to H
until $E^+ = \emptyset$ (*Sufficiency stopping criterion*)

Generate one clause c:
Select a predicate p that must be learned
Initialize c to be $p(\overline{X}) \leftarrow$.
repeat (*Specialization loop*)
    Select a literal L from the language bias
    Add L to the body of c
    if c does not cover any positive example
        then backtrack to different choices for L
until c does not cover any negative example (*Necessity stopping criterion*)
return c
(or fail if backtracking exhausts all choices for L)

Fig. 1. Basic top-down ILP algorithm

There are two broad categories of ILP learning methods: *bottom-up* methods and *top-down* methods. In bottom-up methods clauses in P are generated by starting with a clause that covers one or more positive examples and no negative example, and by generalizing it as much as possible without covering any negative example. In top-down methods clauses in P are constructed starting with a general clause that covers all positive and negative examples and by specializing it until it does no longer cover any negative example while still covering at least one positive. In this paper, we concentrate on top-down methods. A basic top-down inductive algorithm [7,31] learns programs by generating clauses one after the other. A clause is generated by starting with an empty body and iteratively adding literals to the body. The basic inductive algorithm, adapted from [7] and [31], is sketched in Figure 1.

2.3   The New Learning Framework

We consider a new definition of the learning problem where both the background and target theory are abductive theories and the notion of deductive coverage above is replaced by abductive coverage.

Let us first define the *correctness* of an abductive logic program T with respect to the training set E^+, E^-. This notion replaces those of completeness and consistency for logic programs.

Definition 1 (Correctness). *An abductive logic program T is* correct, *with respect to E^+ and E^-, iff there exists $\Delta \subseteq \mathcal{L}^A$ such that*

$$T \vdash_\emptyset^\Delta E^+, not\_E^-$$

where $not\_E^- = \{not\_e^- | e^- \in E^-\}$ and E^+, not_E^- stands for the conjunction of each atom in E^+ and not_E^-

Definition 2 (Abductive Learning Problem).
Given:

- *a set $\mathcal{T}$ of possible abductive logic programs*
- *a set of positive examples E^+*
- *a set of negative examples E^-*
- *an abductive program $T = \langle P, A, IC \rangle$ as background theory*

Find:
A new abductive program $T' = \langle P \cup P', A, IC \rangle$ such that $T' \in \mathcal{T}$ and T' is correct wrt E^+ and E^-.

We say that a positive example e^+ is *covered* if $T \vdash_\emptyset^\Delta e^+$. We say that a negative example e^- is *not covered* (or *ruled out*) if $T \vdash_\emptyset^\Delta not\_e^-$. By employing the abductive proof procedure for the coverage of examples, we allow the system to make assumptions in order to cover positive examples and to avoid the coverage of negative examples. In this way, the system is able to complete a possibly incomplete background knowledge. Integrity constraints give some confidence in the correctness of the assumptions made.

Differently from the ILP problem, we require the conjunction of examples, instead of each example singularly, to be derivable. In this way we ensure that the abductive explanations for different examples are consistent with each other.

The abductive program that is learned can contain new rules (possibly containing abducibles in the body), but not new abducible predicates and new integrity constraints.

3 An Algorithm for Learning Abductive Logic Programs

In this section, we present the system LAP that is able to learn abductive logic programs according to definition 2. The algorithm is obtained from the basic top-down ILP algorithm (Figure 1), by adopting the abductive proof procedure, instead of the Prolog proof procedure, for testing the coverage of examples.

As the basic inductive algorithm, LAP is constituted by two nested loops: the covering loop (Figure 2) and the specialization loop (Figure 3). At each iteration of the covering loop, a new clause is generated such that it covers at least one

---

procedure LAP(
    inputs : E^+, E^- : training sets,
        $AT = \langle T, A, IC \rangle$: background abductive theory,
    outputs : H : learned theory, Δ : abduced literals)

$H := \emptyset$
$\Delta := \emptyset$
repeat
    GenerateRule(in: AT, E^+, E^-, H, Δ; out: $Rule, E^+_{Rule}, \Delta_{Rule}$)
    Add to E^+ all the positive literals of target predicates in Δ_{Rule}
    Add to E^- all the atoms corresponding to
        negative literals of target predicates in Δ_{Rule}
    $E^+ := E^+ - E^+_{Rule}$
    $H := H \cup \{Rule\}$
    $\Delta := \Delta \cup \Delta_{Rule}$
until $E^+ = \emptyset$ (Sufficiency stopping criterion)
output H

Fig. 2. The covering loop

---

procedure GenerateRule(
    inputs : AT, E^+, E^-, H, Δ
    outputs : $Rule$: rule,
        E^+_{Rule} : positive examples covered by $Rule$,
        Δ_{Rule} : abduced literals

Select a predicate to be learned p
Let $Rule = p(X) \leftarrow true$.
repeat (specialization loop)
    select a literal L from the language bias
    add L to the body of $Rule$
    TestCoverage(in: $Rule, AT, H, E^+, E^-, \Delta$,
        out: $E^+_{Rule}, E^-_{Rule}, \Delta_{Rule}$)
    if $E^+_{Rule} = \emptyset$
        backtrack to a different choice for L
until $E^-_{Rule} = \emptyset$ (Necessity stopping criterion)
output $Rule, E^+_{Rule}, \Delta_{Rule}$

Fig. 3. The specialization loop

procedure TestCoverage(
    inputs : $Rule, AT, H, E^+, E^-, \Delta$
    outputs: E^+_{Rule}, E^-_{Rule}: examples covered by $Rule$
       Δ_{Rule} : new set of abduced literals

$E^+_{Rule} = E^-_{Rule} = \emptyset$
$\Delta_{in} = \Delta$
for each $e^+ \in E^+$ **do**
    if AbductiveDerivation($\leftarrow e^+, \langle T \cup H \cup \{Rule\}, A, IC \rangle, \Delta_{in}, \Delta_{out}$)
        succeeds **then** Add e^+ to E^+_{Rule}; $\Delta_{in} = \Delta_{out}$
endfor
for each $e^- \in E^-$ **do**
    if AbductiveDerivation($\leftarrow not\_e^-, \langle T \cup H \cup \{Rule\}, A, IC \rangle, \Delta_{in}, \Delta_{out}$)
        succeeds **then** $\Delta_{in} = \Delta_{out}$
    else Add e^- to E^-_{Rule}
endfor
$\Delta_{Rule} = \Delta_{out} - \Delta$
output $E^+_{Rule}, E^-_{Rule}, \Delta_{Rule}$

Fig. 4. Coverage testing

positive example and no negative one. The positive examples covered by the rule are removed from the training set and a new iteration of the covering loop is started. The algorithm ends when the positive training set becomes empty. The new clause is generated in the specialization loop: we start with a clause with an empty body, and we add literals to the body until the clause does not cover any negative example while still covering at least one positive. The basic top-down algorithm is extended in the following respects.

First, in order to determine the positive examples E^+_{Rule} covered by the generated rule $Rule$ (procedure TestCoverage in Figure 4), an abductive derivation is started for each positive example. This derivation results in a (possibly empty) set of abduced literals. We give as input to the abductive procedure also the set of literals abduced in the derivations of previous examples. In this way, we ensure that the assumptions made during the derivation of the current example are consistent with the assumptions for other examples.

Second, in order to check that no negative example is covered ($E^-_{Rule} = \emptyset$ in Figure 3) by the generated rule $Rule$, an abductive derivation is started for the default negation of each negative example ($\leftarrow not\_e^-$). Also in this case, each derivation starts from the set of abducibles previously assumed. The set of abducibles is initialized to the empty set at the beginning of the computation, and is gradually extended as it is passed on from derivation to derivation. This is done as well across different clauses.

Third, after the generation of each clause, the literals of target predicates that have been abduced are added to the training set, so that they become new training examples. For each positive abduced literal of the form $abd(c^+)$ where c^+ is a tuple of constants, the new positive example $abd(c^+)$ is added to E^+

set, while for each negative literal of the form $not\_abd(c^-)$ the negative example $abd(c^-)$ is added to E^-.

In order to be able to learn exceptions to rules, we include a number of predicates of the form not_abnorm_i/n in the bias of each target predicate of the form p/n. Moreover, $abnorm_i/n$ and not_abnorm_i/n are added to the set of abducible predicates and the constraint

$$\leftarrow abnorm_i(X), not\_abnorm_i(X).$$

is added to the background knowledge. In this way, when the current partial rule in the specialization loop still covers some negative examples and no other literal can be added that would make it consistent, the rule is specialized by adding the literal $not\_abnorm_i(X)$ to its body. Negative examples previously covered are ruled out by abducing for them facts of the form $abnorm_i(c^-)$, while positive examples will be covered by abducing the facts $not\_abnorm_i(c^+)$ and these facts are added to the training set.

We are now able to learn rules for $abnorm_i/n$, thus resulting in a definition for the exceptions to the current rule. For this purpose, predicates $abnorm_i/n$ are considered as target predicates, and we define a bias for them. Since we may have exceptions to exceptions, we may also include a number of literals of the form $not\_abnorm_j(X)$ in the bias for $abnorm_i/n$.

The system has been implemented in Prolog using Sicstus Prolog 3#5.

4   Properties of the Algorithm

LAP is sound, under some restrictions, but not complete. In this section we give a proof of its soundness, and we point out the reasons of incompleteness.

Let us first adapt the definitions of soundness and completeness for an inductive inference machine, as given by [7], to the new problem definition. We will call Abductive Inductive Inference Machine (AIIM) an algorithm that solves the Abductive Learning Problem. If M is an AIIM, we write $M(\mathcal{T}, E^+, E^-, B) = T$ to indicate that, given the hypothesis space $\mathcal{T}$, positive and negative examples E^+ and E^-, and a background knowledge B, the machine outputs a program T. We write $M(\mathcal{T}, E^+, E^-, B) = \bot$ when M does not produce any output.

With respect to the abductive learning problem (definition 2), the definitions of soundness and completeness are:

Definition 3 (Soundness). *An AIIM M is sound iff if $M(\mathcal{T}, E^+, E^-, B) = T$, then $T \in \mathcal{T}$ and T is correct with respect to E^+ and E^-.*

Definition 4 (Completeness). *An AIIM M is complete iff if $M(\mathcal{T}, E^+, E^-, B) = \bot$, then there is no $T \in \mathcal{T}$ that is correct with respect to E^+ and E^-.*

The proof of LAP soundness is based on the theorems of soundness and weak completeness of the abductive proof procedure given in [9]. We will first present the results of soundness and completeness for the proof procedure and then we will prove the soundness of our algorithm.

The theorems of soundness and weak completeness (theorems 7.3 and 7.4 in [9]) have been extended by considering the goal to be proved as a conjunction of abducible and non-abducible atoms (instead of a single non-abducible atom) and by considering an initial set of assumptions Δ_i. The proofs are straightforward, given the original theorems.

Theorem 1 (Soundness). *Let us consider an abductive logic program T. Let L be a conjunction of atoms. If $T \vdash^{\Delta_o}_{\Delta_i} L$, then there exists an abductive model M of T such that $M \models L$ and $\Delta_o \subseteq M \cap \mathcal{L}^{\mathcal{A}}$.*

Theorem 2 (Weak completeness). *Let us consider an abductive logic program T. Let L be a conjunction of atoms. Suppose that every selection of rules in the proof procedure for L terminates with either success or failure. If there exists an abductive model M of T such that $M \models L$, then there exists a selection of rules such that the derivation procedure for L succeeds in T returning Δ, where $\Delta \subseteq M \cap \mathcal{L}^{\mathcal{A}}$.*

We need as well the following lemma.

Lemma 1. *Let us consider an abductive logic program $T = \langle P, A, I \rangle$. Let L be a conjunction of atoms. If $T \vdash^A_\emptyset L$ then $lhm(P \cup \Delta) \models L$, where $lhm(P \cup \Delta)$ is the least Herbrand model of $P \cup \Delta$.*

Proof. Follows directly from theorem 5 in [18].

The theorems of soundness and weak completeness for the abductive proof procedure are true under a number of assumptions:

- the abductive logic program must be ground
- the abducibles must not have a definition in the program
- the integrity constraints are denials with at least one abducible in each constraint.

Moreover, the weak completeness theorem is limited by the assumption that the proof procedure for L always terminates.

The soundness of LAP is limited as well by these assumptions. However, they do not severely restrict the generality of the system. In fact, the requirement that the program is ground can be met for programs with no function symbols. In this case the Herbrand universe is finite and we obtain a finite ground program from a non-ground one by grounding in all possible ways the rules and constraints in the program. This restriction is also assumed in many ILP systems (such as FOIL [37], RUTH [1], [11]).

The restriction on the absence of a (partial) definition for the abducible does not reduce the generality of the results since, when abducible predicates have definitions in T, we can apply a transformation to T so that the resulting program T' has no definition for abducible predicates. This is done by introducing an auxiliary predicate δ_a/n for each abducible predicate a/n and by adding the clause:

$$a(x) \leftarrow \delta_a(x).$$

The predicate a/n is no longer abducible, whereas δ_a/n is now abducible. In this way, we are able to deal as well with partial definitions for abducible predicates, and this is particularly important when learning from incomplete data, because the typical situation is exactly to have a partial definition for some predicates, as will be shown in Section 5.2.

The requirement that each integrity constraint contains an abducible literal is not restrictive because we use constraints only for limiting assumptions and therefore a constraint without an abducible literal would be useless.

The most restrictive requirement is the one on the termination of the proof procedure. However, it can be proved that the procedure always terminates for *call-consistent* programs, i.e. if no predicate depends on itself through an odd number of negative recursive calls (e.g., $p \leftarrow not\_p$).

We need as well the following theorem. It expresses a restricted form of monotonicity that holds for abductive logic programs.

Theorem 3. *Let* $T = \langle P, A, I \rangle$ *and* $T' = \langle P \cup P', A, I \rangle$ *be abductive logic programs. If* $T \vdash_{\emptyset}^{\Delta_1} L_1$ *and* $T' \vdash_{\Delta_1}^{\Delta_2} L_2$, *where* L_1 *and* L_2 *are two conjunctions of atoms, then* $T \vdash_{\emptyset}^{\Delta_2} L_1 \wedge L_2$.

Proof. From $T \vdash_{\emptyset}^{\Delta_1} L_1$ and lemma 1 we have that

$$lhm(P \cup \Delta_1) \models L_1$$

From the definition of abductive proof procedure we have that $\Delta_1 \subseteq \Delta_2$. Since we consider the positive version of programs, $P \cup \Delta_1$ and $P \cup P' \cup \Delta_2$ are definite logic programs. From the monotonicity of definite logic programs $lhm(P \cup \Delta_1) \subseteq lhm(P \cup P' \cup \Delta_2)$ therefore

$$lhm(P \cup P' \cup \Delta_2) \models L_1$$

From $T' \vdash_{\Delta_1}^{\Delta_2} L_2$, by the soundness of the abductive proof procedure, we have that there exists an abductive model M_2 such that $M_2 \models L_2$ and $\Delta_2 \subseteq M_2 \cap \mathcal{L}^A$. From proposition 1, there exists a set $H_2 \subseteq \mathcal{L}^A$ such that $M_2 = lhm(P \cup P' \cup H_2)$. Since abducible and default predicates have no definition in $P \cup P'$, we have that $M_2 \cap \mathcal{L}^A = H_2$ and $\Delta_2 \subseteq H_2$. Therefore $M_2 \supseteq lhm(P \cap P' \cap \Delta_2)$ and

$$M_2 \models L_1$$

From $M_2 \models L_2$ and from the weak completeness of the abductive proof procedure, we have that

$$T' \vdash_{\Delta_1}^{\Delta_2} L_1 \wedge L_2$$

We can now give the soundness theorem for our algorithm.

Theorem 4 (Soundness). *The AIIM LAP is sound.*

Proof. Let us consider first the case in which the target predicates are not abducible and therefore no assumption is added to the training set during the computation. In order to prove that the algorithm is sound, we have to prove that, for any given sets E^+ and E^-, the program T' that is output by the algorithm is such that

$$T' \vdash_\emptyset^\Delta E^+, not\_E^-$$

LAP learns the program T' by iteratively adding a new clause to the current hypothesis, initially empty. Each clause is tested by trying an abductive derivation for each positive and for complement of each negative example. Let $E_c^+ = \{e_1^+ \ldots e_{n_c}^+\}$ be the set of positive examples whose conjunction is covered by clause c and let $E^- = \{e_1^- \ldots e_m^-\}$. Clause c is added to the current hypothesis H when:

$$\exists E_c^+ \subseteq E^+ : \quad E_c^+ \neq \emptyset, \ \forall i \in \{1 \ldots n_c\} : \quad P \cup H \cup \{c\} \vdash_{\Delta_{i-1}^+}^{\Delta_i^+} e_i^+$$

$$\forall j \in \{1 \ldots m\} : \quad P \cup H \cup \{c\} \vdash_{\Delta_{j-1}^-}^{\Delta_j^-} not\_e_j^-$$

where $\Delta_0^+ = \Delta_H$, $\Delta_{i-1}^+ \subseteq \Delta_i^+$ and $\Delta_0^- = \Delta_{n_c}^+$. By induction on the examples and by theorem 3 with $P' = \emptyset$, we can prove that

$$\langle P \cup H \cup \{c\}, A, IC \rangle \vdash_{\Delta_H}^{\Delta_{H \cup \{c\}}} E_c^+, not\_E^-$$

where $\Delta_{H \cup \{c\}} = \Delta_m^-$. At this point, it is possible to prove that

$$T' \vdash_\emptyset^\Delta E_{c_1}^+ \cup \ldots \cup E_{c_k}^+, not\_E^-$$

by induction on the clauses and by theorem 3. From this and from the sufficiency stopping criterion (see Figure 2) we have that $E_{c_1}^+ \cup \ldots \cup E_{c_k}^+ = E^+$.

We now have to prove soundness when the target predicates are abducible as well and the training set is enlarged during the computation. In this case, if the final training sets are E_F^+ and E_F^-, we have to prove that

$$T' \vdash_\emptyset^\Delta E_F^+, not\_E_F^-$$

If a positive assumption is added to E^+, then the resulting program will contain a clause that will cover it because of the sufficiency stopping criterion. If a negative assumption not_e^- is added to E^- obtaining E'^-, clauses that are added afterwards will derive $not\_E'^-$. We have to prove also that clauses generated before allow $not\_E'^-$ to be derived. Consider a situation where not_e^- has been assumed during the testing of the last clause added to H. We have to prove that

$$\langle P \cup H, A, IC \rangle \vdash_\emptyset^\Delta E_H^+, not\_E^- \Rightarrow \langle P \cup H, A, IC \rangle \vdash_\emptyset^\Delta E_H^+, not\_E'^-$$

where $not\_e^- \in \Delta$ and $e^- \in E'^-$. From the left part of the implication and for the soundness of the abductive proof procedure, we have that there exists an abductive model M such that $\Delta \subseteq M \cap \mathcal{L}^A$. From $not\_e^- \in \Delta$, we have that $not\_e^- \in M$ and therefore by weak completeness

$$\langle P \cup H, A, IC \rangle \vdash_\emptyset^\Delta not\_e^-$$

By induction and by theorem 3, we have the right part of the implication.

We turn now to the incompleteness of the algorithm. LAP is incomplete because a number of choice points have been overlooked in order to reduce the computational complexity. The first source of incompleteness comes from the fact that, after a clause is added to the theory, it is never retracted. Thus, it can be the case that a clause not in the solution is learned and the restrictions imposed on the rest of the learning process by the clause (through the examples covered and their respective assumptions) prevent the system from finding a solution even if there is one. In fact, the algorithm performs only a greedy search in the space of possible programs, exploring completely only the smaller space of possible clauses. However, this source of incompleteness is not specific to LAP because most ILP systems perform such a greedy search in the programs space.

The following source of incompleteness, instead, is specific to LAP. For each example, there may be more than one explanation and, depending on the one we choose, the coverage of other examples can be influenced. An explanation Δ_1 for the example e_1 may prevent the coverage of example e_2, because there may not be an explanation for e_2 that is consistent with Δ_1, while a different choice for Δ_1 would have allowed such a coverage. Thus, in case of a failure in finding a solution, we should backtrack on example explanations.

We decided to overlook these choice points in order to obtain an algorithm that is more effective in the average case, but we might not have done so. In fact, these choice points have a high computational cost, and they must be considered only when a high number of different explanations is available for each example. However, this happens only for the cases in which examples are highly interrelated, i.e., there are relations between them or between objects (constants) related to them. This case is not very common in concept learning, where examples represent instances of a concept and the background represents information about each instance and its possible parts. In most cases, instances are separate entities that have few relations with other entities.

5   Examples

5.1   Learning Exceptions

In this section, we show how LAP learns exceptions to classification rules. The example is taken from [16].

Let us consider the following abductive background theory $B = \langle P, A, IC \rangle$ and training sets E^+ and E^-:

$P = \{bird(X) \quad \leftarrow penguin(X).$
$\quad penguin(X) \leftarrow superpenguin(X).$
$\quad bird(a). \quad bird(b). \quad penguin(c). \quad penguin(d).$
$\quad superpenguin(e). \quad superpenguin(f).\}$
$A = \{abnorm_1/1, abnorm_2/1, not\_abnorm_1/1, not\_abnorm_2/1\}$
$IC = \{\leftarrow abnorm_1(X), not\_abnorm_1(X).$
$\quad \leftarrow abnorm_2(X), not\_abnorm_2(X).\}$
$\quad \leftarrow flies(X), not\_flies(X).\}$

$E^+ = \{flies(a), flies(b), flies(e), flies(f)\}$
$E^- = \{flies(c), flies(d)\}$

Moreover, let the bias be:

$flies(X) \leftarrow \alpha$ where $\alpha \subset \{superpenguin(X), penguin(X), bird(X),$
$\qquad\qquad\qquad\qquad\quad not\_abnorm_1(X), not\_abnorm_2(X)\}$
$abnorm_1(X) \leftarrow \beta$ and $abnorm_2(X) \leftarrow \beta$ where
$\qquad\qquad\qquad \beta \subset \{superpenguin(X), penguin(X), bird(X)\}$

The algorithm first generates the following rule (R_1):

$\quad flies(X) \leftarrow superpenguin(X).$

which covers $flies(e)$ and $flies(f)$ that are removed from E^+. Then, in the specialization loop, the rule $R_2 = flies(X) \leftarrow bird(X).$ is generated which covers all the remaining positive examples $flies(a)$ and $flies(b)$, but also the negative ones. In fact, the abductive derivations for $not\_flies(c)$ and $not\_flies(d)$ fail. Therefore, the rule must be further specialized by adding a new literal. The abducible literal not_abnorm_1 is added to the body of R_2 obtaining R_3:

$\quad flies(X) \leftarrow bird(X), not\_abnorm_1(X).$

Now, the abductive derivations for the negative examples $flies(a)$ and $flies(b)$ succeed abducing $\{not\_abnorm_1(a), not\_abnorm_1(b)\}$ and the derivations $not\_flies(c)$ and $not\_flies(d)$ succeed abducing $\{abnorm_1(c), abnorm_1(d)\}$.

At this point the system adds the literals abduced to the training set and tries to generalize them, by generating a rule for $abnorm_1/1$. Positive abduced literals for $abnorm_1/1$ form the set E^+, while negative abduced literals form the set E^-. The resulting induced rule is (R_4):

$\quad abnorm_1(X) \leftarrow penguin(X).$

No positive example is now left in the training set therefore the algorithm ends by producing the following abductive rules:

$\quad flies(X) \leftarrow superpenguin(X).$
$\quad flies(X) \leftarrow bird(X), not\_abnorm_1(X).$
$\quad abnorm_1(X) \leftarrow penguin(X).$

A result similar to ours is obtained in [16], but exploiting "classical" negation and priority relations between rules rather than abduction. By integrating induction and abduction, we obtain a system that is more general than [16].

5.2   Learning from Incomplete Knowledge

Abduction is particularly suitable for modelling domains in which there is incomplete knowledge. In this example, we want to learn a definition for the concept *father* from a background knowledge containing facts about the concepts *parent* and *male*. Knowledge about *male* is incomplete and we can make assumptions about it by considering it as an abducible. We have the abductive background theory $B = \langle P, A, IC \rangle$ and training set:

$P = \{$ $parent(john, mary).$ $male(john).$
    $parent(david, steve).$ $parent(kathy, ellen).$
    $female(kathy).\}$
$A = \{male/1, female/1\}$
$IC = \{\leftarrow male(X), female(X).\}$
$E^+ = \{father(john, mary), father(david, steve)\}$
$E^- = \{father(john, steve), father(kathy, ellen)\}$

Moreover, let the bias be

$father(X, Y) \leftarrow \alpha$ where $\alpha \subset \{parent(X, Y), parent(Y, X),$
                    $male(X), male(Y), female(X), female(Y)\}$

At the first iteration of the specialization loop, the algorithm generates the rule
    $father(X, Y) \leftarrow .$
which covers all the positive examples but also all the negative ones. Therefore another iteration is started and the literal $parent(X, Y)$ is added to the rule
    $father(X, Y) \leftarrow parent(X, Y).$
This clause also covers all the positive examples but also the negative example
    $father(kathy, ellen).$
Note that up to this point no abducible literal has been added to the rule, therefore no abduction has been made and the set Δ is still empty. Now, an abducible literal is added to the rule, $male(X)$, obtaining
    $father(X, Y) \leftarrow parent(X, Y), male(X).$
At this point the coverage of examples is tested. $father(john, mary)$ is covered abducing nothing because we have the fact $male(john)$ in the background. The other positive example, $father(david, steve)$, is covered with the abduction of the following set: $\{male(david), not\_female(david)\}$.

Then the coverage of negative examples is tested by starting the abductive derivations

    $\leftarrow not\_father(john, steve).$

    $\leftarrow not\_father(kathy, ellen).$

The first derivation succeeds with an empty explanation while the second succeeds abducing $not\_male(kathy)$ which is consistent with the fact $female(kathy)$ and the constraint $\leftarrow male(X), female(X)$. Now, no negative example is covered, therefore the specialization loop ends. No atom from Δ is added to the training set because the predicates of abduced literals are not target. The positive examples covered by the rules are removed from the training set which becomes empty. Therefore also the covering loop terminates and the algorithm ends, returning the rule

    $father(X, Y) \leftarrow parent(X, Y), male(X).$
and the assumptions

    $\Delta = \{male(david), not\_female(david), not\_male(kathy)\}.$

6   Related Work

We will first mention our previous work in the field, and then related work by other authors.

In [29] we have presented the definition of the extended learning problem and a preliminary version of the algorithm for learning abductive rules.

In [30] we have proposed an algorithm for learning abductive rules obtained modifying the extensional ILP system FOIL [37]. Extensional systems differ from intensional ones (as the one presented in this paper) because they employ a different notion of coverage, namely *extensional coverage*. We say that the program P *extensionally covers* example e if there exists a clause of P, $l \leftarrow l_1, \ldots, l_n$ such that $l = e$ and for all i, $l_i \in E^+ \cup lhm(B)$. Thus examples can be used also for the coverage of other examples. This has the advantage of allowing the system to learn clauses independently from each other, avoiding the need for considering different orders in learning the clauses and the need for backtracking on clause addition. However, it has also a number of disadvantages (see [13] for a discussion about them). In [30] we have shown how the integration of abduction and induction can solve some of the problems of extensional systems when dealing with recursive predicates and programs with negation.

In [17] the authors discuss various approaches for the integration of abduction and induction. They examine how abduction can be related to induction specifically in the case of Explanation Based Learning, Inductive Learning and Theory Revision. The authors introduce the definition of a learning problem integrating abduction (called Abductive Concept Learning) that has much inspired our work. Rather than considering it as the definition of a problem to be solved and presenting an algorithm for it, they employ the definition as a general framework where to describe specific cases of integration.

Our definition differs from Abductive Concept Learning on the condition that is imposed on negative examples: in [17] the authors require that negative examples not be abductively entailed by the theory. Our condition is weaker because it requires that there be an explanation for not_e^-, which is easier to be met than requiring that there is no explanation for e^-. In fact, if there is an explanation for not_e^-, this does not exclude that there is an explanation also for e^-, while if there is no explanation for e^- then there is certainly an explanation for not_e^-. We consider a weaker condition on negative examples because the strong condition is difficult to be satisfied without learning integrity constraints. For example, in section 5.2, the learned program also satisfies the stronger condition of [17], because for the negative example $father(kathy, ellen)$ the only abductive explanation $\{male(kathy)\}$ is inconsistent with the integrity constraint $\leftarrow male(X), female(X)$. However, if that constraint was not available in the background, the stronger condition would not be satisfiable.

Moreover, in [17] the authors suggest another approach for the integration of abduction in learning that consists in explaining the training data of a learning problem in order to generate suitable or relevant background data on which to base the inductive generalization. Differently from us, the authors allow the use of integrity constraints for rule specialization, while we rely only on the addition of a literal to the body of the clause. Adding integrity constraints for specializing rules means that each atom derived by using the rules must be checked against the constraints, which can be computationally expensive. Moreover, the results of soundness and weak completeness can not be used anymore for the extended proof procedure.

In [2] an integrated abductive and inductive framework is proposed in which abductive explanations that may include general rules can be generated by incorporating an inductive learning method into abduction. The authors transform a proof procedure for abduction, namely SLDNFA, into a proof procedure for induction, called SLDNFAI. Informally, SLDNFA is modified so that abduction is replaced by induction: when a goal can not be proven, instead of adding it to the theory as a fact, an inductive procedure is called that generates a rule covering the goal. However, the resulting learning is not able to a learn a rule and, at the same time, make specific assumptions about missing data in order to cover examples.

The integration of induction and abduction for knowledge base updating has been studied in [11] and [1]. Both systems proposed in these papers perform incremental theory revision: they automatically modify a knowledge base when it violates a newly supplied integrity constraint. When a constraint is violated, they first extract an uncovered positive example or a covered negative example from the constraint and then they revise the theory in order to make it consistent with the example, using techniques from incremental concept learning. The system in [11] differs from the system in [1] (called RUTH) because it relies on an oracle for the extraction of examples from constraints, while RUTH works non interactively. Once the example has been extracted from the constraint, both systems call similar inductive operators in order to update the knowledge base. In [11] the authors use the inductive operators of Shapiro's MIS system [38].

In [28], we have shown that LAP can be used to perform the knowledge base updating tasks addressed by the systems in [11] and [1], by exploiting the abductive proof procedure in order to extract new examples from a constraint on target predicates. While systems in [11, 1] can generate examples that violate other integrity constraints and new inconsistencies have to be recovered at the next iteration of the learning loop, in [28] we are able to select the examples that allow the minimal revision of the theory. Another relevant difference is that our system is a batch learner while the systems in [11, 1] are incremental learners: since we have all the examples available at the beginning of the learning process, we generate only clauses that do not cover negative examples and therefore we do not have to revise the theory to handle covered negative examples, i.e., to retract clauses. As regards the operators that are used in order to handle uncovered positive examples, we are able to generate a clause that covers a positive example by also making some assumptions, while in [11] they can cover an example either by generating a clause or by assuming a fact for covering it, but not the two things at the same time. RUTH, instead, is able to do this, and therefore would be able to solve the problem presented in Section 5.2. Moreover,

RUTH considers abduced literals as new examples, therefore it would be able to solve as well the problems in Section 5.1.

As concerns the treatment of exceptions to induced rules, it is worth mentioning that our treatment of exceptions by means of the addition of a non-abnormality literal to each rule is similar to the one in [35]. The difference is that the system in [35] performs declarative debugging, not learning, therefore no rule is generated. In order to debug a logic program, in [35] the authors first transform it by adding a different default literal to each rule in order to cope with inconsistency, and add a rule (with an abducible in the body) for each predicate in order to cope with predicate incompleteness. These literals are then used as assumptions of the correctness of the rule, to be possibly revised in the face of a wrong solution. The debugging algorithm determines, by means of abduction, the assumptions that led to the wrong solution, thus identifying the incorrect rules.

In [5] the authors have shown that is not possible, in general, to preserve correct information when incrementally specializing within a classical logic framework, and when learning exceptions in particular. They avoid this drawback by using learning algorithms which employ a nonmonotonic knowledge representation. Several other authors have also addressed this problem, in the context of Logic Programming, by allowing for exceptions to (possibly induced) rules [16, 10]. In these frameworks, nonmonotonicity and exceptions are dealt with by learning logic programs with negation. Our approach in the treatment of exceptions is very related to [16]. They rely on a language which uses a limited form of "classical" (or, better, syntactic) negation together with a priority relation among the sentences of the program [25]. However, in [20] it has been shown that negation by default can be seen as a special case of abduction. Thus, in our framework, by relying on ALP, we can achieve greater generality than [16]: besides learning exceptions, LAP is able to learn from incomplete knowledge and to learn theories for abductive reasoning.

In what concerns learning from incomplete information, many ILP systems include facilities in order to handle this problem, for example FOIL [37], Progol [34], mFOIL [19]. The approach that is followed by all these systems is fundamentally different with respect to ours: they are all based on the use of heuristic necessity and sufficiency stopping criteria and of special heuristic functions for guiding the search. The heuristic stopping criteria relaxes the requirements of consistency and completeness of the learned theory: the theory must cover (not cover) "most" positive (negative) examples, where the exact amount of "most" is determined heuristically. These techniques allow the systems to deal with imperfect data in general, including noisy data (data with random errors in training examples and in the background knowledge) and incomplete data. In this sense, their approach is more general than ours, because we are not able to deal with noisy data. Their approach is equivalent to discarding some examples, considering them as noisy or insufficiently specified, while in our approach no example is discarded, the theory must be complete and consistent (in the abductive sense) with each example.

7   Conclusions and Future Work

We have presented the system LAP for learning abductive logic programs. We consider an extended ILP problem in which both the background and target theory are abductive theories and coverage by deduction is replaced with coverage by abduction.

In the system, abduction is used for making assumptions about incomplete predicates of the background knowledge in order to cover the examples. In this way, general rules are generated together with specific assumptions relative to single examples. If these assumptions regard an abnormality literal, they can be used as examples for learning a definition for the class of exceptions.

LAP is obtained from the basic top-down ILP algorithm by substituting, for the coverage testing, the Prolog proof procedure with an abductive proof procedure. LAP has been implemented in Sicstus Prolog 3#5: the code of the system and of the examples shown in the paper are available at <URL:http://www-lia.deis.unibo.it/Staff/FabrizioRiguzzi/LAP.html}>.

In the future, we will test the algorithm on real domains where there is incompleteness of the data. As regards the theoretical aspects, we will investigate the problem of extending the proposed algorithm in order to learn full abductive theories, including integrity constraints as well. The integration of the algorithm with other systems for learning constraints, such as Claudien [12] and ICL [14], as proposed in [27], seems very promising in this respect.

Our approach seems also promising for learning logic programs with two kinds of negation (e.g., default negation and explicit negation), provided that positive and negative examples are exchanged when learning a definition for the (explicit) negation of a concept, and suitable integrity constraints are added to the learned theory so as to ensure non-contradictoriness. This is also subject for future work.

Acknowledgment

We would like to thank the anonymous referees and participants of the post-ILPS97 Workshop on Logic Programming and Knowledge Representation for useful comments and insights on this work. Fabrizio Riguzzi would like to thank Antonis Kakas for many interesting discussions on the topics of this paper they had while he was visiting the University of Cyprus.

References

1. H. Adé and M. Denecker. RUTH: An ILP theory revision system. In *Proceedings of the 8th International Symposium on Methodologies for Intelligent Systems*, 1994.
2. H. Adé and M. Denecker. AILP: Abductive inductive logic programming. In *Proceedings of the 14th International Joint Conference on Artificial Intelligence*, 1995.

3. J. J. Alferes and L. M. Pereira. *Reasoning with Logic Programming*, volume 1111 of *LNAI*. SV, Heidelberg, 1996.
4. M. Bain and S. Muggleton. Non-monotonic learning. In S. Muggleton, editor, *Inductive Logic Programming*, chapter 7, pages 145–161. Academic Press, 1992.
5. M. Bain and S. Muggleton. Non-monotonic learning. In S. Muggleton, editor, *Inductive Logic Programming*, pages 145–161. Academic Press, 1992.
6. F. Bergadano and D. Gunetti. Learning Clauses by Tracing Derivations. In *Proceedings 4th Int. Workshop on Inductive Logic Programming*, 1994.
7. F. Bergadano and D. Gunetti. *Inductive Logic Programming*. MIT press, 1995.
8. F. Bergadano, D. Gunetti, M. Nicosia, and G. Ruffo. Learning logic programs with negation as failure. In L. De Raedt, editor, *Advances in Inductive Logic Programming*, pages 107–123. IOS Press, 1996.
9. A. Brogi, E. Lamma, P. Mancarella, and P. Mello. A unifying view for logic programming with non-monotonic reasoning. *Theoretical Computer Science*, 184:1–59, 1997.
10. L. De Raedt and M. Bruynooghe. On negation and three-valued logic in interactive concept learning. In *Proceedings of the 9th European Conference on Artificial Intelligence*, 1990.
11. L. De Raedt and M. Bruynooghe. Belief updating from integrity constraints and queries. *Artificial Intelligence*, 53:291–307, 1992.
12. L. De Raedt and M. Bruynooghe. A theory of clausal discovery. In *Proceedings of the 13th International Joint Conference on Artificial Intelligence*, 1993.
13. L. De Raedt, N. Lavrač, and S. Džeroski. Multiple predicate learning. In S. Muggleton, editor, *Proceedings of the 3rd International Workshop on Inductive Logic Programming*, pages 221–240. J. Stefan Institute, 1993.
14. L. De Raedt and W. Van Lear. Inductive constraint logic. In *Proceedings of the 5th International Workshop on Algorithmic Learning Theory*, 1995.
15. M. Denecker, L. De Raedt, P. Flach, and A. Kakas, editors. *Proceedings of ECAI96 Workshop on Abductive and Inductive Reasoning*. Catholic University of Leuven, 1996.
16. Y. Dimopoulos and A. Kakas. Learning Non-monotonic Logic Programs: Learning Exceptions. In *Proceedings of the 8th European Conference on Machine Learning*, 1995.
17. Y. Dimopoulos and A. Kakas. Abduction and inductive learning. In *Advances in Inductive Logic Programming*. IOS Press, 1996.
18. P.M. Dung. Negation as hypothesis: An abductive foundation for logic programming. In K. Furukawa, editor, *Proceedings of the 8th International Conference on Logic Programming*, pages 3–17. MIT Press, 1991.
19. S. Džeroski. Handling noise in inductive logic programming. Master's thesis, Faculty of Electrical Engineering and Computer Science, University of Ljubljana, 1991.
20. K. Eshghi and R.A. Kowalski. Abduction compared with Negation by Failure. In *Proceedings of the 6th International Conference on Logic Programming*, 1989.
21. F. Esposito, E. Lamma, D. Malerba, P. Mello, M. Milano, F. Riguzzi, and G. Semeraro. Learning abductive logic programs. In Denecker et al. [15].
22. C. Hartshorne and P. Weiss, editors. *Collected Papers of Charles Sanders Peirce, 1931-1958*, volume 2. Harvards University Press, 1965.
23. A.C. Kakas, R.A. Kowalski, and F. Toni. Abductive logic programming. *Journal of Logic and Computation*, 2:719–770, 1993.

24. A.C. Kakas and P. Mancarella. On the relation between truth maintenance and abduction. In *Proceedings of the 2nd Pacific Rim International Conference on Artificial Intelligence*, 1990.
25. A.C. Kakas, P. Mancarella, and P.M. Dung. The acceptability semantics for logic programs. In *Proceedings of the 11th International Conference on Logic Programming*, 1994.
26. A.C. Kakas and F. Riguzzi. Learning with abduction. Technical Report TR-96-15, University of Cyprus, Computer Science Department, 1996.
27. A.C. Kakas and F. Riguzzi. Learning with abduction. In *Proceedings of the 7th International Workshop on Inductive Logic Programming*, 1997.
28. E. Lamma, P. Mello, M. Milano, and F. Riguzzi. Integrating induction and abduction in logic programming. To appear on Information Sciences.
29. E. Lamma, P. Mello, M. Milano, and F. Riguzzi. Integrating Induction and Abduction in Logic Programming. In P. P. Wang, editor, *Proceedings of the Third Joint Conference on Information Sciences*, volume 2, pages 203–206, 1997.
30. E. Lamma, P. Mello, M. Milano, and F. Riguzzi. Introducing Abduction into (Extensional) Inductive Logic Programming Systems. In M. Lenzerini, editor, *AI*IA97, Advances in Artificial Intelligence, Proceedings of the 5th Congress of the Italian Association for Artificial Intelligence*, number 1321 in LNAI. Springer-Verlag, 1997.
31. N. Lavrač and S. Džeroski. *Inductive Logic Programming: Techniques and Applications*. Ellis Horwood, 1994.
32. L. Martin and C. Vrain. A three-valued framework for the induction of general logic programs. In *Advances in Inductive Logic Programming*. IOS Press, 1996.
33. R. Michalski, J.G. Carbonell, and T.M. Mitchell (eds). *Machine Learning - An Artificial Intelligence Approach*. Springer-Verlag, 1984.
34. S. Muggleton. Inverse entailment and Progol. *New Generation Computing, Special issue on Inductive Logic Programming*, 13(3-4):245–286, 1995.
35. L. M. Pereira, C. V. Damásio, and J. J. Alferes. Diagnosis and debugging as contradiction removal. In L. M. Pereira and A. Nerode, editors, *Proceedings of the 2nd International Workshop on Logic Programming and Non-monotonic Reasoning*, pages 316–330. MIT Press, 1993.
36. D.L. Poole. A logical framework for default reasoning. *Artificial Intelligence*, 32, 1988.
37. J. R. Quinlan and R.M. Cameron-Jones. Induction of Logic Programs: FOIL and Related Systems. *New Generation Computing*, 13:287–312, 1995.
38. E. Shapiro. *Algorithmic Program Debugging*. MIT Press, 1983.

Refining Action Theories through Abductive Logic Programming

Renwei Li[1], Luis Moniz Pereira[1], and Veronica Dahl[2]

[1] Center for Artificial Intelligence (CENTRIA)
Department of Computer Science
Universidade Nova de Lisboa
2825 Monte de Caparica, Portugal
{renwei,lmp}@di.fct.unl.pt

[2] School of Computing Science
Simon Fraser University
Burnaby, B.C. V5A 1S6, Canada
veronica@cs.sfu.ca

Abstract. Reasoning about actions and changes often starts with an action theory which is then used for planning, prediction or explanation. In practice it is sometimes not simple to give an immediately available action theory. In this paper we will present an abductive methodology for describing action domains. We start with an action theory which is not complete, i.e., has more than one model. Then, after some tests are done, we can abduce a complete action theory. Technically, we use a high level action language to describe incomplete domains and tests. Then, we present a translation from domain descriptions to abductive logic programs. Using tests, we then abductively refine an original domain description to a new one which is closer to the domain in reality. The translation has been shown to be both sound and complete. The result of this paper can be used not only for refinement of domain descriptions but also for abductive planning, prediction and explanation. The methodology presented in this paper has been implemented by an abductive logic programming system.

1 Introduction

When reasoning about actions and changes, we often assume that an action theory has been given and described in a formal language or in a framework, e.g. situation calculus [15], event calculus [10], action description languages $\mathcal{A}$ [7] and ADL [16],

the fluent-features framework (FFF) [19], and their variants or extensions. But little work has been reported on how to obtain an action theory. Assume that we want to generate a plan to make the world in a definite state (goal), but we are not certain about the initial state and the effects of available actions. For example, let's consider Vladimir Lifschitz' challenge problem[1]:

---

[1] Vladimir Lifschitz's email message to lmp@di.fct.unl.pt and renwei@di.fct.unl.pt on March 25, 1996.

The room has two lamps, say Big and Small, and two light switches, say Left and Right. A switch controls one and only one light. Both lights are off. Initially we don't know whether the wiring is this way or the other way around, but we can find out by toggling a switch.

In this example, we have two actions: to toggle the left switch and to toggle the right switch, denoted by *toggle(left)* and *toggle(right)*, and we have two fluents: the big light is on and the small light is on, denoted by *on(big)* and *on(small)*. If we knew the way in which the circuit is connected, then we could generate plans, predict the future, or explain the past. The problem is that no such an immediately available theory exists. An intelligent agent should be able to perform some tests and then obtain a complete action theory. In this paper we will present an abductive methodology for reasoning about actions and changes starting from an incomplete action theory, i.e., an action theory with more than one model, then refining it by testing and abductive reasoning so as to have a complete action theory, which can then be used for planning, predicting and explaining. Our methodology consists of a high-level action description language $\mathcal{A}^+$, a translation from $\mathcal{A}^+$ to abductive logic programs, and an abductive logic programming system used as the underlying inference engine for refinement.

Now suppose that we have an action description language obtained by extending $\mathcal{A}$ [7] with propositional conjunctions and disjunctions on effect propositions. Then, the above domain can be described by the following propositions:

$$
\{[toggle(left) \textbf{ causes } on(big) \textbf{ if } \neg on(big)] \\
\wedge [toggle(left) \textbf{ causes } \neg on(big) \textbf{ if } on(big))]\} \\
\dot{\vee} \\
\{[toggle(left) \textbf{ causes } on(small) \textbf{ if } \neg on(small)] \\
\wedge [toggle(left) \textbf{ causes } \neg on(small) \textbf{ if } on(small))]\}
$$

$$
\{[toggle(right) \textbf{ causes } on(big) \textbf{ if } \neg on(big)] \\
\wedge [toggle(right) \textbf{ causes } \neg on(big) \textbf{ if } on(big))]\} \\
\dot{\vee} \\
\{[toggle(right) \textbf{ causes } on(small) \textbf{ if } \neg on(small)] \\
\wedge [toggle(right) \textbf{ causes } \neg on(small) \textbf{ if } on(small))]\}
$$

$$
\{[toggle(left) \textbf{ causes } on(big) \textbf{ if } \neg on(big)] \\
\wedge [toggle(left) \textbf{ causes } \neg on(big) \textbf{ if } on(big))]\} \\
\dot{\vee} \\
\{[toggle(right) \textbf{ causes } on(big) \textbf{ if } \neg on(big)] \\
\wedge [toggle(right) \textbf{ causes } \neg on(big) \textbf{ if } on(big))]\}
$$

$$
\{[toggle(left) \textbf{ causes } on(small) \textbf{ if } \neg on(small)] \\
\wedge [toggle(left) \textbf{ causes } \neg on(small) \textbf{ if } on(small))]\} \\
\dot{\vee} \\
\{[toggle(right) \textbf{ causes } on(small) \textbf{ if } \neg on(small)] \\
\wedge [toggle(right) \textbf{ causes } \neg on(small) \textbf{ if } on(small))]\}
$$

It can be seen that finite uncertainties have been represented by exclusive disjunction $\dot{\vee}$. Intuitively, one of the following two domain descriptions should be real.

$toggle(left)$ **causes** $on(small)$ **if** $\neg on(small)$
$toggle(left)$ **causes** $\neg on(small)$ **if** $on(small)$
$toggle(right)$ **causes** $on(big)$ **if** $\neg on(big)$
$toggle(right)$ **causes** $\neg on(big)$ **if** $on(big)$

and

$toggle(left)$ **causes** $on(big)$ **if** $\neg on(big)$
$toggle(left)$ **causes** $\neg on(big)$ **if** $on(big)$
$toggle(right)$ **causes** $on(small)$ **if** $\neg on(small)$
$toggle(right)$ **causes** $\neg on(small)$ **if** $on(small)$

Later we will see that our methodology works well and produces what is intuitively acceptable. The rest of the paper is organized as follows. In Section 2 we present an action description language, denoted $\mathcal{A}^+$, which is an extension to $\mathcal{A}$. The reason we choose $\mathcal{A}$ is simply that $\mathcal{A}$ has been shown to be a simple, extensible and expressive action description language, and to be equivalent to other three major formalisms [9] proposed by Pednault [16], Reiter [18] and Baker [2], respectively. In Section 3 we will present a translation from domain descriptions in $\mathcal{A}^+$ to abductive logic programs. This translation will serve to bridge the reasoning about actions and abductive logic programming. Generally it is not easy or simple to refine action theories or to predict and explain in $\mathcal{A}^+$. The translation will effectively reduce working in $\mathcal{A}^+$ to working in an abductive logic programming system, thereby being automated. In Section 4 we will show that our translation is both sound and complete. In Section 5 we will discuss tests and refinements by using abductive logic programming. In Section 6 we return to Lifschitz' challenge problem. In Section 7 we conclude this paper with a few remarks.

2   Domain Descriptions

In this section we present an action description language $\mathcal{A}^+$, an extension to $\mathcal{A}$ of [7].

2.1   Syntax

We begin with three disjoint non-empty sets of symbols, called *proposition names*, *fluent names*, and *action names*, respectively. For convenience we will also use parameterized names. *Actions* and *propositions* are defined to be action names and proposition names, respectively. A *fluent expression*, or simply *fluent*, is defined to be a fluent name possibly preceded by $\neg$. A fluent expression is also called a *positive fluent* if it only consists of a fluent name; otherwise it is called a *negative fluent*.

In $\mathcal{A}^+$, a domain description is defined to be a set of effect assertions and constraints. An effect assertion is defined to be a statement of the form

$$A \text{ causes } F \text{ if } P_1, \ldots, P_m, Q_1, \ldots, Q_n$$

where A is an action, each of F, P_1, ..., P_m $(m \geq 0)$ is a fluent expression, and each of $Q_1, \ldots, Q_m$ $(n \geq 0)$ is a proposition name. If $m = n = 0$, then we will simply write it as A **causes** F. A constraint is defined as follows:

– A proposition name is an atomic constraint.
– A statement of the form

$$F \text{ after } A_1, \ldots, A_n$$

where F is a fluent and A_i is an action, is an atomic constraint, also called *value assertion*. When $n = 0$, the value assertion above is abbreviated to **initially** F.
– If C_1 and C_2 are constraints, then $\neg C_1$, $C_1 \wedge C_2$, $C_1 \vee C_2$ are constraints, called complex constraints. Other propositional connectives can be defined in terms of them as derived connectives.

It can be seen that $\mathcal{A}^+$ is an extension of $\mathcal{A}$ by allowing propositions and more types of constraints. However, the detailed discussion on relations between $\mathcal{A}$ and $\mathcal{A}^+$ is out of this paper.

2.2 Remarks

It seems that we would increase the expressive power if we defined the effect assertions in the following way: (1) A basic effect assertion is a statement of the form A **causes** F **if** $C_1, \ldots, C_n$; (2) An effect assertion is a statement of the form $(E_{11} \wedge \ldots \wedge E_{1m_1}) \vee \ldots \vee (E_{n1} \wedge \ldots \wedge E_{nm_n})$, where each E_{ij} is a basic effect assertion. In fact, combining with proposition names, we can reduce the above complex effect assertion to simpler ones of $\mathcal{A}^+$. We can systematically do so by introducing a few new proposition names and then transform effect assertions. For example, consider:

$$(A_1 \text{ causes } F_1 \text{ if } C_{11}, \ldots, C_{1n_1})$$
$$\vee \ldots$$
$$\vee (A_m \text{ causes } F_m \text{ if } C_{m1}, \ldots, C_{mn})$$

Let h_i, $1 \leq i \leq m$ be m new proposition symbols. Then, the above complex effect assertions can be transformed into m basic effect assertions and a new constraint as follows:

$$A_1 \text{ causes } F_1 \text{ if } C_{11}, \ldots, C_{1n_1}, h_1$$
$$\ldots$$
$$A_m \text{ causes } F_m \text{ if } C_{m1}, \ldots, C_{mn}, h_m$$
$$h_1 \vee \ldots \vee h_m$$

On the other hand, it also seems that we would increase the expressive power if we allowed general well-formed propositional formulas in the preconditions of effect assertions. For example, let A be an action, P_1 a fluent, and Q_1, Q_2, Q_3 be proposition names. Consider

$$A \text{ causes } F \text{ if } P_1, (Q_1 \wedge Q_2) \vee \neg Q_3$$

This kind of seemingly more expressive effect assertions can also be reduced to effect assertions in $\mathcal{A}^+$. Let Q_4 be a new proposition name. The following effect assertion and a constraint is equivalent to the above assertion:

$$A \text{ causes } F \text{ if } P_1, Q_4$$
$$Q_4 \leftrightarrow (Q_1 \wedge Q_2) \vee \neg Q_3$$

2.3 Semantics

The semantics of a domain description is defined by using proposition assignment, states, and transitions.

A proposition assignment α is a set of proposition names. Given a proposition name P and an assignment α, we say that P is true if $P \in \alpha$, and $\neg P$ is true if $P \notin \alpha$. A *state* is a set of fluent names. Given a fluent name F and a state σ, we say that F holds in σ if $F \in \sigma$; $\neg F$ holds in σ if $F \notin \sigma$. A *transition function* Φ is a mapping from the set of pairs (A, σ), where A is an action expression and σ is a state, to the set of states.

An *interpretation structure* is a triple (α, σ_0, Φ), where α is an assignment, σ_0 is a state, called the *initial state* of (σ_0, Φ), and Φ is a transition function. For any interpretation structure $M = (\alpha, \sigma_0, \Phi)$ and any sequence of action expressions $A_1; \ldots; A_m$ in M, by $\Phi(A_1; \ldots; A_m, \sigma_0)$ we denote the state $\Phi(A_m, \Phi(A_{m-1}, \ldots, \Phi(A_1, \sigma_0) \ldots))$.

Given an interpretation structure (α, σ_0, Φ), a constraint C is said to be true with respect to it iff

- if C is a proposition name, then $C \in \alpha$;
- if C is a value assertion of the form F **after** $A_1, \ldots, A_n$, then F holds in the state $\Phi(A_1; \ldots; A_n, \sigma_0)$;
- if C is a complex constraint, then it is true according to the usual propositional connective evaluation method.

An interpretation structure (α, σ_0, Φ) is a *model* of a domain description D iff

- Every constraint is true with respect to the interpretation structure.
- For every action A, every fluent name F, and every state σ: (i) If D includes an effect assertion A **causes** F **if** $P_1, \ldots, P_m, Q_1, \ldots, Q_n$, such that fluents $P_1, \ldots, P_m$ hold in σ and propositions $Q_1, \ldots, Q_n$ are true with respect to (α, σ_0, Φ), then $F \in \Phi(A, \sigma)$; (ii) If D includes an effect assertion A **causes** $\neg F$ **if** $P_1, \ldots, P_m, Q_1, \ldots, Q_n$, such that fluents $P_1, \ldots, P_n$ hold

in σ and propositions $Q_1, \ldots, Q_n$ are true with respect to (α, σ_0, Φ), then $F \notin \Phi(A, \sigma)$; (iii) If D does not include any such effect assertions, then $F \in \Phi(A, \sigma)$ iff $F \in \sigma$.

A domain description is *consistent* if it has a model. A domain description is *complete* if it has exactly one model. A domain description D entails a value assertion V if V is true in all models of D. It can be shown that different models of the same domain description differ only in different initial states and/or proposition assignments. In addition, the interpretation of a proposition name is independent of states.

In reality a practical domain should have only one model. The task of refining domain descriptions is to construct a new domain description which has fewer models than the original domain description. We will achieve this purpose by first performing some actions and observing their outcome, then we will abductively infer the truth values of propositions and initial states. We will make use of abductive logic programming for the purpose of abductive reasoning.

3   Translation into Abductive Programs

In this section we will present a translation from domain descriptions into abductive logic programs. An abductive logic program is a triple $< P, IC, \Delta >$, where P is a set of logic programming rules, IC is a set of first-order sentences as constraints, and Δ is a set of predicates, called abducible predicates. An abductive answer δ to a query Q in $< P, IC, \Delta >$ is a finite subset of ground instances of Δ such that (i) $Q \in SEM(P \cup \{a \leftarrow : a \in \delta\}, IC)$; (ii) $P \cup \{a \leftarrow : a \in \delta\} \cup IC$ is consistent according to definition of SEM; (iii) δ is minimal in the sense that no subset of it satisfies the previous two conditions, where $SEM(P, IC)$ denotes the semantics of the program P with constraints IC. There have been a few competing semantics in the literature: predicate completion semantics, stable model semantics, and well-founded model semantics. Later we will see that our logic program translations are acyclic, and thus all of these major semantics agree. Therefore we will define the semantics of logic programs as the predicate completion semantics. For abductive logic programs, we will complete all predicates except the abducible ones [3].

Let D be a domain description. The translation πD includes a set of programming rules and a set of constraints defined as follows:

1. Initialization: $holds(F, s_0) \leftarrow initially(F)$.
2. Law of Inertia:

$$holds(F, result(A, S)) \leftarrow holds(F, S), not\ noninertial(F, S, A).$$

where not is the negation-as-failure operator. By the law of inertia, F is true at a new situation by doing A on S if it was true at S.
3. Each effect assertion a **causes** f **if** $p_1, \ldots, p_m, q_1, \ldots, q_n$, with f being positive, p_i being a fluent, and q_i being a proposition, is translated into

$$holds(f, result(a, S)) \leftarrow holds(p_1, S), \ldots, holds(p_m, S), q_1, \ldots, q_n.$$

where $holds(\neg p, S)$ with p being positive stands for $not\ holds(p, S)$. This convention is also used in the rest of this paper.

4. Each effect assertion a **causes** $\neg f$ **if** $p_1, \ldots, p_m, q_1, \ldots, q_n$, with f being positive, p_i being a fluent, and q_i being a proposition, is translated into

$$noninertial(f, S, a) \leftarrow holds(p_1, S), \ldots, holds(p_m, S), q_1, \ldots, q_n.$$

5. For every constraint C of D: (i) if C is a proposition name, $\pi C = C$; (ii) if C is f **after** $a_1, \ldots, a_n$ with f being positive, then $\pi C = holds(f, result(a_1;$ $\ldots; a_n, s_0))$; (iii) if C is $\neg f$ **after** $a_1, \ldots, a_n$, with f being positive, then $\pi C = \neg holds(f, result(a_1; \ldots; a_n, s_0))$; (iv) $\pi(\neg C_1) = \neg(\pi C_1)$, $\pi(C_1 \wedge C_2)$ $= \pi C_1 \wedge \pi C_2$, $\pi(C_1 \vee C_2) = \pi C_1 \vee \pi C_2$.

We will define abducible predicates to be $initially(F)$ and all proposition names. The semantics of πD, denoted by $Comp(\pi D)$, is defined to be the first-order theory by completing all predicates except $initially(F)$ and proposition names, jointly with Clark's theory of equality, and the constraints [3, 6].

Theorem 31 *Let D be any domain description in $\mathcal{A}^+$. πD is an acyclic logic program with first-order constraints in the sense of [1].*

Proof It suffices to give a level mapping λ for all ground atoms. Note that $initially(f)$ and all propositions appear only on the right-hand side of $\leftarrow$, and thus can be assigned to 0. Observe that the number of occurrences of $result$ in $holds(F, S)$ on the left-hand side of $\leftarrow$ is more than right-hand side of $\leftarrow$. Hence, a level mapping λ can be defined as follows:

$$\lambda(Initially(f)) = 0$$
$$\lambda(p) = 0 \ \text{ for any proposition } p$$
$$\lambda(holds(f, result(a, s))) = 2 \times |s| + 1$$
$$\lambda(noninertial(f, a, s)) = 2 \times |s| + 2$$

where $|s|$ denotes the number of occurrences of $result$ plus 1. Then it is straight-forward to verify the above λ is a level mapping. We should point out that the above level mapping is a slight modification of that in [5, 6].   □

Corollary 32 *The completion semantics $Comp(\pi D)$ of πD agrees with its generalized stable model semantics [8] and generalized well-founded model semantics [17].*

Proof Since πD is an acyclic logic program, According to [5], the completion semantics of any acyclic abductive logic program with constraints coincides with its generalized stable model semantics [8] and generalized well-founded model semantics [17].   □

The above corollary means that the result of this paper can be experimented with any abductive logic programming system with one of the three major semantics. The detailed proof follows from [5]. A short summary of partial results of [5] can also be found in [6].

4   Soundness and Completeness

In general it is very difficult to reason about actions in $\mathcal{A}^+$. The purpose of the translation is to reduce the reasoning work in $\mathcal{A}^+$ to abductive querying in an abductive logic programming system. This section will show that reasoning in $\mathcal{A}^+$ is equivalent to abductive querying through two technical results, whose proofs are slight modifications of [5] by consolidating α component in the interpretation structure.

Theorem 41 *The translation π is sound. That is, for any domain description D and any value assertion V, if $Comp(\pi D) \models \pi V$, then D entails V.*

Proof   If the domain description is not consistent, the above theorem holds trivially since there is no model. Now assume D is consistent. We want to show every model of D is also a model of V. It suffices to prove that for every model (α, σ_0, Φ) of D, there is a model M of πD such that V is true in (α, σ_0, Φ) iff πV holds in M. The same technique of [5] can be used to construct such a model M from (α, σ_0, Φ). The only difference is that [5] does not consider α. In order to have α, just let it be the same in both (α, σ_0, Φ) and M.   □

Definition 42 *A domain description D is effect consistent iff for each pair of effect assertions,*

$$A \text{ causes } F \text{ if } C_1, \ldots, C_m$$
$$A \text{ causes } \neg F \text{ if } C_{m+1}, \ldots, C_n$$

in D, there exists i, $1 \leq i \leq m$, and j, $m + 1 \leq j \leq n$, such that C_i is the complement of C_j.

Note that if $C_1, \ldots, C_m$ contain complement elements, then effect assertion A **causes** F **if** $C_1, \ldots, C_m$ in a domain description has no effect on its models. And thus, in this paper we assume that any domain description does not have such kind of effect assertions.

Theorem 43 *The translation π is complete for any effect consistent domain descriptions. That is, for any effect consistent domain description D and any value assertion V, if D entails V, then $Comp(\pi D) \models \pi V$.*

Proof   Since D is effect consistent, there is a unique translation Φ which satisfies the effect assertions when α is given. Then it suffices to prove that for each model M of πD there is a model (α, σ_0, Φ) of D such that for each value assertion V, $M \models \pi V$ iff V holds in (α, σ_0, Φ). This will immediately implies all value assertions of D hold in (α, σ_0, Φ) since M is a model of πV for every value assertion of D. We can still follow [5] to show it.   □

The requirement for a domain description to be effect consistent is necessary. If a domain description D is not effect consistent, no transition functions exist to satisfy its effect assertions, thus it has no models, and hence it entails every value assertion. On the other hand, its translation is consistent and thus has at least one model which entails a proper subset of what D entails.

The above soundness and completeness theorems signify that our translation can actually be used for the general purposes of reasoning about actions and changes such as abductive planning, prediction, explanation. That is to say, our result of this paper goes beyond refinement of action theories. But we will not delve into detailed discussion on how to use our translation for abductive planning, temporal prediction and explanation. In the next section we will concentrate on refinement of action theories.

5   Refinement

Let D be a domain description. D may have more than one model. If D has more than one model, we may only predict a disjunctive future instead of a definite future. That is to say, after a sequence of actions is done, we cannot predict whether a fluent is definitely true or not. When a domain description is complete, we can always predict whether a fluent is true or not after an action is done. This is sometimes a very important factor in reasoning about actions, as shown as in [14].

When a domain description is not complete, all its models differ in their initial states and/or proposition assignments. In order to determine initial states and proposition assignments, one may perform some tests: doing some actions, observing their effects, and then abductively determining initial states and proposition names.

Now suppose that we are given a domain description D_0. We want to refine it. The way to do it, as said as before, is to perform some actions and observe their effects. This process is called *test*. The purpose of tests is to generate new value assertions. And thus we can formally define a test to be a set of value assertions.

Definition 51 *A test τ in an action domain is a set of value assertions. Let D be a domain description. The pair (D, τ) is called a refinement problem.*

Theorem 52 *Let D be a domain description, and τ a test. Then, every model of $D \cup \tau$ is a model of D.*

Proof Let M be any model of $D \cup \tau$. It is straightforward to see that all effect assertions and constraints are true with respect to M. And thus M is also a model of D.   □

Note that the converse of the above theorem does not hold in general cases. The above theorem means that simply adding tests to a domain description will definitely give a better and new domain description. But syntactically $D \cup \tau$ is more complicated than D. We may prefer simpler and finer descriptions. Note that in an interpretation structure, all proposition names will be either true or false. In the reality, all these proposition names can and can only be either true or false. When we do enough tests, the refinement of the domain will be closer and closer to a complete domain description. This implies that the complete domain description is a limit of all refinements of domain descriptions. When the domain description has only one model, all proposition names can be removed from the domain description by substituting them with their truth values, and thus syntactically simplifying the domain description. Hence, we have the following definition of refinements:

Definition 53 *Let D_1 and D_2 be two domain descriptions. D_2 is said to be a refinement of D_1 iff the following conditions are satisfied:*

- *Every model of D_2 is a model of D_1;*
- *There is no proposition name in D_2 which is true in every model of D_2;*
- *There is no proposition name in D_2 which is false in every model of D_2.*

In what follows we want to show how to compute refinements with abductive logic programming. In Section 3 we presented a translation from domain descriptions to abductive logic programs. However, many existing abductive logic programming systems do not directly support our constraints. Instead, they support constraints of the form

$$\bot \leftarrow L_1, \ldots, L_n$$

First we need to translate all constraints into the above form.

The translation, still denoted by π, is as follows. Let C be a constraint in the program πD. Then C can be equivalently transformed into a conjunctive normal form:

$$(C_{11} \vee \ldots \vee C_{1m_1}) \wedge \ldots \wedge (C_{m1} \vee \ldots \vee C_{mn})$$

Then, it will be translated into

$$\bot \leftarrow not\ C_{11}, \ldots, not\ C_{1m_1}$$
$$\cdots$$
$$\bot \leftarrow not\ C_{m1}, \ldots, not\ C_{mn}$$

where $not\ \neg L$ is taken as L.

After constraints are translated into a logic program, we can run it in any abductive logic programming system. Before proceeding, we need to guarantee that the correctness of the translation is preserved.

Theorem 54 *The translation π is both sound and complete for any effect consistent domain descriptions.*

Proof By the use of the soundness and completeness theorems of the last section, it is sufficient to show that the handing of constraints does not change the semantics. For this purpose, completing

$$\bot \leftarrow not\ C_{11}, \ldots, not\ C_{1m_1}$$
$$\cdots$$
$$\bot \leftarrow not\ C_{m1}, \ldots, not\ C_{mn}$$

we will have

$$\perp \leftrightarrow (\neg C_{11} \wedge \ldots \wedge \neg C_{1m_1}) \vee$$
$$\ldots \vee$$
$$(\neg C_{m1} \wedge \ldots \wedge \neg C_{mn})$$

It is equivalent to

$$(C_{11} \vee \ldots \vee C_{1m_1}) \wedge \ldots \wedge (C_{m1} \vee \ldots \vee C_{mn})$$

Thus the translation of the constraints does not change its semantics. Therefore, the semantics of new programs is the same as before.   □

Let $\tau = \{V_1, \ldots, V_n\}$ be a test. Then, τ can be transformed into a query:

$$\leftarrow \pi V_1, \ldots, \pi V_n$$

where for each i, πV_i is defined as follows: Let V_i be F **after** $A_1, \ldots, A_n$ in τ. If F is positive, then πV_i is defined to be $holds(F, result(A_1; \ldots; A_n, s_0))$; if F is negative and equal to $\neg G$, then πV_i is defined to be $not\ holds(G, result(A_1; \ldots; A_n, s_0))$.

Submitting the query to an abductive logic programming system, we will get abductive answers to it. In what follows we will write $\mathcal{R}(D, \tau)$ to stand for the set of all abductive answers to the query $\leftarrow \pi\tau$ against the abductive logic program πD. Now we are in a position to define the procedure of refining action theories.

Definition 55 *Let D be a domain description and τ a test. Let $\mathcal{R}(D, \tau) = \{R_1, \ldots, R_n\}$. Perform:*

1. *For every proposition name P, if $P \notin R_1 \cup \ldots \cup R_n$, remove from D all effect assertions containing P in the precondition list, and replace P with false in every constraint of D;*
2. *For every proposition name P, if $P \in R_1 \cap \ldots \cap R_n$, remove P from all effect assertions of D, and replace P with true in every constraint of D;*
3. *Simplify constraints of D in the usual way by using of true and false in the formulas. For example, if C is of the form $\neg false$ or $C_1 \vee true$, C is removed.*

Then, Define $\mathcal{S}(D, \tau)$ to be the set of the resulting effect assertions, constraints, and the test τ.

The following theorem says that the new domain description $\mathcal{S}(D, \tau)$ is a refinement of D.

Theorem 56 *Let D be a domain description, τ a test. Then, $\mathcal{S}(D, \tau)$ is a refinement of D.*

Proof To show that $\mathcal{S}(D, \tau)$ is a refinement of D, we need to show

(a) Every model of $\mathcal{S}(D, \tau)$ is a model of D;

(b) There is no proposition name in $\mathcal{S}(D, \tau)$ which is true in every model of $\mathcal{S}(D, \tau)$;

(c) There is no proposition name in $\mathcal{S}(D, \tau)$ which is false in every model of $\mathcal{S}(D, \tau)$.

To see (a), note that it suffices to show that every model of $\mathcal{S}(D, \tau)$ is a model of $D \cup \tau$ according to Theorem 5.2. Let $\mathcal{R}(D, \tau) = \{R_1, \ldots, R_n\}$. Since R_i is an abductive answer to $\pi\tau$, we have

$$Comp(\pi D \cup a \leftarrow \ : a \in R_i) \models \pi\tau$$

Thus for every proposition P, if $P \notin R_1 \cup \ldots \cup R_n$, it is always assigned to "false" in α since our model is two-valued. Since it is always false, if a disjunct on the right-hand side of a completion equivalence of $holds(F, S)$ and $noninertial(F, A, S)$ contains it, it can be removed from $Comp(\pi D)$. Removing it amounts to removing the corresponding effect assertion which has P as one of preconditions. And thus the corresponding effect assertion can be deleted from D. This is what Step 1 does in Def.5.5. On the other hand, if $P \in R_1 \cap \ldots \cap R_n$, it is always assigned to "true", and thus can be vacuumly removed from all the disjuncts on the right-hand side of a completion equivalence of $holds(F, S)$ and $noninertial(F, A, S)$. This amounts to removing the occurrence of P from $Comp(\pi D)$. And thus, P can be removed from the corresponding effect assertions. This is what Step 2 does in Def.5.5. Note that Step 3 in Def.5.5 is in fact an equivalence transformation in logic, and thus does not change models of $Comp(\pi D)$. Therefore, every model of $\mathcal{S}(D, \tau)$ is a model of $D \cup \tau$.

To see (b), suppose that P is true in every model of $\mathcal{S}(D, \tau)$. Since P is an abducible predicate, it must appear in $R_1 \cap \ldots \cap R_n$ as $\{R_1, \ldots, R_n\}$ is the set of all abductive answers, and is thus deleted in Step 2, and hence cannot appear in $\mathcal{S}(D, \tau)$.

To see (c), suppose that P is false in every model of $\mathcal{S}(D, \tau)$. Then we would have $P \notin R_1 \cup \ldots \cup R_n$. And thus all effect assertions with it as a precondition would have been deleted in Step 1, and hence cannot appear in $\mathcal{S}(D, \tau)$.   □

6   An Example

Now we return to the example in the Introduction. Let $controls(S, L)$ be a parameterized proposition name to denote that switch S controls light L. Then, we can have the following domain description D:

$$controls(left, small) \leftrightarrow controls(right, big)$$
$$controls(left, big) \leftrightarrow controls(right, small)$$
$$controls(left, small) \dot{\lor} controls(left, big)$$
$$controls(right, small) \dot{\lor} controls(right, big)$$
$$toggle(left) \textbf{ causes } on(small) \textbf{ if } \neg on(small), controls(left, small)$$
$$toggle(left) \textbf{ causes } \neg on(small) \textbf{ if } on(small), controls(left, small)$$
$$toggle(right) \textbf{ causes } on(small) \textbf{ if } \neg on(small), controls(right, small)$$
$$toggle(right) \textbf{ causes } \neg on(small) \textbf{ if } on(small), controls(right, small)$$
$$toggle(left) \textbf{ causes } on(big) \textbf{ if } \neg on(big), controls(left, big)$$
$$toggle(left) \textbf{ causes } \neg on(big) \textbf{ if } on(big), controls(left, big)$$
$$toggle(right) \textbf{ causes } on(big) \textbf{ if } \neg on(big), controls(right, big)$$
$$toggle(right) \textbf{ causes } \neg on(big) \textbf{ if } on(big), controls(right, big)$$
$$\textbf{initially } \neg on(big)$$
$$\textbf{initially } \neg on(small)$$

Then, we have an abductive logic program πD. Now suppose we have a test τ = $\{on(big) \textbf{ after } toggle(left)\}$. Then we can evaluate it in an abductive logic programming system. The following is the version of πD and $\pi \tau$ in the abductive logic programming system REVISE [4]:

```
%the following are translations of \pi D.
holds(F, init) <- initially(F).
holds(F, result(A, S))
      <- holds(F, S), not noninertial(F, S, A).
holds(on(small), result(toggle(left), S))
      <- controls(left, small), not holds(on(small), S).
noninertial(on(small), S, toggle(left))
      <- controls(left, small), holds(on(small), S).
holds(on(small), result(toggle(right), S))
      <- controls(right, small), not holds(on(small), S).
noninertial(on(small), S, toggle(right))
      <- controls(right, small), holds(on(small), S) .
holds(on(big), result(toggle(left), S))
      <- controls(left, big), not holds(on(big), S).
noninertial(on(big), S, toggle(left))
      <- controls(left, big), holds(on(big), S).
holds(on(big), result(toggle(right), S))
      <- controls(right, big), not holds(on(big), S) .
noninertial(on(big), S, toggle(right))
      <- controls(right, big), holds(on(big), S).
% the following are constraints
<- controls(left, small), not controls(right, big).
<- not controls(left, small), controls(right, big).
<- controls(left, big), not controls(right, small).
<- not controls(left, big), controls(right, small).
```

```
<- controls(left, big), controls(left, small).
<- not controls(left, big), not controls(left, small).
<- controls(right, big), controls(right, small).
<- not controls(right, big), not controls(right, small).
<- holds(on(small), init).
<- holds(on(big), init).
% The following are declarations of abducible predicates
:- revisable(initially(_)).
:- revisable(controls(_, _)).
% The following is the translation of the test.
<- not holds(on(big), result(toggle(left), init)).
```

In the REVISE system, the following answer $\mathcal{R}(D, \tau)$ will be output by issuing the *solution* command:

$$\{\{controls(right, small), controls(left, big)\}\}$$

Then, by definition we have the following new domain description $\mathcal{S}(D, \tau)$:

$$toggle(right) \textbf{ causes } on(small) \textbf{ if } \neg on(small)$$
$$toggle(right) \textbf{ causes } \neg on(small) \textbf{ if } on(small)$$
$$toggle(left) \textbf{ causes } on(big) \textbf{ if } \neg on(big)$$
$$toggle(left) \textbf{ causes } \neg on(big) \textbf{ if } on(big)$$
$$\textbf{initially } \neg on(big)$$
$$\textbf{initially } \neg on(small)$$
$$on(big) \textbf{ after } toggle(left)$$

Thus we have obtained a complete domain description which enables us to generate plan, to predict the future, or to explain the past, as what we expected and intended.

7   Concluding Remarks

In this paper we have presented an experiment on using the abductive logic programming paradigm to refine an action theory in line with [11, 12] starting from [7]. An action theory, also called domain description, describes effects of actions and initial states in a dynamic domain. A complete action theory should enable us to determine which fluent will be true and which fluent will be false after an action is performed. A complete action theory can be used for planning, prediction and explanation. In practice we may encounter incomplete domains with finite uncertainties. The finite uncertainties may be removed by doing some tests and abductive reasoning. Technically we presented an action description language $\mathcal{A}^+$ for domain descriptions, then we presented a translation from $\mathcal{A}^+$ to abductive logic programs. The translation has been shown to be both sound and complete. Thus, the task of reasoning about actions in $\mathcal{A}^+$

amounts to abductive query evaluation in abductive logic programming systems. We also indicate that our abductive logic program is acyclic, and thus we can use any abductive query evaluation procedure, no matter whether their semantics is based on predicate completion, stable models, or well-founded models. The test on a domain is a set of observed effects of a sequence of specific actions. The test can be used to determine truth values of proposition names which serve to represent uncertainties. This has been tested with the latest version of a meta-interpreter of abductive logic programs [4]. To the best of our knowledge, there is no similar work in this topic, although there have been many reports on $\mathcal{A}$ family languages. In general, the refinement of action theories can be regarded as learning. But this kind of learning is different from the main-trend work on learning, where generalization, specialization, and induction is often used as the inference mechanism. In this paper we have used abduction as the underlying inference mechanism. The result of this paper is currently used to develop intelligent situated agent [13], which is able to observe, act and reason in the real world.

Acknowledgement

This work was partially supported by JNICT of Portugal under PRAXIS 2/2.1/ TIT/1593/95 and PRAXIS XXI/BPD/4165/94 and NSERC of Canada under 31-611024. We have benefited from discussions with Vladimir Lifschitz in the early stage of this work. We would also like to thank the anonymous referees for their comments on an early version of this paper.

References

1. K. R. Apt and M. Bezem. Acyclic programs. In *Proc. of ICLP 90*, pages 579–597. MIT Press, 1990.
2. A. B. Baker. Nonmonotonic reasoning in the framework of situation calculus. *Artificial Intelligence*, 49:5–23, 1991.
3. L. Console, D. T. Dupre, and P. Torasso. On the relationship between abduction and deduction. *Journal of Logic and Computation*, 1(5):661–690, 1991.
4. C. V. Damásio, L.M. Pereira, and W. Nejdle. Revise: An extended logic programming system for revising knowledge bases. In *Proc. of KR'94*, 1994.
5. M. Denecker. Knowledge representation and reasoning in incomplete logic programming. Ph.D. thesis, Department of Computer Science, K.U.Leuven, 1993.
6. M. Denecker, and D. Schreye. Representing incomplete knowledge in abductive logic programming. In Proc. of ILPS'93, 1993, pp. 147–163
7. M. Gelfond and V. Lifschitz. Representing action and change by logic programs. *Journal of Logic Programming*, 17:301–322, 1993.
8. A.C. Kakas and P. Mancarella. Generalized stable models: A semantics for abduction. In *Proc. of ECAI'90*, 1990.
9. G.N. Kartha. Soundness and completeness theorems for three formalizations of action. In *Proc. IJCAI93*, pages 712–718. MIT Press, 1993.
10. R.A. Kowalski and F. Sadri. The situation calculus and event calculus compared. In *Proc. of ILPS 94*, pages 539–553. MIT Press, 1994.

11. R. Li and L.M. Pereira. Temporal reasoning with abductive logic programming. In W. Wahsler, editor, *Proc. of ECAI'96*, pages 13–17. John Wiley & Sons, 1996.
12. R. Li and L.M. Pereira. What is believed is what is explained (sometimes). In *Proc. of AAAI'96*, pages 550–555, 1996.
13. R. Li and L.M. Pereira. Knowledge-based situated agents among us. In J. P. Muller, M. J. Wooldridge, and N. R. Jennings, editors, *Intelligent Agents III – Proc. of the Third International Workshop on Agent Theories, Architectures, and Languages (ATAL-96), LNAI 1193*, pages 375–389. Springer, 1997.
14. F. Lin and Y. Shoham. Provably correct theories of actions: preliminary report. In *Proc. of AAAI-91*, 1991.
15. J. McCarthy and P.J. Hayes. Some philosophical problems from the stand-point of artificial intelligence. In B. Meltzer and D. Michie, editors, *Machine Intelligence*, volume 4, pages 463–502, Edinburgh, 1969.
16. E. P. D. Pednault. Adl: Exploring the middle ground between strips and the situation calculus. In R. J. Brachman, H. Levesque, and R. Reiter, editors, *Proc. of KR'89*, pages 324–332. Morgan Kaufmann Publishers, Inc., 1989.
17. L. M. Pereira, J. J. Alferes, and J. N. Aparício. Nonmonotonic reasoning with well founded semantics. In K. Furukawa, editor, *Proc. of 8th ICLP*, pages 475–489. MIT Press, 1991.
18. R. Reiter. The frame problem in the situation calculus: A simple solution (sometimes) and a completeness result for goal regression. In V. Lifschitz, editor, *Artificial Intelligence and Mathematical Theory of Computation: Papers in Honor of John McCarthy*, pages 359–380. Academic Press, San Diego, CA, 1991.
19. E. Sandewall. *Features and Fluents: The Representation of Knowledge about Dynamic Systems, Vol. 1*. Oxford University Press, 1994.

Abduction, Argumentation and Bi-Disjunctive Logic Programs

Kewen Wang and Huowang Chen

School of Computer
Changsha Institute of Technology
410073, P.R. China
E-mail: wkw@nudt.edu.cn

Abstract. We study the relationship between argumentation (abduction) and disjunctive logic programming. Based on the paradigm of argumentation, an abductive semantic framework for disjunctive logic programming is presented, in which the disjunctions of negative literals are taken as possible assumptions rather than only negative literals as the case of non-disjunctive logic programming. In our framework, three semantics PDH, CDH and WFDH are defined by three kinds of acceptable hypotheses to represent credulous reasoning, moderate reasoning and skeptical reasoning in AI, respectively. On the other hand, our semantic framework could be established in a broader class than that of disjunctive programs (called bi-disjunctive logic programs) and, hence, the corresponding abductive framework is abbreviated as BDAS (Bi-Disjunctive Argumentation-theoretic Semantics). Besides its rich expressive power and nondeterminism, BDAS integrates and naturally extends many key semantics, such as the minimal models, EGCWA, the well-founded model, and the stable models. In particular, a novel and interesting argumentation-theoretic characterization of EGCWA is shown. Thus the framework in this paper does not only provides a new way of performing argumentation (abduction) in disjunctive logic programming, but also is a simple, intuitive and unifying semantic framework for disjunctive logic programming.

1 Introduction

In our everyday life as well as in various artificial intelligence (AI) applications, we are often required to deal with disjunctive information. It suffices to enumerate only a few areas of using disjunctive information: reasoning by cases, approximate reasoning, legal reasoning, diagnosis, and natural language understanding [10, 26]. For example, if we know only that '*Mike will work in Havard or in Stanford* ' but we do not know exactly in which university he will work, then this information can be conveniently transformed into a rule of disjunctive logic programs. In fact, it is known that disjunctive programs have more expressive power than non-disjunctive programs and permit a direct and natural representation of disjunctive information from natural language and informal specifications. To conveniently and properly handle the representation and reasoning of disjunctive information in logic programming, a great deal of efforts have been given to the problem of finding suitable extensions of logic programming. The problem of defining an intended (declarative) meaning for disjunctive logic programs, however, has been proved to be more difficult than the case of non-disjunctive logic programs. The semantics of stratified non-disjunctive programs leads to unique minimal model (that is, the perfect model) [1], which is well accepted as the intended meaning of stratified programs. However, this is not the case when we consider the class of non-stratified programs or disjunctive programs (even positive disjunctive programs) and a lot of approaches have been proposed to determine semantics for non-stratified programs and/or disjunctive programs. Though some of semantics, such as the well-founded semantics for non-disjunctive programs [19], the extended generalized closed world assumption (EGCWA) for positive disjunctive programs [41]and the stable semantics for non-disjunctive/disjunctive logic programs [18, 28] etc., are widely studied and shown to be promising in deductive databases, and nonmonotonic reasoning, but also they are often criticized in the literature for their shortcomings. For example, the problem of the (disjunctive) stable semantics is its incompleteness: some disjunctive programs do not possess any stable models; the well-founded semantics is not able to express the nondeterministic nature of non-stratified programs. The diversity of various approaches in semantics for (disjunctive) logic programs shows that there is probably not a unique suitable semantics for applications in logic programming. Therefore, in our opinion, a suitable semantic framework rather than only a single semantics for disjunctive logic programming should be provided, in which most of the existing key semantics should be embedded and their shortcomings be overcome. In addition, a suitable semantic framework for disjunctive logic programming can provide a unifying mechanism for the implementation of various disjunctive semantics as well as it is used in studying the relationship between different formalisms of nonmonotonic reasoning.

On the other hand, the paradigm of disjunctive logic programming is still not expressive enough to give direct representation for some problems in commonsense reasoning. Thus, it would be also desirable that the syntax of disjunctive programs should be extended to a broader class of logic programs so that the syntax of this class resembles that of traditional logic programs and the new class should include disjunctive programs as a subclass. Brass, Dix and Przymusinki [10] propose a generalization for the syntax of disjunctive programs (called *super logic programs*) and the static semantics [30] of super logic programs is discussed. However, argumentation does not be treated in their work. In fact, as far as we know, the problem of performing argumentation-based abduction in disjunctive logic programming is rarely discussed [6].

Abduction is usually defined as inferring the best or most reasonable explanation (or hypothesis) for a given set of facts. Moreover, it is a form of nonmonotonic reasoning, since explanations which are consistent in a given context may become inconsistent when new information is obtained. In fact, abduction plays an important role in much of human inference. It is relevant in our everyday commonsense reasoning as well as in many expert problem-solving tasks. Several efforts have been recently devoted to extending non-disjunctive logic programming to perform abductive reasoning, such as [15, 20, 22, 37]. Two key forms of approaches to abduction are consistency-based and argumentation-based ones. The first kind of approaches exploit a certain logical consistency and an acceptable hypothesis is specified as the corresponding consistent sets (some other constraints might also be applied), such as [2, 3, 11, 17, 23]; the latter kind of approches depend on an attack relation among hypotheses and acceptable hypotheses are defined through a kind of stability conditions [14, 15, 36, 37]. However, the approaches to argumentation-based abduction in logic programming are mainly concentrated on non-disjunctive logic programs and these approaches can not be directly extended to the class of disjunctive programs.

Since argumentation has applications in areas such as law and practical reasoning, it should be investigated and implemented in the setting of disjunctive logic programming. And more, as the results of this paper will show, an argumentation-theoretic framework can suggest many new semantics for disjunctive programs and can overcome the shortcomings of some major semantics. In this paper, we mainly concentrate on two problems: (1) The relationship between argumentation-based abduction and various semantics for disjunctive programs (the consistency-based abduction has been studied by some authors such as [3, 11, 34]; (2) The extension of disjunctive logic programming from both syntax (allowing disjunction in the bodies of program clauses) and semantics (by argumentation). For this purpose, we first define a moderate extension for the syntax of disjunctive logic programs (referred to as bi-disjunctive logic programs) by allowing the disjunctions of negative literals to appear in the bodies of program clauses. We shall see that the class of bi-disjunctive programs is broader than that of traditional disjunctive programs and can be considered as a subclass of super logic programs. More importantly, an argumentation-theoretic semantic framework for (bi-)disjunctive logic programs is presented, called the bi-disjunctive argumentation-theoretic semantics (abbreviated as BDAS), which is a generalization of Dung's preferred scenarios [14, 15] and Torres' non-deterministic well-founded semantics [36, 37]. In fact, this paper is heavily influenced by their work. Our work also shows that this is a non-trivial generalization. The basic idea of this paper is to introduce a special resolution for default negation and interpreting the disjunctions of negative literals as abducibles (or, assumptions) rather than only negative literals as the case of non-disjunctive programs. As a result, we transform a given bi-disjunctive program P into an argument framework $\mathbf{F}_P = < P, DB_P^-, \leadsto_P >$, where DB_P^- is the set of all disjunctions of (ground) negative literals in P, a subset Δ of DB_P^- is called a disjunctive hypothesis (or simply, hypothesis) of P, and $\leadsto_P$ is an attack relation among the hypotheses of P. An admissible hypothesis Δ is one that can attack every hypothesis which attacks it. Based on this basic idea, we introduce mainly three subclasses of admissible hypotheses: preferred disjunctive hypothesis (PDH); complete disjunctive hypothesis (CDH); well-founded disjunctive hypothesis (WFDH). Each of these subclasses defines an abductive semantics for bi-disjunctive programs and they are all complete for disjunctive programs, that is, every disjunctive program has at least one corresponding hypothesis. BDAS can not only handle the problems of commonsense reasoning properly, but many interesting results are obtained. In particular, we show that BDAS characterizes and extends many key semantics. For example, our Theorem 6.2 states that WFDH extends both the well-found semantics for non-disjunctive logic programs [19] and the extended generalized closed world assumption (EGCWA) [41] (and thus provides a unifying characterization for these two different semantics by abduction). This theorem has many implications and it might be one of the most interesting results in this paper; we will also show that PDH extends the stable models [18] for (disjunctive) logic programs to the whole class of disjunctive logic programs. As noted in [15], the skepticism and credulism are two major semantic intuitions for knowledge representation. A skeptical reasoner does not infer any conclusion in uncertainty conditions, but a credulous reasoner tries to give conclusions as much as possible. BDAS integrates these two opposite semantic intuitions and, in particular, PDH and WFDH characterize credulism and skepticism, respectively.

The rest of this paper is arranged as follows: Section 2 will briefly define some necessary notions and definitions for disjunctive logic programming; In Section 3 we extends the class of disjunctive programs to bi-disjunctive programs. By introducing a natural attack relation and a special resolution for default negation, our basic argument framework BDAS is established; In Section 4, three interesting acceptable hypotheses (PDH, CDH, WFDH) for bi-disjunctive programs are identified and hence they are three declarative semantics for disjunctive logic programming; Some fundamental properties of BDAS are shown in Section 5; Section 6 studies the relationship between BDAS and some key approaches for non-disjunctive/disjunctive programs; Section 7 is our conclusion, in which some future work is pointed out. The proofs are omitted here and can be found in [39].

2   Basic Notions and Definitions

In this section, we first introduce some necessary definitions and notions. Since only Herbrand models of logic programs are mentioned, without loss of generality, we consider only propositional logic programs, this means that a logic program is often understood as its ground instantiation.

Throughout the paper we will refer to the following different classes of logic programs:

A *Horn logic program* is a set of Horn clauses of the form

$$a \leftarrow a_1, \ldots, a_m,$$

where a and a_i $(i = 1, \ldots, m)$ are atoms and $m \geq 0$.

A *non-disjunctive logic program* is a set of non-disjunctive clauses of the form

$$a \leftarrow a_1, \ldots, a_s, \sim a_{s+1}, \ldots, \sim a_t,$$

where a and a_i $(i = 1, \ldots, t)$ are atoms and $t \geq s \geq 0$. The symbol $\sim$ denotes negation by default, rather than classical negation.

A *disjunctive logic program* is a set of disjunctive clauses of the form

$$a_1| \cdots |a_r \leftarrow a_{r+1}, \ldots, a_s, \sim a_{s+1}, \ldots, \sim a_t,$$

where a_i $(i = 1, \ldots, t)$ are atoms and $t \geq s \geq r > 0$. The symbol $|$ is the disjunction, sometimes called the *epistemic disjunction* to distinguish it from the classical disjunction $\vee$.

A *positive disjunctive logic program* is a set of positive disjunctive clauses of the form

$$a_1| \cdots |a_r \leftarrow a_{r+1}, \ldots, a_s,$$

where a_i $(i = 1, \ldots, s)$ are atoms and $s \geq r > 0$.

As usual, B_P denotes the *Herbrand base* of disjunctive logic program P, that is, the set of all (ground) atoms in P. The set DB_P^+ of all disjuncts of the atoms in P is called the *disjunctive Herbrand base* of P; the set DB_P^- of all disjuncts of the negative literals in P is called the *negative disjunctive Herbrand base* of P. $\perp$ denotes the empty disjuncts.

If S is an expression, then $atoms(S)$ is the set of all atoms appearing in S.

For $\alpha, \beta \in DB_P^+$, if $atoms(\alpha) \subseteq atoms(\beta)$ then we say α implies β, denoted as $\alpha \Rightarrow \beta$. For example, $a|b \Rightarrow a|b|c$. If $\alpha \in DB_P^+$, then the smallest factor $sfac(\alpha)$ of α is the disjunction of atoms obtained from α by deleting all repeated occurrence of atoms in α (if α is not propositional, the definition will not be so simple, see [24]). For instance, the smallest factor of $a|b|a$ is $a|b$. For $S \subseteq DB_P^+$, $sfac(S) = \{sfac(\alpha) : \alpha \in S\}$. The *expansion* of α is defined as $\| \alpha \| = \{\beta \in DB_P^+ : \alpha \Rightarrow \beta\}$; the expansion of S is $\| S \| = \{\beta \in DB_P^+ : \text{there exists } \alpha \in S \text{ such that } \alpha \Rightarrow \beta\}$.

The *canonical form* of S is defined as $can(S) = \{\alpha \in sfac(S) : \text{there exists no } \alpha' \in sfac(S) \text{ such that } \alpha' \Rightarrow \alpha \text{ and } \alpha' \neq \alpha\}$.

For $\alpha \in DB_P^-$ and $S \subseteq DB_P^-$, the notions of $sfac(\alpha)$, $sfac(S)$, $\| \alpha \|$ and $\| S \|$ can be defined similarly.

A subset of DB_P^+ is called a *state* of the disjunctive logic program P; a *state pair* of P is defined as $S = < S^+; S^- >$, where $S^+ \subseteq DB_P^+$ and $S^- \subseteq DB_P^-$.

The minimal models and the least model state are two important declarative semantics for positive disjunctive programs, both of which extend the least model theory of Horn logic programs. The minimal model semantics captures the disjunctive consequences from a positive disjunctive program as a set of models. The least model state captures the disjunctive consequences as a set of disjuncts of atoms and leads to a unique 'model' characterization.

Let P be a positive disjunctive program, then the *least model state* of P is defined as

$$ms(P) = \{\alpha \in DB_P^+ : P \vdash \alpha\},$$

where $\vdash$ is the inference of the first-order logic and P is considered as the corresponding first-order formulas. For example, the corresponding first-order formulae of disjuncts $a_1| \cdots |a_m$ and $\sim a_1| \cdots | \sim a_m$ are $a_1 \vee \cdots \vee a_m$ and $\neg a_1 \vee \cdots \vee \neg a_m$, respectively.

The least model state $ms(P)$ of a positive disjunctive P can be characterized by the operator $T_P^S : 2^{DB_P^+} \to 2^{DB_P^+}$: for any $J \subseteq DB_P^+$,

$T_P^S(J) = \{\alpha \in DB_P^+ :$ there exists a disjunctive clause $\alpha' \leftarrow a_1, \ldots, a_n$ in P and $a_i | \alpha_i \in J, i = 1, \ldots, n$, such that $\alpha'' = \alpha' | \alpha_1 | \cdots | \alpha_n$, where $\alpha_1, \ldots, \alpha_n \in DB_P^+ \cup \{\bot\}$, and $\alpha = sfac(\alpha'')\}$.

Minker and Rajasekar [27] have shown that T_P^S has the least fixpoint $lfp(T_P^S) = T_P^S \uparrow \omega$, and the following result:

Theorem 2.1. *Let P be a positive disjunctive program, then $ms(P) = \| T_P^S \uparrow \omega \|$, and $ms(P)$ has the same set of minimal models as P.*

3 Argumentation in Bi-disjunctive Logic Programs

As noted in the introduction, we know that some disjunctive information should be given a more direct and more convenient representation than with only traditional disjunctive programs (this will be further explained later). Another motivation of extending the syntax of disjunctive programs is that, when we set to study the relationship between argumentation (abduction) and disjunctive logic programming, we found that our argumentation-theoretic framework for disjunctive programs seems more natural in the case of bi-disjunctive logic programs. Now, we first introduce the class of bi-disjunctive logic programs and then the basic argumentation-theoretic framework for bi-disjunctive programs is established.

Definition 3.1. A bi-disjunctive clause C is a rule of the form

$$a_1 | \cdots | a_r \leftarrow a_{r+1}, \ldots, a_s, \beta_{s+1}, \ldots, \beta_t,$$

where a_i $(i = 1, \ldots, s)$ are atoms, β_j $(j = s+1, \ldots, t)$ are disjuncts of negative literals, and $t \geq s \geq r > 0$, where $|$ is the epistemic disjunction and $\sim$ is default negation.

A *bi-disjunctive logic program* P is defined as a set of bi-disjunctive clauses.

For example, the following program is a bi-disjunctive program:

$$a|b \leftarrow$$
$$e|c \leftarrow d, \sim a| \sim b$$
$$d \leftarrow \sim e$$

We consider another example.

Example 3.1 Suppose that we have a knowledge base consisting of the following four rules (a variant of an example in [10]):

R_1 Mike is able to visit London or Paris

R_2 If Mike is able to visit London, he will be happy

R_3 If Mike is able to visit Paris, he will be happy

R_4 If Mike is not able to visit both London and Paris, he will be prudent

It is easy to see that the knowledge base can be easily expressed as the following bi-disjunctive logic program:

$r_1 : Visit - London | Visit - Paris \leftarrow$

$r_2 : \qquad\qquad\qquad Happy \leftarrow Visit - London$

$r_3 : \qquad\qquad\qquad Happy \leftarrow Visit - Paris$

$r_4 : \qquad\qquad Prudent \leftarrow\; \sim VisitLondon | \sim VisitParis$

Notice that the rule R_4 possesses a more direct transformation with bi-disjunctive logic programs than with traditional disjunctive programs.

We again stress the difference between the epistemic disjunction | and the classical disjunction $\vee$. For example, $a \vee \neg a$ is a tautology but the truth of the disjunction $a | \sim a$ is unknown in the disjunctive program $P = \{a|b \leftarrow\}$ since both of them may be unknown. In particular, the intended meaning of a disjunction $\beta =\sim b_1 | \cdots | \sim b_n$ of negative literals is similar to the default atom $\sim (b_1 \wedge \cdots \wedge b_n)$ in super logic programs [10]. That is, β means that $b_1, \ldots,$ and b_n can not be proved at the same time. Therefore, bi-disjunctive programs can be regarded as a subclass of super programs.

It is obvious that the following inclusions hold:

Super Logic Programs $\supset$ *Bi-Disjunctive Programs* $\supset$ *Disjunctive Programs* $\supset$ *Non-disjunctive Programs*

Notice that we can also allow positive disjunctions to appear in the bodies of bi-disjunctive clauses as well as negative disjunctions. The semantic framework in this paper can be similarly defined for such bi-disjunctive programs by only trivially generalizing the notion of the least model state [25]. For simplicity, we will not make such a generalization here.

In general, argumentation-based abduction is based on argument frameworks defined as triples $\mathbf{F} =< K, H, \rightsquigarrow >$, where K is a first order theory representing the given knowledge, H is a set of first order formulae representing the possible hypotheses, and $\rightsquigarrow$ is an attack relation among the hypotheses.

Given a bi-disjunctive program P, an assumption of P is an element of DB_P^-; a hypothesis of P is defined a subset Δ of DB_P^- such that Δ is expansion-closed: $\| \Delta \| = \Delta$. In this paper, we will consider a bi-disjunctive program P as an argument framework $\mathbf{F}_P =< P, H(P), \rightsquigarrow_P >$, where $H(P)$ is the set of all hypotheses of P, and $\rightsquigarrow_P$ is a binary relation on $H(P)$, called the attack relation of $\mathbf{F}_P$ (or P).

To define the attack relation of $\mathbf{F}_P$, similar to GL-transformation [18], we first introduce a generalized GL-transformation for the class of bi-disjunctive programs, by which a positive disjunctive program P_Δ^+ is obtained from any given bi-disjunctive program P with a (disjunctive) hypothesis Δ of P.

Definition 3.2. Let Δ be a hypothesis of a bi-disjunctive program P, then

(1) For each bi-disjunctive clause C in P, delete all the disjuncts of negative literals in the body of C that belong to Δ. The resulting bi-disjunctive program is denoted as P_Δ;

(2) The positive disjunctive program consisting of all the positive disjunctive clauses of P_Δ is denoted as P_Δ^+, and is called the *generalized GL-transformation* of P.

Example 3.2.   Let P be the following bi-disjunctive program:

$$a|b \leftarrow$$
$$e|c \leftarrow d, \sim a| \sim b$$
$$d \leftarrow \sim e$$

If $\Delta_1 =\| \sim a| \sim b \|$, then $P_{\Delta_1} = \{a|b \leftarrow; \ e|c \leftarrow d; \ d \leftarrow \sim e\}$, and $P_{\Delta_1}^+ = \{a|b \leftarrow; \ e|c \leftarrow d\}$. If $\Delta_2 =\| \sim a| \sim b, \sim e \|$, then $P_{\Delta_2}^+ = P_{\Delta_2} = \{a|b \leftarrow; \ e|c \leftarrow d; \ d \leftarrow\}$.

Based on the above transformation, we can define a special resolution $\vdash_P$ for default-negation, which can be intuitively illustrated as the following principle:

If there is an agent who
(1) holds the assumptions $\sim b_1, \ldots, \sim b_m$;and
(2) can 'derive' $b_1| \ldots |b_m|b_{m+1}| \ldots |b_n$ from the knowledge base P with
these assumptions.
Then the disjunctive information $b_{m+1}| \ldots |b_n$ is obtained.

The following definition precisely formulates this principle with bi-disjunctive programs.

Definition 3.3.   Let Δ be a (disjunctive) hypothesis of a bi-disjunctive program P, $\alpha \in DB_P^+$ and $\sim b_1, \ldots, \sim b_m \in \Delta$ such that the following two conditions are satisfied:
(1) $\beta = \alpha|b_1| \cdots |b_m$; and
(2) $\beta \in can(ms(P_\Delta^+))$.
Then we call Δ is a *supporting hypothesis* for α, denoted as $\Delta \vdash_P \alpha$.

The condition (2) above means that β is a logical consequence of P_Δ^+ with respect to the least model state. The set of all disjuncts of positive literals that are supported by Δ is denoted as $V_P(\Delta)$. That is,

$$V_P(\Delta) = \{\alpha \in DB_P^+ : \ \Delta \vdash_P \alpha\}.$$

In Example 3.2, $V_P(\Delta_1) =\| a|b \|$, $V_P(\Delta_2) =\| a|b, c, d \|$.

Definition 3.4.   Let Δ be a hypothesis of P, then $S_\Delta =<\| V_P(\Delta) \|; \Delta >$ is called a supported state pair of P.

Though each hypothesis Δ corresponds to a state pair of P, not every state pair represent the intended meaning of P. For example $P = \{a|b \leftarrow \sim a, \sim b\}$. If $\Delta =\| \sim a, \sim b \|$, then $V_P(\Delta) = \{a|b\}$ and thus $S_\Delta =<\| a|b \|; \| \sim a, \sim b \|>$. It is obvious that S_Δ does not represent the correct meaning of P. This is similar to the problem caused by the closed world assumption (CWA) which is first observed by Minker [25].

To derive suitable hypotheses for a given bi-disjunctive program, some constraints will be required, which can be realized though the following definition.

Definition 3.5.   Let Δ and Δ' be two hypotheses of a bi-disjunctive program P. If at least one of the following conditions holds:

(1) There exists $\beta = \sim b_1 | \cdots | \sim b_m \in \Delta'$, $m > 0$, such that $\Delta \vdash_P b_i, i = 1, \ldots, m$; or

(2) There exist $\sim b_1, \ldots, \sim b_m \in \Delta', m > 0$, such that $\Delta \vdash_P b_1 | \cdots | b_m$.

Then we say Δ *attacks* Δ', and denoted as $\Delta \rightsquigarrow_P \Delta'$.

Intuitively, $\Delta \rightsquigarrow_P \Delta'$ means that Δ causes the direct contradiction with Δ', which may come from any one of the above two cases.

Example 3.3.   Let P be the bi-disjunctive program of Example 3.2. Take $\Delta = \|\sim a | \sim b, \sim e \|$, $\Delta' = \|\sim c | \sim d \|$. Since $V_P(\Delta) = \{a|b, c, d\}$, that is, $\Delta \vdash_P c, d$ thus $\Delta \rightsquigarrow_P \Delta'$, but not $\Delta' \rightsquigarrow_P \Delta$.

This example shows that the relation $\rightsquigarrow_P$ is not symmetric. Otherwise, the attack relation would have no much use.

In the remaining of this subsection, we seek to define suitable constraints on (disjunctive) hypotheses by using the above fundamental definition (Definition 3.5).

Consider again the logic program $P = \{a|b \leftarrow \sim a | \sim b\}$ and $\Delta = \|\sim a | \sim b \|$, it is not hard to see that $\Delta \rightsquigarrow_P \Delta$, this means that Δ attacks itself.

Firstly, a plausible hypothesis should not attack itself.

Definition 3.6.   A hypothesis Δ of a bi-disjunctive program P is self-consistent if $\Delta \not\rightsquigarrow_P \Delta$.

The empty hypothesis $\emptyset$ is always self-consistent, called *trivial hypothesis*. The above example shows that there exist non-trivial hypotheses that are not self-consistent.

The following easy corollary will be often used in proofs of some results in subsequent sections.

Corollary 3.1.   *A hypothesis Δ of P is not self-consistent if and only if there exists $\sim b_1 | \cdots | \sim b_n \in \Delta$ such that $\Delta \vdash_P b_i$, $i = 1, \ldots, n$.*

Definition 3.7. For any self-consistent hypothesis Δ of a bi-disjunctive program P, the corresponding state pair S_Δ is called a self-consistent state pair of P.

By Definition 3.3 and 3.5, it is not hard to see that the self-consistency of a hypothesis guarantees that there exists no direct contradiction within the corresponding state pair of this hypothesis. That is, given a self-consistent hypothesis Δ of P, neither of the following two conditions hold for the state S of Δ:

(1) there exist $a_1, \ldots, a_r \in S^+$, such that $\sim a_1 | \cdots | \sim a_r \in S^-$; or

(2) there exists $a_1 | \cdots | a_r \in S^+$, such that $\sim a_1, \ldots, \sim a_r \in S^-$.

Definition 3.8. A state pair $S = < S^+; S^- >$ is consistent if the set of the corresponding first-order formulas of $S^+ \cup S^-$ is consistent.

A self-consistent state pair is not necessarily consistent though there is no direct contradiction within it.

Example 3.4.   Let P be the following disjunctive program:

$$a|b \leftarrow$$
$$b|c \leftarrow$$
$$c|a \leftarrow$$

Take $\Delta = \|\sim a| \sim b, \sim b| \sim c, \sim c| \sim a \|$, then Δ is a self-consistent hypothesis. However, $V_P(\Delta) = \{a|b, b|c, c|a\}$ and $\| V_P(\Delta) \| \cup \Delta$ being considered as a set of first-order formulas is not consistent, thus the state pair $S_\Delta = <\| V_P(\Delta) \|; \Delta >$ is not consistent.

In particular, in many cases, self-consistency of state pairs can still not provide suitable constraints for abductive semantics of bi-disjunctive programs. For example, the disjunctive program P consisting of

$$Sleeping | ListeningFootballGameByRadio \leftarrow \sim ElectricitySupplied$$
$$PossessGoodTV \leftarrow$$

This disjunctive program has two self-consistent hypotheses $\Delta_1 = \|\sim Electricity$ $Supplied \|>$ and $\Delta_2 = \|\sim Sleeping, \sim ListeningFootballGameByRadio, \|$. But it is widely accepted that Δ_1 rather than Δ_2 is the acceptable hypothesis of P.

How can we determine the self-consistent hypotheses of P that capture the intended semantics. In other words, we must specify when a hypothesis of P is acceptable. To accomplish this task, we need to exploit an intuitive and useful principle in argument reasoning: *If one hypothesis can attack each hypothesis that attacks it, then this hypothesis is acceptable* . Ref.[16] illustrates this principle by some examples and study its application in non-disjunctive logic programming.

Now, we formulate this principle in the setting of bi-disjunctive logic programming, which can really provide a suitable criteria for specifying acceptable hypotheses for bi-disjunctive programs and forms the basis of our argumentation-theoretic framework for disjunctive logic programming.

For short, if $\beta = \sim b_1| \cdots | \sim b_m \in DB_P^-$, and Δ' is a hypothesis such that $\Delta' \vdash_P b_i$, for any $i = 1, \ldots, m$, then we say Δ' denies β .

Definition 3.9.   Let Δ be a hypothesis of a bi-disjunctive program P, an assumption β of P is *admissible* with respect to Δ if $\Delta \leadsto_P \Delta'$ holds for any hypothesis Δ' of P such that Δ' denies β. Write $\mathbf{A}_P(\Delta) = \{\beta \in DB_P^- : \beta$ is admissible wrt. $\Delta\}$.

Consider the bi-disjunctive program in Example 3.2 and the hypothesis Δ_1 of P. It is easy to see that $\sim a| \sim b$ is admissible, since any hypothesis Δ' of P that denies $\sim a| \sim b$ must contain the hypothesis $\|\sim a, \sim b \|$ but $\Delta_1 \leadsto_P \|\sim a, \sim b \|$.

$\mathbf{A}_P$ has the following two properties, which are fundamental to the main results in this paper:

Corollary 3.2.   *If Δ and Δ' are two hypotheses of disjunctive program P, then*

(1) $\| \mathbf{A}_P(\Delta) \| = \mathbf{A}_P(\Delta)$, that is, $\mathbf{A}_P(\Delta)$ is a hypothesis of P;

(2) If $\Delta \subseteq \Delta'$, then $\mathbf{A}_P(\Delta) \subseteq \mathbf{A}_P(\Delta')$. This means that $\mathbf{A}_P$ is a monotonic operator.

Intuitively, an acceptable hypothesis should be such one whose assumptions are all admissible with respect to it. Thus the following definition is in order.

Definition 3.10. A hypothesis Δ of a bi-disjunctive program P is said to be admissible if Δ is self-consistent and $\Delta \subseteq A_P(\Delta)$. An admissible (disjunctive) hypothesis of P will be abbreviated as ADH.

An intuitive and equivalent definition for admissible hypotheses will be shown in Section 5 (Theorem 5.1). Before giving examples, we first show a simple lemma.

Lemma 3.1. *Let Δ be a hypothesis of a disjunctive program P. If an assumption $\beta =\sim b_1|\cdots| \sim b_r$ of P is admissible with respect to Δ, then $\beta' =\sim b_1|\cdots| \sim b_r| \sim b_{r+1}|\cdots| \sim b_n$ is also admissible with respect to Δ for any atoms $b_{r+1},\ldots,b_n$ in P and $r \leq n$.*

This lemma is useful when we want to show that a hypothesis of a disjunctive program is admissible: To show that a hypothesis $\Delta =\| \beta_1,\ldots,\beta_n \|$ is admissible, it suffices to show that all assumptions β_i $(i = 1,\ldots,n)$ (the representatives of Δ) are admissible with respect to Δ.

Example 3.5. Consider the following disjunctive program P:

$$a \leftarrow \sim a$$
$$b \leftarrow$$

P has five possible hypotheses: $\Delta_0 = \emptyset$, $\Delta_1 =\| \sim a \|$, $\Delta_2 =\| \sim b \|$, $\Delta_3 =\| \sim a| \sim b \|$, $\Delta_4 =\| \sim a, \sim b \|$, among which Δ_1, Δ_2 and Δ_4 are not self-consistent. Since $\Delta_1 \leadsto_P \Delta_3$ but $\Delta_3 \not\leadsto_P \Delta_1$, Δ_3 is not an ADH of P, thus P has only one ADH $\Delta_0 = \emptyset$ and the corresponding state pair $S_{\Delta_0} =<\| b \|;\emptyset >$.

Example 3.6. The disjunctive program $P = \{a|b \leftarrow \sim a\}$ also has five possible hypotheses as the program in Example 3.5. For $\Delta_1 =\| \sim a \|$, the assumption $\sim a$ is admissible with respect to Δ_1, since $\Delta_4 =\| \sim a, \sim b \|$ is the only hypothesis that can attack Δ_1 and $\Delta_1 \leadsto_P \Delta_4$.

Now we have established the basic argumentation-theoretic framework BDAS for bi-disjunctive logic programs, in which various semantics for performing argumentation-based abduction with bi-disjunctive programs can be defined. Each semantics in our framework will be specified as a subclass of admissible hypotheses (equivalently, admissible state pairs).

4   Some Important Classes of Hypotheses for Bi-disjunctive Programs

As mentioned in Section 1, a suitable semantic framework rather than a single semantics should be defined, in which most of the existing key semantics could be embedded and their shortcomings could be overcome. As well as investigating the inherent relationship between argumentation (abduction) and disjunctive logic programming, we shall attempts to show that our abductive framework defined in section 2 can provide a (at least potentially) suitable framework, in a certain extent, for disjunctive logic programming by defining some abductive semantics and relating to some important semantics, such as the well-founded model, minimal models, stable models and EGCWA.

Definition 4.1. Let Δ be a hypothesis of a bi-disjunctive program P:

(1) A preferred disjunctive hypothesis (PDH) Δ of P is defined as a maximal ADH of P with respect to set inclusion;

(2) If Δ is self-consistent and $\Delta = \mathbf{A}_P(\Delta)$, then Δ is called a complete disjunctive hypothesis (CDH) of P;

(3) If the hypothesis $\mathbf{A}_P \uparrow \omega$ is self-consistent, then it is called the well-founded disjunctive hypothesis of P, denoted as $WFDH(P)$.

If Δ is an ADH (res. PDH, CDH, WFDH), then the corresponding state pair S_Δ is called an ADS (res. PDS, CDS, WFDS) of P.

Definition 4.2. The ADH (res. PDH, CDH, WFDH) semantics for a bi-disjunctive program P is defined as the class of its all ADS (res. PDS, CDS, WFDS).

It follows easily from the above definition that a CDH must be an ADH; In Section 5 we will show that a PDH is a CDH. However, the converses do not hold.

Example 4.1. P consists of only one program clause: $a|b \leftarrow$. Take $\Delta_0 = \emptyset$, then $\mathbf{A}_P(\Delta_0) = \|\sim a| \sim b \|$. Hence Δ_0 is an ADH of P but not a CDH. If $\Delta_1 = \|\sim a| \sim b \|$, then $\mathbf{A}_P(\Delta_1) = \Delta_1$ and thus Δ_1 is a CDH of P but not a PDH, since $\Delta_2 = \|\sim a \|$ is an ADH of P and $\Delta_1 \subset \Delta_2$.

Since $\emptyset$ is always an admissible hypothesis, each bi-disjunctive program has at least one PDH.

Theorem 4.1. *The semantics ADH is complete for the class of bi-disjunctive programs. That is, each bi-disjunctive program has at least one PDH.*

The completeness of CDH and WFDH will be delayed to Section 5. In the remaining of this section, by some examples, we will show the difference of BDAS from other semantics and illustrate behaviors of our argumentation-theoretic semantic framework BDAS in knowledge representation.

Example 4.2. Let P be the following disjunctive program:

$$a|b \leftarrow$$
$$a \leftarrow$$

Most of semantics for disjunctive programs assign the truth of b to false with respect the above program (credulous reasoning), , except the possible model semantics [33] and the WGCWA [31](skeptical reasoning). In BDAS, P has three admissible hypotheses $\Delta_1 = \emptyset$, $\Delta_2 = \|\sim a| \sim b \|$ and $\Delta_3 = \|\sim b \|$. In particular, the WFDS of P is $S_1 = <\| a \|; \emptyset >$ and the PDH is $<\| a \|; \|\sim b \|>$. Thus,

$\sim b$ is unknown with respect to WFDH but is true with respect to PDH , and this implies that both the skeptical and credulous reasoning of P can all be represented in BDAS.

Example 4.3.   Let P be the program :

$$a \leftarrow \sim a$$
$$b \leftarrow$$

We know from Example 3.5 that P has only one ADH $\Delta_0 = \emptyset$ and the corresponding state pair $S_{\Delta_0} =<\| b \|; \emptyset >$. This conclusion coincides our intuition on P, that is, P provides no information about a for us and thus, from P, we can infer neither a nor $\sim a$, but can infer b. This example shows that BDAS can handle the inconsistency of disjunctive programs properly. Notice that the Clark completion of P is not consistent and P has no stable model.

5   Characterizations of BDAS

As the basis for further investigation, this section is devoted to study some fundamental properties of BDAS. First, we give an intuitive and equivalent characterization of admissible hypotheses, which will be often used as an alternative definition for Definition 3.10.

Theorem 5.1.   *Let Δ be a self-consistent hypothesis of a bi-disjunctive program P. Then Δ is an ADH of P if and only if $\Delta \leadsto_P \Delta'$ for any hypothesis Δ' of P satisfying $\Delta' \leadsto_P \Delta$.*

This theorem shows that an ADH is such a hypothesis that can attack any hypothesis that attacks it.

In the following we will characterize ADHs in another way.

Definition 5.1. Let Δ and Δ' be two ADHs of a bi-disjunctive program P. If $\Delta \subseteq \Delta'$, then Δ' is called an admissible extension of Δ. In particular, Δ' is called a non-trivial admissible extension of Δ if $\Delta \neq \Delta'$.

Definition 5.2.
Let Δ be an ADH of a bi-disjunctive program P. If Δ' satisfies the following two conditions:
(1) $\Delta \cup \Delta'$ is self-consistent; and
(2) $\Delta' \subseteq A_P(\Delta \cup \Delta')$.
Then Δ' is called a plausible hypothesis with respect to Δ.

The following three corollaries can be easily obtained by Definition 5.1 and Definition 5.2.

Corollary 5.1.   *If Δ' is a plausible hypothesis wrt an ADH Δ, then $\Delta \cup \Delta'$ is an ADH.*

Corollary 5.2.   *Δ' is an admissible extension of Δ if and only if $\Delta \subseteq \Delta'$ and $\Delta' \setminus \Delta$ is plausible with respect to Δ.*

Corollary 5.3. *For any bi-disjunctive program P, the following statements are equivalent:*

   (1) Δ is an ADH of P;

   (2) Δ is an admissible extension of the empty hypothesis $\emptyset$;

   (3) Δ is plausible with respect to $\emptyset$.

Definition 5.3. An admissible sequence of a bi-disjunctive program P is a sequence $\Delta_1, \Delta_2, \ldots, \Delta_n, \ldots$ of ADHs of P such that $\Delta_n \subseteq \Delta_{n+1}$ for any $n > 0$.

The following proposition states that the sequences of bi-disjunctive program P possess the property of completeness.

Proposition 5.1. *For any admissible sequence $\Delta_1, \Delta_2, \ldots, \Delta_n, \ldots$ of a bi-disjunc- tive program P, the hypothesis $\Delta = \cup_{n=1}^{\infty} \Delta_n$ is an ADH of P.*

In particular, we have the following result:

Corollary 5.4. *Every ADH of a bi-disjunctive program P is contained in a PDH.*

The following proposition is fundamental and our many results in BDAS for disjunctive programs will be based on it.

Proposition 5.2. *For any ADH Δ of a disjunctive program P, if $\alpha \in DB_P^-$ is admissible wrt. Δ, that is, $\alpha \in \mathbf{A}_P(\Delta)$, then $\Delta' = \| \Delta \cup \{\alpha\} \|$ is also an ADH of P.*

This result guarantees that, for any ADH Δ of a disjunctive program P, if α is admissible wrt. Δ and $\alpha \notin \Delta$ then we can obtain a non-trivial admissible extension of Δ by simply adding α to Δ.

As a direct corollary of Theorem 5.1, it is not hard to see that a PDH of a disjunctive program must be a CDH.

Proposition 5.3. *If Δ is a PDH of a disjunctive program P, then Δ is also a CDH of P.*

Corollary 5.5. *Each disjunctive program has at least one CDH. That is, semantics CDH is complete for the class of all disjunctive programs.*

In the rest of this section, we will show the existence and completeness of WFDH. P will be a disjunctive program if it is not stated explicitly. $H(P)$ is the set of all disjunctive hypotheses of P and it can be easily verified that the partial order set $(H(P), \subseteq)$ is a complete lattice. From Definition 3.9, $\mathbf{A}_P$ can be considered as an operator on $H(P)$, called the admissible operator of P, and we will show that $\mathbf{A}_P$ is continuous.

Lemma 5.1. *For any disjunctive program P, its admissible operator $\mathbf{A}_P : H(P) \to H(P)$ is continuous. That is, for any directed subset $\mathbf{D}$ of $H(P)$, the following holds:*

$$\mathbf{A}_P(\cup\{\Delta : \Delta \in \mathbf{D}\}) = \cup\{\mathbf{A}_P(\Delta) : \Delta \in \mathbf{D}\}.$$

Remark: A subset **D** of a complete lattice is directed if every finite subset of **D** has an upper bound in **D**.

It follows from Lemma 5.1 and Tarski's theorem [35] that $\mathbf{A}_P$ has the least fixpoint $lfp(\mathbf{A}_P)$ and $lfp(\mathbf{A}_P) = \mathbf{A}_P \uparrow \omega$, that is, the closure cardinal of $\mathbf{A}_P$ is ω. Therefore, the following theorem is obtained.

Theorem 5.2. *Every disjunctive program P possesses the unique well-founded disjunctive hypothesis (WFDH).*

From Theorem 4.1, Corollary 5.5 and Theorem 5.2, it follows that the three semantics PDH, CDH and WFDH are all complete for disjunctive programs.

6   Relationship Between BDAS and Some Other Approaches

In this section we investigate the relationship between BDAS and some other semantics for (disjunctive) logic programs. The main results of this section can be summarized as the following:

(1) PDH coincides with the stable semantics for an extensive subclass of disjunctive programs.

(2) WFDH for non-disjunctive programs coincides with the well-founded semantics.

(3) In particular, we show that the WFDH provides a quite new characterization of EGCWA [41] by argumentation (abduction).

Thus, WFDH integrates and extends both the well-founded semantics for non-disjunctive logic programs and EGCWA for positive disjunctive programs. As a result, EGCWA can be used to implement argumentative reasoning in deductive databases.

6.1   BDAS for Non-disjunctive Programs

As a special case, we consider the BDAS of non-disjunctive logic programs. In this subsection, P will be a non-disjunctive program. Let Δ be a (disjunctive) hypothesis of P, that is, $\Delta \subseteq DB_P^-$, and $L(\Delta)$ denotes the set of all negative literals in Δ.

Definition 6.1. A hypothesis Δ of P is a non-disjunctive hypothesis of P if $L(\Delta) = can(\Delta)$. That is, the set of representatives of a non-disjunctive hypothesis consists of only negative literals.

It follows from Definition 3.3 that, for any non-disjunctive program P and $a \in B_P$,

$$\Delta \vdash_P a \text{ iff } a \in Min(P_\Delta^+) \text{ iff } a \in Min(P_{L(\Delta)}^+).$$

Corollary 6.1. *If Δ is a CDH of non-disjunctive program P, then $L(\Delta) = can(\Delta)$, that is, the CDHs of a non-disjunctive program are non-disjunctive.*

It follows from Corollary 6.1 and the result in Ref.[21, 22] that, for any non-disjunctive program P, we will get the equivalent definition of Definition 3.5 if the basic inference $\Delta \vdash_P a$ is replaced by $P \cup \Delta \vdash a$. This means that our CDH and Dung's complete extension are equivalent concepts for the class of non-disjunctive programs.

Theorem 6.1.   *If Δ is a non-disjunctive hypothesis of non-disjunctive program P, then the following two statements are equivalent:*

(1) *Δ is a CDH of P;*
(2) *$P \cup L(\Delta)$ is a complete extension.*

This theorem shows that BDAS generalizes the frameworks of Dung [15] and Torres [37].

6.2   BDAS for Positive Disjunctive Programs

In this subsection we investigate the relationship between BDAS and some semantics for positive disjunctive programs (without negation in the bodies of program clauses). In particular, we show that the well-founded disjunctive hypotheses (WFDHs) provide a quite new characterization of EGCWA by argumentation (abduction). As a result, WFDH integrates and extends both the well-founded semantics for non-disjunctive logic programs and EGCWA for positive disjunctive programs.

If we do not state explicitly, P will denote a positive disjunctive program in this subsection.

Proposition 6.1.   *If $ms(P)$ is the least model state of a positive disjunctive program P, then the state pair corresponding to the ADH $\emptyset$ is $S_\emptyset = < ms(P); \emptyset >$.*

This result shows that the ADH $\emptyset$ characterizes the least model state for positive disjunctive programs.

Proposition 6.2.   *Let Δ be a hypothesis of a positive disjunctive program P:*
(1) If Δ is a PDH of P and Δ is consistent (i. e. the first-order formulas $V_P(\Delta) \cup \Delta$ is consistent), then $I_\Delta = B_P \setminus \{a \in B_P | \sim a \in \Delta\}$ is a minimal model of P;
(2) If I is a minimal model of P then $\Delta = \|\sim \bar{I}\|$ is a PDH of P, where $\bar{I} = B_P \setminus I$ and $\sim \bar{I} = \{\sim a| a \in \bar{I}\}$.

We believe that the condition 'Δ is consistent 'is unnecessary. Moreover, we guess that the ADHs (including the PDHs, CDHs, and WFDHs) are all consistent but we have not found such a precise proof at present.

For any positive disjunctive program P, its WFDH does not only exist, but also can be obtained by one step iteration of $\mathbf{A}_P$ from $\emptyset$.

Proposition 6.3.   *Let P be a positive disjunctive program, then the closure ordinal of $\mathbf{A}_P$ is 1, that is, the (unique) WFDH of P is $\mathbf{A}_P(\emptyset)$.*

To characterize EGCWA in BDAS, we first give the model-theoretic definition of EGCWA [41].

Definition 6.2. *Let P be a positive disjunctive program, then*

$$EGCWA(P) = \{\beta \in DB_P^- : P \models_{min} \beta\}$$

The following theorem shows that $EGCWA$ coincides with $WFDH$ for the class of positive disjunctive programs.

Theorem 6.2.(Characterization of EGCWA by Argumentation)   *For positive disjunctive program P, $EGCWA(P) = WFDH(P)$.*

As noted before, this theorem may be the most interesting result in this paper in that it is not only quite intuitive but also useful in performing argumentation (abduction) in deductive databases by exploiting EGCWA.

The following corollaries are directly obtained from Theorem 6.2 and the results in Ref.[24, 41].

Corollary 6.2.   *For any positive disjunctive program P, its WFDH is consistent.*

The generalized closed world assumption (GCWA) can also be characterized by WFDH.

Corollary 6.3. $GCWA(P) = L(WFDH(P)) = \{\sim a : \sim a \in WFDH(P)\}.$

Corollary 6.4.   *M is a minimal model of P if and only if M is a minimal model of $P \cup WFDH(P)$.*

6.3 The Relationship Between PDH and the Disjunctive Stable Semantics

Both the disjunctive stable semantics and our PDH represents credulous reasoning in disjunctive logic programming but the former is not complete. In this section we will study PDH and its relation to the disjunctive stable semantics. To this end, we first define a program transformation Lft [38, 40] for disjunctive logic programs (called the least fixpoint transformation) and then, an extensive class of disjunctive programs, called the strongly stable disjunctive programs, are introduced, for which we show that PDHs and stable models have a one-to-one correspondence. Hence the abductive semantics PDH is not only complete but can also be considered as a natural and complete extension of the disjunctive stable semantics. Moreover, Lft also provides an optimization technique for the computation of various semantics in BDAS (including many semantics that can be embedded in BDAS).

The program transformation Lft is based on the idea of Dung and Kanchansut [13] and Bry [12]. It is also independently defined by Brass and Dix [8, 7]. To define Lft for disjunctive programs, we first extend the notion of the Herbrand base B_P to *the generalized disjunctive base GDB_P* of a disjunctive logic program P.

GDB_P is defined as the set of all negative disjunctive programs whose atoms are in B_P:

$$GDB_P = \{a_1| \cdots |a_r \leftarrow \sim b_1, \ldots, \sim b_s : a_i, b_j \in B_P, i = 1, \ldots, r; j = 1, \ldots, s\}$$

and $\leftarrow$ the empty clause.

Thus, we can introduce an immediate consequence operator T_P^G for general disjunctive program P, which is similar to the immediate consequence operator $T_{P'}^S$ for positive program P'. The operator T_P^G will provide a basis for defining our program transformation Lft.

Definition 6.3. For any disjunctive program P, the generalized consequence operator $T_P^G : 2^{GDB_P} \to 2^{GDB_P}$ is defined as, for any $J \subseteq GDB_P$,

$$T_P^G(J) = \{C \in GDB_P : \text{There exist a disjunctive clause } \alpha' \leftarrow b_1, \ldots, b_m, \sim b_{m+1}$$

$$, \ldots, \sim b_s \text{ and } C_1, \ldots, C_m \in GDB_P \cup \{\leftarrow\} \text{ such that} (1) \ b_i|head(C_i) \leftarrow body(C_i)$$

$$\text{is in } J, \text{ for all } i = 1, \ldots, m; (2) \ C \text{ is the clause } can(\alpha'|head(C_1)| \cdots |head(C_m))$$

$$\leftarrow body(C_1), \ldots, body(C_m), \sim b_{m+1}, \ldots, \sim b_s\}.$$

This definition looks a little tedious at first sight. In fact, its intuition is quite simple and it defines the following form of resolution:

$$\frac{\alpha' \leftarrow b_1, \ldots, b_m, \beta_1, \ldots, \beta_s; \ b_1|\alpha_1 \leftarrow \beta_{11}, \ldots, \beta_{1t_1}; \ \cdots; b_m|\alpha_m \leftarrow \beta_{m1}, \ldots, \beta_{mt_m}}{\alpha'|\alpha_1| \cdots |\alpha_m \leftarrow \beta_{11}, \ldots, \beta_{1t_1}, \cdots, \beta_{m1}, \ldots, \beta_{mt_m}, \beta_1, \ldots, \beta_s}$$

where αs with subscripts are positive disjunctive literals and βs with subscripts are negative disjunctive literals.

Example 6.1. Suppose that $P = \{a_1|a_2 \leftarrow a_3, \sim a_4; \ a_3|a_5 \leftarrow \sim a_6\}$ and $J = T_P^G(\emptyset)$. Then $T_P^G(\emptyset) = \{a_3|a_5 \leftarrow \sim a_6\}$; If $J' = T_P^G(T_P^G(\emptyset))$. Then $T_P^G(J') = T_P^G(T_P^G(\emptyset)) = \{a_3|a_5 \leftarrow \sim a_6; \ a_1|a_2|a_5 \leftarrow \sim a_4, \sim a_6\}$.

Notice that T_P^G is a generalization of T_P^S if a disjunctive program clause $a_1| \cdots |a_n \leftarrow$ is treated as the disjunct $a_1| \cdots |a_n$. The following proposition shows that T_P^G possesses the least fixpoint.

Lemma 6.1. *For any disjunctive program P, its generalized consequence operator T_P^G is continuous and hence possesses the least fixpoint $T_P^G \uparrow \omega$.*

It is obvious that the least fixpoint of T_P^G does not only exist but also is computable. Since $T_P^G \uparrow \omega$ is a negative disjunctive program, T_P^G results in a computable program transformation which will be defined in the next definition.

Definition 6.4. Denote $T_P^G \uparrow \omega$ as $Lft(P)$, then $Lft : P \to Lft(P)$ defines a transformation from the set of all disjunctive programs to the set of all negative disjunctive programs, and we say that $Lft(P)$ is the least fixpoint transformation of P.

The following lemma asserts that $Lft(P)$ has the same least model-state as P and it is fundamental to prove some invariance properties of Lft under various semantics for disjunctive programs.

Lemma 6.2 *For any hypothesis Δ of disjunctive program P, $(Lft(P)^+_\Delta)$ possesses the same least model-state as P^+_Δ :*

$$ms(Lft(P)^+_\Delta) = ms(P^+_\Delta).$$

Firstly, we show that the program transformation $Lft(P)$ preserves our abductive semantics.

Theorem 6.3. *For any disjunctive program P, P is equivalent to its least fixpoint transformation $Lft(P)$ with respect to BDAS. As a result, $Lft(P)$ has the same ADH (res. CDH, PDH) as P.*

The following proposition, which is also independently given by Brass and Dix in [7], shows that the least fixpoint transformation also preserves the (disjunctive) stable models.

For any disjunctive program P, and $M \subseteq B_P$. Set

$$P/M = \{a_1| \cdots |a_r \leftarrow a_{r+1}, \ldots, a_s : \text{ there exists a clause of } P: a_1| \cdots |a_r \leftarrow$$

$$a_{r+1}, \ldots, a_s, \sim a_{s+1}, \ldots, \sim a_t \text{ such that } a_{s+1}, \ldots, a_t \notin M\}.$$

If M is a minimal model of P/M, then it is a (disjunctive) stable model of P. The disjunctive stable semantics of P is defined as the set of its all disjunctive table models.

Proposition 6.4. *For any disjunctive program P, P is equivalent to its least fixpoint transformation $Lft(P)$ with respect to the stable semantics. That is, P has the same set of the stable models as $Lft(P)$.*

Let Δ be a hypothesis of disjunctive program P, P^*_Δ is defined as the disjunctive program obtained by the following transformations:

1. For any clause C in P, if $a \in head(C)$ and $\sim a \in \Delta$, then delete a from the head of C; if $\sim b \in body(C)$ and $\sim b \in \Delta$, then delete $\sim b$ from the body of C;

2. From the program obtained by the step 1, delete all the clauses that have empty heads;

3. For any $a \in B_P$ such that all the clauses containing a or $\sim a$ have been deleted by the above two steps, add a new clause $a \leftarrow a$.

Notice that the step 3 is technical, which is to keep P^*_Δ has the same Herbrand base as P. But the step 2 is necessary and it can guarantees that P^*_Δ has a stable model if P has at least one. For example, if $P = \{a|b \leftarrow c\}$ and $\Delta = \|\sim a, \sim b\|$, then P will be transformed to the program $\{\leftarrow c\}$, which has no stable model.

Definition 6.5. A disjunctive program P is strongly stable if, for any $\Delta \in H(P)$, P^*_Δ possesses at least one stable model.

It is obvious that positive disjunctive programs are strongly stable. More generally, the class of (local) stratified disjunctive programs are strongly stable. Thus, the class of strongly stable disjunctive programs is extensive enough.

The main theorem of this subsection can be stated as follows.

Theorem 6.4. *Suppose that disjunctive program P is strongly stable and its all PDHs are consistent:*

1. *If Δ is a PDH of P, then $I_\Delta = \{a \in B_P : \sim a \notin \Delta\}$ is a stable model of P.*

2. *If M is a stable model of P, then $\Delta_M =\|\{\sim a : a \in B_P \setminus M\}\|$ is a PDH of P.*

As mentioned before, we believe that the condition 'the PDHs of P are consistent' is unnecessary.

This theorem establishes a one-one correspondence between the PDHs and the stable models for any strongly stable programs. Therefore, PDH extends the stable semantics to the whole class of disjunctive programs. Moreover, this result reveals the relationship between credulous argumentation and the stable semantics for disjunctive logic programming.

Corollary 6.5. *Any (local) stratified disjunctive program P has the unique PDH.*

6.4   Relations to Some Other Approaches

Becides the semantics discussed in the previous subsections of Section 6, there have been proposed some other interesting approaches of defining semantics for disjunctive logic programs, such as the static semantics [30], the D-WFS [7, 9]. In this subsection we will compare our BDAS to these semantics.

Example 6.2.   Consider disjunctive program P:

$$a|b \leftarrow$$
$$c \leftarrow \sim a$$
$$c \leftarrow \sim b$$

We need to consider only the following seven assumptions of P:

$$\sim a, \sim b, \sim c, \sim a| \sim b, \sim b| \sim c, \sim c| \sim a, , \sim a| \sim b| \sim c.$$

The possible hypotheses of P has 19:

$$
\begin{aligned}
&\Delta_0 = \emptyset, &&\Delta_1 =\|\sim a\|, \\
&\Delta_2 =\|\sim b\|, &&\Delta_3 =\|\sim c\|, \\
&\Delta_4 =\|\sim a|\sim b\|, &&\Delta_5 =\|\sim b|\sim c\|, \\
&\Delta_6 =\|\sim a|\sim c\|, &&\Delta_7 =\|\sim a|\sim b|\sim c\|, \\
&\Delta_8 =\|\sim a,\sim b\|, &&\Delta_9 =\|\sim a,\sim c\|, \\
&\Delta_{10} =\|\sim b,\sim c\|, &&\Delta_{11} =\|\sim a,\sim b|\sim c\|, \\
&\Delta_{12} =\|\sim a|\sim c,\sim b\|, &&\Delta_{13} =\|\sim a|\sim b,\sim c\|, \\
&\Delta_{14} =\|\sim a|\sim b,\sim c|\sim a\|, &&\Delta_{15} =\|\sim a|\sim b,\sim b|\sim c\|, \\
&\Delta_{16} =\|\sim b|\sim c,\sim c|\sim a\|, &&\Delta_{17} =\|\sim a,\sim b,\sim c\|, \\
&\Delta_{18} =\|\sim a|\sim b,\sim b|\sim c,\sim c|\sim a\|,
\end{aligned}
$$

where $\Delta_0, \Delta_1, \Delta_2, \Delta_4, \Delta_{17}$ are all the ADHs of P; $\Delta_1, \Delta_2, \Delta_4$ are CDHs; the PDHs Δ_1, Δ_2 correspond to the stable models $\{b, c\}$ and $\{a, c\}$. WFDH of P is Δ_4 and the state pair $WFDH(P) = S_{\Delta_4} = <\| \, a|b \, \|; \| \sim a| \sim b \, \|>$.

The least stationary model [29] and the static model of P coincide and equal to $\tilde{S} = <\| \, a|b, c \, \|, \| \sim a| \sim b \, \|>$. It is obvious that $WFDH(P)^- = \tilde{S}^-$ but c can not be inferred in WFDH from P.

This example has been used by many authors to show the suitability of their semantics. It is known that, from this program, the extended well-founded semantics [32] and the GDWFS [4] do not infer c to be true; but the static semantics [30] and the disjunctive stable semantics [28] infer a to be true. This phenomenon is caused because different semantics provide deferent meaning for the disjunction. An interesting problem is that: Can these two disjunctions (classical and epistemic) be represented in the bodies of rules by one single semantics for disjunctive logic programming. To solve this problem, it is necessary that the syntax should be extended. Now, we show this problem can be treated in our WFDH semantics for bi-disjunctive programs. In particular, the classical disjunction in program $P_1 = \{c \leftarrow \sim a \vee \sim b\}$ can be represented by changing P_1 into $\{c \leftarrow \sim a; \; c \leftarrow \sim b\}$ and the program $P_2 = \{c \leftarrow \sim a| \sim b\}$ represents the epistemic disjunction of $\sim a| \sim b$.

Example 6.3.   Let P' be the bi-disjunctive program:

$$a|b \leftarrow$$
$$c \leftarrow \sim a| \sim b$$

Similar to Example 6.2, it can be shown that $WFDH(P') = <\| \, a|b, c \, \|, \| \sim a| \sim b \, \|>$. It is obvious that we can infer c from P'.

By Theorem 6.4, the relationship between the stationary semantics and PDH can be formulated as the following result.

Corollary 6.6.   *For any strongly stable disjunctive program P, stationary models coincide with preferred disjunctive state-pairs (PDSs).*

Dix and Brass [7] propose an interesting and general approach to define semantics for disjunctive programs simply by postulating some semantic properties. In particular, they define a generalization of the well-founded semantics called D-WFS. Though D-WFS and WFDH have quite different intuitions, D-WFS bears some similarities with our WFDH: (1) it extends the well-founded model for non-disjunctive programs and (E)GCWA for positive disjuntive programs; (2) it represents also a form of skeptical reasoning in disjunctive logic programming. However, we will show that WFDH is different from D-WFS. In fact, D-WFS is more skeptical than WFDH.

As shown by Dix and Brass in [7], for any disjunctive program P, the negative disjunctive program $Lft(P)$ can be further reduced to the so-called residual program $res(P)$.

Lemma 6.3. *For any disjunctive program P, P is equivalent to $res(P)$ wrt. BDAS. In particular, $WFDH(P) = WFDH(res(P))$.*

By Lemma 6.3, it is direct to prove the following result.

Proposition 6.5. *WFDH is less skeptical than D-WFS. That is, $D\text{-}WFS(P) \subseteq WFDH(P)$ but '$\subseteq$'can not be replaced by '$=$'in general.*

Notice that D-WFS and WFDH have some other differences. For example, if $\alpha =\sim a_1| \cdots | \sim a_r$ is a disjunctive hypothesis of P with $\alpha \in D\text{-}WFS$ then there exists at least one $i(1 \leq i \leq r)$ such that $\sim a_i \in D\text{-}WFS(P)$. However, WFDH allows one concludes 'true 'disjunctive information. Take $P = \{a|b \leftarrow\}$, it is not hard to see that $D\text{-}WFS(P)$ contains no negative (disjunctive) literals. However, $\sim a| \sim b \in WFDH(P)$ even though neither $\sim a \in WFDH(P)$ nor $\sim b \in WFDH(P)$.

Moreover, $WFDH(P)$ and $D\text{-}WFS(P)$ may have distinct sets of non-disjunctive literals as the following example shows.

Example 6.4. Let P consist of only one clause:

$$a|b \leftarrow \sim a$$

Since $P = res(P)$, it is easy to see that $\sim a \in WFDH(P)$ but $\sim a \notin D\text{-}WFS(P)$. For this program, it seems that WFDH should be the intended meaning of negation as failure.

Consider another similar example.

Example 6.5. Let P be the following disjunctive program:

$$a|b \leftarrow$$
$$c \leftarrow \sim a$$

Then it can be verified that $WFDH(P) =<\| b, c \|; \| \sim a \|>$ and $D\text{-}WFS(P) = <\| a|b \|; \emptyset >$.

Thus, our result further convinces that D-WFS is the most skeptical semantics for disjunctive logic programs.

7   Conclusion

In this paper, we have provided an extension of disjunctive logic programming both from semantics and syntax. Syntactically, the class of bi-disjunctive programs is defined, which includes disjunctive programs and can be considered as a subclass of super logic programs; Semantically, an argumentation-theoretic framework BDAS for bi-disjunctive programs is established, which is a simple, unifying and intuitive framework for disjunctive logic programming. In BDAS three semantics PDH, CDH and WFDH for bi-disjunctive programs are defined by three kinds of admissible hypotheses to represent credulous reasoning, moderate reasoning and skeptical reasoning in AI, respectively. Besides its rich expressive power and nondeterminism, BDAS integrates and naturally extends many key semantics, such as the minimal models, EGCWA, the well-founded model, and the stable models.

Besides the unifying frameworks mentioned in the previous sections, Bonatti [5] has also defined a unifying framework for disjunctive logic programs by viewing a disjunctive program as an epistemic theory. In our opinion, this framework and some of existing ones are not so intuitive as BDAS and argumentation is not treated. An interesting problem to be further investigated is the relationship between BDAS and some other major semantics for disjunctive programs. Some of the most interesting applications of BDAS have to also be left for future work. Another problem that has not been touched in this paper is the relationship between argumentation and extended disjunctive logic programming. Since the situation becomes quite complicated when the explicit negation is allowed in BDAS, this problem has to be discussed in a separate paper. A weak form of cumulativity of nonmonotonic reasoning defined by WFDH is given in [38] and further work is needed.

Acknowledgements

We would like to thank Juergen Dix, Teodor Przymusinski and the two anonymous referees for their useful comments. This work has been partially supported by the National High Tech. Development Program of China (863-306).

References

1. Apt,K., Blair,H., and Walker,A., "Towards a theory of declarative knowledge ", in *Foundations of Deductive Databases and Logic Programming*, Morgan Kaufmann, San Mateo, CA, pp.89-148, 1988.
2. Alfereira,J.and Pereira,L., "An argumentation theoretic semantics based on non-refutable falsity.", in *Proceedings of International Workshop on Nonmonotonic Extensions of Logic Programming* (LNCS), 1994.
3. Aravindan,C., "An abductive framework for negation in disjunctive logic programming, "Tech. report, University of Koblenz-Landau, 1996.
4. Baral,C., Lobo,J., and Minker,J., "Generalized disjunctive well-founded semantics for logic programs. "*Annals of Math and AI*, 5, pp.89-132, 1992
5. Bonatti,P., "Autoepistemic logics as a unifying framework for the semantics of logic programs ", in *Proceedings of the Joint International Conference and Symposium on Logic Programming*, MIT Press, pp.69-86, 1992
6. Bondarenko,A., Toni,F. and Kowalski,R., "An assumption-based framework for non-monotonic reasoning, "in *Proceedings of the 2nd International Workshop on LNMR*, MIT Press, pp.171-189, 1993.
7. Brass,S. and Dix J. Semantics of disjunctive logic programs based on partial evaluation. *Journal of Logic Programming*(to appear), 1998. Extended abstract appeared in Disjunctive semantics based upon partial and bottom-up evaluation. In *Proceedings of the 12th International Logic Programming Conference*, MIT Press, pp. 199–213, 1995.
8. Brass,S. and Dix J. Characterizations of the disjunctive stable semantics by partial evaluation. *Journal of Logic Programming*, 32(3), pp.207-228, 1997. Extended

abstract appeared in: Characterizations of the stable semantics by partial evaluation, in *LPNMR, Proceedings of the Third International Conference* (LNCS928), Springer, pp.85-98, 1995.

9. Brass,S. and Dix J. Characterizations of the disjunctive well-founded semantics: confluent calculi and iterated GCWA. *Journal of Automated Reasoning*, 20(1), pp.143–165, 1998. Extended abstract appeared in: Characterizing DWFS: Confluence and Iterated GCWA, in *Logics in Artificial Intelligence, JELIA '96* (LNCS 1126), Springer, pp. 268–283, 1996.

10. Brass,S.,Dix, J. and Przymusinki,T., "Super logic programs, "in *Principles of Knowledge Representation and Reasoning: Proceedings of the Fifth International Conference (KR '96)*, (L. C. Aiello and J. Doyle and S. C. Shapiro, editors), Morgan Kaufmann, pp. 529–541, 1996.

11. Brewka,G.,"An abductive framework for generalized logic programs,"in *Proceedings of the 2nd Workshop on Logic Programming and Nonmonotonic Reasoning* (Marek, W. and Subrahmanian,V. eds.), MIT Press, pp. 266-282, 1993.

12. Bry, F., "Negation in logic programming: A formalization in constructive logic,"in *Information Systems and Artificial Intelligence: Integration Aspects* (Karagiannis D. ed.), Springer, pp.30-46, 1990.

13. Dung, P., Kanchansut K., "A fixpoint approach to declarative semantics of logic programs,"in *Proceedings of North American Conference* (Lusk E. and Overbeek R. eds.), MIT Press, 1989.

14. Dung,P., "Negation as hypothesis: an abductive foundation to logic programming,"in *Proceedings of the 8th International Conference on Logic Programming*, MIT Press, pp.3-17, 1991.

15. Dung,P., "An argumentation-theoretic foundation for logic programming," *J. Logic Programming*, 24, pp.151-177, 1995.

16. Dung,P., "On the acceptability of arguments and its fundamental roles in nonmonotonic reasoning and n-person games ", *Artificial Intelligence*, 77, pp.321-357, 1995.

17. Eshghi,K. and Kowalski,R., "Abduction compared with negation by failure,"in *Proceedings of the 6th International Conference on Logic Programming*, MIT Press, pp.234-255, 1989.

18. Gelfond,M. and Lifschitz,J., "The stable model semantics for logic programming,"in *Proceedings of the 5th Symposium on Logic Programming*, MIT Press, pp.1070-1080,1988.

19. van Gelder,A., Ross,K. and Schlipf,J., "Unfounded sets and well-founded semantics for general logic programs,"in *Proceedings of the 7th ACM Symposium on Principles Of Database Systems*, pp.221-230,1988. Full version in *J. ACM*, 38, pp. 620-650,1992.

20. Kakas,A., Kowalski,R. and Toni,F., "Abductive logic programming," *J. Logic and Computation*, 2, pp.719-770,1992.

21. Kakas,A. and Mancarella,P., "Generalized stable models: a semantics for abduction,"in *Proceedings of the 9th European Conference Artificial Intelligence*, pp.385-391, 1990.

22. Kakas,A. and Mancarella,P., "Negation as stable hypotheses,"in *Proceedings of the 1st Workshop on Logic Programming and Nonmonotonic Reasoning* (Marek, W. and Subrahmanian,V. eds.), MIT Press, pp. 275-288, 1991.

23. Lifschitz,V. and Turner,H., "From disjunctive programs to abduction,"in *Proceedings of the Workshop on Nonmonotonic Extensions of Logic Programming*, (Dix,J., Pereira,L. and Przymunski,T. eds.), pp. 111-125, 1994.

24. Lobo,J., Minker,J. and Rajasekar,A., *Foundations of Disjunctive Logic Programming*, MIT Press, 1992.
25. Minker,J., "On indefinite databases and the closed world assumption ", in *LNCS 138*, Springer, pp.292-308, 1982.
26. Minker,J., "Overview of disjunctive logic programming," *Ann. Math. AI.*, 12, pp.1-24, 1994.
27. Minker,J. and Rajasekar,A., A fixed point semantics for disjunctive logic programs, *"J. Logic Programming*, 9, 45-74, 1990.
28. Przymunski,T., "Stable semantics for disjunctive programs," *New Generation Computing*, 9, pp.401-424, 1991.
29. Przymunski,T., "Stationary semantics for disjunctive logic programs and deductive databases,"in *Proceedings of the North American Conference on Logic Programming* (Debray,S. and Hemenegildo,M. eds.), MIT Press, pp. 42-59,1991.
30. Przymunski,T., "Static semantics of logic programs," *Ann. Math. AI.*, 14, 323-357, 1995.
31. Rajasekar,A., Lobo,J., and Minker,J., "Weak Generalized Closed World assumption ", *Journal of Automated Reasoning*, 5, pp.293-307, 1989.
32. Ross,K. "Well-founded semantics for disjunctive logic programming. "*Proceedings of the first Conference on Deductive and Object-Oriented Databases*, pp.337-351, 1989.
33. Sakama,C., "Possible model semantics for disjunctive databases ", in *Proc. the First Int'l Conf. on Deductive and Object Oriented Databases*, pp.1055-1060, 1989.
34. Sakama,C. and Inoue,K., "On the equivalence between disjunctive and abductive logic programming,"in *Proceedings of the 11th International Conference on Logic Programming* (Van Hentenryck ed.), MIT Press, pp.489-503, 1994.
35. Tarski,A., "A lattice-theoretic fixpoint theorem and its applications,"*Pacific J. Math.*, 5, pp.285-309, 1955.
36. Torres,A., "Negation as failure to support,"in *Proceedings of the 2nd International Workshop on Logic Programming and Nonmonotonic Reasoning* (Marek, W. and Subrahmanian,V. eds.), MIT Press, pp.223-243, 1993.
37. Torres,A., "A nondeterministic semantics,"*J. Math. AI.*, 14, pp.37-73, 1995.
38. Wang,K., "Abduction and Disjunctive Logic Programming,"Ph. D. Thesis (in Chinese, Abstract in English), Nankai University, March 1996.
39. Wang, K., "An argumentation-based semantic framework for bi-disjunctive logic programs,"Tech. report NUDT97-14, Changsha Institute of Technology, 1997.
40. Wang, K., Chen H. and Wu Q., "The least fixpoint transformation for disjunctive logic programs, "*Journal of Computer Science and Technology*, 13(3), pp.193-201.
41. Yahya,A. and Henschen,L., "Deduction in non-Horn databases,"*J. Automated Reasoning*, 1, pp.141-160, 1985.

Reasoning with Prioritized Defaults

Michael Gelfond and Tran Cao Son

Computer Science Department
University of Texas at El Paso
El Paso, Texas 79968
{mgelfond,tson}@cs.utep.edu

Abstract. The purpose of this paper is to investigate the methodology of reasoning with prioritized defaults in the language of logic programs under the answer set semantics. We present a domain independent system of axioms, written as an extended logic program, which defines reasoning with prioritized defaults. These axioms are used in conjunction with a description of a particular domain encoded in a simple language allowing representation of defaults and their priorities. Such domain descriptions are of course domain dependent and should be specified by the users. We give sufficient conditions for consistency of domain descriptions and illustrate the use of our system by formalizing various examples from the literature. Unlike many other approaches to formalizing reasoning with priorities ours does not require development of the new semantics of the language. Instead, the meaning of statements in the domain description is given by the system of (domain independent) axioms. We believe that in many cases this leads to simpler and more intuitive formalization of reasoning examples. We also present some discussion of differences between various formalizations.

1 Introduction

The purpose of this paper is to investigate the methodology of reasoning with prioritized defaults in the language of logic programs under the answer set semantics. Information about relative strengths of defaults can be commonly found in natural language descriptions of various domains. For instance, in legal reasoning it is often used to state preference of some laws over others, e.g., federal laws in the U.S. can, in some cases, override the laws of a particular state. Preferences are also used in reasoning with expert's knowledge where they are assigned in accordance with the degree of our confidence in different experts. Sometimes preferences in the natural language description of the domain are given implicitly, e.g., a conflict between two contradictory defaults can be resolved by selecting the one which is based on more specific information. All these examples suggest that it may be useful to consider knowledge representation languages capable of describing defaults and preferences between them. There is a sizeable body of literature devoted to design and investigation of such languages [1, 5–7, 11, 23, 30, 32, 33, 36]. The work is too diverse and our knowledge of it is not sufficient to allow a good classification but we will try to mention several important differences in approaches taken by the different authors. To shorten the discussion we limit our attention to approaches based on logic programming and default logics.

Many differences in design seem to be caused by the ambiguity of the very notion of default. Sometimes defaults are understood as statements of natural language, of the form "Elements of a class C *normally* (regularly, as a rule) satisfy property P". Sometimes this understanding is broadened to include all statements with defeasible conclusions. The following example is meant to illustrate the difference.

Suppose we are given a list t of people and want to define the class of people not listed in t. This, of course, can be done by the rule

r1. $unlisted(X) \leftarrow not\ t(X)$.

The conclusion of this statement can be defeated by expanding the table t but cannot be defeated by adding a fact of the form $\neg unlisted(x)$ where $x \notin t$. The attempt to do the latter will (justifiably) lead to contradiction. The statement $r1$ is not a default according to the first, narrow view. It is rather a universally true statement which does not allow exceptions and can not be defeated by other (preferred) statements; of course, according to the second view, $r1$ is a default. Notice, that the statement "Table *unlisted* normally contains all the people not contained in t" is a default according to the both views. Its logic programming representation can have a form

r2. $unlisted(X) \leftarrow not\ t(X), not\ \neg unlisted(X)$.

This time the addition of $\neg unlisted(x)$ where $x \notin t$ cause no contradiction.

This (and similar) differences in understanding of defaults seems to sometimes determine the syntax of the corresponding "default" languages. The first view seems to lead to introducing special syntax for defaults while the second uses standard logic programming syntax augmented by the preference relation among the rules. According to the second view it seems to be also more natural to consider static preference relation, i.e., to prohibit occurrence of the preference relation in the rules of the program.

Even more important differences can be found on determining the correct modes of default reasoning. To demonstrate the problem let us accept a narrow view of defaults and consider the theory consisting of three defaults:

d1. "Normally a";

d2. "Normally b"

d1. "Normally c"

and three rules

r1. "b's are always $\neg a$'s";

r2.   "b's are always d's";

r3.   "a's are always d's";

There seems to be at least three equally reasonable ways to deal with this theory. We can assume that it is inconsistent and entail everything (or nothing); We can be cautious and refuse to apply defaults $d1$ and $d2$. In this case the only conclusion is c. We can be less cautious and reason by cases entailing d supported by two different arguments. With preference relation the situation will become even less clear since we will have an additional difficult question of defining what we mean by a conflict between defaults.

Different choices made by the authors of default languages are expressed in their semantics given by defining the entailment and/or the derivability relation for the language. The corresponding new logics can often be viewed as "prioritized" versions of the existing general purpose non-monotonic formalisms [1, 5–7, 32, 28] with new level of complexity added in fixpoint (or other) constructions defining the semantics. The viability of new logics is normally demonstrated by using it for formalization of some examples of default reasoning aimed to illustrate special features of the logic and the inadequacy of other formalisms. This process, even though useful and necessary, is often complicated by our collective lack of experience in representing knowledge about defaults and their preferences. It is often unclear for instance, if unintuitive answers to queries given by various formalisms can be blamed on the formalism itself or on the inadequate representation of the original problem. Moreover, it is often unclear what is the "common-sense", natural language description of the original problem of which the corresponding formal theory claims to be a representation. This, together with technical complexity of definitions, lack of the developed mathematical theories for new logics and the absence of clearly understood parameters which determine the choice of the semantics make their use for knowledge representation a rather difficult task.

This paper is the result of the authors attempts to understand some of the issues discussed above. We wanted to design a simple language, $\mathcal{L}$, capable of expressing and reasoning with prioritized defaults satisfying (among others) the following requirements:

• Understand defaults in a narrow sense as statements of the form a's are normally b's.

• Allow dynamic priorities, i.e., defaults and rules about the preference relation.

• Give semantics of $\mathcal{L}$ without developing new general purpose nonmonotonic formalism.

• Make sure that changes in informal parameters of the language such as properties of the preference relation, the definitions of conflicting defaults, cautiousness or bravery in reasoning are reflected by comparatively simple changes in the formalism.

- Make sure that some inference mechanism is available to reason with theories of $\mathcal{L}$ and some mathematical theory is available to prove properties of these theories.

We achieve these goals by mapping theories of $\mathcal{L}$ (also called domain descriptions) into a class of extended logic programs under the answer sets semantics [21]. This is done by presenting a logic program $\mathcal{P}$ consisting of (domain independent) axioms defining the use of prioritized defaults; viewing domain descriptions of $\mathcal{L}$ as collections of atoms; and defining the notion of entailment between query q and a domain description $\mathcal{D}$ in $\mathcal{L}$ via answer set entailment in logic programming. In other words, we say that a domain description $\mathcal{D}$ entails a query q if q is entailed by the logic program $\mathcal{P} \cup \mathcal{D}$.

This approach appears to be similar in principle to the one suggested recently in [11] (which was not yet published when this work was completed). The resulting formalisms however are quite different technically. The precise relationship between the two is not yet fully investigated.

The use of the language will be illustrated by various examples from the literature. All the examples were run using the SLG inference engine [9, 10]. We believe that the study of the class of logic programs described by $\mathcal{P}_0$ and its variants can complement the existing work and help to understand reasoning with prioritized defaults.

The paper is organized as follows. In the next section, we introduce the language of prioritized defaults $\mathcal{L}_0$ and present a collection of axioms $\mathcal{P}_0$. In Section 3 we show examples of the use of domain descriptions in $\mathcal{L}_0$. Section 4 contains the brief discussion of several extensions of $\mathcal{D}_0$. Section 5 is devoted to the class of hierarchical domain descriptions. Finally, in Section 6, we discuss the relationship between our work and that of Brewka.

2   The Language of Prioritized Defaults

We start with describing the class $\mathcal{L}_0(\sigma)$ of languages used for representing various domains of discourse. $\mathcal{L}_0(\sigma)$ is parameterized by a multi-sorted signature σ containing names for objects, functions and relations of the user's domain. By $lit(\sigma)$ and $atoms(\sigma)$ we denote the set of all (ground) literals and atoms of σ. Literal $\neg\neg l$ will be identified with l. We assume that $atoms(\sigma)$ contain two special collections of atoms, called *default names* and *rule names* which will be used to name defaults and strict (non-defeasible) rules of the language. Domain knowledge in $\mathcal{L}_0(\sigma)$ will be described by a collection of literals of σ (called σ-literals) together with statements describing strict rules, defaults, and preferences between defaults. The syntax of such descriptions is given by the following definitions:

Definition 1.

- σ-literals are literals of $\mathcal{L}_0(\sigma)$;

– if d, d_1, d_2 are default names, $l_0, \ldots, l_n$ are literals of $\mathcal{L}_0(\sigma)$ and $[\,]$ is the list operator of Prolog then

$$rule(r, l_0, [l_1, \ldots, l_m]); \tag{$\mathcal{L}_0$.1}$$

$$default(d, l_0, [l_1, \ldots, l_m]); \tag{$\mathcal{L}_0$.2}$$

$$conflict(d_1, d_2); \tag{$\mathcal{L}_0$.3}$$

$$prefer(d_1, d_2); \tag{$\mathcal{L}_0$.4}$$

are literals of $\mathcal{L}_0(\sigma)$.

A set D of ground literals of $\mathcal{L}_0(\sigma)$ will be called *domain description* (with underlying signature σ).

We assume that symbols *default*, *rule*, *conflict* and *prefer* do not belong to σ. Relations, denoted by these symbols will be called *domain independent*.

A set S of $\mathcal{L}_0(\sigma)$ literals containing variables (ranging over objects of various types) will be viewed as a shorthand for the set of all (properly typed) ground instantiations of literals from S. Statements ($\mathcal{L}_0$.1) and ($\mathcal{L}_0$.2) will be called *definitions* of rule r and default d respectively. Intuitively, the statement ($\mathcal{L}_0$.1) defines the rule r which says that if literals $l_1, \ldots, l_m$ are true in a domain description $\mathcal{D}$ then so is the literal l_0. It can be viewed as a counterpart of the logic programming rule

$$l_0 \leftarrow l_1, \ldots, l_m.$$

Literals l_0 and $l_1, \ldots, l_m$ are called the head and the body of r and are denoted by $head(r)$ and $body(r)$ respectively.

The statement ($\mathcal{L}_0$.2) is a definition of the default d which says that *normally*, if $l_1, \ldots, l_m$ are true in $\mathcal{D}$ then l_0 is true in $\mathcal{D}$. The logic programming counterpart of d is the rule

$$l_0 \leftarrow l_1, \ldots, l_m, not \, \neg l_0.$$

As before we refer to l_0 as the head of d ($head(d)$) and to $l_1, \ldots, l_m$ as its body ($body(d)$).

The statement ($\mathcal{L}_0$.3) indicates that d_1 and d_2 are conflicting defaults. In many interesting cases $conflict(d_1, d_2)$ will be true iff heads of defaults d_1 and d_2 are contrary literals, but other defaults can also be declared as conflicting by the designer of the domain description. Finally, the statement ($\mathcal{L}_0$.4) stops the application of default d_2 if defaults d_1 and d_2 are in conflict with each other and the default d_1 is applicable.

This informal explanation of the meaning of domain independent relations of $\mathcal{L}_0(\sigma)$ will be replaced by the precise definition in the next section. But first we will attempt to clarify this meaning with the following examples.

Example 1. Let us assume that we are given complete lists of students enrolled in various university departments. We know that in general, students can not write computer programs and that computer science students do it regularly. Let us represent this information by a domain description $\mathcal{D}_0$.

The underlying signature σ of $\mathcal{D}_0$ contains student names, *mary, mike, sam,* ..., department names *cs, cis, art,* ..., appropriately typed predicate symbols *is_in(S, D)* and *can_progr(S)* read as "Student S is in department D" and "Student S can program", and default names of the form $d_1(S)$, $d_2(S)$, and $d_3(S, D)$.

The defaults from our informal description can be represented by statements

$default(d1(S), \neg can\_progr(S), [student(S)])$.
$default(d2(S), can\_progr(S), [student(S), is\_in(S, cs)])$.

Finally, the lists of students mentioned in the informal description will be represented by the collection F of facts:

$student(mary)$. $dept(cs)$. $is\_in(mary, cs)$.
$student(mike)$. $dept(art)$. $is\_in(mike, art)$.
$student(sam)$. $dept(cis)$. $is\_in(sam, cis)$.
$\ldots$ $\ldots$ $\ldots$

We also need the closed world assumption [34] for *is_in*, written as the default

$default(d3(S, D), \neg is\_in(S, D), [\ ])$.

Relations *student* and *dept* are, of course, not necessary. They are playing the role of types and will later allow us to avoid floundering when applying the *SLG* inference engine to this example.

We will assume that our domain description contain statements of the form $conflict(d_1, d_2)$ for any two defaults with contrary heads and that the relation *conflict* is symmetric. This will guarantee that $\mathcal{D}_0$ will contain $conflict(d_1(X), d_2(X))$ and $conflict(d_2(X), d_1(X))$. (These assumptions will be of course enforced later by the corresponding axioms).

Informally, the domain description $\mathcal{D}_0$ should allow us to conclude that Mike and Sam do not know how to program, while we should remain undecided about programming skills of Mary. This is the case only as long as we do not assume that the second default overrides the first one, due to the specificity principle. We can use the relation *prefer* from our language to record this preference by stating

$prefer(d2(X), d1(X))$.

From the new domain description $\mathcal{D}_1$ we should be able to conclude that Mary can write programs.   ◇

The next example is meant to illustrate the behavior of conflicting defaults in the presence of strict rules.

Example 2. Consider the domain description $\mathcal{D}_2$ consisting of two defaults

$default(d_1, p, [])$

$default(d_2, q, [r])$,

the rules

$rule(r_1, \neg p, [q])$

$rule(r_2, \neg q, [p])$

and the fact

r.

(Intuitively, the logic programming counterpart of $\mathcal{D}_2$ consists of the rules

$p \leftarrow not \neg p$

$q \leftarrow r, not \neg q$

$\neg p \leftarrow q$

$\neg q \leftarrow p$

Notice that the last two rules can be viewed as a translation into the logic programming language of the conditional q's are always not p's.)

The intended meaning of $\mathcal{D}_2$ should sanction two alternative sets of conclusions: one, containing p and $\neg q$, and another containing q and $\neg p$. If we expand $\mathcal{D}_2$ by

$conflict(d_2, d_1)$

$prefer(d_2, d_1)$

the application of d_1 should be blocked and the new domain description $\mathcal{D}_3$ should entail q and $\neg p$. Notice, that if $conflict(d_2, d_1)$ were not added to the domain description then addition of $prefer(d_2, d_1)$ would not alter the conclusions of $\mathcal{D}_2$. This is because preference only influences application of conflicting defaults.   ◇

More examples of the use of the language $\mathcal{L}_0$ for describing various domains will be found in the following sections. In the next section we give a precise definition of entailment from domain descriptions of $\mathcal{L}_0$.

2.1   Axioms of $\mathcal{P}_0$

In this section we present a collection $\mathcal{P}_{0,\sigma}$ of axioms defining the meaning of the domain independent relations of $\mathcal{L}_0(\sigma)$. The axioms are stated in the language of logic programs under the answer set semantics. They are intended to be used in conjunction with domain descriptions of $\mathcal{L}_0(\sigma)$ and to define the collection of statements which (strictly and/or defeasibly) follow from a given domain description $\mathcal{D}$. More precisely, we consider two basic relations $holds(l)$ and $holds\_by\_default(l)$ defined on literals of $\mathcal{L}_0(\sigma)$ which stand for "strictly holds" and "defeasibly holds", respectively. The *query language* associated with domain descriptions of $\mathcal{L}_0(\sigma)$ will consist of ground atoms of the form $holds\_by\_default(l)$, $holds(l)$, and their negations. In what follows, by $laws(\mathcal{D})$ we denote the set of statements of the forms ($\mathcal{L}_0.1$) and ($\mathcal{L}_0.2$) from definition 1 which belong to $\mathcal{D}$; $facts(\mathcal{D}) = \mathcal{D} \setminus laws(\mathcal{D})$.

Definition 2. We say that a domain description $\mathcal{D}$ entails a query q ($\mathcal{D} \models q$) if q belongs to every answer set of the program $\mathcal{P}_{0,\sigma}(\mathcal{D}) = \mathcal{P}_{0,\sigma} \cup \{holds(l) \mid l \in facts(\mathcal{D})\} \cup laws(\mathcal{D})$.

Program $\mathcal{P}_0$[1] consists of the following rules:

Non-defeasible Inference:

$$holds(L) \leftarrow rule(R, L, Body),$$
$$hold(Body). \qquad\qquad (\mathcal{P}_0.1)$$

$$hold([\,]). \qquad\qquad (\mathcal{P}_0.2)$$

$$hold([H|T]) \leftarrow holds(H),$$
$$hold(T). \qquad\qquad (\mathcal{P}_0.3)$$

The first axiom describes how the rules can be used to prove that a $\mathcal{L}_0(\sigma)$ literal l is non-defeasibly true in a domain description $\mathcal{D}$. The next two axioms define similar relation on the lists of literals in $\mathcal{L}_0(\sigma)$, i.e., $hold([l_1, \ldots, l_n])$ iff all the l's from the list are true in $\mathcal{D}$.

Defeasible Inference:

$$holds\_by\_default(L) \leftarrow holds(L). \qquad\qquad (\mathcal{P}_0.4)$$

$$holds\_by\_default(L) \leftarrow rule(R, L, Body), \qquad\qquad (\mathcal{P}_0.5)$$
$$hold\_by\_default(Body).$$

$$holds\_by\_default(L) \leftarrow default(D, L, Body), \qquad\qquad (\mathcal{P}_0.6)$$
$$hold\_by\_default(Body),$$

---

[1] In what follows we assume that σ is fixed and omit reference to it whenever possible.

$$not\ defeated(D),$$
$$not\ holds\_by\_default(\neg L).$$

$$hold\_by\_default([\ ]). \hspace{5cm} (\mathcal{P}_0.7)$$

$$hold\_by\_default([H|T]) \leftarrow holds\_by\_default(H), \hspace{2cm} (\mathcal{P}_0.8)$$
$$hold\_by\_default(T).$$

The first axiom in this group ensures that strictly true statements are also true by default. The next one allows application of rules for defeasible inference. The third axiom states that defaults with proven premises imply their conclusions unless they are defeated by other rules and defaults of the domain description. The condition $not\ holds\_by\_default(\neg L)$ is used when the domain contains two undefeated defaults d_1 and d_2 with conflicting conclusions. In this case $\mathcal{P}_0(\mathcal{D})$ will have multiple answer sets, one containing the conclusion of d_1 and the other containing the conclusion of d_2. The alternative solution here is to stop applications of both defaults, but we believe that in some circumstances (like those described by the extended *"Nixon Diamond"*) our solution is preferable.

The last two rules from this group define relation $hold\_by\_default(List)$ which holds if all literals from the list hold by default.

Defeating defaults:

$$defeated(D) \leftarrow default(D, L, Body), \hspace{3cm} (\mathcal{P}_0.9)$$
$$holds(\neg L).$$

$$defeated(D) \leftarrow default(D, L, Body), \hspace{3cm} (\mathcal{P}_0.10)$$
$$default(D_1, L_1, Body_1),$$
$$holds(conflict(D_1, D)),$$
$$holds\_by\_default(prefer(D1, D)),$$
$$hold\_by\_default(Body_1),$$
$$not\ defeated(D_1).$$

These axioms describe two possible ways to defeat a default d. The first axiom describes a stronger type of defeat when the conclusion of the default is proven to be false by non-defeasible means. The axiom $(\mathcal{P}_0.10)$ allows defeating of d by conflicting undefeated defaults of higher priority. They represents the "bravery" approach in the application of defaults. In the next section, we show how our axioms can be expanded or changed to allow other ways of defeating defaults.

Now we are left with the task of defining conflicts between defaults. There are several interesting ways to define this notion. Different definitions will lead to different theories of default reasoning. The investigation of ramifications of different choices is, however, beyond the limits of this paper. Instead we introduce the following three axioms which constitute the minimal requirement for this relation.

$$holds(conflict(d_1, d_2)) \leftarrow default(d_1, L_1, Body_1), \qquad (\mathcal{P}_0.11)$$
$$default(d_2, L_2, Body_2),$$
$$contrary(L_1, L_2).$$

for any two defaults with contrary literals in their heads and for any two defaults whose heads are of the form $prefer(d_i, d_j)$ and $prefer(d_j, d_i)$ respectively. The precise definition of *contrary* is given by the rules $(\mathcal{P}_0.21)$ and $(\mathcal{P}_0.22)$.

$$\neg holds(conflict(D, D)). \qquad (\mathcal{P}_0.12)$$

$$holds(conflict(D_1, D_2)) \leftarrow holds(conflict(D_2, D_1)). \qquad (\mathcal{P}_0.13)$$

Finally, we include axioms stating asymmetry of the preference relation:

$$\neg holds(prefer(D_1, D_2)) \leftarrow holds(prefer(D_2, D_1)), \qquad (\mathcal{P}_0.14)$$
$$D_1 \neq D_2.$$

$$\neg holds\_by\_default(prefer(D_1, D_2)) \leftarrow holds\_by\_default(prefer(D_2, D_1)), \qquad (\mathcal{P}_0.15)$$
$$D_1 \neq D_2.$$

Without the loss of generality we can view these axioms as schemes where D_1 and D_2 stand for defaults present in $\mathcal{D}$. The equality used in these axioms is interpreted as identity. Notice, that our minimal requirements on the preference relation do not include transitivity. On the discussion of nontransitive preference relations see [18], [25].

Uniqueness of names for defaults and rules:

These three axioms guarantee uniqueness of names for defaults and rules used in the domain description.

$$\neg rule(R, F_1, B_1) \leftarrow default(R, F_2, B_2). \tag{$\mathcal{P}_0$.16}$$

$$\neg rule(R, F_1, B_1) \leftarrow rule(R, F_2, B_2), \tag{$\mathcal{P}_0$.17}$$
$$rule(R, F_1, B_1) \neq rule(R, F_2, B_2)$$

$$\neg default(D, F_1, B_1) \leftarrow default(D, F_2, B_2), \tag{$\mathcal{P}_0$.18}$$
$$default(D, F_1, B_1) \neq default(D, F_2, B_2).$$

Addition of these axioms is needed only to make domain descriptions containing statements $default(d, l_1, \Gamma_1)$ and $default(d, l_2, \Gamma_2)$, $rule(r1, l_1, \Gamma_1)$ and $rule(r1, l_2, \Gamma_2)$, etc, inconsistent.

Auxiliary

Finally we have the axioms

$$\neg holds(L) \leftarrow holds(\neg L). \tag{$\mathcal{P}_0$.19}$$

$$\neg holds\_by\_default(L) \leftarrow holds\_by\_default(\neg L). \tag{$\mathcal{P}_0$.20}$$

$$contrary(L, \neg L). \tag{$\mathcal{P}_0$.21}$$

$$contrary(prefer(D_1, D_2), prefer(D_2, D_1)) \leftarrow D_1 \neq D_2. \tag{$\mathcal{P}_0$.22}$$

whose meaning is self-explanatory.

We believe that $\mathcal{P}_0(\mathcal{D})$ captures a substantial part of our intuition about reasoning with prioritized defaults and therefore deserves some study.

3 Using the Axioms

In this section we illustrate the use of our approach by formalizing several examples of reasoning with priorities. In what follows we will refer to running our programs using SLG inference engine. Since the syntax of SLG does not allow "$\neg$" we treat it as a new function symbol and consider only those stable models of $\mathcal{P}_0(\mathcal{D})$ which do not contain literals of the form a and $neg(a)$.

Example 3. (Example 1 revisited)
It is easy to check that the program $\mathcal{P}_0(\mathcal{D}_0)$ (where $\mathcal{D}_0$ is the domain description from Example 1) has two answer sets, containing

$$\{\neg hd(can\_progr(mary)), \neg hd(can\_progr(mike)), \neg hd(can\_progr(sam))\}$$

and

$$\{hd(can\_progr(mary)), \neg hd(can\_progr(mike)), \neg hd(can\_progr(sam))\},$$

respectively, where hd is a shorthand for *holds_by_default*. Hence, we can conclude that Mike and Sam do not know how to program but we have to stay undecided on the same question about Mary.

If we expand the domain by adding the statement $prefer(d_2, d_1)$ then the first answer set will disappear which of course corresponds exactly to our intention. It may be instructive to expand our domain by the following information: "Bad students never know how to program. Bob is a bad computer science student". This can be represented by facts

$student(bob).$
$bad(bob).$
$is\_in(bob, cs).$

and the rule

$rule(r_2(S), \neg can\_progr(S), [student(S), bad(S)]).$

The new domain description $\mathcal{D}_4$ will correctly entail that Bob does not know how to program. Notice, that if the above rule were changed to the default

$default(d_3(S), \neg can\_progr(S), [student(S), bad(S)])$

we would again get two answer sets with contradictory conclusions about Bob, and that again the conflict could be resolved by adding, say,

$prefer(d_3(S), d_2(S)).$ ◊

The previous example had an introductory character and could have been nicely formalized without using the preference relation. The next example (from [5], which attributes it to [24]) is more sophisticated: Not only does it require the ability to apply preferences to resolve conflicts between defaults, but also the ability of using defaults to *reason about such preferences*. Brewka in [5] argues that the ability to reason about preferences between defaults in the same language in which defaults are stated is important for various applications. In legal reasoning similar arguments were made by Gordon, Prakken, and Sartor [24, 32]. On the other hand, many formalisms developed for reasoning with prioritized defaults treat preferences as something statically given and specified separately from the corresponding default theory.

Example 4. (Legal Reasoning [5]) Assume that a person wants to find out if her security interest in a certain ship is perfected. She currently has possession of the ship. According to the Uniform Commercial Code (UCC) a security interest in goods may be perfected by taking possession of the collateral. However, there is a federal law called Ship Mortgage Act (SMA) according to which a security interest in a ship may only be perfected by filing a financing statement. Such a statement has not been filed. Now, the question is whether the UCC or the SMA takes precedence in this case. There are two known legal principles for resolving conflicts of this kind. The principle of *Lex Posterior* gives preference to newer law. In our case the UCC is newer than the SMA. On the other hand, the principle of *Lex Superior* gives precedence to laws supported by the higher authority. In our case the SMA has higher authority since it is federal law.

Let us build the domain description $\mathcal{D}_5$ which represents the above information. We will follow the formalization from [5] which uses symbols *possession* for "ship is a possession of the lady from the above story", *perfected* for "the ownership of the ship is perfected", and *filed* for "financial statement about possession of the ship is filed". The domain also contains symbols $state(D), federal(D)$, and $more\_recent(D_1, D_2)$ representing properties and relations between legal laws.

The UCC and SMA defaults of $\mathcal{D}_5$ can be represented by

$default(d_1, perfected, [possession])$.
$default(d_2, \neg perfected, [\neg filed])$.

The two legal principles for resolving conflicts are represented by the next two defaults:

$default(d_3(D_1, D_2), prefer(D_1, D_2), [more\_recent(D_1, D_2)])$.
$default(d_4(D_1, D_2), prefer(D_1, D_2), [federal(D_1), state(D_2)])$.

The next defaults will express the closed world assumptions for relations $more\_recent, federal$ and $state$. Presumably, a reasoning legal agent must have complete knowledge about the laws. The following defaults are added to $\mathcal{D}_5$ to represent this CWA assumption.

$default(d_5(D_1, D_2), \neg more\_recent(D_1, D_2), [\ ])$.
$default(d_6(D), \neg federal(D), [\ ])$.
$default(d_7(D), \neg state(D), [\ ])$.

To complete our formalization we need the following facts:

$\neg filed$.
$possession$.
$more\_recent(d_1, d_2)$.
$federal(d_2)$.
$state(d_1)$.

It is not difficult to check (using SLG if necessary) that the program $\mathcal{P}_0(\mathcal{D}_5)$ has two answer sets where

   (i) $holds\_by\_default(perfected)$

belongs to one answer set and

   (ii) $\neg holds\_by\_default(perfected)$

belongs to the other. This is because we have two defaults d_1 and d_2: the former supports the first conclusion, the latter - the second one, and preference between them cannot be resolved using defaults d_3 and d_4. Thus, neither (i) nor (ii) is entailed by $\mathcal{P}_0(\mathcal{D}_5)$. This is also Brewka's result in [5].

However, if we know that d_4 has a preference over d_3 the situation changes; To see that, let us expand our domain description by

   $prefer(d4(D_1, D_2), d3(D_2, D_1)).$

and denote the new domain description by $\mathcal{D}_6$; as a result, program $\mathcal{P}_0(\mathcal{D}_6)$ has then only one answer set, which contains (ii). This is again the desired behavior, according to [5]. It may be worth noticing that the closed world assumptions d_5, d_6 and d_7 have no role in the above arguments and could be removed from the domain description. They are important, however, for general correctness of our representation. The example can be substantially expanded by introducing more realistic representation of the story and by using more complex strategies of assigning preferences to conflicting defaults. We found that the corresponding domain descriptions remain natural and correct.   ◇

Example 5. (Simple Inheritance Hierarchy) Now let us consider a simple inheritance hierarchy of the form depicted in fig (1).

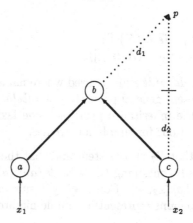

Figure 1. The Inheritance Hierarchy of $\mathcal{D}_7$

A simple hierarchy consists of two parts: an acyclic graph representing the proper subclass relation between classes of objects and a collection of positive and negative defaults from these subclasses to properties of objects. In fig (1) we have three class nodes, a, b, and c. The strict link between the class nodes, say, a

and b can be read as "a is a proper subclass of b". Dotted lines from b and c to property p represent positive and negative defaults respectively. The simple hierarchy is used in conjunction with a collection of statements $is\_in(x, c)$ read as "x is an elements of a class c". For simplicity we assume completeness of information about relations $subclass$ and is_in. (For discussion of hierarchies with incomplete information, see [20]).

The encoding of simple hierarchies will consists of two parts: the first representing a particular graph and the second containing general properties of a hierarchy together with the inheritance principle. Notice, that the second part is common to all simple hierarchies.

In our case, the domain description $\mathcal{D}_7$ encoding the hierarchy from fig (1) consists of domain dependent axioms

$$subclass(a, b).$$
$$subclass(c, b).$$
$$is\_in(x_1, a)$$
$$is\_in(x_2, c)$$
$$default(d_1(X), has(X, p), [is\_in(X, b)])$$
$$default(d_2(X), \neg has(X, p), [is\_in(X, c)])$$

(where $has(X, P)$ stands for "element X has a property P") and the domain independent axioms

$$rule(r_1(C_0, C_2), subclass(C_0, C_2), [subclass(C_0, C_1), subclass(C_1, C_2)]).$$
$$rule(r_2(X, C_1), is\_in(X, C_1), [subclass(C_0, C_1), is\_in(X, C_0)]).$$
$$rule(r_3(D_1(X), D_2(X)), prefer(D_1(X), D_2(X)), [d(D_1(X), \_, [is(X, A)]),$$
$$d(D_2(X), \_, [is(X, B)]),$$
$$subclass(A, B)]).$$
$$default(d_3(X), \neg is\_in(X), []).$$
$$default(d_4, \neg subclass(A, B), []).$$

(where d stands for $default$ and $\_$ is used where names are not important). The first two rules represent general properties of $subclass$ and is_in. The next rule is an encoding of the inheritance principle. The last two defaults express the closed world assumptions for simple hierarchies.

It is easy to check that $\mathcal{D}_7$ is consistent and that the logic program $\mathcal{P}_0(\mathcal{D}_7)$ has the unique answer set containing $holds\_by\_default(has(x_1, p))$ and $holds\_by\_default(\neg has(x_2, p))$. Consistency result can be easily expanded to "rule-consistent" domains representing simple hierarchies.

We use the next example from Brewka [7] to illustrate differences between our theory and several other formalisms dealing with prioritized defaults.

Example 6. (Gray Area) Brewka considers the following defaults:

1. "Penguins normally do not fly;",
2. "Birds normally fly;", and

3. "Birds that can swim are normally penguins;",

under the assumption that default (1) is preferred over (2), and (2) is preferred over (3). (Notice, that Brewka assumes transitivity of the preference relation).

These defaults are represented in his formalism by a program

> $bird.$
> $swims.$
> (d_1) $\neg flies \leftarrow not\ flies, penguin.$
> (d_2) $flies \leftarrow not\ \neg flies, bird.$
> (d_3) $penguin \leftarrow not\ \neg penguin, bird, swims.$

According to Brewka, the prioritized default theories from $[1, 5, 28]$ are applicable to this case and produce single extension $E_1 = \{swims,\ bird,\ flies,\ penguin\}$ which seems contrary to intuition. According to the semantics from [7] the corresponding program has one prioritized answer set, $E_2 = \{swims,\ bird,\ penguin,\ \neg flies\}$ which is a more intuitive result. The information above is naturally encoded in the domain description $\mathcal{D}_8$ by the following statements

> $bird.$
> $swims.$
>
> $default(d_1, \neg flies, [penguin]).$
> $default(d_2, flies, [bird]).$
> $default(d_3, penguin, [bird, swims]).$
>
> $prefer(d_1, d_2).$
> $prefer(d_2, d_3).$
> $prefer(d_1, d_3).$

The program $\mathcal{P}_0(\mathcal{D}_8)$ has only one answer set which contains
$S_1 = \{holds\_by\_default(bird), holds\_by\_default(swim),$
$\qquad holds\_by\_default(penguin), \neg holds\_by\_default(flies)\}.$
which coincides with the approach from [7]. This happens because the default d_3 is in conflict with neither d_1 nor d_2 and therefore its application is not influenced by the preference relation. If we expand the domain description $\mathcal{D}_8$ by a statement

$conflict(d_2, d_3)$

the situation changes. Now we will have the second answer set,

$S_2 = \{holds\_by\_default(bird), holds\_by\_default(swim), holds\_by\_default(flies)\}.$

which corresponds to the following line of reasoning: We are initially confronted with "ready to fire" defaults (d_2) and (d_3). Since (d_2) has a higher priority and d_2 and d_3 are conflicting defaults, d_2 wins and we conclude $flies$. Now, (d_1) is not applicable and hence we stop.

To obtain S_1, we can apply defaults (d_1) and (d_3). Since (d_2) is then defeated by (d_1) it will not block (d_3).   ◊

We realize of course that this example belongs to the *gray area* and can be viewed differently. The main lesson from this observation is that in the process of expressing ourself (while programming or otherwise) we should try to avoid making unclear statements. Of course, we hope that further work on semantics will help to clarify some statements which so far remain unclear. We also hope that the reader is not left with the impression that we claim success in following our own advice.

4   Extending $\mathcal{L}_0(\sigma)$

In this section we briefly outline and discuss several extensions of the language $\mathcal{L}_0(\sigma)$. We show how to extend the language and the corresponding collection of axioms to allow the representation of more powerful defaults and default defeaters.

4.1   Beyond Normal Defaults

The domain descriptions of $\mathcal{L}_0(\sigma)$ contain defaults whose logic programming counterparts are of the form

(ND) $l_0 \leftarrow l_1, \ldots, l_n, not \; \neg l_0.$

These rules can be viewed as normal defaults in the sense of Reiter [35]. Even though the ability to express priorities between the defaults gives the domain descriptions of $\mathcal{L}_0(\sigma)$ expressive power that exceeds that of default theories of Reiter consisting of (ND)-rules, this power is not sufficient for some applications. In this section we expand the language $\mathcal{L}_0(\sigma)$ and the corresponding system of axioms to make it possible to represent more general types of defaults. To this end we replace the definition of default description in $\mathcal{L}_0(\sigma)$ (see $\mathcal{L}_0.2$ in the Definition 1) by the more powerful construct

$$default(d, l_0, [l_1, \ldots, l_m], [l_{m+1}, \ldots, l_n]) \tag{$\mathcal{L}.2$}$$

The intuitive meaning of this statement is that *normally*, if $l_1, \ldots, l_m$ are true in $\mathcal{D}$ and there is no reason to believe that $l_{m+1}, \ldots, l_n$ are true in $\mathcal{D}$ then l_0 is true in $\mathcal{D}$. In other words, the statement $(\mathcal{L}.2)$ corresponds to the logic programming rule

$$l_0 \leftarrow l_1, \ldots, l_m, not \; l_{m+1}, \ldots, not \; l_n, not \; \neg l_0.$$

Literals $l_1, \ldots, l_m$ and $l_{m+1}, \ldots, l_n$ are called positive and negative preconditions of d respectively. Both sets of preconditions will be sometimes referred to as the body of statement $(\mathcal{L}.2)$.

Our set of axioms $\mathcal{P}_0$ will be modified as follows: axioms $(\mathcal{P}_0.6)$ and $(\mathcal{P}_0.10)$ will be replaced by axioms

$$holds\_by\_default(L) \leftarrow holds(default(D, L, Positive, Negative)), \quad (\mathcal{P}.6)$$
$$hold\_by\_default(Positive),$$
$$fail\_by\_default(Negative),$$
$$not\ defeated(D),$$
$$not\ \neg holds\_by\_default(L).$$

$$defeated(D) \leftarrow holds(default(D1, L, Positive, Negative)), \quad (\mathcal{P}.10)$$
$$holds\_by\_default(prefer(D1, D)),$$
$$hold\_by\_default(Positive),$$
$$fail\_by\_default(Negative),$$
$$not\ defeated(D_1).$$

where $fail\_by\_default$ is defined as follows:

$$fail\_by\_default([\ ]). \qquad (\mathcal{P}.23)$$

$$fail\_by\_default([H|T]) \leftarrow not\ holds\_by\_default(H), \qquad (\mathcal{P}.24)$$
$$fail\_by\_default(T).$$

We hope that the modification is self-explanatory.

The following example, taken from [32], illustrates the use of the new language.

Example 7. [33] Consider the following two legal default rules:

1. Normally, a person who cannot be shown to be a minor has the capacity to perform legal acts.
2. In order to exercise the right to vote the person has to demonstrate that he is not a minor.

The first default can be represented as

$$default(d_1(x), has\_legal\_capacity(x), [\ ], [minor(x)])$$

which requires a negative precondition. The second default has the form

$$default(d_2(x), has\_right\_to\_vote(x), [\neg minor(x)], [\ ]).$$

These defaults, used in conjunction with statement $\neg minor(jim)$ entail that Jim has legal capacity and the right to vote. If the system is asked the same questions about Mary whose legal age is not known it will conclude that Mary has legal capacity but will remain in the dark about Mary's right to vote. If we expand our domain description by the closed world assumption for *has_right_to_vote*

$$default(d_3(x), \neg has\_right\_to\_vote(x), [\,], [\,])$$

then the answer to the last question will be *no*.   ◇

4.2 Weak Exceptions to Defaults

So far our language allowed only strong exceptions to defaults, i.e., a default *d* could be defeated by rules and by defaults conflicting with *d*. Many authors argued for a need for so called weak exceptions - statements of the form "do not apply default *d* to objects satisfying property *p*". (For the discussion of the difference between weak and strong exceptions see, for instance, [2].) Weak exceptions of this type can be easily incorporated in our language. First we expand the language by allowing literals of the form

$$exception(d(x_1, \ldots, x_k), [l_1, \ldots, l_n], [l_{n+1}, \ldots, l_{n+m}]) \qquad (\mathcal{L}.5)$$

read as "the default *d* is not applicable to $x_1, \ldots, x_k$ which satisfy $l_1, \ldots, l_n$ and *not* $l_{n+1}, \ldots,$ *not* l_{n+m}". The formal meaning of this statement is defined by an axiom

$$
\begin{aligned}
defeated(D) \leftarrow\ &exception(D, Positive, Negative), \qquad\qquad (\mathcal{P}.25)\\
&hold\_by\_default(Positive),\\
&fail\_by\_default(Negative).
\end{aligned}
$$

added to $\mathcal{P}_0$.

Consider a domain description $\mathcal{D}_9$.

$$default(d(X), p(X), [q(X)], [\,]).$$
$$exception(d(X), [r(X)], [\,]).$$
$$q(x_1).$$
$$q(x_2).$$
$$r(x_2).$$

It is easy to check, that the corresponding program $\mathcal{P}_0(\mathcal{D}_9)$ (and hence $\mathcal{D}_9$) entails $p(x_1)$ but remains undecided about $p(x_2)$. Notice, that we were able to entail $p(x_1)$ even though x_1 may satisfy property r, i.e. $\mathcal{D}_9 \not\models \neg r(x_1)$. In some cases we need to be able to say something like "do not apply d to x if x may satisfy property r". This can be achieved by replacing the exception clause in $\mathcal{D}_9$ by

$$exception(d(X), [\,], [\neg r(X)]). \qquad\qquad (\mathcal{L}.6)$$

The new domain description entails neither $p(x_1)$ nor $p(x_2)$.

We will denote the language and the system of axioms described in this section by $\mathcal{L}$ and $\mathcal{P}$ respectively. We believe that the system is useful for reasoning with prioritized defaults and deserves careful investigation. In this paper however we present only several illustrative results about $\mathcal{P}_0$. A more detailed analysis of $\mathcal{P}$ will be done elsewhere. Before presenting these results we would like to mention another possible extension/modification of the system.

4.3   Changing the Mode of Reasoning

In our theory $\mathcal{P}_0$ we formalized a " brave" mode of applying defaults. In this section we briefly mention how the axioms can be changed to allow for cautious reasoning. This can be achieved by adding to $\mathcal{P}_0$ the axiom

$$defeated(D) \leftarrow default(D, L, Body), \qquad (\mathcal{P}.26)$$
$$default(D_1, L_1, Body_1),$$
$$holds(conflict(D_1, D)),$$
$$not\ holds\_by\_default(prefer(D1, D)),$$
$$not\ holds\_by\_default(prefer(D, D1)),$$
$$hold\_by\_default(Body),$$
$$hold\_by\_default(Body_1)$$

Let us denote the resulting program by $\mathcal{P}_{0,c}$. Now let us consider the domain description $\mathcal{D}_{10}$ consisting of defaults and conditionals mentioned in the introduction

$default(d_1, a, []).$
$default(d_2, b, []).$
$default(d_3, c, []).$
$conflict(d_1, d_2).$
$rule(r_1, \neg a, [b]).$ $\qquad\qquad$ $rule(r'_1, \neg b, [a]).$
$rule(r_2, d, [b]).$ $\qquad\qquad$ $rule(r'_2, \neg b, [\neg d]).$
$rule(r_3, d, [a]).$ $\qquad\qquad$ $rule(r'_3, \neg a, [\neg d]).$

It is easy to check that $\mathcal{P}_0(\mathcal{D}_{10})$ has two answer sets containing $\{c, a, d, \neg b\}$ and $\{c, b, d, \neg a\}$ and therefore entails d and c. In contrast $\mathcal{P}_{0,c}(\mathcal{D}_{10})$ has one answer set containing c and not containing d.

It is worth mentioning that it may be possible in this framework to introduce two types of defaults - those requiring brave and cautious reasoning and add the above axiom for the latter.

5   Hierarchical Domain Descriptions

Definition 3. We will say that a domain description D is *consistent* if $P_0(D)$ is consistent, i.e., has a consistent answer set.

Obviously, not all domain descriptions are consistent; $D = \{p, \neg p, q\}$, for instance, is not.

(Notice that this is the intended meaning. We believe that the question of drawing conclusions in the presence of inconsistency is somewhat orthogonal to the problem we address in this paper and should be studied separately.)

In the next example inconsistency is slightly less obvious.

Example 8. The domain description D_{11} consists of the following three literals:

$default(d, a, [])$.
$rule(r_1, \neg c, [a])$.
c.

It is easy to see that $P_0(D_{11})$ does not have a consistent answer set. This happens because nothing prevents rule $(P_0.6)$ of P_0 from concluding that a holds by default. This conclusion, together with fact c and rule r_1 from D_{11} leads to inconsistency. Notice, that addition of the rule

$rule(r_2, \neg a, [c])$.

blocks the application of $(P_0.6)$ and restore consistency.   ◊

In this section we give a simple condition guaranteeing consistency of domain descriptions of $\mathcal{L}_0$. The condition can be expanded to domain descriptions of $\mathcal{L}$ but we will not do it in this paper. From now on, by *domain descriptions we will mean domain descriptions of $\mathcal{L}_0$*.

We will need the following definitions.

Definition 4. The domain description D is said to be *rule-consistent* if the non-defeasible part of $P_0(D)$ has a consistent answer set. (By the non-defeasible part of $P_0(D)$ we mean the program $P_0^s(D)$ consisting of the set $\{holds(l) \mid l \in facts(D)\} \cup laws(D)$ and nondefeasible rules (rules $(P_0.1)$-$(P_0.3)$, $(P_0.9)$, $(P_0.12)$-$(P_0.14)$, $(P_0.16)$-$(P_0.19)$, and $(P_0.21)$-$(P_0.22)$ of P_0).

Definition 5. A domain description D over signature σ will be called *hierarchical* if it satisfies the following conditions:

1. D is rule-consistent;
2. D does not contain statements of the form $\mathcal{L}_0.3$ (i.e., there are no conflicts except those specified in P_0);
3. heads of defaults in D are σ-literals or literals of the form $prefer(d_1, d_2)$;
4. no literal from the head of a default in D belongs to the body of a rule in D;

5. there is a function *rank* from the set $heads(\mathcal{D})$ of literals belonging to the heads of defaults in $\mathcal{D}$ to the set of ordinals such that

   (a) if $l \in head(\mathcal{D})$ and $\neg l \in head(\mathcal{D})$ then $rank(l) = rank(\neg l)$;
   (b) if $prefer(d_1, d_2)) \in head(\mathcal{D})$ and $prefer(d_2, d_1) \in head(\mathcal{D})$ then $rank(prefer(d_1, d_2)) = rank(prefer(d_2, d_1))$;
   (c) if $default(d, l, [l_1, \ldots, l_n]) \in \mathcal{D}$ and $l_i \in heads(\mathcal{D})$ then $rank(l) > rank(l_i)$;
   (d) if $prefer(d_1, d_2) \in heads(\mathcal{D})$ and $d_1, d_2 \in \mathcal{D}$ then $rank(head(d_i)) > rank(prefer(d_1, d_2))$ for $i = 1, 2$;

It is easy to check that domain descriptions $\mathcal{D}_0$, $\mathcal{D}_1$, $\mathcal{D}_4$, and $\mathcal{D}_6$ are hierarchical while $\mathcal{D}_2, \mathcal{D}_3, \mathcal{D}_7$ are not. In $\mathcal{D}_2$ and $\mathcal{D}_7$, the condition (4) is violated while (2) is not true in $\mathcal{D}_3$. Domain description $\mathcal{D}_5$ is also hierarchical. The rank function for $\mathcal{D}_5$ can be given by $rank(l) = 1$ for $l \notin \{perfected, \neg perfected\}$, $rank(perfected) = rank(\neg perfected) = 4$, and $rank(prefer(d1(X), d2(X))) = rank(prefer(d2(X), d1(X))) = 2$.

Theorem 1. Hierarchical domain descriptions are consistent.

Proof. *(Sketch)* To prove the theorem we first simplify the program $\mathcal{P}_0(\mathcal{D})$ by

(i) replacing all the occurrences of literals of the form $hold([l_1, \ldots, l_n])$ and $hold\_by\_default([l_1, \ldots, l_n])$ in the bodies of the rules from $\mathcal{P}_0(\mathcal{D})$ by $holds(l_1), \ldots, holds(l_n)$ and $holds\_by\_default(l_1), \ldots, holds\_by\_default(l_n)$ respectively and

(ii) dropping the rules with these literals in the heads.

It is easy to verify that $\mathcal{P}_0(\mathcal{D})$ is a conservative extension of the resulting program $\mathcal{P}_2(\mathcal{D})$ (whose language does not contain predicate symbols *hold* and *hold_by_default*).

Now let us notice that, since $\mathcal{D}$ is a hierarchical domain description, the non-defeasible part $\mathcal{P}_0^s(\mathcal{D})$ of $\mathcal{P}_0(\mathcal{D})$ has a unique consistent answer set, say H. This answer set can be used to further simplify $\mathcal{P}_2(\mathcal{D})$ by eliminating all the occurrences of literals from H. This is done by using the splitting set theorem of [27] and removing some useless rules. Finally, we drop the rule $(\mathcal{P}_0.20)$ and replace the occurrences of $holds\_by\_default(l)$ and $defeated(d)$ in $\mathcal{P}_0(\mathcal{D})$ by l and d

respectively. We call the resulting program $Q(\mathcal{D})$ the *defeasible counterpart* of $\mathcal{D}$.

$$Q(\mathcal{D}) = \begin{cases} l. & \text{if } holds(l) \in H \quad (1) \\[2ex] l & \leftarrow l_1, \ldots, l_n, \quad (2) \\ & \quad not\ d, \\ & \quad not\ \neg l. \\[1ex] & \quad \text{if } default(d, l, [l_1, \ldots, l_n]) \in \mathcal{D} \\ & \quad \text{and } holds(l) \notin H, \\ & \quad \text{and } holds(\neg l) \notin H \\[2ex] d_2 & \leftarrow l_1, \ldots, l_n, \quad (3) \\ & \quad prefer(d_1, d_2), \\ & \quad not\ d_1. \\[1ex] & \quad \text{if } d_2 \in \mathcal{D}, \\ & \quad default(d_1, l, [l_1, \ldots, l_n]) \in \mathcal{D}, \\ & \quad holds(conflict(d_1, d_2)) \in H \\ & \quad \text{and } holds(l) \notin H \\ & \quad \text{and } holds(\neg l) \notin H, \\[2ex] \neg prefer(d_1, d_2) \leftarrow prefer(d_2, d_1). \quad (4) \\[1ex] & \quad \text{if } holds(prefer(d_1, d_2)) \notin H \\ & \quad \text{and } holds(prefer(d_2, d_1)) \notin H \\ & \quad \text{and } d_1, d_2 \in \mathcal{D} \end{cases}$$

Using the splitting sequence theorem, and the assumption that $\mathcal{D}$ is hierarchical, we can prove that for any σ-literal l

$$\mathcal{P}_0(\mathcal{D}) \models holds\_by\_default(l) \text{ iff } Q(\mathcal{D}) \models l.$$

In the last part of the proof we show that $Q(\mathcal{D})$ is consistent. This implies the consistency of $\mathcal{P}_0(\mathcal{D})$. $\Diamond$

The detailed proof of the theorem 1 can be found in appendix A.

The last example in this section demonstrates the importance of the requirement for existence of the rank function in definition 5.

Example 9. Let us consider the following domain description, $\mathcal{D}_{12}$.

> $default(d_1, l, []).$
> $default(d_2, \neg l, [l]).$
> $prefer(d_2, d_1).$

It is easy to see that $\mathcal{D}_{12}$ has no rank function. To show that $\mathcal{D}_{12}$ is inconsistent it suffices to verify that $\mathcal{P}_0(\mathcal{D}_{12})$ is consistent iff the following program R is consistent:

$$l \;\leftarrow\; not\; d_1, not\; \neg l$$
$$\neg l \leftarrow l, not\; d_2, not\; l$$
$$d_1 \leftarrow l, not\; d_2$$

Obviously, R is inconsistent. $\Diamond$

It is worth mentioning that the domain description $\mathcal{D}_{13}$ which is obtained from $\mathcal{D}_{12}$ by removing the preference $prefer(d_2, d_1)$ is consistent. This demonstrates the difference between prioritized defaults and preferential model approaches (see e.g. [22]). In these approaches existence of preferred models is guaranteed if the original theory has a model and the preference relation is transitive.

6   Domain Descriptions and Prioritized Logic Programs

In this section we discuss the relationship between our theory of prioritized defaults and the prioritized logic programs recently introduced by G. Brewka [7]. In Brewka's approach, a domain description is represented by a prioritized logic program $(P, <)$ where P is a logic program with the answer set semantics representing the domain without preferences and $<$ is a preference relation among rules of P. The semantics of $(P, <)$ is defined by its *preferred answer set* - answer sets of P satisfying some conditions determined by $<$.

We will recall the notion of preferred answer sets from [7] and show that for a restricted class of hierarchical domain descriptions Brewka's approach and our approach are equivalent. In what follows, we will use the following terminology.

A binary relation R on a set S is called *strict partial order* (or *order*) if R is irreflexive and transitive. An order R is *total* if for every pair $a, b \in S$, either $(a, b) \in R$ or $(b, a) \in R$; R is *well-founded* if every set $X \subseteq S$ has a minimal element; R is *well-ordered* if it is total and well-founded.

Let P be a collection of rules of the form

$$r: \qquad\qquad l_0 \leftarrow l_1, \ldots, l_m, not\; l_{m+1}, \ldots, not\; l_n$$

where l_i's are ground literals. Literals $l_1, \ldots, l_m$ are called the *prerequisites* of r. If $m = 0$ then r is said to be *prerequisite free*. A rule r is *defeated* by a literal l if $l = l_i$ for some $i \in \{m + 1, \ldots, n\}$; r is defeated by a set of literal X if X contains a literal that defeats r. A program P is *prerequisite free* if every rule in P is prerequisite free.

For a program P and a set of literals X, the *reduct of P with respect to X*, denoted by $^X P$, is the program obtained from P by

- deleting all rules with prerequisite l such that $l \notin X$; and

    – deleting all prerequisites of the remaining rules.

Definition 6. *(Brewka [7])* Let $(P, <)$ be a prioritized logic program where P is prerequisite free and $<$ is a total order among rules of P. Let $C_<(P) = \bigcup_{i=1}^{\infty} S_i$ where

$$S_0 = \emptyset$$

$$S_n = \begin{cases} S_{n-1} & \text{if } r_n \text{ is defeated by } S_{n-1} \\ S_{n-1} \cup \{head(r_n)\} & \text{otherwise} \end{cases}$$

and r_n is the nth rule in the order $<$. Then

– An answer set A of P is called a *preferred answer set*[2] of $(P, <)$ if $A = C_<(P)$.
– For an arbitrary prioritized logic program $(P, <)$, a set of literals A is called a preferred answer set of $(P, <)$ if it is an answer set of P and $A = C_{<'}(^A P)$ for some total order $<'$ that extends $<$.
– A prioritized program $(P, <)$ entails a query q, denoted by $(P, <) \hspace{0.1em}\vdash\hspace{-0.5em}\sim q$, if for every preferred answer set A of $(P, <)$, $q \in A$.

There are several substantial differences between domain descriptions of $\mathcal{L}_0$ and prioritized logic programs. To compare the two approaches we need to limit ourself to domain descriptions without dynamic priorities whose preference relation is transitive and is defined only on conflicting defaults. More precisely:

Definition 7. A domain description $\mathcal{D}$ of $\mathcal{L}_0$ is said to be *static* if it satisfies the following conditions:

– laws of $\mathcal{D}$ do not contain occurrences of the predicate symbol *prefer*;
– the transitive closure of the preference relation $\{\langle d_1, d_2 \rangle : d_1, d_2$ are defaults in $\mathcal{D}$ such that $prefer(d_1, d_2) \in \mathcal{D}\}$, denoted by $prefer_\mathcal{D}^*$, is an order on defaults of $\mathcal{D}$;
– for every literal of the form $prefer(d_1, d_2) \in \mathcal{D}$, $head(d_1)$ and $head(d_2)$ are contrary literals.

A static domain description $\mathcal{D}$ can be naturally encoded by a prioritized logic program $\Pi(\mathcal{D}) = (\mathcal{B}(\mathcal{D}), <_\mathcal{D})$ defined as follows.

$$\Pi(\mathcal{D}) = \begin{cases} \mathcal{B}(\mathcal{D}) = \begin{cases} l. & \text{if } l \text{ is a } \sigma\text{-literal in } \mathcal{D} & (1) \\ \\ l \leftarrow l_1, \ldots, l_n. & (2) \\ & \text{if } rule(r, l, [l_1, \ldots, l_n]) \in \mathcal{D} \\ \\ d: \quad l \leftarrow l_1, \ldots, l_n, not \ \neg l. & (3) \\ & \text{if } default(d, l, [l_1, \ldots, l_n]) \in \mathcal{D} \end{cases} \\ \\ d_1 <_\mathcal{D} d_2 \qquad \text{if } \langle d_1, d_2 \rangle \in prefer_\mathcal{D}^* & (4) \end{cases}$$

---

[2] Strongly preferred answer set in Brewka's terminology.

We say that a domain description $\mathcal{D}$ entails a σ-literal l in the sense of Brewka if $\Pi(\mathcal{D}) \hspace{0.1em}\vert\!\!\sim q$.

The following theorem shows that for static and hierarchical domain descriptions Brewka's approach coincides with ours.

Theorem 2. For every hierarchical and static domain description $\mathcal{D}$ and for every σ-literal l,

$$\mathcal{D} \models holds\_by\_default(l) \quad \text{if and only if} \quad \Pi(\mathcal{D}) \hspace{0.1em}\vert\!\!\sim l.$$

Proof. *(Sketch)* First, by "partially evaluating" $\mathcal{D}$ with respect to non-defeasible information and removing various useless statements we reduce $\mathcal{D}$ to a simpler domain description $\mathcal{D}_N$ with the following property:

(i) $\mathcal{D} \models holds\_by\_default(l)$ iff $\mathcal{D} \models holds(l)$ or $\mathcal{D}_N \models holds\_by\_default(l)$ and

(ii) $\Pi(\mathcal{D}) \hspace{0.1em}\vert\!\!\sim l$ iff $\mathcal{D} \models holds(l)$ or $\Pi(\mathcal{D}_N) \hspace{0.1em}\vert\!\!\sim l$.

The domain description $\mathcal{D}_N$ can be represented by the program $\mathcal{R}(\mathcal{D}_N)$ consisting of the rules

$$\mathcal{R}(\mathcal{D}_N) \begin{cases} l \leftarrow l_1, \ldots, l_n, not\ d, not\ \neg l. & (1) \\[1em] \quad \text{if } default(d, l, [l_1, \ldots, l_n]) \in \mathcal{D}_N \\[1em] d_2 \leftarrow l_1, \ldots, l_n, not\ d_1. & (2) \\[1em] \quad \text{if } d_2 \in \mathcal{D}_N, \\ \quad default(d_1, l, [l_1, \ldots, l_n]) \in \mathcal{D}_N, \\ \quad prefer(d_1, d_2) \in \mathcal{D}_N, \\ \quad \text{and } head(d_2) = \neg l \end{cases}$$

and the set $pref = \{prefer(d_1, d_2) : prefer(d_1, d_2) \in \mathcal{D}_N\}$.

$\mathcal{D}_N$ can also be represented by the prioritized logic program $\Pi(\mathcal{D}_N) = (\mathcal{B}(\mathcal{D}_N), <_{\mathcal{D}_N})$ where $\mathcal{B}(\mathcal{D}_N)$ consists of the following rules:

$$\mathcal{B}(\mathcal{D}_N) \begin{cases} l \leftarrow l_1, \ldots, l_n, not\ \neg l. & (1) \\[1em] \quad \text{if } default(d, l, [l_1, \ldots, l_n]) \in \mathcal{D}_N \end{cases}$$

We then show that

(iii) for each answer set A of $\mathcal{R}(\mathcal{D}_N)$, the set $B = A \cap lit(\sigma)$ is a preferred answer set of $\Pi(\mathcal{D}_N)$; and

(iv) for each preferred answer set A of $\Pi(\mathcal{D}_N)$ there exists an answer set B of $\mathcal{R}(\mathcal{D})$ such that $B \cap lit(\sigma) = A$.

The conclusion of the theorem follows from (i)-(iv). $\diamond$

Detailed proof of the theorem can be found in appendix B.

The theorem 2 can be used to better understand properties of both formalizations. It implies, for instance, that queries to Brewka's prioritized programs corresponding to domain descriptions of $\mathcal{L}_0$ can be answered by the SLG inference engine. It can also be used for a simple proof of the fact that static, hierarchical domain descriptions are monotonic with respect to *prefer*, i.e. for any such $\mathcal{D}$ and $\mathcal{D}'$ with preference relations P and P' if $P \subseteq P'$ and $\mathcal{D} \models l$ then $\mathcal{D}' \models l$.

The next example demonstrates differences between reasoning with domain descriptions and prioritized logic programs.

Example 10. Let us consider the domain description $\mathcal{D}_{14}$ which consists of the following $\mathcal{L}_0$-literals:

$$rule(r_1, \neg l_1, [l_2]).$$
$$rule(r_2, \neg l_2, [l_1]).$$
$$default(d_1, l_1, []).$$
$$default(d_2, l_2, []).$$
$$conflict(d_1, d_2).$$
$$prefer(d_2, d_1).$$

It is easy to see that in this domain description d_2 is applicable, d_1 is defeated and hence, the program $\mathcal{P}_0(\mathcal{D}_{14})$ has a unique answer set containing l_2 and $\neg l_1$.

The prioritized logic program $\mathcal{B}(\mathcal{D}_{14})$ which corresponds to $\mathcal{D}_{14}$ consists of the following rules:

$$
\begin{array}{lll}
r_1 : & \neg l_1 \leftarrow l_2. \\
r_2 : & \neg l_2 \leftarrow l_1. \\
d_1 : & l_1 \leftarrow not\ \neg l_1. \\
d_2 : & l_2 \leftarrow not\ \neg l_2. \\
d_2 < d_1.
\end{array}
$$

and has two preferred answer sets: $\{l_2, \neg l_1\}$ and $\{l_1, \neg l_2\}$. The former corresponds to the preference orders in which $r_2 < r_1$ and the latter to the preference order $r_1 < r_2 < d_2 < d_1$. $\lozenge$

The above example shows that Brewka's approach differs from ours in the way priority is dealt with. In our approach, we distinguish rules from defaults and only priority between defaults are considered and enforced. This is not so in Brewka's approach where priority is defined among rules of the logic program representing the domain in consideration. The completion of the preference order could "overwrite" the preference order between defaults as the above example has shown.

7   Conclusions

In this paper we

• introduced a language $\mathcal{L}(\sigma)$ capable of expressing strict rules, defaults with exceptions, and the preference relation between defaults;

• gave a collection of axioms, $\mathcal{P}$, defining the entailment relation between domain descriptions of $\mathcal{L}(\sigma)$ and queries of the form $holds(l)$ and $holds\_by\_default(l)$;

• demonstrated, by way of examples, that the language and the entailment relation is capable of expressing rather complex forms of reasoning with prioritized defaults;

• gave sufficient conditions for consistency of domain descriptions;

• described a class of domain descriptions for which our treatment of prioritized defaults coincides with that suggested by G. Brewka in [7].

Defining reasoning with prioritized defaults via axioms of $\mathcal{P}$ allows to use logic programming theory to prove consistency and other properties of domain descriptions of $\mathcal{L}$. Logic programming also provides algorithms for answering queries to such domain descriptions. This work can be extended in several directions. First, the results presented in the paper can be generalized to much broader classes of theories of $\mathcal{L}$. We also plan a more systematic study of the class of logic programs defined by $\mathcal{P}$ (i.e., programs of the form $\mathcal{P} \cup \mathcal{D}$). It may be interesting and useful to check if cautious monotony [19] or other general properties of defeasible inference ([26, 12–14]) hold for this class of programs. Another interesting class of questions is related to investigating the relationship between various versions of $\mathcal{P}$. Under what conditions on $\mathcal{D}$, for instance, we can guarantee that $\mathcal{P}(\mathcal{D})$ is equivalent to $\mathcal{P}_0(\mathcal{D})$? What is the effect of expanding $\mathcal{P}$ by the transitivity axiom for $prefer$? Should this axiom to be made defeasible? etc. Finally, we want to see if a better language can be obtained by removing from it the notion of $conflict$. In the current language the statement $prefer(d_1, d_2)$ stops the application of default d_2 if defaults d_1 and d_2 are in conflict with each other and the default d_1 is applicable. It may be more convenient to make $prefer(d_1, d_2)$ simply mean that d_2 is stoped if d_1 is applicable. More experience with both languages is needed to make a justified design decision. We hope that answers to these and similar questions will shed new light on representation and reasoning with prioritized defaults.

Acknowledgment

We are grateful to Gerhard Brewka for an illuminating discussion on reasoning with prioritized defaults. We also would like to thank Alfredo Gabaldon for useful discussions and help with running our examples on SLG. Special thanks also to Vladik Kreinovich who helped us to better understand the use of priorities in the utility theory and hence our own work. This work was partially supported by United Space Alliance under contract # NAS9-20000.

Appendix A

In this appendix we prove theorem 1. We need the following lemmas.

Lemma 1. [3]Let $\mathcal{T}$ be a logic program and

$$q \leftarrow \Gamma_1$$
$$q \leftarrow \Gamma_2$$
$$\dots$$

be the collection of all rules of $\mathcal{T}$ with the head q. Then the program $\mathcal{Q}$ obtained from $\mathcal{T}$ by replacing rules of the form

$$p \leftarrow \Delta_1, q, \Delta_2$$

by the set of rules

$$p \leftarrow \Delta_1, \Gamma_1, \Delta_2$$
$$p \leftarrow \Delta_1, \Gamma_2, \Delta_2$$
$$\dots$$

is equivalent to $\mathcal{T}$, i.e., $\mathcal{T}$ and $\mathcal{Q}$ have the same consistent answer sets.

Proof. Let us denote the set of all rules removed from $\mathcal{T}$ by $\mathcal{S}$ and let

$$\mathcal{R} = \mathcal{Q} \cup \mathcal{S}.$$

$\mathcal{R}$ can be viewed as a union of $\mathcal{T}$ and the set of new rules obtain from $\mathcal{T}$ by the application of the cut inference rule. Since the cut is sound with respect to constructive logic N_2 [31] which is an extension of the logic N from [29], $\mathcal{T}$ and $\mathcal{R}$ are equivalent in N_2. As shown in [31], programs equivalent in N_2 have the same consistent answer sets, i.e.,

(a) programs $\mathcal{T}$ and $\mathcal{R}$ are equivalent.

This means that to prove our lemma it suffices to show equivalence of $\mathcal{R}$ and $\mathcal{Q}$.

Let $\mathcal{Q}^A$ and $\mathcal{S}^A$ be reducts of $\mathcal{Q}$ and $\mathcal{S}$ with respect to set A of literals (as in the definition of answer sets). We show that A is the minimal set closed under $\mathcal{Q}^A$ iff it is the minimal set closed under $\mathcal{Q}^A \cup \mathcal{S}^A$.

(b) Let A be the minimal set closed under $\mathcal{Q}^A$. We show that it is closed under $\mathcal{S}^A$.

Consider a rule

$$p \leftarrow \Delta_1^A, q, \Delta_2^A \in \mathcal{S}^A$$

s.t. $\{\Delta_1^A, q, \Delta_2^A\} \subseteq A$. (Here by Δ_i^A we denote the result of removing from Δ_i all the occurrences of $not\ l$ s.t. $l \notin A$. Obviously, Δ_i^A's above do not contain not .) From the assumption of (b) and the fact that $q \in A$ we have that there is i s.t. a rule

---

[3] This is a well-know property of logic programs called "partial evaluation" in [3, 4]. We were, however, unable to find a proof of it for an infinite P.

$$q \leftarrow \Gamma_i^A \in \mathcal{Q}^A$$

with $\Gamma_i^A \subseteq A$. This implies that there is a rule

$$p \leftarrow \Delta_1^A, \Gamma_i^A, \Delta_2^A \in \mathcal{Q}^A$$

whose body is satisfied by A, and therefore $p \in A$. This implies that A is the minimal set closed under $\mathcal{Q}^A \cup \mathcal{S}^A$.

(c) Let A be the minimal set closed under $\mathcal{Q}^A \cup \mathcal{S}^A$. We will show that it is the minimal set closed under $\mathcal{Q}^A$.

A is obviously closed under $\mathcal{Q}^A$. Suppose that there is $B \subset A$ closed under $\mathcal{Q}^A$. As was shown above it would be also closed under $\mathcal{S}^A$ which contradicts our assumption.

From (b), (c) and the definition of answer set we have that $\mathcal{R}$ and $\mathcal{Q}$ are equivalent, which, together with (a), proves the lemma.   ◇

To formulate the next lemma we need the following notation: Let $\mathcal{T}$ be a (ground) logic program not containing negative literals $\neg l$ and let p be a unary predicate symbol from the language of $\mathcal{T}$. By $\mathcal{T}^*$ we denote the result of replacing all occurrences of atoms of the form $p(t)$ in $\mathcal{T}$ by t. Notice, that $\mathcal{T}^*$ can be viewed as a propositional logic program with different terms viewed as different propositional letters. Let us also assume that terms of the language of $\mathcal{T}$ do not belong to the set of atoms in this language.

Lemma 2. Let $\mathcal{T}$ and p be as above. Then A is an answer set of $\mathcal{T}$ iff A^* is an answer set of $\mathcal{T}^*$.

Proof. If $\mathcal{T}$ does not contain *not* the lemma is obvious. Otherwise, notice that by definition of answer set, A is an answer set of $\mathcal{T}$ iff it is an answer set of $\mathcal{T}^A$. Since $\mathcal{T}^A$ does not contain *not* this happens iff A^* is the answer set of $(\mathcal{T}^A)^*$. To complete the proof it remains to notice that $(\mathcal{T}^A)^* = (\mathcal{T}^*)^{A^*}$.   ◇

Lemma 3. Let $\mathcal{D}$ be a domain description. By $\mathcal{P}_2(\mathcal{D})$ we denote the program obtained from $\mathcal{P}_0(\mathcal{D})$ by

- replacing all occurrences of literals $hold([l_1, \ldots, l_n])$
  and $hold\_by\_default([l_1, \ldots, l_n])$ in the bodies of the rules from $\mathcal{P}_0(\mathcal{D})$ by
  $holds(l_1), \ldots, holds(l_n)$ and $holds\_by\_default(l_1), \ldots, holds\_by\_default(l_n)$ respectively (we denote the resulting program by $\mathcal{P}_1(\mathcal{D})$);
- Dropping the rules with heads formed by literals $hold$ and $hold\_by\_default$.

Then

(a) if A is an answer set of $\mathcal{P}_0(\mathcal{D})$ then $A \setminus lit(\{hold, hold\_by\_default\})$ is an answer set of $\mathcal{P}_2(\mathcal{D})$;

(b) if A is an answer set of $\mathcal{P}_2(\mathcal{D})$ then

$$A \cup \{hold([l_1,\ldots,l_n]) : holds(l_1),\ldots,holds(l_n) \in A\} \cup$$
$$\{hold\_by\_default([l_1,\ldots,l_n]) : holds\_by\_default(l_1) \in A,\ldots,$$
$$holds\_by\_default(l_n) \in A\}$$

is an answer set of $\mathcal{P}_0(\mathcal{D})$.

Proof. First notice that by Lemma 1, programs $\mathcal{P}_0(\mathcal{D})$ and $\mathcal{P}_1(\mathcal{D})$ are equivalent. Then observe that atoms formed by predicate symbols $hold$ and $hold\_by\_default$ form the complement of a splitting set of program $\mathcal{P}_1$. The conclusion of the lemma follows immediately from the splitting set theorem ([27]) and the fact that rules defining $hold$ and $hold\_by\_default$ contains neither not nor $\neg$. ◇

Lemma 4. Let $\mathcal{D}$ be a hierarchical domain description over signature σ and

$$H = \{holds(l) : \mathcal{P}_0^s(\mathcal{D}) \models holds(l)\} \cup \{defeated(d) : \mathcal{P}_0^s(\mathcal{D}) \models defeated(d)\}.$$

By $\mathcal{P}_3(\mathcal{D})$ we denote the program consisting of the following rules

$$holds\_by\_default(l). \quad \text{if } holds(l) \in H \tag{1}$$

$$holds\_by\_default(l) \leftarrow holds\_by\_default(l_1), \tag{2}$$
$$\vdots$$
$$holds\_by\_default(l_n),$$
$$not\ defeated(d),$$
$$not\ holds\_by\_default(\neg l).$$

$$\text{if } default(d,l,[l_1,\ldots,l_n]) \in \mathcal{D}$$
$$\text{and } holds(l) \notin H,$$
$$\text{and } holds(\neg l) \notin H$$

$$defeated(d_2) \leftarrow holds\_by\_default(l_1), \tag{3}$$
$$\vdots$$
$$holds\_by\_default(l_n),$$
$$holds\_by\_default(prefer(d_1,d_2))$$
$$not\ defeated(d_1).$$

$$\text{if } d_2 \in \mathcal{D},$$
$$default(d_1,l,[l_1,\ldots,l_n]) \in \mathcal{D},$$
$$holds(conflict(d_1,d_2)) \in H,$$

$$\text{and } holds(l) \notin H,$$
$$\text{and } holds(\neg l) \notin H$$

$$holds\_by\_default(\neg prefer(d_1, d_2)) \leftarrow holds\_by\_default(prefer(d_2, d_1)) \quad (4)$$

$$\text{if } holds(prefer(d_1, d_2)) \notin H,$$
$$\text{and } holds(prefer(d_2, d_1)) \notin H,$$
$$\text{and } d_1, d_2 \in \mathcal{D}$$

$$\neg holds\_by\_default(l) \leftarrow holds\_by\_default(\neg l). \quad (5)$$

Then, A is an answer set of $\mathcal{P}_2(\mathcal{D})$ iff $A = laws(\mathcal{D}) \cup H \cup B$ where B is an answer set of $\mathcal{P}_3(\mathcal{D})$.

Proof. Let U_0 be the set of literals formed by predicate symbols $holds$, $rule$ and $default$. U_0 is a splitting set of program $\mathcal{P}_2(\mathcal{D})$ and hence A is an answer set of $\mathcal{P}_2(\mathcal{D})$ iff $A = A_0 \cup A_1$ where A_0 is the answer set of program $b_{U_0}(\mathcal{P}_0(\mathcal{D}))$ consisting of rules of $\mathcal{P}_2(\mathcal{D})$ whose heads belong to U_0 and A_1 is an answer set of the partial evaluation, $\mathcal{R} = e_{U_0}(t_{U_0}(\mathcal{P}_0(\mathcal{D})), A_0)$, of the rest of the program with respect to U_0 and A_0. It is easy to see that the program $\mathcal{R}$ consists of the rules of $\mathcal{P}_3(\mathcal{D})$ and

(a) rules of the type (2) where $holds(l)$ or $holds(\neg l)$ is in H;

(b) rules of the type (3) where $holds(l) \in H$ or $holds(\neg l) \in H$;

(c) rules of the type

$$holds\_by\_default(l) \leftarrow holds\_by\_default(l_1),$$
$$\ldots$$
$$holds\_by\_default(l_n),$$

for each rule $rule(r, l, [l_1, \ldots, l_n]) \in \mathcal{D}$;

(d) rules of the type (4) where $holds(prefer(d_1, d_2)) \in H$ or $holds(prefer(d_2, d_1)) \in H$;

(e) facts of the type $defeated(d)$ where d is a default in $\mathcal{D}$ with the head l s.t. $holds(\neg l) \in H$.

From the rule $(\mathcal{P}_0.9)$ of program $\mathcal{P}_0$ we have that facts of the type (e) belong to H and hence to prove the lemma it is enough to show that the rules of the type (a)-(d) can be eliminated from $\mathcal{R}$ without changing its answer sets. To do that let us first make the following simple observation. Consider a program $\mathcal{Q}_1$ containing a rule $p \leftarrow \Gamma$ and the fact p and let $\mathcal{Q}_2$ be obtained from $\mathcal{Q}_1$ by removing the rule. $\mathcal{Q}_1$ and $\mathcal{Q}_2$ are obviously equivalent in the logic N_2 and hence have the same answer sets. Similarly, we can show that a rule whose body contradicts a fact of the program can be removed from the program.

(1a) Consider a rule r of $\mathcal{R}$ of the type (a).
If $holds(l) \in H$ then, from rule (4) of $\mathcal{P}_0$ we have that $holds\_by\_default(l) \in \mathcal{R}$. Hence, by the above observation, r can be removed from $\mathcal{R}$ without changing its answer sets.
If $holds(\neg l) \in H$ then from rule (4) of $\mathcal{P}_0$ we have that $holds\_by\_default(\neg l) \in \mathcal{R}$ which contradicts the body of r. Hence r is useless and can be safely removed.

(1b) Now consider a rule r of the type (b). We will show that its head, $defeated(d_2)$, is a fact of $\mathcal{R}$.

First notice that, if $holds(\neg l) \in H$ then $\mathcal{P}_0^s(\mathcal{D}) \models defeated(d_1)$. Therefore, $defeated(d_1) \in A_0$ and hence, in this case, $r \notin \mathcal{R}$.

Suppose now that $holds(l) \in H$. Consider two cases:

(i) The head l of d_2 is σ literal.
By definition of rules of type (b) we have that $holds(conflict(d_1, d_2)) \in H$. From condition (2) of definition 5 of hierarchical domain description and the rules $(\mathcal{P}_0.11)$, $(\mathcal{P}_0.21)$, and $(\mathcal{P}_0.22)$ of $\mathcal{P}_0$ we conclude that the head of default d_1 is literal $\neg l$. Since r is of type (b), this means that $holds(\neg l) \in H$ and, from the rule $(\mathcal{P}_0.9)$ of $\mathcal{P}_0$ we have that $defeated(d_2) \in H$.

(ii) The head l of d_2 is of the form $prefer(d_i, d_j)$.
From conditions (2), (3) of definition 5 and the rule $(\mathcal{P}_0.11)$, $(\mathcal{P}_0.21)$, and $(\mathcal{P}_0.22)$ of $\mathcal{D}$ we have that the head of d_1 is $prefer(d_j, d_i)$. From rule $(\mathcal{P}_0.14)$ of $\mathcal{P}_0$ we have that $\neg prefer(d_i, d_j) \in H$. Finally, from rule $(\mathcal{P}_0.9)$ of $\mathcal{P}_0$ we have that $defeated(d_2) \in H$.
This demonstrates that the rules of the type (b) can be removed from $\mathcal{R}$ without changing its answer sets.

(1c) It is easy to check that by the condition (4) of definition 5 the body of a rule of the type (d) is satisfied iff $holds(l_1), \ldots, holds(l_n) \in H$ and hence the head of such a rule is in H or the rule is useless.

(1d) Similar argument can be used for the rules of the type (c). The conclusion of the lemma follows now from the observation above and the splitting set theorem. $\Diamond$

Let us consider a logic program $\mathcal{Q}(\mathcal{D})$ obtained from program $\mathcal{P}_3(\mathcal{D})$ by

(a) removing rules of the type (5);

(b) replacing literals of the form $holds\_by\_default(l)$ and $defeated(d)$ by l and d respectively.

The program $Q(D)$ is called the defeasible counterpart of D and consists the following rules:

$$Q(D) = \begin{cases}
\begin{array}{ll}
l. & \text{if } holds(l) \in H \hfill (1) \\[2mm]
l & \leftarrow l_1, \ldots, l_n, \hfill (2) \\
& not\ d, \\
& not\ \neg l. \\[2mm]
& \text{if } default(d, l, [l_1, \ldots, l_n]) \in D \\
& \text{and } holds(l) \notin H, \\
& \text{and } holds(\neg l) \notin H \\[3mm]
d_2 & \leftarrow l_1, \ldots, l_n, \hfill (3) \\
& prefer(d_1, d_2) \\
& not\ d_1. \\[2mm]
& \text{if } d_2 \in D, \\
& default(d_1, l, [l_1, \ldots, l_n]) \in D, \\
& holds(conflict(d_1, d_2)) \in H \\
& \text{and } holds(l) \notin H \\
& \text{and } holds(\neg l) \notin H \\[3mm]
\neg prefer(d_1, d_2) & \leftarrow prefer(d_2, d_1). \hfill (4) \\[2mm]
& \text{if } holds(prefer(d_1, d_2)) \notin H \\
& \text{and } holds(prefer(d_2, d_1)) \notin H \\
& \text{and } d_1, d_2 \in D
\end{array}
\end{cases}$$

Lemma 5. Let D be a hierarchical domain description over signature σ and let H be the set of literals defined as in Lemma 4. Then the program $Q(D)$ is consistent.

Proof. First let us notice that the set F of facts of the form (1) from the program $Q(D)$ form a splitting set of this program. Since D is rule-consistent so is F. This implies that $Q(D)$ is consistent iff the result Q_0 of partial evaluation of $Q(D)$ with respect to F is consistent. Let Q_1 be the result of removal from Q_0 all the rules whose bodies contain literals not belonging to the heads of rules from Q_0. Obviously, $Q(D)$ is equivalent to Q_1.

To prove consistency of Q_1 we construct its splitting sequence and use the splitting sequence theorem from [27].

Since D is hierarchical it has a rank function $rank$. Let μ be the smallest ordinal number such that $rank(l) < \mu$ for every l from the domain of $rank$. Let $heads(Q_1)$ be the set of literals from the heads of rules in Q_1 and

$U_\alpha = \{l : l \in lit(\sigma) \cap heads(\mathcal{Q}_1) \text{ s.t. } rank(l) < \alpha\} \cup$
$\qquad \{d \in heads(\mathcal{Q}_1) : rank(head(d)) < \alpha\} \cup$
$\qquad \{prefer(d_1, d_2) \in heads(\mathcal{Q}_1) : rank(prefer(d_1, d_2)) < \alpha\} \cup$
$\qquad \{\neg prefer(d_1, d_2) : prefer(d_2, d_1) \in heads(\mathcal{Q}_1), rank(prefer(d_2, d_1)) < \alpha\}$

The sequence $U = \langle U_\alpha \rangle_{\alpha < \mu}$ is monotone ($U_\alpha \subset U_\beta$ whenever $\alpha < \beta$) and continuous (for each limit ordinal $\alpha < \mu$, $U_\alpha = \bigcup_{\beta < \alpha} U_\beta$). Using the property of the $rank$ function from the definition of hierarchical domain description it is not difficult to check that for each $\alpha < \mu$, U_α is a splitting set of $\mathcal{Q}_1$ and that $\bigcup_{\alpha < \mu} U_\alpha$ is equal to the set of all literals occurring in $\mathcal{Q}_1$. Hence, U is a splitting sequence of $\mathcal{Q}_1$. By the splitting sequence theorem existence of an answer set of $\mathcal{Q}_1$ follows from existence of a solution to $\mathcal{Q}_1$ (with respect to U). Let T_α be a collection of all the rules from $\mathcal{Q}_1$ whose heads belong to U_α. To show existence of such a solution it suffices to

(i) assume that for α such that $\alpha + 1 < \mu$ the program T_α has a consistent answer set A_α;

(ii) use this assumption to show that $T_{\alpha+1}$ also has a consistent answer set;

(iii) show that $\bigcup_{\alpha < \mu} A_\alpha$ is consistent.

Let us show (ii) and (iii). Let T be the result of partial evaluation of the program $T_{\alpha+1}$ with respect to the set A_α. T can be divided into three parts consisting of rules of the form

(a) $d_2 \leftarrow not\ d_1$.

and

(b) $l \leftarrow not\ d, not\ \neg l$ where l is a σ-literal

and

(c1) $prefer(d_i, d_j) \leftarrow not\ d, not\ \neg prefer(d_i, d_j)$

(c2) $\neg prefer(d_m, d_n) \leftarrow prefer(d_n, d_m)$.

respectively.

To show consistency of the program $T(a)$ consisting of rules (a) we first observe that, by construction, if a rule r of type (a) is in T then d_1, d_2 are conflicting defaults and hence, by condition 2 of definition 5 and the rule $(\mathcal{P}_0.11)$, $(\mathcal{P}_0.21)$, and $(\mathcal{P}_0.22)$ of $\mathcal{P}_0$, their heads are either contrary σ-literals or of the form $prefer(d_i, d_j)$ and $prefer(d_j, d_i)$ where $i \neq j$. Consider the dependency graph D of S_1. D obviously does not contain cycles with positive edges. We will show that it does not contain odd cycles with negative edges. (Programs with this property are called call-consistent). Suppose that $d_1, \ldots, d_{2n+1}, d_1$ is such a cycle. Since d_i and d_{i+1} ($i = 1, \ldots, 2n$) are conflicting defaults we have that d_1 and d_{2n+1} have the same heads (clause (2) of the definition and rules $(\mathcal{P}_0.11)$,

$(\mathcal{P}_0.21)$, and $(\mathcal{P}_0.22)$ of $\mathcal{P}_0$). Since d_1 and d_{2n+1} are conflicting their heads must be different. Hence our program has no odd cycles. As was shown by Fages [17] (see also [15]), call consistent programs with dependency graphs without positive cycles have an answer set.

To show consistency of the program $T(a,b)$ consisting of rules (a) and (b) of T it suffices to take an arbitrary answer set of program $T(a)$ and use the splitting set theorem. The corresponding reduct R will consist of rules of the form $l \leftarrow not \neg l$. Let X_0 be the set of all positive literals from the heads of R and X_1 be the set of negative literals of the form $\neg l$ from the heads of R such that $l \notin X_0$. It is easy to see that the set $X_0 \cup X_1$ is a consistent answer set of R.

Now we need to show consistency of the partial evaluation T_r of T with respect to some answer set of $T(a,b)$. T_r consists of rules

$$prefer(d_i, d_j) \leftarrow not \neg prefer(d_i, d_j)$$

and

$$\neg prefer(d_m, d_n) \leftarrow prefer(d_n, d_m).$$

Let $heads(T_r)$ be the set of the heads of the rules of T_r and let us assume that each default is associated with a unique index i. Consider a set X_0

$$X_0 = \{prefer(d_i, d_j) : prefer(d_i, d_j) \in heads(T_r), prefer(d_j, d_i) \notin heads(T_r)\} \cup$$
$$\{prefer(d_i, d_j) : i < j \text{ if } prefer(d_i, d_j) \in heads(T_r) \text{ and } prefer(d_j, d_i) \in heads(T_r)\}$$

Now let

$$X = X_0 \cup \{\neg prefer(d_n, d_m) : prefer(d_m, d_n) \in X_0\}$$

Obviously, X is consistent. To show that it is a consistent answer set of T_r let us construct T_r^X and show that

$$prefer(d_i, d_j) \in T_r^X \text{ iff } prefer(d_i, d_j) \in X.$$

Let

$$prefer(d_i, d_j) \in X.$$

Then, by construction of X,

$$prefer(d_j, d_i) \notin X, \text{ hence}$$

$$\neg prefer(d_i, d_j) \notin X, \text{ i.e.}$$

$$prefer(d_i, d_j) \in T_r^X.$$

Similar argument demonstrates equivalence in the opposite direction. This implies that X is a consistent answer set of T_r. By the splitting set theorem we conclude consistency of T and $T_{\alpha+1}$. Statement (iii) follows immediately from the above construction of answer set of $T_{\alpha+1}$ and hence, from the splitting sequence theorem we have that $\mathcal{Q}(\mathcal{D})$ is consistent.   ◇

Lemma 6. Let $\mathcal{D}$ be a hierarchical domain description over signature σ and let $\mathcal{Q}(\mathcal{D})$ be the program defined as in Lemma 5. Then for any literal l of $\mathcal{L}_0(\sigma)$

$\mathcal{D} \models holds\_by\_default(l)$ iff $\mathcal{Q}(\mathcal{D}) \models l$.

Proof. By definition,

1. $\mathcal{D} \models holds\_by\_default(l)$ iff $\mathcal{P}_0(\mathcal{D}) \models holds\_by\_default(l)$.

From (1) and lemma 3 we have that

2. $\mathcal{D} \models holds\_by\_default(l)$ iff $\mathcal{P}_2(\mathcal{D}) \models holds\_by\_default(l)$.

From (2) and lemma 4 we have that

3. $\mathcal{D} \models holds\_by\_default(l)$ iff $\mathcal{P}_3(\mathcal{D}) \models holds\_by\_default(l)$.

Let $\mathcal{P}_4(\mathcal{D})$ be the program obtained from the program $\mathcal{P}_3(\mathcal{D})$ by removing the rules of type (5) from $\mathcal{P}_3(\mathcal{D})$. It is easy to see that $\mathcal{P}_4(\mathcal{D})$ is the bottom program of $\mathcal{P}_3(\mathcal{D})$ with respect to the splitting set consisting of all positive literals of the program $\mathcal{P}_3(\mathcal{D})$.

Now let us consider the program $\mathcal{Q}_p(\mathcal{D})$ obtained from $\mathcal{Q}(\mathcal{D})$ by replacing every negative literal $l = \neg p(t)$ by the atom $\bar{l} = \bar{p}(t)$ where $\bar{p}$ is a new predicate symbol.

From (3) and lemma 2 we have that

4. $\mathcal{P}_4(\mathcal{D}) \models holds\_by\_default(l)$ iff $\mathcal{Q}_p(\mathcal{D}) \models l$.

As was shown in [21] answer sets of $\mathcal{Q}(\mathcal{D})$ coincide with answer sets (stable models) of $\mathcal{Q}_p(\mathcal{D})$ which do not contain pairs of atoms of the form $l, \bar{l}$. Let us show that no answer set A of $\mathcal{Q}_p(\mathcal{D})$ contains such literals. Consider two cases:

(i) l is a σ-literal. Suppose that $l \in A$. Obviously there is no rule of the type (2) in $\mathcal{Q}_p(\mathcal{D})$ whose head is $\bar{l}$ and whose body is satisfied by A. Since $\mathcal{D}$ is rule-consistent $\bar{l} \notin \mathcal{Q}_p(\mathcal{D})$ and hence $\bar{l} \notin A$.

(ii) $l = prefer(d_i, d_j)$. There are free types of rules in $\mathcal{Q}_p(\mathcal{D})$ which contain literals formed by $prefer$ in the heads:

(a). $prefer(d_i, d_j)$.

from rule (1) of $\mathcal{Q}(\mathcal{D})$

(b). $prefer(d_i, d_j) \leftarrow \Gamma, not\ \overline{prefer}(d_i, d_j)$.

from rule (2) of $\mathcal{Q}(\mathcal{D})$ and

(c). $\overline{prefer}(d_i, d_j) \leftarrow prefer(d_j, d_i)$.

from rule (2) of $\mathcal{Q}(\mathcal{D})$.

Suppose that $prefer(d_i, d_j) \in A$. Then, from the rule consistency of $\mathcal{D}$ we have that $prefer(d_j, d_i)$ does not belong to (a). Since, by rule (c) we have that $\overline{prefer}(d_j, d_i) \in A$ and hence $prefer(d_j, d_i) \notin A$. This implies that $\overline{prefer}(d_i, d_j) \notin A$.

Hence, we have that

5. $\mathcal{Q}_p(\mathcal{D}) \models l$ iff $\mathcal{Q}(\mathcal{D}) \models l$.

It follows from (5) and (4) that

6. $\mathcal{P}_4(\mathcal{D}) \models holds\_by\_default(l)$ iff $\mathcal{Q}(\mathcal{D}) \models l$.

Since $\mathcal{Q}(\mathcal{D})$ is consistent, we can conclude that no answer set of $\mathcal{P}_4(\mathcal{D})$ containing $holds\_by\_default(l)$ and $holds\_by\_default(\neg l)$. By the splitting theorem, we have that $\mathcal{P}_3(\mathcal{D})$ is consistent and moreover,

7. $\mathcal{P}_3(\mathcal{D}) \models holds\_by\_default(l)$ iff $\mathcal{P}_4(\mathcal{D}) \models holds\_by\_default(l)$.

The proof of the lemma follows from (7), (6), and (3). $\Diamond$

The proof of the theorem 1 follows immediately from Lemmas 5 and 6.

Appendix B

In this appendix we prove the theorem 2. By Lemma 6, we have that for any σ-literal l

$$\mathcal{D} \models holds\_by\_default(l) \text{ iff } \mathcal{Q}(\mathcal{D}) \models l$$

where $\mathcal{Q}(\mathcal{D})$ is the program defined in Lemma 5. Hence, to prove the theorem, it suffices to show that

$$\mathcal{Q}(\mathcal{D}) \models l \text{ iff } \Pi(\mathcal{D}) \hspace{2pt}\vdash\hspace{-10pt}\sim\hspace{4pt} l.$$

Let us introduce some useful terminology and notation. Let $\mathcal{D}$ be a hierarchical domain description and

$$U(\mathcal{D}) = \{l : l \text{ is a } \mathcal{L}_0(\sigma) \text{ literal and } \mathcal{P}_0^s(\mathcal{D}) \models holds(l)\}$$

where $\mathcal{P}_0^s(\mathcal{D})$ is the non-defeasible part of $\mathcal{P}_0(\mathcal{D})$.

To simplify the proof let us assume that the set of defaults in $\mathcal{D}$ has the cardinality less than or equal to ω and that the minimal value of the rank function of $\mathcal{D}$ is 1. Let $\mathcal{D}_N$ be the domain description obtained from $\mathcal{D}$ as follows:

(i) removing all rules and σ-literals from $\mathcal{D}$;
(ii) removing all defaults $d \in \mathcal{D}$ such that $head(d) \in U(\mathcal{D})$ or $\neg head(d) \in U(\mathcal{D})$;
(iii) removing every occurrence of σ-literal $l \in U(\mathcal{D})$ from the bodies of the remaining defaults of $\mathcal{D}$; We denote the resulting domain description $\mathcal{D}_0$.
(iv) Let $\mathcal{D}_M = \cap_{r=0}^{\omega} \mathcal{D}_r$ where $\mathcal{D}_r$ is obtained from $\mathcal{D}_{r-1}$ by removing from it every default of the rank r whose body contains a literal not belonging to the head of any default in $\mathcal{D}_{r-1}$; $\mathcal{D}_N$ is obtained from $\mathcal{D}_M$ by removing all literals of the form $prefer(d_1, d_2)$ such that $d_1 \notin \mathcal{D}_M$ or $d_2 \notin \mathcal{D}_M$.

The domain description $\mathcal{D}_N$ will be called *the normalization of $\mathcal{D}$*.

A hierarchical domain description $\mathcal{D}$ is said to be *normalized* if $\mathcal{D} = \mathcal{D}_N$.

Let $\mathcal{Q}(\mathcal{D})$ be the defeasible counterpart of a static domain description $\mathcal{D}$ and let $\mathcal{R}(\mathcal{D})$ be obtained from $\mathcal{Q}(\mathcal{D})$ by

(a) removing rules of the type (4);
(b) performing partial evaluation of the resulting program with respect to $U(\mathcal{D})$.

This construction, together with the following simple lemma, will be frequently used in our proof.

Lemma 7. For any static and hierarchical domain description $\mathcal{D}$ and σ-literal $l \notin U(\mathcal{D})$,

$$\mathcal{Q}(\mathcal{D}) \models l \text{ iff } \mathcal{R}(\mathcal{D}) \models l.$$

Proof. First notice that since $\mathcal{D}$ is static $\neg prefer(d_1, d_2) \in U(\mathcal{D})$ or $prefer(d_2, d_1) \notin U(\mathcal{D})$. Hence the program $\mathcal{Q}_a(\mathcal{D})$ obtained from $\mathcal{Q}(\mathcal{D})$ by step (a) has the same answer sets as $\mathcal{Q}(\mathcal{D})$.

Now notice that since $\mathcal{D}$ is static the heads of rules of the type (2) in $\mathcal{Q}(\mathcal{D})$ belong to $lit(\sigma)$. By construction of $\mathcal{Q}(\mathcal{D})$ these heads do not belong to $U(\mathcal{D})$. Therefore, $U(\mathcal{D})$ is a splitting set of $\mathcal{Q}_a(\mathcal{D})$ and conclusion of the lemma follows from the splitting set theorem. $\diamond$

The proof of the theorem 2 will be based on the following lemmas.

Lemma 8. Let $\mathcal{D}_N$ be the normalization of a static and hierarchical domain description $\mathcal{D}$. Then, for every σ-literal l such that $l \notin U(\mathcal{D})$

$$\mathcal{D} \models holds\_by\_default(l) \quad \text{iff} \quad \mathcal{D}_N \models holds\_by\_default(l).$$

Proof. Let l be a σ-literal such that $l \notin U(\mathcal{D})$. Since $\mathcal{D}$ is hierarchical we have that by Lemma 6 it suffices to show that

a. $\mathcal{Q}(\mathcal{D}) \models l$ iff $\mathcal{Q}(\mathcal{D}_N) \models l$.

Domain descriptions $\mathcal{D}$ and $\mathcal{D}_N$ are static and hierarchical and hence, by Lemma 7 we have that (a) is true iff

b. $\mathcal{R}(\mathcal{D}) \models l$ iff $\mathcal{R}(\mathcal{D}_N) \models l$.

Let $\mathcal{D}^*$ be the domain description obtained from $\mathcal{D}$ by performing the steps (i), (ii), and (iii) in the construction of $\mathcal{D}_N$. Obviously, $\mathcal{D}_N \subseteq \mathcal{D}^*$. We first prove that

c. $\mathcal{R}(\mathcal{D})$ and $\mathcal{R}(\mathcal{D}^*)$ are identical.

Let

c1. $r \in \mathcal{R}(\mathcal{D})$

We consider two cases:

(i) $head(r) \in lit(\sigma)$, i.e.,

r is of the form $l_0 \leftarrow \Gamma, not\ d, not\ \neg l_0$

where Γ consists of σ-literals not belonging to $U(\mathcal{D})$. By construction of $\mathcal{R}(\mathcal{D})$ and $\mathcal{Q}(\mathcal{D})$ this is possible iff

c2. neither l_0 nor $\neg l_0$ is in $U(\mathcal{D})$ and there is a set of literals $\Delta \subseteq U(\mathcal{D})$ such that $default(d, l_0, [\Delta, \Gamma]) \in \mathcal{D}$.

From definition of $\mathcal{D}_N$ we have that (c2) holds iff

c3. $default(d, l_0, [\Gamma]) \in \mathcal{D}^*$.

Notice also that, by the same definition, $U(\mathcal{D}^*)$ consists of literals formed by *prefer* and *conflict* and hence do not contain σ-literals. This implies that (c3) holds iff

c4. $r \in \mathcal{Q}(\mathcal{D}^*)$.

Since $\mathcal{D}$ is static, literals from $U(\mathcal{D}^*)$ do not belong to rules (2) of $\mathcal{Q}(\mathcal{D}^*)$. This implies that (c4) holds iff

c5. $r \in \mathcal{R}(\mathcal{D}^*)$.

(ii) $head(r) \notin lit(\sigma)$, i.e.

r is of the form $d_2 \leftarrow \Gamma, not\ d_1$

where Γ consists of σ-literals not belonging to $U(\mathcal{D})$.

By construction of $\mathcal{R}(\mathcal{D})$ this is possible iff

c6. $default(d_1, l_0, [\Delta, \Gamma]), default(d_2, \neg l_0, [\Delta_1, \Gamma_1]) \in \mathcal{D}$

for some $\Delta \subseteq U(\mathcal{D})$, $\Delta_1 \subseteq U(\mathcal{D})$ and Γ_1 consisting of σ-literals not belonging to $U(\mathcal{D})$; $l_0, \neg l_0 \notin U(\mathcal{D})$, and $prefer(d_1, d_2) \in \mathcal{D}$.

It follows from definition of $\mathcal{D}^*$ that (c6) holds iff

c7. $default(d_1, l_0, [\Gamma]) \in \mathcal{D}^*$, $default(d_2, \neg l_0, [\Gamma_1]) \in \mathcal{D}^*$ and $prefer(d_1, d_2) \in \mathcal{D}^*$.

which holds iff

c8. $r \in \mathcal{R}(\mathcal{D}^*)$.

From (c1), (c5) and (c8) we have that $\mathcal{R}(\mathcal{D})$ and $\mathcal{R}(\mathcal{D}^*)$ are identical. Therefore, to prove (b) we will show

d. $\mathcal{R}(\mathcal{D}^*) \models l$ iff $\mathcal{R}(\mathcal{D}_N) \models l$.

Let

e. A be an answer set of $\mathcal{R}(\mathcal{D}^*)$.

Let

f. $B = A \setminus \{d : d \in \mathcal{D}^* \setminus \mathcal{D}_N\}$.

We will prove that

d1. B is an answer set of $\mathcal{R}(\mathcal{D}_N)$.

By construction of $\mathcal{R}(\mathcal{D}^*)$ and $\mathcal{R}(\mathcal{D}_N)$ it is easy to see that

d2. $(\mathcal{R}(\mathcal{D}_N))^B \subseteq (\mathcal{R}(\mathcal{D}))^A$.

Hence,

d3. B is closed under the rules of $(\mathcal{R}(\mathcal{D}_N))^B$.

Assume that there exists a set of literals $C \subset B$, which is closed under the rules of $(\mathcal{R}(\mathcal{D}_N))^B$. Let

d4. $D = (C \cap lit(\sigma)) \cup (A \setminus lit(\sigma))$.

We will prove that

d5. D is closed under the rules of $(\mathcal{R}(\mathcal{D}^*))^A$.

By construction of D,

d6. D is closed under the rules of $(\mathcal{R}(\mathcal{D}^*))^A$ whose heads do not belong to $lit(\sigma)$.

Consider a rule

e0. $l_0 \leftarrow \Gamma \in (\mathcal{R}(\mathcal{D}^*))^A$ such that

e1. $\Gamma \subseteq B$.

By construction of $(\mathcal{R}(\mathcal{D}^*))^A$, this is possible if there exists a default d,

e2. $default(d, l_0, [\Gamma]) \in \mathcal{D}^*$,

e3. $\neg l_0 \notin B, d \notin A$,

From (e2) and the fact that C is closed under the rules of $(\mathcal{R}(\mathcal{D}_N))^B$, by construction of $\mathcal{D}_N$, we conclude that

e4. $default(d, l_0, [\Gamma]) \in \mathcal{D}_N$.

which, together with (e3), implies that

e5. $l_0 \leftarrow \Gamma \in (\mathcal{R}(\mathcal{D}_N))^B$

Since C is closed under the rules of $(\mathcal{R}(\mathcal{D}_N))^B$, (e5) together with (e1), implies that $l_0 \in C$. This proves that D is closed under the rules of $(\mathcal{R}(\mathcal{D}^*))^A$ with σ-literals in their heads. This, together with (d6), implies (d5), and hence, implies that, A is not an answer set of $\mathcal{R}(\mathcal{D}^*)$. This contradiction proves (d1).

Now, let

f1. A be an answer set of $\mathcal{R}(\mathcal{D}_N)$,

and

f2. $B = A \cup \{d : d \in \mathcal{D}^* \setminus \mathcal{D}_N, \exists d' \in \mathcal{D}_N, prefer(d', d) \in \mathcal{D}^*, body(d') \subseteq A\}$.

We will prove that B is an answer set of $\mathcal{R}(\mathcal{D}^*)$ by showing that B is a minimal set of literals closed under the rules of $(\mathcal{R}(\mathcal{D}^*))^B$.

Since A is an answer set of $\mathcal{R}(\mathcal{D}_N)$ we can conclude that

f3. for any $d \in \mathcal{D}^* \setminus \mathcal{D}_N$, $body(d)$ is not satisfied by A.

This, together with the construction of B and the fact that every rule of $(\mathcal{R}(\mathcal{D}^*))^B$ is of the form $l \leftarrow \Gamma$ or $d \leftarrow \Gamma$ where Γ is the body of some default in $\mathcal{D}^*$, implies that

f4. B is closed under the rules of $(\mathcal{R}(\mathcal{D}^*))^B$.

We need to prove the minimality of B. Assume the contrary, there exists a set of literals $C \subset B$ that is closed under the rules of $(\mathcal{R}(\mathcal{D}^*))^B$. Let

f5. $D = C \setminus (B \setminus A)$.

Obviously, $D \subset A$. Since $(\mathcal{R}(\mathcal{D}_N))^A \subseteq (\mathcal{R}(\mathcal{D}^*))^B)$, it is easy to check that D is closed under the rules of $(\mathcal{R}(\mathcal{D}_N))^A$ which contradicts the fact that A is an answer set of $\mathcal{R}(\mathcal{D}_N)$, i.e., we have proved that

f6. B is an answer set of $\mathcal{R}(\mathcal{D}^*)$.

From (e), (d1), (f1), and (f6) we can conclude (d). which, together with (a), (b), and (c) proves the lemma. $\diamond$

The next lemma shows that for a static and hierarchical domain description, the program $\mathcal{B}(\mathcal{D})$ can also be simplified.

Lemma 9. Let $\mathcal{D}$ be a static and hierarchical domain description and $\mathcal{D}_N$ be its normalization. Then, for each σ-literal l such that $l \notin U(\mathcal{D})$,

$$\Pi(\mathcal{D}) \hspace{0.3em}\mid\!\sim l \qquad \text{if and only if} \qquad \Pi(\mathcal{D}_N) \hspace{0.3em}\mid\!\sim l.$$

Proof. First, observe the following for prioritized programs.

Let $(Q, <)$ be a prioritized program where Q is a defeasible program without facts, i.e., each rule in Q contains at least a negation-as-failure literal. Let P be a strict program, i.e., no rule in P contains a negation-as-failure literal. Let $head(Q)$ be the set of literals belonging to the heads of Q and $body(P)$ be the set of literals belonging to the body of rules of P. Assume that $head(Q) \cap body(P) = \emptyset$. Then, we have that

(i) A is a preferred answer set of $(P \cup Q, <)$ iff $A = A_P \cup A_Q$ where A_P is the answer set of P and A_Q is a preferred answer set of $(Q_P, <)$ where Q_P is the partial evaluation of Q with respect to A_P.

(ii) Let P' be a strict program equivalent to P. Then, $(P \cup Q, <)$ and $(P' \cup Q, <)$ are equivalent.

(iii) Let R be the set of rules in Q such that for every $r \in R$, $P \models head(r)$ or $P \models \neg head(r)$. Then, $(P \cup Q, <)$ and $(P \cup Q \setminus R, <)$ are equivalent.

Let us denote the program consisting of rules (3) of $\mathcal{B}(\mathcal{D})$ by Q and $P = \mathcal{B}(\mathcal{D})\backslash Q$. Obviously,

a. Q is a defeasible logic program without facts and P is a strict program.

Since $\mathcal{D}$ is hierarchical, we have that

b. $head(Q) \cap body(P) = \emptyset$.

Let $U_0(\mathcal{D})$ be the set of σ-literals belonging to $U(\mathcal{D})$. It is easy to see that $U_0(\mathcal{D})$ is the unique answer set of P, i.e., $U_0(\mathcal{D})$ and P are equivalent. Therefore, together with (a) and (b), by (ii) we can conclude that

c. $\Pi(\mathcal{D}) \hspace{0.3em}\sim\hspace{-0.9em}\mid\hspace{0.6em} l$ iff $(U_0(\mathcal{D}) \cup Q, <_\mathcal{D}) \hspace{0.3em}\sim\hspace{-0.9em}\mid\hspace{0.6em} l$.

Let R be the set of rules in Q such that for every $r \in R$, $head(r) \in U_0(\mathcal{D})$ or $\neg head(r) \in U_0(\mathcal{D})$, then by (iii) we know that

d. $(U_0(\mathcal{D}) \cup Q, <_\mathcal{D}) \hspace{0.3em}\sim\hspace{-0.9em}\mid\hspace{0.6em} l$ iff $(U_0(\mathcal{D}) \cup Q \setminus R, <_\mathcal{D}) \hspace{0.3em}\sim\hspace{-0.9em}\mid\hspace{0.6em} l$.

It is easy to see that $U_0(\mathcal{D})$ is a splitting set of $U_0(\mathcal{D}) \cup Q \setminus R$. Let S be the reduct of $U_0(\mathcal{D}) \cup Q \setminus R$ with respect to $U_0(\mathcal{D})$.

As in the previous proof, let $\mathcal{D}^*$ be the domain description obtained from $\mathcal{D}$ by performing the steps (i), (ii), and (iii) in the construction of $\mathcal{D}_N$. We will prove that S is identical to $\mathcal{B}(\mathcal{D}^*)$. Let

e1. $r \in S$.

It means that r has the form

e2. $l \leftarrow \Gamma, not \neg l$.

where Γ is a set of σ-literals containing no literals from $U_0(\mathcal{D})$. By construction of S, (e2) holds iff

e3. $l \notin U_0(\mathcal{D})$, $\neg l \notin U_0(\mathcal{D})$, and there exists a set of literals $\Delta \subseteq U_0(\mathcal{D})$ such that $default(d, l, [\Gamma, \Delta]) \in \mathcal{D}$.

From the definition of $\mathcal{D}^*$, (e3) holds iff

e4. $default(d, l, [\Gamma]) \in \mathcal{D}^*$

By definition of $\mathcal{B}(\mathcal{D}^*)$ and the definition of $\mathcal{D}^*$, (e4) holds iff

e5. r is a rule in $\mathcal{B}(\mathcal{D}^*)$.

From (e1) and (e5) we can conclude that

e. S is identical to $\mathcal{B}(\mathcal{D}^*)$.

From (e), (i), (c), and (d), and the splitting set theorem, we have that

f. $\Pi(\mathcal{D}) \hspace{0.3em}\sim\hspace{-0.9em}\mid\hspace{0.6em} l$ iff $l \in U(\mathcal{D})$ or $\Pi(\mathcal{D}^*) \hspace{0.3em}\sim\hspace{-0.9em}\mid\hspace{0.6em} l$.

This, implies that to prove the lemma, it suffices to show that

g. $\Pi(\mathcal{D}^*) \hspace{0.3em}\sim\hspace{-0.9em}\mid\hspace{0.6em} l$ iff $\Pi(\mathcal{D}_N) \hspace{0.3em}\sim\hspace{-0.9em}\mid\hspace{0.6em} l$.

To prove (g) we first prove that

g1. $\mathcal{B}(\mathcal{D}^*)$ and $\mathcal{B}(\mathcal{D}_N)$ are equivalent.

Let

g2. A be an answer set of $\mathcal{B}(\mathcal{D}^*)$.

Since $\mathcal{D}_N \subseteq \mathcal{D}^*$, we have that

g3. $(\mathcal{B}(\mathcal{D}_N))^A \subseteq (\mathcal{B}(\mathcal{D}^*))^A$

which immediately implies that

g4. A is closed under the rules of $(\mathcal{B}(\mathcal{D}_N))^A$.

Furthermore, it is easy to prove that if $B \subset A$ is closed under the rules of $(\mathcal{B}(\mathcal{D}_N))^A$ then B is closed under the rules of $(\mathcal{B}(\mathcal{D}^*))^A$. This, together with (g4), implies that

g5. A is an answer set of $\mathcal{B}(\mathcal{D}_N)$.

Now, let

g6. A be an answer set of $\mathcal{B}(\mathcal{D}_N)$.

Since for any rule

g7. $l \leftarrow \Gamma \in (\mathcal{B}(\mathcal{D}^*))^A \setminus (\mathcal{B}(\mathcal{D}_N))^A$

there exists a default d such that

g8. $default(d, l, [\Gamma]) \in \mathcal{D}^* \setminus \mathcal{D}_N$.

Hence, we can conclude that

g9. if r is a logic programming rule in $(\mathcal{B}(\mathcal{D}^*))^A \setminus (\mathcal{B}(\mathcal{D}_N))^A$ then $body(r)$ is not satisfied by A.

This, together with (g6) and the fact that $(\mathcal{B}(\mathcal{D}_N))^A \subseteq (\mathcal{B}(\mathcal{D}^*))^A$, implies that

g10. A is an answer set of $\mathcal{B}(\mathcal{D}^*)$.

From (g2), (g5), (g6), and (g10) we can conclude (g1).

The conclusion (g) follows from (g1) and the fact that $^A(\mathcal{B}(\mathcal{D}^*)$ is identical to $^A(\mathcal{B}(\mathcal{D}_N)$. $\Diamond$

The above two lemmas show that for any static and hierarchical domain description $\mathcal{D}$ and σ-literal $l \notin U(\mathcal{D})$

(i) $\mathcal{Q}(\mathcal{D}) \models l$ iff $\mathcal{R}(\mathcal{D}_N) \models l$ and

(ii) $\Pi(\mathcal{D}) \hspace{1pt}\vert\!\sim\hspace{1pt} l$ iff $\Pi(\mathcal{D}_N) \hspace{1pt}\vert\!\sim\hspace{1pt} l$.

where $\mathcal{D}_N$ is the normalization of $\mathcal{D}$.

Furthermore, for $l \in U(\mathcal{D})$, $\mathcal{Q}(\mathcal{D}) \models l$ and $\Pi(\mathcal{D}) \hspace{1pt}\vert\!\sim\hspace{1pt} l$.

Therefore, to prove the theorem 2, we will show that for $l \notin U(\mathcal{D})$, $\mathcal{R}(\mathcal{D}_N) \models l$ iff $\Pi(\mathcal{D}_N) \mathrel{\vdash\!\!\!\sim} l$.

The above observation shows that in proving theorem 2 we can limit ourself to static and normalized domain descriptions. Since for a static and normalized domain description $\mathcal{D}$, the programs $\mathcal{R}(\mathcal{D})$ and $\Pi(\mathcal{D})$ are simpler than for general cases, for future references, we define these programs before continuing with the proof of theorem 2.

For a static and normalized domain description $\mathcal{D}$, the program $\mathcal{R}(\mathcal{D})$ consists of the following rules

$$
\mathcal{R}(\mathcal{D}) \begin{cases} l & \leftarrow l_1, \ldots, l_n, not\ d, not\ \neg l. \qquad (1) \\[4pt] & \text{if } default(d, l, [l_1, \ldots, l_n]) \in \mathcal{D} \\[10pt] d_2 & \leftarrow l_1, \ldots, l_n, not\ d_1. \qquad (2) \\[6pt] & \text{if } d_2 \in \mathcal{D}, \\ & default(d_1, l, [l_1, \ldots, l_n]) \in \mathcal{D}, \\ & prefer(d_1, d_2) \in \mathcal{D}, \\ & \text{and } head(d_2) = \neg l \end{cases}
$$

and the program $\mathcal{B}(\mathcal{D})$ of $\Pi(\mathcal{D})$ consists of the following rules:

$$
\mathcal{B}(\mathcal{D}) \begin{cases} l \leftarrow l_1, \ldots, l_n, not\ \neg l. \qquad (1) \\[4pt] \text{if } default(d, l, [l_1, \ldots, l_n]) \in \mathcal{D} \end{cases}
$$

To continue with the proof we need the following definitions.

Definition 8. Let $\mathcal{D}$ be a static domain description with the preference relation P_0. Let P_1 be a well-ordered order defined on defaults in $\mathcal{D}$ which extends P_0. The domain description $\tilde{\mathcal{D}} = \mathcal{D} \cup \{prefer(d_1, d_2) : \langle d_1, d_2 \rangle \in P_1\}$ is called a *completion* of $\mathcal{D}$.

We will need the following technical observations.

Lemma 10. Let $\mathcal{D}$ be a static and normalized domain description. Let A be an answer set of $\mathcal{R}(\mathcal{D})$ and $default(d, l, [\Gamma])$ be a default in $\mathcal{D}$ such that $l \notin A$ and $\Gamma \subseteq A$. Then, $\neg l \in A$.

Proof. First notice that, since $\mathcal{D}$ is normalized, it is hierarchical. Therefore, in virtue of theorem 1, $\mathcal{D}$ is consistent. By Lemmas 6 and 7 this implies that $\mathcal{R}(\mathcal{D})$ is consistent. As was shown in [21] every answer set of consistent program is consistent which implies consistency of A.

Since $l \leftarrow \Gamma, not\ d, not\ \neg l$ is a rule in $\mathcal{R}(\mathcal{D})$, $\Gamma \subseteq A$, $l \notin A$, and A is a consistent answer set of $\mathcal{R}(\mathcal{D})$, we have two cases:

(i) $\neg l \in A$; or

(ii) $d \in A$.

Consider the second case: $d \in A$. Then there exists a rule (2) of $\mathcal{R}(\mathcal{D})$ with the head d whose body is satisfied by A. From construction of $\mathcal{R}$ this implies that there exists a default

1. $default(d_1, \neg l, [\Delta]) \in \mathcal{D}$

such that

2. $\Delta \subseteq A$ and $d_1 \notin A$.

From (1) and construction of $\mathcal{R}$ we can conclude that $\mathcal{R}$ contains the rule

3. $\neg l \leftarrow \Delta, not\, d_1, not\, l$.

Recall, that, by condition of the lemma, $l \notin A$. This, together with (2), implies that the body of the rule (3) is satisfied by A. Therefore, $\neg l \in A$.   ◇

Let X be a set of literals in the language of $\mathcal{R}(\mathcal{D})$. By $X|_l$ we denote $X \cap lit(\sigma)$.

Lemma 11. Let $\mathcal{D}$ be a static and normalized domain description and $\tilde{\mathcal{D}}$ be one of its completions. Then, for every answer set $\tilde{A}$ of $\mathcal{R}(\tilde{\mathcal{D}})$ there exists an answer set A of $\mathcal{R}(\mathcal{D})$ such that $\tilde{A}|_l = A|_l$.

Proof. Since the preference relation in $\tilde{\mathcal{D}}$ is a well-ordered order among defaults, we can enumerate the set of defaults in $\mathcal{D}$ by the sequence $d_0, d_1, \ldots, d_n, \ldots$[4]

Let $\tilde{A}$ be an answer set of $\mathcal{R}(\tilde{\mathcal{D}})$. It is easy to see that, since $\mathcal{D}$ is normalized, $\tilde{A}$ is consistent.

We define a sequence of sets of literals $A_{i=0}^{\infty}$ in the language of $\mathcal{R}(\mathcal{D})$ as follows:

$$A_0 = \tilde{A}|_l$$

$$A_{n+1} = \begin{cases} A_n \cup \{d_{n+1}\} \text{ if there exists } d_i \text{ s.t.} \\ \qquad \text{(0a) } default(d_i, \neg head(d_{n+1}), [\Gamma]) \in \mathcal{D}, \\ \qquad \text{(0b) } prefer(d_i, d_{n+1}) \in \mathcal{D}, \\ \qquad \text{(0c) } \Gamma \subseteq A_n, \text{ and} \\ \qquad \text{(0d) } d_i \notin A_n. \\ \\ A_n \qquad \text{otherwise} \end{cases}$$

Let $A = \cup_{i=0}^{\infty} A_i$. Obviously, A is consistent. We will prove that A is an answer set of $\mathcal{R}(\mathcal{D})$ and $A|_l = \tilde{A}|_l$.

---

[4] For simplicity, here and in the following lemmas we assume that the set of defaults in $\mathcal{D}$ has the cardinality less than or equal to the ordinal number ω. However, the proofs presented in this paper can be expanded to the general case.

By the construction of A, we have that $A|_l = \tilde{A}|_l$. Hence, to prove the lemma we need to prove that A is an answer set of $\mathcal{R}(\mathcal{D})$. To do that, we will show that A is a minimal set of literals which is closed under the rules of $(\mathcal{R}(\mathcal{D}))^A$.

Since $\mathcal{D}$ is a normalized domain description, $(\mathcal{R}(\mathcal{D}))^A$ consists of the following rules:

$$(\mathcal{R}(\mathcal{D}))^A = \begin{cases} l \;\leftarrow \Gamma. & (1) \\[4pt] \quad \text{if there is } d \text{ s.t.} \\ \quad (1a)\ default(d, l, [\Gamma]) \in \mathcal{D}, \\ \quad (1b)\ d \notin A, \text{ and } \neg l \notin A \\[8pt] d_2 \leftarrow \Gamma. & (2) \\[4pt] \quad \text{if there is } d_1 \text{ s.t.} \\ \quad (2a)\ default(d_1, \neg head(d_2), [\Gamma]) \in \mathcal{D}, \\ \quad (2b)\ prefer(d_1, d_2) \in \mathcal{D}, \text{ and} \\ \quad (2c)\ d_1 \notin A. \end{cases}$$

Let r be a rule of $(\mathcal{R}(\mathcal{D}))^A$ whose body is satisfied by A, i.e.,

a. $\Gamma \subseteq A$.

We consider two cases:

(i) r is of the form (1).

Since $A|_l = \tilde{A}|_l$, from (1b) and (a) we conclude that

b. $\neg l \notin \tilde{A}$ and $\Gamma \subseteq \tilde{A}$.

By Lemma 10, this, together with (1a) implies that $l \in \tilde{A}$ and hence $l \in A$, i.e.,

c. A is closed under the rules of type (1) of $(\mathcal{R}(\mathcal{D}))^A$.

(ii) r is of the form (2). From (2a)-(2c) and (a), by the construction of A, we conclude that $d_2 \in A$, i.e.,

d. A is closed under the rules of type (2) of $(\mathcal{R}(\mathcal{D}))^A$.

From (c) and (d) we can conclude that

e. A is closed under the rules of $(\mathcal{R}(\mathcal{D}))^A$.

We now prove the minimality of A.

Assume that there exists a set $B \subset A$ which is closed under the rules of $(\mathcal{R}(\mathcal{D}))^A$. We consider two cases:

(i) $A|_l \setminus B|_l \neq \emptyset$.

Since $\mathcal{D}$ is hierarchical, there exists a rank function $rank$ of $\mathcal{D}$ that satisfies the conditions of Definition 5.

Let $l \in A|_l \setminus B|_l$ such that

f. $rank(l) = \min\{rank(p) : p \in A|_l \setminus B|_l\}$.

Since $l \in A$ and $A|_l = \tilde{A}|_l$, we have that $l \in \tilde{A}$. Let

f1. $\Delta_l^+ = \{d : default(d, l, [\Gamma]) \in \mathcal{D}, \Gamma \subseteq \tilde{A}\}$.

Since $\tilde{A}$ is an answer set of $\mathcal{R}(\tilde{\mathcal{D}})$, we have that

f2. $\Delta_l^+ \neq \emptyset$.

Since the preference relation in $\tilde{\mathcal{D}}$ is well-ordered, there exists a minimal element d_j of Δ_l^+ such that

f3. $prefer(d_j, d_k) \in \tilde{\mathcal{D}}$ for $d_k \in \Delta_l^+ \setminus \{d_j\}$.

We will prove that

g. $d_j \notin \tilde{A}$.

Assume the contrary, $d_j \in \tilde{A}$. By construction of $\mathcal{R}(\tilde{\mathcal{D}})$, we conclude that there exists a default d_n such that

g1. $default(d_n, \neg l, [\Lambda]) \in \mathcal{D}$,

g2. $\Lambda \subseteq \tilde{A}$, and

g3. $prefer(d_n, d_j) \in \tilde{\mathcal{D}}$.

It follows from (f3) and (g3) and the fact that the preference order in $\tilde{\mathcal{D}}$ is well-ordered that

g3. $prefer(d_n, d) \in \tilde{\mathcal{D}}$ for $d \in \Delta_l^+$.

This, together with (g1) and (g2), implies that

g4. $d \in \tilde{A}$ for $d \in \Delta_l^+$.

which, in turn, implies that there exists no rule with the head l in $\mathcal{R}(\tilde{\mathcal{D}})$ whose body is satisfied by $\tilde{A}$, i.e., $l \notin \tilde{A}$. This contradiction proves (g).

We now prove that

h. $d_j \notin A$.

Assume that (h) does not hold, i.e.,

h1. $d_j \in A$.

Using the definition of A and the fact that A and $\tilde{A}$ coincide on σ-literals we can easily check that there is d_i such that

h2. $default(d_i, \neg l, [\Gamma]) \in \tilde{\mathcal{D}}$

h3. $prefer(d_i, d_j) \in \tilde{\mathcal{D}}$

h4. $\Gamma \subseteq \tilde{A}$

From construction of $\mathcal{R}(\tilde{\mathcal{D}})$ and conditions (h2), (h3) we have that

h5. $d_j \leftarrow \Gamma, not\ d_i \in \mathcal{R}(\tilde{\mathcal{D}})$

First assume that

h6: $d_i \notin \tilde{A}$

Then, from (h4), (h5), and the fact that $\tilde{A}$ is an answer set of $\mathcal{R}(\tilde{\mathcal{D}})$ we conclude that $d_j \in \tilde{A}$ which contradicts (g). Therefore,

h7. $d_i \in \tilde{A}$

This implies that there is a default d_k of the form $default(d_k, l, [\Delta]) \in \tilde{\mathcal{D}}$ such that

h8. $\Delta \subseteq \tilde{A}$

h9. $prefer(d_k, d_i) \in \tilde{\mathcal{D}}$

Since the preference relation in $\tilde{\mathcal{D}}$ is total from (h3) and (h9) we conclude that

h10. $prefer(d_k, d_j) \in \tilde{\mathcal{D}}$

which contradicts d_j being the minimal element of Δ_l^+. This contradiction proves (h).

Recall that $head(d_j) = l$ and let Θ be its body. Since d_j is best for l in A we have that

k. $\Theta \subseteq A$

Since $l \in A$ and A is consistent, $\neg l \notin A$. This, together with (h), implies that

l. $l \leftarrow \Theta \in (\mathcal{R}(\mathcal{D}))^A$.

Since $l \notin B$ and B is closed under the rules of $(\mathcal{R}(\mathcal{D}))^A$, from (l) we can conclude that there exists a literal $l' \in \Theta$ such that $l' \notin B$. This, together with (k), implies that

m. $l' \in A \setminus B$.

Since $\mathcal{D}$ is normalized and hence hierarchical, from condition 5 of Definition 5 we have that $rank(l') < rank(l)$. This, together with (m), contradicts with (f) which implies that $A|_l \setminus B|_l = \emptyset$.

(ii) $A|_l = B|_l$. Since $B \subset A$, there exists $d_j \in A \setminus B$. By the construction of A,

n. there exists a default $d_i \in \mathcal{D}$ of the form $default(d_i, \neg head(d_j), [\Gamma])$ such that

n1. $prefer(d_i, d_j) \in \mathcal{D}, d_i \notin A$ and

n2. $\Gamma \subseteq A$.

(n1), together with the definition of $(\mathcal{R}(\mathcal{D}))^A$ implies that

n3. $d_j \leftarrow \Gamma \in (\mathcal{R}(\mathcal{D}))^A$.

This, together with the assumption that B is closed under the rules of $(\mathcal{R}(\mathcal{D}))^A$ and $B|_l = A|_l$, implies that $d_j \in B$ which contradicts the selection of d_j.

We showed that no proper subset B of A is closed under the rules of $(\mathcal{R}(\mathcal{D}))^A$ and hence A is an answer set of $\mathcal{R}(\mathcal{D})$. ◇

The next lemma is the reverse of Lemma 11.

Lemma 12. Let $\mathcal{D}$ be a static and normalized domain description and A be an answer set of $\mathcal{R}(\mathcal{D})$. Then, there exists a completion $\tilde{\mathcal{D}}$ of $\mathcal{D}$ and an answer set $\tilde{A}$ of $\mathcal{R}(\tilde{\mathcal{D}})$ such that $\tilde{A}|_l = A|_l$.

Proof. We start with introducing some notation. Let P be a binary relation. By P^* we denote the transitive closure of P. For a σ-literal l, we define,

$\Delta_l^+ = \{d : default(d, l, [\Gamma]) \in \mathcal{D}, \ \Gamma \subseteq A\}$,

$\Delta_l^- = \{d : default(d, \neg l, [\Gamma]) \in \mathcal{D}, \ \Gamma \subseteq A\}$,

$\Delta_l = \Delta_l^+ \cup \Delta_l^-$, and

$\Delta^l = \{d \in \mathcal{D} : head(d) \in \{l, \neg l\}\}$

By $<_l$ we denote the order induced on Δ_l by the preference relation of $\mathcal{D}$.

In our further discussion we need the following well known result:

(*) if P is a well-founded strict partial order then there exists a well-founded total order containing P.

Now we start our construction of $\tilde{\mathcal{D}}$. Notice that if $l \in A$ then, since $<_l$ is well-founded, it is easy to prove that there exists a default $d \in \Delta_l^+$ which is a minimal element in Δ_l. Let us denote such a default by $d(l)$.

Let

$X_1(l) = \{prefer(d(l), d) : d \in \Delta_l^-\}$.

$X_2(l) = \{prefer(d_1, d_2) : prefer(d_1, d_2) \in \mathcal{D}, d_1, d_2 \in \Delta^l\}$.

For every atom $p \in lit(\sigma)$ we define the set X_p as follows:

$$
X_p = \begin{cases}
(X_1(p) \cup X_2(p))^* & \text{if } p \in A \\
(X_1(\neg p) \cup X_2(p))^* & \text{if } \neg p \in A \\
X_2(p) & \text{otherwise}
\end{cases}
$$

It is easy to see that X_p is a well-founded, strict partial order on Δ^p. Let Y_p be a well-founded, total order on Δ^p which extends X_p (existence of Y_p is ensured by (*)). Obviously, $\bigcup_{p \in atom(\sigma)} Y_p$ is a well-founded, strict partial order on the set of defaults of $\mathcal{D}$ which extends the preference relation in $\mathcal{D}$.

Let Y be a well-founded, total order on the set of defaults of $\mathcal{D}$ which extends $\bigcup_{p \in atom(\sigma)} Y_p$.

Let

$$\tilde{\mathcal{D}} = \mathcal{D} \cup Y.$$

It is easy to see that $\tilde{\mathcal{D}}$ is a consistent completion of $\mathcal{D}$.

Now we will construct an answer set $\tilde{A}$ of $\mathcal{R}(\tilde{\mathcal{D}})$ such that $\tilde{A}|_l = A|_l$.

$$U_i = \{l : l \in lit(\sigma) \cap heads(\mathcal{R}(\tilde{\mathcal{D}})) \text{ s.t. } rank(l) < i\} \cup$$
$$\{d \in heads(\mathcal{R}(\tilde{\mathcal{D}})) : rank(head(d)) < i\}.$$

The sequence $U = U_0, U_1, \ldots$ is monotone and continuous. Using the property of the $rank$ function from the definition of hierarchical domain description it is not difficult to check that each U_i is a splitting set of $\mathcal{R}(\tilde{\mathcal{D}})$ and that $\bigcup U_i$ is equal to the set of all literals occurring in $\mathcal{R}(\tilde{\mathcal{D}})$. Hence, U is a splitting sequence of $\mathcal{R}(\tilde{\mathcal{D}})$.

Let T_i be a collection of all the rules from $\mathcal{R}(\tilde{\mathcal{D}})$ whose heads belong to U_i and let $A_i = A \cap U_i$.

We define a sequence $\tilde{A}_0, \tilde{A}_1, \ldots$ such that

1a. $\tilde{A}_i$ is an answer set of T_i.

1b. $\tilde{A}_i|_l = A_i|_l$

(i) Let $\tilde{A}_0 = A_0$

Since both sets are empty conditions (1a) and (1b) are satisfied.

(ii) assume that conditions (1a) and (1b) are satisfied by the already constructed set $\tilde{A}_i$ Let T be the result of partial evaluation of the program T_{i+1} with respect to the set $\tilde{A}_i$.

T will consists of the rules

(r2) $l \leftarrow not\ d, not\ \neg l$ where l is a σ-literal.

and

(r1) $d_2 \leftarrow not\ d_1$.

Using the argument from Lemma 6 we can show that the program consisting of the rules of T of the form (r1) contains no negative odd cycles and therefore is consistent. Let S_0 be an answer set of this program and $S_1 = (A_{i+1} \setminus A_i)|_l$. We will show that

2. $S = S_0 \cup S_1$

is an answer set of T. By the splitting set theorem it suffices to show that S_1 is an answer set of the partial evaluation of rules of the type (r2) from T with respect to S_0. We denote this partial evaluation by π. This, in turn, is true iff

3. $S_1 = \pi^{S_1}$.

To prove (3) let us first assume that

4. $l \in S_1$.

This implies that $l \in A$ and hence $\Delta_l \neq \emptyset$. Consider $d \in \Delta_l$ which is minimal with respect to well-ordering induced on Δ_l by the preference relation from $\tilde{D}$. It is easy to check that, since $l \in A$, $head(d) = l$ and $body(d) \subseteq A$. Since $\mathcal{D}$ is hierarchical we have that $body(d) \subseteq A_i$, and hence, by inductive hypothesis,

4a. $body(d) \subseteq \tilde{A}_i$.

Since d is minimal, by construction of $\tilde{D}$ we have that there is no rule in T with d in the head. Hence,

4b. $d \notin S_0$.

By construction of $\mathcal{R}(\tilde{D})$ and conditions (4a) and (4b) we have that

4c. $l \leftarrow not\ \neg l\ \in \pi$.

Since $l \in A$ and A is consistent we conclude that $\neg l \notin A_{i+1}$. Therefore, $\neg l \notin S_1$. Hence,

4d. $l \in \pi^{S_1}$

Suppose now that

5. $l \in \pi^{S_1}$.

This implies that there is d and $\Gamma \subseteq A$ such that

$default(d, l, \Gamma) \in \mathcal{D}$.

From (4d) we have that $\neg l \notin A$ and hence, by Lemma 10 we conclude that $l \in A$. Therefore $l \in S_1$ which concludes the proof of (3).

By the splitting set theorem, $\tilde{A}_{i+1} = \tilde{A}_i \cup S$ is an answer set of T_{i+1}. Obviously, $\tilde{A}_{i+1}$ also satisfies condition (1b). Now let

$\tilde{A} = \bigcup \tilde{A}_i$.

From construction we have that $\tilde{A}|_l = A|_l$. Using the splitting sequence theorem it is easy to check that $\tilde{A}$ is an answer set of $\mathcal{R}(\tilde{D})$. $\Diamond$

Lemma 13. Let $\mathcal{D}$ be a static and normalized domain description and A be an answer set of $\mathcal{R}(\mathcal{D})$. Then, $A|_l$ is an answer set of $\mathcal{B}(\mathcal{D})$.

Proof. Since $\mathcal{D}$ is normalized, A is consistent, it suffices to prove that $A|_l$ is a minimal set of literals closed under the rules of $\mathcal{B}(\mathcal{D})^{A|_l}$.

Let

a. $l \leftarrow \Gamma \in \mathcal{B}(\mathcal{D})^{A|_l}$

and

b. $\Gamma \subseteq A|_l$.

By construction of $\mathcal{B}(\mathcal{D})$ and of $\mathcal{B}(\mathcal{D})^{A|_l}$, (a) implies that there exists a default $d \in \mathcal{D}$ such that

c. $default(d, l, [\Gamma]) \in \mathcal{D}$ and $\neg l \notin A|_l$.

Since A is an answer set of $\mathcal{R}(\mathcal{D})$, from (c), (b), and Lemma 10, we can conclude that $l \in A$ and hence $l \in A|_l$ which proves that

d. $A|_l$ is closed under the rules of $\mathcal{B}(\mathcal{D})^{A|_l}$.

We now prove the minimality of $A|_l$.

Assume that there exists a set $B \subset A|_l$ which is closed under the rules of $\mathcal{B}(\mathcal{D})^{A|_l}$. We will prove that the set of literals

$$C = B \cup \{d_i : d_i \in A\}$$

is closed under the rules of $(\mathcal{R}(\mathcal{D}))^A$.

Since C contains every d_i in A, $C \subset A$, and A is an answer set of $(\mathcal{R}(\mathcal{D}))^A$, we have that

e. C is closed under the rules of the form (2) of $(\mathcal{R}(\mathcal{D}))^A$.

Let r be a rule of the form (1) of $(\mathcal{R}(\mathcal{D}))^A$ whose body is satisfied by C, i.e.,

f1. $l \leftarrow \Gamma \in (\mathcal{R}(\mathcal{D}))^A$ and

f2. $\Gamma \subseteq C$.

By construction of $(\mathcal{R}(\mathcal{D}))^A$, (f1) implies that there exists a default d such that

g1. $default(d, l, [\Gamma]) \in \mathcal{D}$, and

g2. $\neg l \notin A$.

By definition of $\mathcal{B}(\mathcal{D})$ and $\mathcal{B}(\mathcal{D})^{A|_l}$, and from (g1) and (g2) we conclude that

h. $l \leftarrow \Gamma$ is a rule of $\mathcal{B}(\mathcal{D})^{A|_l}$.

which, together with (f2) and the assumption that B is closed under rules of $(\mathcal{B}(\mathcal{D}))^{A|_l}$ implies that $l \in B$ and hence $l \in C$ which, in turn, implies that

j. C is closed under the rule of the form (1) of $(\mathcal{R}(\mathcal{D}))^A$.

From (e) and (j) we can conclude that C is closed under the rules of $(\mathcal{R}(\mathcal{D}))^A$ which together with $C \subset A$ contradicts the fact that A is an answer set of $\mathcal{R}(\mathcal{D})$. This, together with (d), implies that $A|_l$ is an answer set of $\mathcal{B}(\mathcal{D})$.   ◇

Lemma 14. Let $\mathcal{D}$ be a static and normalized domain description with a well-ordered preference order P and let A be an answer set of $\mathcal{R}(\mathcal{D})$. Then, $A|_l$ is a preferred answer set of $\Pi(\mathcal{D})$.

Proof. Lemma 13 shows that $A|_l$ is an answer set of $\mathcal{B}(\mathcal{D})$. We need to show that $A|_l = Z$ where $Z = C_{<_\mathcal{D}}(\mathcal{B}(\mathcal{D}))$ and $C_{<_\mathcal{D}}(\mathcal{B}(\mathcal{D}))$ is defined as in Definition 6.

Let $d_0, d_1, \ldots$ be the sequence of defaults in $\mathcal{D}$, ordered by P.

Notice that

$l \leftarrow not\ \neg l\ \in^{A|_l} \mathcal{B}(\mathcal{D})$

iff there exists a default d such that

0a. $default(d, l, [\Gamma]) \in \mathcal{D}$, and

0b. $\Gamma \subseteq A|_l$.

(i) We first prove that $Z \subseteq A|_l$. Let

   a. $l \in Z$.

   This implies that there exists a default $d_i \in \mathcal{D}$ such that

   b1. d_i satisfies (0a) and (0b), and

   b2. the rule $l \leftarrow not\ l$ is not defeated by S_{i-1}. (see Definition 6).

   Let i be the minimal integer such that

   c. d_i satisfies (b1) and (b2).

   From (c) and (b2) and the definition of Z, we can conclude that

   d. there exists no $j < i$ and $\Delta \subseteq A|_l$ such that $default(d_j, \neg l, [\Delta]) \in \mathcal{D}$.

   By construction of $\mathcal{R}(\mathcal{D})$ and (d), we conclude that there exists no rule of $\mathcal{R}(\mathcal{D})$ with the head d_i whose body is satisfied by A, which implies that

   e. $d_i \notin A$.

   Furthermore, for every default d_k such that $i < k$ and $default(d_k, \neg l, [\Delta]) \in \mathcal{D}$, it follows from (b1), (e), and the construction of $(\mathcal{R}(\mathcal{D}))^A$ that

   f. $d_k \in A$.

   This implies that

   g. there exists no rule of $(\mathcal{R}(\mathcal{D}))^A$ with the head $\neg l$ whose body is satisfied by A.

   This implies that

   h. $\neg l \notin A$.

   From (h), (b1), and Lemma 10, we can conclude that $l \in A$ and hence $l \in A|_l$ which, together with (a) proves that

   j. $Z \subseteq A|_l$.

(ii) We now prove that $A|_l \subseteq Z$. Let

k. $l \in A|_l$.

Since A is an answer set of $\mathcal{R}(\mathcal{D})$, there exists a default d such that

l. $default(d, l, [\Gamma]) \in \mathcal{D}$,

m. $\Gamma \subseteq A$, and $\neg l \notin A$.

which implies that $l \leftarrow not \neg l$ is a rule of $^{A|_l}\mathcal{B}(\mathcal{D})$. This indicates that

n1. $l \in Z$ or

n2. $\neg l \in Z$.

If (n2) holds, then, by (j), $\neg l \in A|_l$, which, together with $l \in A$, contradicts the fact that $A|_l$ is consistent. Hence, (n1) holds, i.e., $l \in Z$ which, together with (k) entails

o. $A|_l \subseteq Z$.

The lemma is proved by (o) and (j).   ◇

We now prove the reverse of Lemma 14.

Lemma 15. Let $\mathcal{D}$ be a static and normalized domain description with a well-ordered preference order P. Let A be a preferred answer set of $\Pi(\mathcal{D})$. Then, there exists an answer set B of $\mathcal{R}(\mathcal{D})$ such that $B|_l = A$.

Proof. First, notice that since $\mathcal{D}$ is normalized, $\mathcal{R}(\mathcal{D})$ is consistent and therefore, by Lemma 14, $\mathcal{B}(\mathcal{D})$ is consistent. Thus, A is consistent.

Let $d_0, d_1, \ldots$ be the sequence of defaults in $\mathcal{D}$, ordered by P. We define a sequence of sets of literals $B_{i=1}^{\infty}$ as follows.

$$B_0 = B$$

$$B_{n+1} = \begin{cases} B_n \cup \{d_{n+1}\} & \text{if there exists } i \leq n \text{ s.t.} \\ & \quad \text{(0a) } default(d_i, \neg head(d_{n+1}), [\Gamma]) \in \mathcal{D}, \\ & \quad \text{(0b) } \Gamma \subseteq B_n, \text{ and} \\ & \quad \text{(0c) } d_i \notin B_n. \\ \\ B_n & \text{otherwise} \end{cases}$$

Let $B = \cup_{i=0}^{\infty} B_i$. Obviously B is consistent and $B|_l = A$. We prove that B is an answer set of $\mathcal{R}(\mathcal{D})$, i.e., B is a minimal set of literals closed under the rules of $(\mathcal{R}(\mathcal{D}))^B$. By definition, $(\mathcal{R}(\mathcal{D}))^B$ consists of the following rules:

$$(\mathcal{R}(\mathcal{D}))^B = \begin{cases} l \leftarrow \Gamma. & (1) \\[4pt] \quad \text{if there is } d \text{ s.t.} \\ \quad \text{(1a) } default(d, l, [\Gamma]) \in \mathcal{D}, \\ \quad \text{(1b) } d \notin B, \text{ and } \neg l \notin B \\[8pt] d_2 \leftarrow \Gamma. & (2) \\[4pt] \quad \text{if there is } d_1 \text{ s.t.} \\ \quad \text{(2a) } default(d_1, l, [\Gamma]) \in \mathcal{D}, \\ \quad \text{(2b) } prefer(d_1, d_2) \in \mathcal{D}, \\ \quad \text{(2c) } head(d_2) = \neg l, \text{ and} \\ \quad \text{(2d) } d_1 \notin B. \end{cases}$$

Let r be a rule of $(\mathcal{R}(\mathcal{D}))^B$ whose body is satisfied by B, i.e.,

a. $\Gamma \subseteq B$.

We consider two cases:

(i) r is of the form (1).

By the construction of $\mathcal{B}(\mathcal{D})$ we have that

b. $l \leftarrow \Gamma, not \, \neg l \in \mathcal{B}(\mathcal{D})$.

From $B|_l = A$, (a), and (1b), we conclude that

c. $\Gamma \subseteq A$ and $\neg l \notin A$.

Since A is an answer set of $\mathcal{B}(\mathcal{D})$, from (b) and (c) we conclude that $l \in A$ and hence, $l \in B$, which proves that

d. B is closed under the rules of the form (1) of $(\mathcal{R}(\mathcal{D}))^B$.

(ii) r is a rule of form (2).

By construction of B and from (a) and (2a)-(2d), we can conclude that $d_2 \in B$ which implies that

e. B is closed under the rules of the form (2) of $(\mathcal{R}(\mathcal{D}))^B$.

It follows from (e) and (d) that

f. B is closed under the rules of $(\mathcal{R}(\mathcal{D}))^B$.

We now prove the minimality of B.

Assume that there exists a set of literals $C \subset B$ and C is closed under the rules of $(\mathcal{R}(\mathcal{D}))^B$. We will prove that

g. $C|_l$ is closed under the rules of $\mathcal{B}(\mathcal{D})^A$.

Let r be a rule of $\mathcal{B}(\mathcal{D})^A$ whose body is satisfied by $C|_l$, i.e., r is of the form

h1. $l \leftarrow \Gamma \in (\mathcal{B}(\mathcal{D}))^A$, and

h2. $\Gamma \subseteq C|_l$.

By construction of $\mathcal{B}(\mathcal{D})^A$, we conclude that there exists a default d_i in $\mathcal{D}$ such that

j1. $default(d_i, l, [\Gamma]) \in \mathcal{D}$, and

j2. $\neg l \notin A$.

(j1) and (h2) imply that the rule $l \leftarrow not\ \neg l$ belongs to $^A\mathcal{B}(\mathcal{D})$ which, together with (j2) and the assumption that A is a preferred answer set of $\Pi(\mathcal{D})$, implies that $l \in A$.

We will prove that

l. $d_i \notin B$.

Assume the contrary, i.e.,

m. $d_i \in B$.

By the construction of B, there exists $j < i$ such that

n1. $default(d_j, \neg l, [\Delta]) \in \mathcal{D}$,

n2. $\Delta \subseteq B$, and

n3. $d_j \notin B$.

From (n1) and (n2) and the construction of $^A\mathcal{B}(\mathcal{D})$, we can conclude that

p. $\neg l \leftarrow not\ l$ is a rule of $^A\mathcal{B}(\mathcal{D})$.

From $l \in A$, the fact that A is a preferred answer set of $\Pi(\mathcal{D})$, and (p), we can conclude that there exists a $k < j$ such that

q1. $default(d_k, l, [\Theta]) \in \mathcal{D}$,

q2. $\Theta \subseteq A$, and

q3. for every o, $o < k$, if $default(d_o, \neg l, [\Lambda]) \in \mathcal{D}$, then $\Lambda \not\subseteq A$.

From (q3) and the definition of $\mathcal{R}(\mathcal{D})^B$ we have that

r. $d_k \notin B$.

From (r), (q1), (q2), and the construction of B we have that

s. $d_j \in A_{j+1} \subseteq B$

which contradicts with (n3), i.e., we have proved (l).

It follows from (j1), (j2), and (l) that $l \leftarrow \Gamma \in (\mathcal{R}(\mathcal{D}))^B$ which, together with the assumption that C is closed under the rules of $(\mathcal{R}(\mathcal{D}))^B$ and $\Gamma \subseteq C$, implies $l \in C$, and hence, $l \in C|_l$ which proves (g).

Since A is an answer set of $\mathcal{B}(\mathcal{D})$, from (g) we can conclude that $C|_l = A$, which, together with the assumption that $C \subset B$, implies that there exists some $d_i \in \mathcal{D}$ such that

t. $d_i \in B \setminus C$.

By the construction of B, (t) implies that there exists a $j < i$ such that

u1. $default(d_j, \neg l, [\Delta]) \in \mathcal{D}$,

u2. $\Delta \subseteq B$, and

u3. $d_j \notin B$.

Since $j < i$, by the ordering P, we conclude that $prefer(d_j, d_i) \in \mathcal{D}$. This, together with (u1) and (u3), implies that

v. $d_i \leftarrow \Delta$ is a rule of $(\mathcal{R}(\mathcal{D}))^B$.

It follows from (u2), (v), and the assumption that C is closed under the rule of $(\mathcal{R}(\mathcal{D}))^B$ that $d_i \in C$ which contradicts with (t). In other words, B is a minimal set of literals which is closed under $(\mathcal{R}(\mathcal{D}))^B$, i.e., B is an answer set of $\mathcal{R}(\mathcal{D})$. $\Diamond$

We are now ready to prove the Theorem 2.

Proof of Theorem 2. Let $\mathcal{D}_N$ be the normalization of a static domain description tion $\mathcal{D}$. By Lemma 8, $\mathcal{D} \models holds\_by\_default(l)$ iff

a. $l \in U(\mathcal{D})$ or $\mathcal{R}(\mathcal{D}_N) \models l$,

and by Lemma 9, $\Pi(\mathcal{D}) \hspace{0.1em}\sim\hspace{-0.8em}\mid\hspace{0.3em} l$ iff

b. $l \in U(\mathcal{D})$ or $\Pi(\mathcal{D}_N) \hspace{0.1em}\sim\hspace{-0.8em}\mid\hspace{0.3em} l$.

By Lemmas 12-14, we have that

c. $\mathcal{R}(\mathcal{D}_N) \models l$ iff $\Pi(\mathcal{D}_N) \hspace{0.1em}\sim\hspace{-0.8em}\mid\hspace{0.3em} l$.

The conclusion of theorem 2 follows immediately from (a), (b), and (c). $\Diamond$

References

1. Baader, F. and Hollunder, B,: Priorities on Defaults with Prerequisite and their Application in Treating Specificity in Terminological Default Logic, Journal of Automated Reasoning, 15:41–68, 1995.
2. Baral, C. and Gelfond M.: Logic Programming and Knowledge Representation, Journal of Logic Programming, 19,20: 73–148, 1994.

3. Brass, S. and Dix, J.: A disjunctive semantics based on unfolding and bottom-up evaluation, in Bernd Wolfinger, editor, *Innovationen bei Rechen- und Kommunikationssystemen*, (IFIP '94-Congress, Workshop FG2: Disjunctive Logic Programming and Disjunctive Databases), pages 83–91, 1994, Springer.

4. Brass, S. and Dix, J.: Characterizations of the Disjunctive Stable Semantics by Partial Evaluation, Journal of Logic Programming, 32(3):207–228, 1997.

5. Brewka, G.: Reasoning about Priorities in Default Logic, Proc. AAAI-94, Seattle, 1994

6. Brewka, G.: Adding Priorities and Specificity to Default Logic, Proc. JELIA 94, Springer LNAI 838, 247–260, 1994

7. Brewka, G.: Preferred Answer Sets, Proc. ILPS'97 Postconference Workshop, 76–88, 1997.

8. Covington M.A., Nute D., and Vellino A.: Prolog Programming in Depth, Prentice Hall, NJ, 1997.

9. Chen, W. and Warren, D.S.: Query Evaluation under the Well-Founded Semantics, The Twelfth ACM Symposium on Principles of Database System, 1993.

10. Chen, W.: Extending Prolog with Nonmonotonic Reasoning, Journal of LP, 169–183, 1996.

11. Delgrande , J.P., Schaub, T.H.: Compiling Reasoning with and about Preferences into Default Logic, IJCAi'97, (1997).

12. Dix, J.: Classifying Semantics of Logics Programs. In Proc. of the International Workshop in Logic Programming and Nonmonotonic Reasoning, 166–180, Washington, DC, 1991.

13. Jürgen Dix. A Classification-Theory of Semantics of Normal Logic Programs: I. Strong Properties, Fundamenta Informaticae, XXII(3):227–255, 1995.

14. Jürgen Dix. A Classification-Theory of Semantics of Normal Logic Programs: II. Weak Properties, Fundamenta Informaticae, XXII(3):257–288, 1995.

15. Dung, P.M.: On the Relations Between Stable and Well-Founded Semantics of Logic Programming, Theoretical Computer Science 105:7-25 (1992).

16. Dung, P.M.: On the Acceptability of Arguments and its Fundamental Role in Nonmonotonic Reasoning and Logic Programming and N-person game. AI (77) 2:321–357 (1995).

17. Fages, F.: Consistency of Clark's Completion and Existence of Stable Models, Technical Report 90-15, Ecole Normale Superieure, 1990.

18. Fishburn, P.C.: Nonlinear Preference and Utility Theory (Johns Hopkins University Press, Baltimore, 1988).

19. Gabbay, D.: Theoretical Foundation for Nonmonotonic Reasoning in Experts System. In K. Apt, editor, Logics and models of Concurrent Systems, 439–457, Springer Verlag, NY, 1985.

20. Gelfond, M., Gabaldon, A.: From Functional Specifications to Logic Programs, 355–370, Proc. of ILPS'97, 1997.

21. Gelfond, M., Lifschitz, V.: Classical Negation in Logic Programs and Disjunctive Databases, New Generation of Computing 365–387, 1991.

22. Geffner, H., Pearl, J.: Conditional Entailment: Bridging two Approaches to Default Reasoning, Artificial Intelligence 53, 209 – 244, 1992.

23. Grosof, B.N: Prioritized Conflict Handling for Logic Programs, 197–212, Proc. of ILPS'97, 1997.

24. Gordon, T.: The Pleadings Game: An Artificial Intelligence Model of Procedural Justice. Ph.D. Dissertation, TU Darmstadt.

25. Kosheleva, O.M. and Kreinovich, V.Ya.: Algorithm Problems of Nontransitive (SSB) Utilities, Mathematical Social Sciences 21 (1991) 95–100.

26. Lehmann, D., Kraus, S., and Magidor, M.: Nonmonotonic Reasoning, Preferential Models and Cumulative Logics, AI (44) 1: 167–207, 1990.
27. Lifschitz, V., Turner, H.: Splitting a Logic Program, Proc. of ICLP, MIT Press, 1994.
28. Marek, W. and Truszczynski, M.: Nonmonotonic Logic: Context-Dependent Reasoning, Springer, 1993.
29. Nelson, D.: Constructible Falsity, JSL 14(1949), 16-26.
30. Nute, D.: A Decidable Quantified Defeasible Logic. In Prawitz, D., Skyrms, B., and Westerstahl, D. (eds): Logic, Methodology and Philosophy of Science IX. Elsevier Science B.V., 263–284, 1994.
31. Pearce, D.: A New Logical Characterization of Stable Models and Answer Sets, NMELP'96, Springer, 57–70, 1997.
32. Prakken, H. and Sartor, G,: On the relation between legal language and legal argument: assumptions, applicability and dynamic priorities. Proc. of the Fifth International Conference on AI and Law, Maryland, College Park, MD USA, 1–10, 1995.
33. Prakken, H. and Sartor, G.: Argument-based extended logic programming with defeasible priorities. Journal of applied non-classical logics, 1,2 (7), 25–77, 1997.
34. Reiter, R.: On closed world data bases. In H. Gallaire and J. Minker, editors, Logic and data bases, 55–76, 1978.
35. Reiter R.: A Logic for Default Reasoning in Readings in Nonmonotonic Reasoning, Edited by M. L. Ginsberg, Morgan Kaufmann Publishers, Inc., Los Altos, California (1987) 68–93
36. Zhang, Y. and Foo , N.Y.: Answer Sets for Prioritized Logic Programs, 69–84, Proc. of ILPS'97, 1997.

Generalizing Updates: From Models to Programs

João Alexandre Leite*,** and Luís Moniz Pereira**

Centro de Inteligência Artificial (CENTRIA)
Departamento de Informática
Universidade Nova de Lisboa
2825 Monte da Caparica, Portugal
(jleite|lmp@di.fct.unl.pt

Abstract. Recently the field of theory update has seen some improvement, in what concerns model updating, by allowing updates to be specified by so-called revision programs. The updating of theory models is governed by their update rules and also by inertia applied to those literals not directly affected by the update program. Though this is important, it remains necessary to tackle as well the updating of programs specifying theories. Some results have been obtained on the issue of updating a logic program which encodes a set of models, to obtain a new program whose models are the desired updates of the initial models. But here the program only plays the rôle of a means to encode the models.

A logic program encodes much more than a set of models: it encodes knowledge in the form of the relationships between the elements of those models. In this paper we advocate that the principle of inertia is advantageously applied to the rules of the initial program rather than to the individual literals in a model. Indeed, we show how this concept of program update generalizes model or interpretation updates. Furthermore, it allows us to conceive what it is to update one program by another, a crucial notion for opening up a whole new range of applications concerning the evolution of knowledge bases. We will consider the updating of normal programs as well as these extended with explicit negation, under the stable semantics.

Keywords: Updates

1 Introduction and Motivation

When dealing with modifications to a knowledge base represented by a propositional theory, two kinds of abstract frameworks have been distinguished both by Keller and Winslett in [KW85] and by Katsuno and Mendelzon in [KM91]. One, theory revision, deals with incorporating new knowledge about a static world. The other, dealing with changing worlds, is known as theory update. This paper concerns only theory update.

So far, most of the work accomplished in the field of theory update [PT95] [MT94] [KM91]has addressed the modification of models on a one by one basis,

---

* Partially supported by PRAXIS XXI scholarship no. BM/437/94.
** Partially supported by project MENTAL (PRAXIS XXI 2/2.1/TIT/1593/95.)

by allowing updates to be specified by so-called revision programs. The field of theory update has seen several major achievements, namely the embedding of revision programs into logic programs [MT94], arbitrary rule updates and, the embedding into default logic [PT95].

The update of models is governed by update rules and also by inertia applied to the literals not directly affected by the update program. Though this is important, it remains necessary to tackle as well the updating of programs specifying theories, as opposed to updating its models. Some results have been obtained in what concerns the updating of a logic program which encodes a set of models, to obtain a new program whose models are the desired justified updates of the initial models [AP97]. But here the program only plays the rôle of a means to encode the models.

A logic program encodes much more than a set of models: it encodes knowledge in the form of the relationships between the elements of those models. In this paper we advocate that the principle of inertia is advantageously applied to the rules of the initial program rather than to the individual literals in a model. Indeed, we show how this concept of program update generalizes model or interpretation updates. Furthermore, it allows us to conceive what it is to update one program by another. A crucial notion for opening up a whole new range of applications concerning the evolution of knowledge bases. We will consider the updating of normal programs as well as these extended with explicit negation, under the stable semantics.

To show that a logic program encodes relationships between the elements of a model, which are lost if we simply envisage updates on a model by model basis, as proposed in [KM91], consider the following situation where an alarm signal is present:

Example 1. Take the normal program P and its single stable model M:

$$P : go\_home \leftarrow not\ money$$
$$go\_restaurant \leftarrow money$$
$$money \leftarrow$$

$$M = \{money, go\_restaurant\}$$

Now consider an update program stating that the person has been robbed and that a robbery leaves the person without any money:

$$U : out(money) \leftarrow in(robbed)$$
$$in(robbed) \leftarrow$$

According to [MT94] and model updating we obtain as the single justified update of M the following model:

$$M_U = \{robbed, go\_restaurant\}$$

Stating that, although we know that the person doesn't have any money, he/she still goes to the restaurant and not home. In [AP97] the authors propose a program transformation that produces a new program whose models are exactly the justified revisions of the models of the initial program, according to the definition proposed in [MT94], and so produces exactly the result above.

But looking at the program and at the update program, we arguably conclude that M_U doesn't represent the intended meaning of the update of P by U for a commonsensical reasoner. Since "*go_restaurant*" was true because the person had "*money*", the removal of "*money*" should make one expect "*go_restaurant*" to become false. The same kind of reasoner expects "*go_home*" to become true. The intended update model of the example presumably is:

$$M'_U = \{robbed, go\_home\} \ \Diamond$$

Another symptomatic example, but using explicit negation is this:

Example 2. Given the statements:

- If I've seen something that is unexplainable then I've seen a miracle.
- If I've seen a miracle then God exists.
- I've seen something.
- It is not explainable.

They can be represented by the following extended logic program:

$$P : seen\_miracle \leftarrow seen\_something, not \ explainable$$
$$god\_exists \leftarrow seen\_miracle$$
$$seen\_something \leftarrow$$
$$\neg explainable \leftarrow$$

whose answer-set M is:

$$M = \{seen\_something, \neg explainable, seen\_miracle, god\_exists\}$$

Now consider the following update program U stating that we now have an explanation:

$$U : in(explainable) \leftarrow$$

According to model updating we obtain as the single justified update of M the following model M_U:

$$M_U = \{seen\_something, explainable, seen\_miracle, god\_exists\}$$

Once again we arguably conclude that this model doesn't represent the intended meaning and that the correct model should be:

$$M_U = \{seen\_something, explainable\} \ \Diamond$$

The purpose of this paper is to generalize model updates to logic program updates. The former are a special case of the latter since they can be coded as factual programs. To do this we must first consider the rôle of inertia in updates.

Newton's first law, also known as the law of inertia, states that: *"every body remains at rest or moves with constant velocity in a straight line, unless it is compelled to change that state by an unbalanced force acting upon it"* (adapted from [Principia]). One often tends to interpret this law in a commonsensical way, as things keeping as they are unless some kind of force is applied to them. This is true but it doesn't exhaust the meaning of the law. It is the result of all applied forces that governs the outcome. Take a body to which several forces are applied, and which is in a state of equilibrium due to those forces canceling out. Later one of those forces is removed and the body starts to move.

The same kind of behaviour presents itself when updating programs. Let us make the parallel between a program rule and a physical body with forces applied to it, the body of the rule being the forces applied to the head. In the same way we have to determine whether the forces are still in a state of equilibrium, before concluding that a physical body is at rest or moves with constant velocity in a straight line due to inertia, when it comes to the updating of a program we have to check if the truth value of a body which determines the truth value of a head hasn't changed before concluding the truth value of the head by inertia. This is so because the truth value of the body may change due to an update rule.

Going back to the previous example, before stating that "god_exists" is true by inertia since it wasn't directly affected by the update program, one should verify for instance whether "explained" is still not true, for otherwise there would be no longer a way to prove "god_exists" and therefore its truth value would no longer be 'true'.

To conclude, we argue that the truth of any element in the updated models should be supported by some rule, i.e. one with a true body, either of the update program or of the given program, in face of new knowledge.

The remainder of this paper is structured as follows: in Sect.2 we recapitulate some background concepts necessary in the sequel; in Sect.3 we formalize the normal logic program update process and present a transformation, reminiscent of the one in [AP97], providing the intended results; we conclude the section by showing that the transformation generalizes the one set forth in [PT95]; in Sect.4 we extend our approach to the case where the program to be updated is a logic program extended with explicit negation, and in Sect.5 we conclude and elaborate on future developments.

2   Review of Interpretation Updates

In this section we summarize some of the definitions related to the issue of theory update. Some of these definitions will be slightly different, though equivalent to the original ones, with the purpose of making their relationship clearer.

For self containment and to eliminate any confusion between updates and revisions, instead of using the original vocabulary of revision rule, revision program and justified revision, we will speak of update rule, update program and justified update, as in [AP97].

The language used is similar to that of logic programming: update programs are collections of update rules, which in turn are built out of atoms by means of the special operators: $\leftarrow$, in, out, and ",".

Definition 1 (Update Programs). *[MT94] Let U be a countable set of atoms. An update in-rule or, simply, an in-rule, is any expression of the form:*

$$in(p) \leftarrow in(q_1), ..., in(q_m), out(s_1), ..., out(s_n) \qquad (1)$$

where p, q_i, $1 \leq i \leq m$, and s_j, $1 \leq j \leq n$, are all in U, and $m, n \geq 0$.
An update out-rule or, simply, an out-rule, is any expression of the form:

$$out(p) \leftarrow in(q_1), ..., in(q_m), out(s_1), ..., out(s_n) \qquad (2)$$

where p, q_i, $1 \leq i \leq m$, and s_j, $1 \leq j \leq n$, are all in U, and $m, n \geq 0$. A collection of in-rules and out-rules is called an update program *(UP).* $\Diamond$

Definition 2 (Necessary Change). *[MT94] Let P be an update program with least model M (treating P as a positive Horn program). The* necessary change *determined by P is the pair (I_P, O_P), where*

$$I_P = \{a : in(a) \in M\} \qquad O_P = \{a : out(a) \in M\} \qquad (3)$$

Atoms in I_P (resp. O_P) are those that must become true (resp. false). If $I \cap O = \{\}$ then P is said coherent. $\Diamond$

Intuitively, the necessary change determined by a program P specifies those atoms that must be added and those that must be deleted as a result of a given update, whatever the initial interpretation.

Definition 3 (P-Justified Update). *[MT94] Let P be an update program and I_i and I_u two total interpretations. The reduct $P_{I_u|I_i}$ with respect to I_i and I_u is obtained by the following operations:*
- *Removing from P all rules whose body contains some $in(a)$ and $a \notin I_u$;*
- *Removing from P all rules whose body contains some $out(a)$ and $a \in I_u$;*
- *Removing from the body of any remaining rules of P all $in(a)$ such that $a \in I_i$;*
- *Removing from the body of any remaining rules of P all $out(a)$ such that $a \notin I_i$.*

Let (I, O) be the necessary change determined by $P_{I_u|I_i}$. Whenever $P_{I_u|I_i}$ is coherent, I_u is a P-justified update of I_i with respect to P iff the following stability *condition holds:*

$$I_u = (I_i - O) \cup I \Diamond \qquad (4)$$

The first two operations delete rules which are useless given I_u. The stability condition preserves the initial interpretation in the final one as much as possible.

3 Normal Logic Program Updating

As we've seen in the introduction, updating on the basis of models isn't enough if we want to take advantage of the information encoded by a logic program and not expressed in the set of its models.

When we generalize the notion of P-justified update, from interpretations to the new case where we want to update programs, the resulting update program should be made to depend only on the initial program and on the update program, but not on any specific initial interpretation. An interpretation should be a model of a normal logic program updated by an update program if the truth of each of its literals is either supported by a rule of the update program with true body in the interpretation or, in case there isn't one, by a rule of the initial program whose conclusion is not contravened by the update program.

Another way to view program updating, and in particular the rôle of inertia, is to say that the rules of the initial program carry over to the updated program, due to inertia, instead of the truth of interpretation literals as in [AP97], just in case they are not overruled by the update program. This is to be preferred because the rules encode more information than the literals. Inertia of literals is a special case of rule inertia since literals can be coded as factual rules. Accordingly, program updating generalizes model updating.

To achieve rule inertia we start by defining the sub-program of the initial program which contains the rules that should persist in the updated program due to inertia. We use this program together with the update program to characterize the models of the resulting updated program, i.e. the program-justified updates, whatever the updated program may be. Finally, we present a joint program transformation of the initial and the update programs, which introduces inertia rules, to produce an updated program whose models are the required program-justified updates. Stable model semantics and its generalization to extended logic programs [GL90] will be used to define the models of programs.

We start by defining a translation of an update program written in a language that does not contain explicit negation, into a normal logic program extended with explicit negation.

Definition 4 (Interpretation Restriction). *Given a language $\mathcal{L}$ that does not contain explicit negation $\neg$, let $M_\neg$ be an interpretation, of the language $\mathcal{L}_\neg$, obtained by augmenting $\mathcal{L}$ with the set $\mathcal{E} = \{\neg A : A \in \mathcal{L}\}$.*

We define the corresponding restricted interpretation M, of $\mathcal{L}$, as:

$$M = M_\neg \text{ restricted to } \mathcal{L} \; \Diamond \tag{5}$$

Definition 5 (Translation of UPs into LPs). *Given an update program UP, in the language $\mathcal{L}$, its translation into an extended logic program U in the language $\mathcal{L}_\neg$ is obtained from UP by replacing each in-rule (1) with the corresponding rule:*

$$p \leftarrow q_1, ...q_m, not\ s_1, ..., not\ s_n \tag{6}$$

and similarly replacing each out-rule (2) with the corresponding rule:

$$\neg p \leftarrow q_1, ...q_m, not\ s_1, ..., not\ s_n \; \Diamond \tag{7}$$

From now onwards, and unless otherwise stated, whenever we refer to an update program we mean its reversible translation into an extended logic program according to the previous definition. Notice that such programs do not contain explicitly negated atoms in the body of its rules.

Definition 6 (Inertial Sub-Program). *Let P be a normal logic program in the language $\mathcal{L}$, U an update program in the language $\mathcal{L}_\neg$ and $M_\neg$ an interpretation of $\mathcal{L}_\neg$. Let:*

$$Rejected(M_\neg) = \{A \leftarrow body \in P : M_\neg \models body \\ and\ \exists \neg A \leftarrow body' \in U : M_\neg \models body' \} \tag{8}$$

where A is an atom. We define Inertial Sub-Program $P_{inertial}(M_\neg)$ *as:*

$$P_{inertial}(M_\neg) = P - Rejected(M_\neg) \ \Diamond \tag{9}$$

Intuitively, the rules for some atom A that belong to $Rejected(M_\neg)$ are those that belong to the initial program but, although their body is still verified by the model, there is an update rule that overrides them, by contravening their conclusion.

Definition 7 (<P,U>-Justified Updates). *Let P be a normal logic program in the language $\mathcal{L}$, U an update program in the language $\mathcal{L}_\neg$, and M an interpretation of the language $\mathcal{L}$. M is a <P,U>-Justified Update of P updated by U, iff there is an interpretation $M_\neg$ of $\mathcal{L}_\neg$ such that $M_\neg$ is an answer-set of P^*, where*

$$P^* = P_{inertial}(M_\neg) + U \ \Diamond \tag{10}$$

Notice that the new definition of program-justified update doesn't depend on any initial model. Once again this is because inertia applies to rules and not model literals. To achieve inertia of model literals it is enough to include them as fact rules, as shown in the sequel.

The following example will show the rôle played by $Rejected(M_\neg)$ when determining the <P,U>-Justified Updates.

Example 3. Consider program P stating that someone is a pacifist and that a pacifist is a reasonable person. Later on, an update U states that it is not clear whether we're at war or at peace, and that a state of war will make that person no longer a pacifist:

$$P : pacifist \leftarrow \qquad\qquad U : \neg pacifist \leftarrow war$$
$$reasonable \leftarrow pacifist \qquad peace \leftarrow not\ war$$
$$war \leftarrow not\ peace$$

Intuitively, when performing the update of P by U, we should obtain two models, namely

$$M_1 = \{pacifist, reasonable, peace\}$$
$$M_2 = \{war\}$$

Let's check whether they are <P,U>-justified updates. M_1 is $M_{\neg 1}$ restricted to the language of P:

$$M_{\neg 1} = \{pacifist, reasonable, peace\}$$

Since

$$Rejected(M_{\neg 1}) = \{\}$$
$$P^* = P + U - \{\}$$

$M_{\neg 1}$ is an answer-set of P^*, and so M_1 is a <P,U>-justified update.

M_2 is $M_{\neg 2}$ restricted to the language of P:

$$M_{\neg 2} = \{war, \neg pacifist\}$$

Since

$$Rejected(M_{\neg 2}) = \{pacifist \leftarrow\}$$
$$P^* = P + U - \{pacifist \leftarrow\}$$

$M_{\neg 2}$ is an answer-set of P^* and so M_2 is a <P,U>-justified update.

Let's check if the model

$$M_X = \{reasonable, war\}$$

is a <P,U>-justified update. Intuitively it should not be one because the truth value of *reasonable* should be determined by the evaluation of the rule of P, *reasonable←pacifist*, on the strength of the truth of *pacifist* in the updated model, and therefore should be false. Note, however, that this model would be a justified update of the only stable model of P, determined according to interpretation updating.

Once again M_X is $M_{\neg X}$ restricted to the language of P:

$$M_{\neg X} = \{reasonable, war, \neg pacifist\}$$

Since

$$Rejected(M_{\neg X}) = \{pacifist \leftarrow\}$$
$$P^* = P + U - \{pacifist \leftarrow\}$$

As expected, $M_{\neg X}$ is not an answer-set of P^*, and therefore M_X is not a <P,U>-justified update.   ◇

Next we present a program transformation that produces an updated program from an initial program and an update program. The answer-sets of the updated program so obtained will be exactly the <P,U>-justified models, according to Theorem 1 below. The updated program can thus be used to compute them.

Definition 8 (Update transformation of a normal program). *Consider an update program U in the language $\mathcal{L}_\neg$. For any normal logic program P in the language $\mathcal{L}$, its updated program P_U with respect to U, written in the extended language $\mathcal{L}_\neg + \{A', A^U, \neg A^U : A \in \mathcal{L}\}$ is obtained via the operations:*

- *All rules of U and P belong to P_U subject to the changes:*
  - *in the head of every rule of P_U originated in U replace literal L by a new literal L^U;*
  - *in the head of every rule of P_U originated in P replace atom A by a new atom A';*
- *Include in P_U, for every atom A of P or U, the defining rules:*

$$A \leftarrow A', not\ \neg A^U \qquad A \leftarrow A^U \qquad \neg A \leftarrow \neg A^U \lozenge \qquad (11)$$

The above definition assumes that in the language $\mathcal{L}$ there are no symbols of the form L' and L^U. This transformation is reminiscent of the one presented in [AP97], where the goal was to update a set of models encoded by a logic program. In [AP97], literals figuring in the head of a rule of U (but it could be for any literal) originate replacement of the corresponding atom in both the head and body of the rules of the initial program, whereas in the above transformation this replacement occurs only in the head (for all rules). This has the effect of exerting inertia on the rules instead of on the model literals because the original rules will be evaluated in the light of the updated model. The defining rules establish that, after the update, a literal is either implied by inertia or forced by an update rule. Note that only update rules are allowed to inhibit the inertia rule, in contrast to the usual inertia rules for model updates. In model updates there are no rule bodies in the coding of the initial interpretation as fact rules, so the conclusion of these rules cannot change, in contradistinction to the case of program updates. Hence the new inertia rule, which applies equally well to model updating (cf. justification in Theorem 2) and so is more general. Their intuitive reading is: A can be true either by inertia or due to the update program.

Example 4. Consider the normal logic program P with a single stable model M:

$$P : a \leftarrow not\ b$$
$$d \leftarrow e$$
$$e \leftarrow$$

$$M = \{a, d, e\}$$

now consider the update program U:

$$U : c \leftarrow not\ a$$
$$b \leftarrow$$
$$\neg e \leftarrow a$$

And the updated program P_U is (where the rules for A stand for all their ground instances):

$$
\begin{array}{lll}
c^U \leftarrow not\ a & a' \leftarrow not\ b & A \leftarrow A', not\ \neg A^U \\
b^U \leftarrow & d' \leftarrow e & A \leftarrow A^U \\
\neg e^U \leftarrow a & e' \leftarrow & \neg A \leftarrow \neg A^U
\end{array}
$$

whose only answer-set (modulo A' and A^U atoms) is:

$$M_U = \{b, c, d, e\}$$

This corresponds to the intended result: the insertion of **b** renders **a** no longer supported and thus false; since **a** is false, **c** becomes true due to the first rule of the update program; the last rule of U is ineffective since **a** is false; **e** is still supported and not updated, so it remains true by inertia; finally **d** remains true because still supported by **e**. ◊

If we consider this same example but performing the updating on a model basis instead, we would get as the only U-justified update of M: $M' = \{a, b, d\}$. The difference, for example in what **a** is concerned, is that in M' **a** is true by inertia because it is true in M and there are no rules for **a** in U. According to our definition, since there aren't any rules (with a true body) in U for **a**, the rule in P for **a** is still valid by inertia and re-evaluated in the final interpretation, where since **b** is true **a** is false.

Example 5. Consider the P and U of example 3. The updated program P_U of P by U is (where the rules for A stand for all their ground instances):

$$
\begin{array}{ll}
pacifist' \leftarrow & \neg pacifist^U \leftarrow war \\
reasonable' \leftarrow pacifist & peace^U \leftarrow not\ war \\
A \leftarrow A', not\ \neg A^U & war^U \leftarrow not\ peace \\
A \leftarrow A^U & \neg A \leftarrow \neg A^U
\end{array}
$$

whose answer-sets (modulo A', A^U and explicitly negated atoms) are:

$$
\begin{array}{l}
M_1 = \{pacifist, reasonable, peace\} \\
M_2 = \{war\}
\end{array}
$$

coinciding with the two <P,U>-justified updates determined in example 3. ◊

The following theorem establishes the relationship between the models of the update transformation of a program and its <P,U>-justified updates.

Theorem 1 (Correctness of the update transformation). *Let P be a normal logic program in the language $\mathcal{L}$ and U a coherent update program in the language $\mathcal{L}\neg$. Modulo any primed and X^U literals, the answer-sets of the updated program P_U are exactly the <P,U>-Justified Updates of P updated by U.* ◊

Proof. Let P be a normal logic program consisting of rules of the form:

$$A \leftarrow B_i, not\ C_i$$

and U an update program consisting of rules of the form:

$$
\begin{array}{l}
A \leftarrow B_j, not\ C_j \\
\neg A \leftarrow B_k, not\ C_k
\end{array}
$$

where A is an atom and each B and C is some finite set of atoms .

Let P_U^* be the program obtained according to Def. 7:

$$P_U^* = U + P_{inertial}(M_\neg)$$

and note that $P_{inertial}(M_\neg) \subseteq P$.

Let P_U be the program obtained according to Def. 8:

$$P_U : A' \leftarrow B_i, not\ C_i \qquad \text{for all rules from } P$$

$$\left.\begin{aligned} A &\leftarrow A', not\ \neg A^U \\ A &\leftarrow A^U \\ \neg A &\leftarrow \neg A^U \end{aligned}\right\} \text{ for all } A$$

$$\left.\begin{aligned} A^U &\leftarrow B_j, not\ C_j \\ \neg A^U &\leftarrow B_k, not\ C_k \end{aligned}\right\} \text{ for all rules from } U$$

We will show that P_U is equivalent to P_U^* for our purposes. Performing on P_U a partial evaluation of A^U and $\neg A^U$ on the rules $A \leftarrow A^U$ and $\neg A \leftarrow \neg A^U$ we obtain:

$$
\begin{aligned}
P_U' : A' &\leftarrow B_i, not\ C_i & (1) \\
A &\leftarrow A', not\ \neg A^U & (2) \\
A &\leftarrow B_j, not\ C_j & (3) \\
\neg A &\leftarrow B_k, not\ C_k & (4) \\
A^U &\leftarrow B_j, not\ C_j & (5) \\
\neg A^U &\leftarrow B_k, not\ C_k & (6)
\end{aligned}
$$

Note that rules (3) and (4) are exactly the update program.

These rules can be simplified. In particular we don't need the rules for A^U and $\neg A^U$. For some arbitrary A, consider first the case where $\neg A^U$ is false. We can then perform the following simplifications on P_U': replace in (2) A' by the body of (1) and remove $not\ \neg A^U$ to obtain (2*): $A \leftarrow B_i, not\ C_i$; now we no longer need rule (6). Since we don't care about primed nor A^U literals in the updated models we can now remove rule (1), as well as rules (5) and (6)). The so mutilated P_U' preserves the semantics of P_U' when $\neg A^U$ is false, apart primed and U literals, and looks like this:

$$
\begin{aligned}
A &\leftarrow B_i, not\ C_i & (2*) \\
A &\leftarrow B_j, not\ C_j & (3) \\
\neg A &\leftarrow B_k, not\ C_k & (4)
\end{aligned}
$$

which corresponds exactly to P_U^* when $P_{inertial}(M_\neg) = P$ when $\neg A^U$ is false, and hence their answer-sets are the same in that case.

For the case where $\neg A^U$ is true, we can delete rule (2); rule (6) is also not needed for we don't care about $\neg A^U$ literals in the updated models. Since we don't care about primed nor A^U literals in the updated models, and A' and A^U don't appear in the body of remaining rules, we can delete rules (1) and (5). The simplified P_U' preserves the semantics of P_U' when $\neg A^U$ is true, apart primed and U literals, and looks like this:

$$
\begin{aligned}
A &\leftarrow B_j, not\ C_j & (4) \\
\neg A &\leftarrow B_k, not\ C_k & (5)
\end{aligned}
$$

which is semantically equal to P_U^*. Indeed, note that when $\neg A^U$ is true, the rules of P for A are rejected if $M_\neg \models B_i, not\ C_i$ and don't belong to P_U^*. So the only possible difference between the simplified P_U' and P_U^* would be the existence of some extra rules in P_U^* such that for any answer-set $M_\neg$ we would have $M_\neg \not\models B_i, not\ C_i$, which does not affect the semantics

The next Theorem establishes the relationship between program update and interpretation update. For this we begin by defining a transformation from an interpretation into the arguably simplest normal logic program that encodes it.

Definition 9 (Factual LP). *Let I be an interpretation of a language $\mathcal{L}$. We define the normal logic program associated with I, $P^*(I)$, as:*

$$P^*(I) = \{L \leftarrow: L \in I\} \ \Diamond \tag{12}$$

We also need the following closeness relationship:

Definition 10 (Closeness relationship). *Given three total interpretations I, I_u and I_u', we say that I_u' is closer to I than I_u if*

$$(I_u' \setminus I \cup I \setminus I_u') \subset (I_u \setminus I \cup I \setminus I_u) \ \Diamond \tag{13}$$

Theorem 2 (Generalization of Updates). *Let U be an update program and I an interpretation. Then:*

1. *Every U-justified update of I is a $<P^*(I), U>$-justified update.*
2. *A $<P^*(I), U>$-justified update I_u is a U-justified update of I iff there is no I_u' closer to I than I_u, where I_u' is a $<P^*(I), U>$-justified update.* $\Diamond$

Proof. 1. Let U be an update program consisting of rules of the form:

$$A \leftarrow B_j, not\ C_j$$
$$\neg A \leftarrow B_k, not\ C_k$$

where A is an atom and each B and C is some finite set of atoms. According to [AP97], an interpretation I_u is a U-justified update of I iff it is a total (or two-valued) WFSX model (modulo primed and explicitly negated elements) of the corresponding program P_U:

$$P_U : A' \leftarrow \qquad\qquad \text{for all } A \in I$$
$$A \leftarrow A', not\ \neg A$$
$$\neg A \leftarrow not\ A', not\ A \qquad \Big\} \text{ for all } A$$
$$A \leftarrow B_j, \neg C_j$$
$$\neg A \leftarrow B_k, \neg C_k \qquad \Big\} \text{ for all rules from } U$$

according to Def. 8, an interpretation I_u' is a $<P^*(I), U>$-justified update iff it is the restriction to the language of I of an answer-set of the program

P'_U:

$$P'_U : A' \leftarrow \qquad\qquad \text{for all } A \in I$$

$$\left.\begin{array}{l} A \leftarrow A', not \ \neg A^U \\ A \leftarrow A^U \\ \neg A \leftarrow \neg A^U \end{array}\right\} \text{for all } A$$

$$\left.\begin{array}{l} A^U \leftarrow B_j, not \ C_j \\ \neg A^U \leftarrow B_k, not \ C_k \end{array}\right\} \text{for all rules from } U$$

Notice the difference in the translation of update rules in what the kind of negation used in their bodies is concerned. We will show that for every total (or two-valued) WFSX model I_u of the program P_U, there is an answer-set I'_u of P'_U such that $I_u = I'_u$ restricted to the language of I.

Performing a partial evaluation of A^U and $\neg A^U$ on the rules $A \leftarrow A^U$ and $\neg A \leftarrow \neg A^U$ we obtain:

$$\begin{array}{ll} P'_U : A' \leftarrow & (1) \\ A \leftarrow A', not \ \neg A^U & (2) \\ A \leftarrow B_j, not \ C_j & (3) \\ \neg A \leftarrow B_k, not \ C_k & (4) \\ A^U \leftarrow B_j, not \ C_j & (5) \\ \neg A^U \leftarrow B_k, not \ C_k & (6) \end{array}$$

We can safely replace $not \ \neg A^U$ by $not \ \neg A$ in rule (2), for the only rules for $\neg A$ and $\neg A^U$ have the same body. Now, and since we don't care about A^U and $\neg A^U$ in the updated models, we can remove rules (5) and (6) and obtain the following program P''_U:

$$\begin{array}{llll} P''_U : A' \leftarrow & (1) & P_U : A' \leftarrow & \\ A \leftarrow A', not \ \neg A & (2) & A \leftarrow A', not \ \neg A & \\ & (3) & \neg A \leftarrow not \ A', not \ A & \\ A \leftarrow B_j, not \ C_j & (4) & A \leftarrow B_j, \neg C_j & \\ \neg A \leftarrow B_k, not \ C_k & (5) & \neg A \leftarrow B_k, \neg C_k & \end{array}$$

It is easy to see that the only differences between P''_U and P_U are the kind of negation used in the body of the rules from the update program, and the extra rule (3) in P_U. Suppose that we add rule (3) to P''_U: if rule (3) has a true body, rule (2) must have a false body; since we are not concerned about $\neg A$ in the final models, and $\neg A$ doesn't appear in the body of any other rules, adding rule (3) to P''_U wouldn't change the restricted models. Now, the only difference is the kind of negation used, but since in answer-sets we have that if $\neg C$ is true then $not \ C$ is also true, we have that all total WFSX models of P_U are also answer-sets of P''_U.

2. There now remains to be proved the closeness part of the theorem, i.e. that the set of interpretations $S = Q - R$, where

$$Q = \{I_u : I_u \text{ is a } < P^*(I), U > \text{-justified update}\}$$
$$R = \{I_u : I_u \text{ is a } U\text{-justified update of } I\}$$

is such that for every I'_u in S, there is an I_u in R such that I_u is closer to I than I'_u, and thus eliminated by the closeness condition. According to [MT94], I_u is a U-justified update of I iff it satisfies the rules of U (as per Def.1 and where I satisfies $in(a)$ (resp. $out(a)$) if $a \in I$ (resp. $a \notin I$)), and is closest to I among such interpretations. From Definition 7, every $<P,U>$-justified update must satisfy the rules of U, of the form:

$$A \leftarrow B_j, not\ C_j$$
$$\neg A \leftarrow B_k, not\ C_k \tag{14}$$

Since for any answer-set if $\neg a \in I$ then $a \notin I$, we have that any $<P,U>$-justified update, because it satisfies the rules of (14), must also satisfy the update rules with in's and out's of the form (15)

$$in(A) \leftarrow in(B_j), out(C_j)$$
$$out(A) \leftarrow in(B_k), out(C_k) \tag{15}$$

Let X be the set of all interpretations that satisfy the rules of (15). Then the interpretations in $X - R$ are the ones eliminated by the closeness condition, to obtain the U-justified updates, according to [MT94]. Since $R \subseteq Q$ (first part of the theorem), and every interpretation of Q satisfies the rules of (15), we have that $S \subseteq X$ and thus any interpretation in S is eliminated by the closeness condition of this theorem.

Therefore the notion of program update presented here is a generalization of the updates carried out on a model basis. Consequently, the program transformation above is a generalization of the program transformation in [AP97], regarding its 2-valued specialization. Elsewhere [Lei97] the 3-valued case is generalised as well.

Remark 1 (Extending the language of initial programs). We could allow for initial programs to be of the same form as update programs, i.e. with explicit negated literals in their heads only, as per Def.5. For this, we would have to change Definitions 6 and 8 by replacing atom A there with objective literal L^1 (see [Lei97]). However, note that, although both programs have explicit negation in their heads, its use is limited, as explicit negation does not appear in rule bodies. Indeed, all its occurrences can be replaced by allowing **not** in heads instead, and then employing a semantics for such generalized programs such as [LW92],[DP96].

---

[1] An updated program can in turn be updated, once the inertia rule is generalized for objective literals: $L \leftarrow L', not\neg L$. Because the inertia rule contains explicitly negated literals in its body, the language of programs has to be extended, as per the next section. However, the inertia rule itself does not need to be updated, only the program and update rules. These will accumulate dashes in their heads as they are updated. For the inertia rule to recurrently strip away successive dashes one needs to introduce the equivalence $(\neg A)' = \neg(A)'$, and define $\neg$ and $'$ as operators to allow unification to do its work. For the details of such a generalization the reader is referred to [Lei97].

4   Extended Logic Program Updating

When we update a normal logic program the result is an extended logic program. In order to update these in turn we need to extend the results of the previous section to cater for explicit negation in programs. Besides this obvious motivation, there is much work done on representing knowledge using extended logic programs, and we want to be able to update them. We begin by extending the definitions of the previous section to allow for the inclusion of explicit negation anywhere in a normal program.

Definition 11 (Update Rules for Objective Literals). *[AP97]Let $\mathcal{K}$ be a countable set of objective literals. Update in-rules or, simply in-rules, and update out-rules or, simply, out-rules, are as (1) and as (2), but with respect to this new set $\mathcal{K}$.*   ◇

Also, for extended update programs their transformation into an extended logic programs is now:

Definition 12 (Translation of extended UPs into ELPs). *[AP97]Given an update program with explicit negation UP, its translation into the extended logic program U is defined as follows[2]:*

1. *Each in-rule*

$$in(L_0) \leftarrow in(L_1), ..., in(L_m), out(L_{m+1}), ..., out(L_n) \qquad (16)$$

   where $m, n \geq 0$, and L_i are objective literals, translates into:

$$L_0^* \leftarrow L_1, ..., L_m, not\ L_{m+1}, ..., not\ L_n \qquad (17)$$

   where $L_0^* = A^p$ if $L_0 = A$, or $L_0^* = A^n$ if $L_0 = \neg A$;
2. *Each out-rule*

$$out(L_0) \leftarrow in(L_1), ..., in(L_m), out(L_{m+1}), ..., out(L_n) \qquad (18)$$

   where $m, n \geq 0$, and L_i are objective literals, translates into:

$$\neg L_0^* \leftarrow L_1, ..., L_m, not\ L_{m+1}, ..., not\ L_n \qquad (19)$$

   where $L_0^* = A^p$ if $L_0 = A$, or $L_0^* = A^n$ if $L_0 = \neg A$;
3. *For every objective literal L such that $in(L)$ belongs to the head of some in-rule of UP, U contains $\neg L^* \leftarrow L$ where $L^* = A^n$ if $L = A$, or $L^* = A^p$ if $L = \neg A$;*
4. *For every atom A, U contains the rules $A \leftarrow A^p$ and $\neg A \leftarrow A^n$.*   ◇

---

[2] This translation employs the results in [DP96], namely the expressive power of WFSX to capture the semantics of extended logic programs with default literals in the heads of rules, via the program transformation P^{not}.

Intuitively, this transformation converts an atom A into a new atom A^p and an explicitly negated atom $\neg A$ into a new atom A^n and ensures coherence. This way, we no longer have explicitly negated atoms in the heads of the rules of update programs and so we can use explicit negation $\neg L$ to code the $out(L)$ in the heads of rules, as for update programs without explicit negation. Operation 4 maps the A^n and A^p back to their original atoms.

Conversely, any extended logic program (ELP) can be seen as an update program, possibly applied to an empty program. Indeed, translate each ELP rule of the form

$$L_0 \leftarrow L_1, ..., L_m, not\ L_{m+1}, ..., not\ L_n \tag{20}$$

where L_i are objective literals, to

$$in(L_0) \leftarrow in(L_1), ..., in(L_m), out(L_{m+1}), ..., out(L_n) \tag{21}$$

It is easy to see that applying the above translation (Def.12) of such an update program back into an ELP preserves the semantics of the original program because of the read-out rules, $A \leftarrow A^p$ and $\neg A \leftarrow A^n$.

The language of update programs is more expressive than that of ELPs because one may additionally have $out(A_0)$ and $out(\neg A_0)$. The semantics of such ELP_{out} programs can be defined simply by the ELP semantics of the translation into an ELP of their corresponding update programs.

Then we can envisage any ELP (or ELP_{out}) program as an update specification for another ELP (or ELP_{out}) program, albeit the empty one. Programs can update one another, in succession.

Definition 13 (Extended Interpretation Restriction). *Given a language $\mathcal{K}$ with explicit negation, let M_{np} be the an interpretation of the language $\mathcal{K}_{np}$, obtained by augmenting $\mathcal{K}$ with the set $\mathcal{E} = \{L^n, L^p : L \in \mathcal{K}\}$ (L^n, L^p and L are objective literals).*

We define the corresponding restricted interpretation M, *of $\mathcal{K}$, as:*

$$M = M_{np}\ restricted\ to\ \mathcal{K} \lozenge \tag{22}$$

Definition 14 (Inertial Sub-Program). *Let P be an extended logic program in the language $\mathcal{K}$, U an update program in the language $\mathcal{K}_{np}$ and M_{np} an interpretation of $\mathcal{K}_{np}$. Let:*

$$
\begin{aligned}
Rejected(M_{np}) = \{&A \leftarrow body \in P : M_{np} \models body \\
&and\ \exists \neg A^p \leftarrow body' \in U : M_{np} \models body'\ \} \cup \\
\cup \{&\neg A \leftarrow body \in P : M_{np} \models body \\
&and\ \exists \neg A^n \leftarrow body' \in U : M_{np} \models body'\ \}
\end{aligned}
\tag{23}
$$

where A is an atom. We define Inertial Sub-Program $P_{inertial}(M_{np})$ *as:*

$$P_{inertial}(M_{np}) = P - Rejected(M_{np}) \lozenge \tag{24}$$

Again, the rules for some objective literal L that belong to $Rejected(M_{np})$ are those that belong to the initial program but, although their body is still verified by the model, there is an update rule that overrides them, by contravening their conclusion. Note that a rule of P for atom A, with true body, is also countervened by a rule of U with true body for A^n (i.e. one translated from $in(\neg A)$). Since every U also contains the rules $\neg A^p \leftarrow \neg A$ and $\neg A \leftarrow A^n$, then $\neg A$ in $\neg A^p \leftarrow \neg A$ is also true, and so that rule of P is rejected in this case too. Similarly for a rule of P with head $\neg A$, but now with respect to A^p.

Definition 15 (<P,U>-Justified Updates). *Let P be an extended logic program in the language $\mathcal{K}$, U an update program in the language $\mathcal{K}_{np}$ and M an interpretation of the language $\mathcal{K}$. M is a <P,U>-Justified Update of P updated by U iff there is an interpretation M_{np} such that M_{np} is an answer-set of P^*, where*

$$P^* = P_{inertial}(M_{np}) + U \, \Diamond \tag{25}$$

Once again we should point out that the extended <P,U>-Justified Update doesn't depend on any initial interpretation. As for the case of normal logic programs, it is the rules that suffer the effects of inertia and not model literals per se.

Example 6. Consider a recoding of the alarm example using explicit negation, where P and UP are:

$$P: sleep \leftarrow \neg alarm \qquad UP: in(\neg alarm) \leftarrow$$
$$panic \leftarrow alarm$$
$$alarm \leftarrow$$

the update program U obtained from UP is:

$$alarm^n \leftarrow$$
$$\neg alarm^p \leftarrow \neg alarm$$
$$alarm \leftarrow alarm^p$$
$$\neg alarm \leftarrow alarm^n$$

Intuitively, when performing the update of P by U, we should obtain a single model, namely

$$M = \{\neg alarm, sleep\}$$

Let's check whether M is an extended <P,U>-justified update. M is M_{np} restricted to the language of P:

$$M_{np} = \{\neg alarm, sleep, alarm^n, \neg alarm^p\}$$

Since

$$Rejected(M_{np}) = \{alarm \leftarrow\}$$
$$P^* = P + U - \{alarm \leftarrow\}$$

M_{np} is an answer-set of P^*, and so M is an extended <P,U>-justified update. $\Diamond$

Definition 16 (Update transformation of an extended LP). *Given an update program UP, consider its corresponding extended logic program U in the language $\mathcal{K}_{np}$. For any extended logic program P in the language $\mathcal{K}$, its updated program P_U with respect to U, written in the extended language $\mathcal{K}_{np} + \{A', \neg A', A^{nU}, \neg A^{nU}, A^{pU}, \neg A^{pU} : A \in \mathcal{K}\}$ is obtained through the operations:*

- *All rules of U and P belong to P_U subject to the changes, where L is a literal:*
  - *in the head of every rule of P_U originated in U, replace L^p (resp. L^n) by a new literal L^{pU} (resp. L^{nU});*
  - *in the head of every rule of P_U originated in P, replace literal L by a new literal L';*
- *Include in P_U, for every atom A of P or U, the defining rules:*

$$\begin{array}{ll} A^n \leftarrow \neg A', not \, \neg A^{nU} & A^p \leftarrow A', not \, \neg A^{pU} \\ A^n \leftarrow A^{nU} & A^p \leftarrow A^{pU} \\ \neg A^n \leftarrow \neg A^{nU} & \neg A^p \leftarrow \neg A^{pU} \qquad \diamond \end{array} \tag{26}$$

As before, the transformation reflects that we want to preserve, by inertia, the rules for those literals in P not affected by the update program. This is accomplished via the renaming of the literals in the head of rules only, whilst preserving the body, plus the inertia rules.

Theorem 3 (Correctness of the update transformation). *Let P be an extended logic program and U a coherent update program. Modulo any primed, A^U, A^p and A^n elements and their defaults, the answer-sets of the updated program P_U of P with respect to U are exactly the $<P,U>$-Justified Updates of P updated by U.* $\diamond$

Proof. (sketch): Let P be an extended logic program consisting of rules of the form:

$$\begin{array}{l} A \leftarrow B_i, not \, C_i \\ \neg A \leftarrow B_j, not \, C_j \end{array}$$

and U an update program consisting of rules of the form:

$$\begin{array}{ll} A^p \leftarrow B_k, not \, C_k & A \leftarrow A^p \\ \neg A^p \leftarrow B_l, not \, C_l & \neg A \leftarrow A^n \\ A^n \leftarrow B_m, not \, C_m & \neg A^n \leftarrow A \\ \neg A^n \leftarrow B_n, not \, C_n & \neg A^p \leftarrow \neg A \end{array}$$

where A is an atom and each B and C is some finite set of objective literals.

Let P_U^* be the program obtained according to Def. 7:

$$P_U^* = U + P_{inertial}(M_{np})$$

and note that $P_{inertial}(M_{np}) \subseteq P$.

Let P_U be the program obtained according to Def. 8:

$$P_U : \begin{array}{l} A' \leftarrow B_i, not\ C_i \\ \neg A' \leftarrow B_j, not\ C_j \end{array} \left.\right\} \text{ for all rules from } P$$

$$\left.\begin{array}{l} A^p \leftarrow A', not\ \neg A^{pU} \\ A^n \leftarrow \neg A', not\ \neg A^{nU} \\ A^p \leftarrow A^{pU} \\ \neg A^p \leftarrow \neg A^{pU} \\ A^n \leftarrow A^{nU} \\ \neg A^n \leftarrow \neg A^{nU} \\ A \leftarrow A^p \\ \neg A \leftarrow A^n \end{array}\right\} \text{ for all } A$$

$$\left.\begin{array}{l} A^{pU} \leftarrow B_k, not\ C_k \\ \neg A^{pU} \leftarrow B_l, not\ C_l \\ A^{nU} \leftarrow B_m, not\ C_m \\ \neg A^{nU} \leftarrow B_n, not\ C_n \\ \neg A^{nU} \leftarrow A \\ \neg A^{pU} \leftarrow \neg A \end{array}\right\} \text{ rules from } U$$

We will show that P_U is equivalent to P_U^* for our purposes. Performing on P_U a partial evaluation of A^{pU}, $\neg A^{pU}$, A^{nU} and $\neg A^{nU}$ on the rules $A^p \leftarrow A^{pU}$, $\neg A^p \leftarrow \neg A^{pU}$, $A^n \leftarrow A^{nU}$ and $\neg A^n \leftarrow \neg A^{nU}$ we obtain:

$$
\begin{array}{llll}
P_U' : A' \leftarrow B_i, not\ C_i & (1) & \neg A^p \leftarrow \neg A & (10) \\
\neg A' \leftarrow B_j, not\ C_j & (2) & A \leftarrow A^p & (11) \\
A^p \leftarrow A', not\ \neg A^{pU} & (3) & \neg A \leftarrow A^n & (12) \\
A^n \leftarrow \neg A', not\ \neg A^{nU} & (4) & A^{pU} \leftarrow B_k, not\ C_k & (13) \\
A^p \leftarrow B_k, not\ C_k & (5) & \neg A^{pU} \leftarrow B_l, not\ C_l & (14) \\
\neg A^p \leftarrow B_l, not\ C_l & (6) & A^{nU} \leftarrow B_m, not\ C_m & (15) \\
A^n \leftarrow B_m, not\ C_m & (7) & \neg A^{nU} \leftarrow B_n, not\ C_n & (16) \\
\neg A^n \leftarrow B_n, not\ C_n & (8) & \neg A^{nU} \leftarrow A & (17) \\
\neg A^n \leftarrow A & (9) & \neg A^{pU} \leftarrow \neg A & (18)
\end{array}
$$

Note that rules (5)-(12) are exactly equal to the rules of the update program.

The structure of the remaining part of the proof is quite similar to the one set forth in Theorem 1. Its details are slightly more extensive for we now have to simplify P_U' eliminating A^{pU}, $\neg A^{pU}$, A^{nU} and $\neg A^{nU}$ whilst in Theorem 1 we only had to consider A^U and $\neg A^U$.

Example 7. Applying this transformation to the alarm example (Ex. 6)

$$
\begin{array}{ll}
P : sleep \leftarrow \neg alarm & \quad U : in(\neg alarm) \leftarrow \\
 panic \leftarrow alarm & \\
 alarm \leftarrow &
\end{array}
$$

we obtain (where the rules for A and $\neg A$ stand for their ground instances):

$$
\begin{aligned}
P_U : \; & sleep' \leftarrow \neg alarm & A^p \leftarrow A', not\ \neg A^{pU} \\
& panic' \leftarrow alarm & A^n \leftarrow \neg A', not\ \neg A^{nU} \\
& alarm' \leftarrow & A^p \leftarrow A^{pU} \\
& alarm^{nU} \leftarrow & \neg A^p \leftarrow \neg A^{pU} \\
& \neg alarm^{pU} \leftarrow \neg alarm & A^n \leftarrow A^{nU} \\
& A \leftarrow A^p & \neg A^n \leftarrow \neg A^{nU} \\
& \neg A \leftarrow A^n &
\end{aligned}
$$

with model (modulo L', L^n, L^p, L^U):

$$
M_U = \{sleep, \neg alarm\} \; \Diamond
$$

Definition 9 and Theorem 2 both now carry over to a language K with explicit negation.

Definition 17 (Extended factual LP). *Let I be an interpretation of a language K with explicit negation. We define the extended logic program associated with I, $P^*(I)$, as:*

$$
P^*(I) = \{L \leftarrow: L \in I\} \tag{27}
$$

where the Ls are objective literals. $\qquad\qquad\qquad\qquad\qquad\qquad\qquad\Diamond$

It is worth pointing out that the translation of update programs into extended logic programs, making use of explicit negation $\neg$ to code the out's in the heads of update rules and default negation *not* to code the out's in the bodies of the same rules, allows for some pairs of answer-sets, one of which will always be closer than the other to the initial interpretation. This is best illustrated by the following example:

Example 8. Let $I = \{a\}$ and $U = \{\neg a \leftarrow not\ a\}$ where U is the translation of $U' = \{out(a) \leftarrow out(a)\}$ according to Def.5. The updated program is:

$$
\begin{aligned}
P_U : \; & a' \leftarrow \\
& a \leftarrow a', not\ \neg a^U \\
& \neg a^U \leftarrow not\ a
\end{aligned}
$$

with two answer-sets whose restrictions are $M_1 = \{a\}$ and $M_2 = \{\}$. Note that M_1 is closer to I than M_2. $\qquad\qquad\qquad\qquad\qquad\qquad\qquad\qquad\qquad\Diamond$

The closeness condition in Theorems 2 and 4 exists to eliminate such farther models in order to obtain the U-justified updates only. As mentioned, this phenomena is due to the translation of the update programs. This is also shared by [AP97] for the case of updates extended with explicit negation, and so their soundness and completeness theorem should also make use of the closeness relationship.

This translation has the virtue of not excluding such models, just in case they are seen as desired. Another approach exists, mentioned in the conclusions, that avoids the need for the closeness relation by excluding the non-closest updates by construction.

Theorem 4 (Generalization of Updates). *Let U be an update program with explicit negation and I an interpretation. Then:*

1. *Every U-justified update of I is a $<P^*(I), U>$-justified update.*
2. *A $<P^*(I), U>$-justified update I_u is a U-justified update of I iff there is no I'_u closer to I than I_u, where I'_u is a $<P^*(I), U>$-justified update.*   ◇

Proof. (sketch): Let U be an update program consisting of rules of the form:

$$
\begin{array}{ll}
A^p \leftarrow B_k, not\ C_k \qquad & A \leftarrow A^p \\
\neg A^p \leftarrow B_l, not\ C_l \qquad & \neg A \leftarrow A^n \\
A^n \leftarrow B_m, not\ C_m \qquad & \neg A^n \leftarrow A \\
\neg A^n \leftarrow B_n, not\ C_n \qquad & \neg A^p \leftarrow \neg A
\end{array}
$$

where A is an atom and each B and C is some finite set of objective literals.

According to [AP97], a total (or two-valued) WFSX model (modulo primed and explicitly negated elements) of the program P_U is a U-justified update iff it is closest to I, among all such models, where P_U is:

$$
\begin{array}{lll}
P_U : A' \leftarrow & & \text{for all } A \in I \\
\quad \neg A' \leftarrow & & \text{for all } \neg A \in I \\
\quad A^p \leftarrow A', not\ \neg A^p & \left.\rule{0pt}{9.5em}\right\} & \\
\quad \neg A^p \leftarrow not\ A', not\ A^p & & \\
\quad A^n \leftarrow \neg A', not\ \neg A^n & & \\
\quad \neg A^n \leftarrow not\ \neg A', not\ A^n & & \\
\quad A \leftarrow A^p & & \text{for all } A \\
\quad \neg A \leftarrow A^n & & \\
\quad \neg A^n \leftarrow A & & \\
\quad \neg A^p \leftarrow \neg A & & \\
\quad A^p \leftarrow B_k, not\ C_k & \left.\rule{0pt}{4.5em}\right\} & \\
\quad \neg A^p \leftarrow B_l, not\ C_l & & \text{rules from } U \\
\quad A^n \leftarrow B_m, not\ C_m & & \\
\quad \neg A^n \leftarrow B_n, not\ C_n & &
\end{array}
$$

according to Def. 8, an interpretation I'_u is a $<P^*(I), U>$-justified update iff it is the restriction of an answer-set of the program P'_U (after the same partial evaluation as done in the proof of Theorem 3):

$$
\begin{array}{llll}
P'_U : A' \leftarrow B_i, not\ C_i & (1) & \neg A^p \leftarrow \neg A & (10) \\
\quad \neg A' \leftarrow B_j, not\ C_j & (2) & A \leftarrow A^p & (11) \\
\quad A^p \leftarrow A', not\ \neg A^{pU} & (3) & \neg A \leftarrow A^n & (12) \\
\quad A^n \leftarrow \neg A', not\ \neg A^{nU} & (4) & A^{pU} \leftarrow B_k, not\ C_k & (13) \\
\quad A^p \leftarrow B_k, not\ C_k & (5) & \neg A^{pU} \leftarrow B_l, not\ C_l & (14) \\
\quad \neg A^p \leftarrow B_l, not\ C_l & (6) & A^{nU} \leftarrow B_m, not\ C_m & (15) \\
\quad A^n \leftarrow B_m, not\ C_m & (7) & \neg A^{nU} \leftarrow B_n, not\ C_n & (16) \\
\quad \neg A^n \leftarrow B_n, not\ C_n & (8) & \neg A^{nU} \leftarrow A & (17) \\
\quad \neg A^n \leftarrow A & (9) & \neg A^{pU} \leftarrow \neg A & (18)
\end{array}
$$

We will have to show that these two transformed programs have the same models, apart from irrelevant elements.

Following similar, though slightly more complex, arguments as in the proof of Theorem 2, we can replace A^{pU}, $\neg A^{pU}$, A^{nU} and $\neg A^{nU}$ by A^p, $\neg A^p$, A^n and $\neg A^n$ in rules (3)-(6), and deleting rules (15)-(20). Also rules $\neg A^p \leftarrow not\ A', not\ A^p$ and $\neg A^n \leftarrow not\ \neg A', not\ A^n$ of P_U are irrelevant for the only rules with $\neg A^p$ and $\neg A^n$ in their body also have A' and $\neg A'$ in their body, respectively, which could never be true. Removing those rules from P_U, it would be exactly equal to P'_U, after the simplifications mentioned, thus proving the theorem.

5   Conclusions

In this paper we have generalized the notion of updates to the case where we want to update programs instead of just their models. We have shown that since a program encodes more information than a set of models, the law of inertia should be applied to rules instead of to model literals, as had been done so far. We presented a transformation which, given an initial program and an update program, generates the desired updated program. Our results have been further extended to allow for both programs and update programs extended with explicit negation. This is important inasmuch as it permits our updated programs to be updated in turn, and allows us to conceive what it is to successively update one program by another, and so to define the evolution of knowledge bases by means of updates[3].

Future foundational work involves dealing with partial interpretations and non-coherent update programs and their contradiction removal requirements, among other developments. Indeed, as the world changes, so must logic programs that represent it. Program updating is a crucial notion opening up a whole new range of applications, from specification of software updates to temporal databases, from reasoning about actions to active databases, and in general as a means for better representing reasoning, including belief revision.

Acknowledgments We thank José Júlio Alferes, Halina Przymusinska and Teodor Przymusinski for their insightful discussions and suggestions, and the anonymous referees for their comments. A joint paper together with them is well under way, improving on and generalizing the results presented here, as well as exploring some of the application areas mentioned above. (A Prolog implementation of this more general theory is already available.)

---

[3] Iterated updates are made easier by a similar approach to that of Footnote 1, where instead the equivalences $(A_n)' = (A')_n$, $(A_p)' = (A')_p$, $(A_n^U)' = (A')_n^U$ and $(A_n^U)' = (A')_n^U$ are introduced. Lack of space prevents us to elaborate further on iterated updates, and garbage collection techniques to do away with rules rendered useless. For the details on these topics the reader is referred to [Lei97].

References

[AP96] J. J. Alferes, L. M. Pereira. *Reasoning with logic programming*, LNAI 1111, Berlin, Springer-Verlag, 1996.

[AP97] J. J. Alferes, L. M. Pereira. *Update-programs can update programs*. In J. Dix, L. M. Pereira and T. Przymusinski, editors, Selected papers from the ICLP'96 ws NMELP'96, vol. 1216 of LNAI, pages 110-131. Springer-Verlag, 1997.

[APP96] J. J. Alferes, L. M. Pereira and T. Przymusinski. *Strong and Explicit Negation in Nonmonotonic Reasoning and Logic Programming*. In J. J. Alferes, L. M. Pereira and E. Orlowska, editors, JELIA '96, volume 1126 of LNAI, pages 143-163. Springer-Verlag, 1996.

[BD95] S. Brass and J. Dix. *Disjunctive Semantics based upon Partial and Bottom-Up Evaluation*. In Leon Sterling, editor, Procs. of the 12th Int. Conf. on Logic Programming, Tokyo, pag. 85-98, Berlin, June 1995. Springer-Verlag.

[DP96] C. V. Damásio and L. M. Pereira. *Default negated conclusions: why not?* In R. Dyckhoff, H. Herre and P. Schroeder-Heister, editors, Procs. of ELP'96, volume 1050 of LNAI, pages 103-118. Springer-Verlag, 1996.

[GL90] M. Gelfond and V. Lifschitz. *Logic Programs with classical negation*. In Warren and Szeredi, editors, 7th Int. Conf. on LP, pages 579-597. MIT Press, 1990.

[KM91] H. Katsuno and A. Mendelzon. *On the difference between updating a knowledge base and revising it*. In James Allen, Richard Fikes and Erik Sandewall, editors, Principles of Knowledge Representation and Reasoning: Proc. of the Second Int'l Conf. (KR91), pages 230-237, Morgan Kaufmann 1991.

[KW85] A. Keller and M. Winslett Wilkins. *On the use of an extended relational model to handle changing incomplete information*. IEEE Trans. on Software Engineering, SE-11:7, pages 620-633, 1985.

[Lei97] João A. Leite. *Logic Program Updates*. MSc dissertation, Universidade Nova de Lisboa, 1997.

[LW92] V. Lifschitz and T. Woo. *Answer sets in general nonmonotonic reasoning (preliminary report)*. In B. Nebel, C. Rich and W. Swartout, editors, Principles of Knowledge Representation and Reasoning, Proc. of the Third Int'l Conf (KR92), pages 603-614. Morgan-Kaufmann, 1992

[MT94] V.Marek and M. Truszczynski. *Revision specifications by means of programs*. In C. MacNish, D. Pearce and L. M. Pereira, editors, JELIA '94, volume 838 of LNAI, pages 122-136. Springer-Verlag, 1994.

[Principia] Isaaco Newtono. *Philosophiæ Naturalis Principia Mathematica*. Editio tertia aucta & emendata. Apud Guil & Joh. Innys, Regiæ Societatis typographos. Londini, MDCCXXVI. Original quotation:"*Corpus omne perseverare in statu suo quiescendi vel movendi uniformiter in directum, nisi quatenus illud a viribus impressis cogitur statum suum mutare.*".

[PA92] L. M. Pereira and J. J. Alferes. *Well founded semantics for logic programs with explicit negation*. In B. Neumann, editor, European Conf. on AI, pages 102-106. John Wiley & Sons, 1992.

[PT95] T. Przymusinski and H. Turner. *Update by means of inference rules*. In V. Marek, A. Nerode, and M. Truszczynski, editors, LPNMR'95, volume 928 of LNAI, pages 156-174. Springer-Verlag, 1995.

Springer
and the
environment

At Springer we firmly believe that an
international science publisher has a
special obligation to the environment,
and our corporate policies consistently
reflect this conviction.
We also expect our business partners –
paper mills, printers, packaging
manufacturers, etc. – to commit
themselves to using materials and
production processes that do not harm
the environment. The paper in this
book is made from low- or no-chlorine
pulp and is acid free, in conformance
with international standards for paper
permanency.

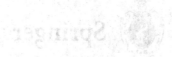

Lecture Notes in Artificial Intelligence (LNAI)

Lecture Notes in Computer Science